On Jewish Music

Joachim Braun

On Jewish Music

Past and Present

2nd Revised Edition

Peter Lang
Frankfurt am Main · Berlin · Bern · Bruxelles · New York · Oxford · Wien

Bibliographic Information published by the Deutsche Nationalbibliothek
The Deutsche Nationalbibliothek lists this publication in the Deutsche Nationalbibliografie; detailed bibliographic data is available in the internet at http://dnb.d-nb.de.

Cover Design:
© Olaf Gloeckler, Atelier Platen, Friedberg

Cover illustration:
Hebrew Psalm Ms Biblioteca Palatina Ms 1870, fol. 105R (Ps. 76).

Reproduction by kind permission
of the Ministerio per i Beni e le Attività Culturali.

ISBN 978-3-631-63038-9
© Peter Lang GmbH
Internationaler Verlag der Wissenschaften
Frankfurt am Main 2011
All rights reserved.

All parts of this publication are protected by copyright. Any utilisation outside the strict limits of the copyright law, without the permission of the publisher, is forbidden and liable to prosecution. This applies in particular to reproductions, translations, microfilming, and storage and processing in electronic retrieval systems.

www.peterlang.de

*In loving memory of our
grandson Ariel
1976-2004*

Introduction

This book *On Jewish Music* presents a retrospective of studies on the latest topic of my research interests, mostly published during the years 1977-2004.[*] It includes sections from the history of Jewish musical culture from the earliest times of artifactual evidence in ancient Israel/Palestine through the centuries of the Diaspora to modern Israel. This approach of combining research on ancient cultures with current problems of these cultures stems from my strong belief in a lasting tradition at the roots of any culture, which can hardly disappear.

Without special initial intent and without a later tenor of action, the particular pieces of this volume fall together in a historical narrative. The part on ancient Israel/Palestine (chs. I-III), containing mainly excerpts from my book on this subject, is an overview of the origin and ancient period of Jewish musical culture, which at the present state of our knowledge can be recreated only on the basis of archaeological evidence and indirect textual or ethno-comparative material. Chapter III (not published before) attempts a reconsideration of the disputable question of ethnicity in ancient musical cultures. The next two chapters (IV and V), still dealing with the past, although devoted to a seemingly contingent occurrence – the acceptance of the pagan lute and Christian organ into Jewish musical culture – reveal the sources of a dramatic process of acculturation. The relatively short time of ancient independence and its aftermath turned into the lasting years of a painful Diaspora. I concentrated here on what I seemed to know best, not only from archives and libraries but also from experience – the years of the Diaspora in the former Soviet Union (chs. VI-XIII). It is not by accident that much of this part was written right at the beginning of my new life in Israel, and putting on paper this time of the past was for me some kind of liberation. The hope for a nor-

---

- Previous and parallel subjects of my work were mainly targeting the musical cultures of ancient Israel/Palestine, the Baltics, in particular Latvia, matters of hermeneutics, organology and iconography of music.

mal life with equality for the Jewish people after centuries of suppression, promised by the ideologists of communism; the frustrating disappointments of the 1930s and 40s; the decades of Stalinism and Gulags, of life in fear with the sword of Damocles over them, Jewish culture being on the border of permitted but undesired, even forbidden, and the necessity of a permanent double-life – all this created an atmosphere unique in history and a musical culture nearly impossible to describe (chs VIII-X). The phenomenon of the latent musical language, which existed, lived and provided communication, and which may be described as the oral musical tradition of 20th-century totalitarian systems, is analyzed here for the first time on examples of Jewish elements in Dmitri Shostakovich's music (ch. XI). This Aesopian musical language, as any oral tradition in the danger of sinking into oblivion remains a major desiderata of musicology. In the last part of the book (chs. XIV-XVI) I strive for an understanding of musical life in modern Israel, its strains in retaining Jewish musical cultures and the creation of the new multicultural music of Israel/Palestine.

This kind of historical overview or bridging requires some working definition of the discussed subject, which as well known, was and is by itself an endless subject of discourse. By accepting Jewish music as no longer anchored in myth and stiff tradition, and regardless of attempts to move it into different forms of multipartite-ethnicity, -territoriality, -culture etc., we may suggest a solution based on Allan Merriams's comprehension of music in general. Using his definition of music in a broader sense as "patterned behavior," we may claim that ethnic, respectively national music, is ethnic, respectively national patterned behavior. In the case of the Jewish people – Jewish conditioned patterned behavior, or in other words, music that shows historical, stylistic and/or semantic codes of Jewish culture, *transmits paradigma of Jewish culture.*

I would like to conclude this short introduction to *On Jewish Music* which reflects more than thirty years of apprehension, doubts and work, by expressing thanks and appreciation to my wife Aviva, the person without whose daily patient support and critical eye this volume would never have been fulfilled. My gratitude also to everyone who has contributed to this work, each in his own way, with encouragement, suggestions or necessary information, especially the staff members of libraries and archives who were helpful with photographic and other material, as well as the publishers and editors who have kindly permitted the reprint of the chapters indicated in the Contents.

The publication of this book was made possible by the financial support of the Bar-Ilan University Research Fund.

Joachim Braun
Jerusalem, June 2005

Contents

Introduction _____ 7

List of Figures _____ 15

Musical Examples _____ 19

Past _____ 21

I. Music in Ancient Israel/Palestine, the Biblical Terminology
of Music Instruments and the Near Eastern Context ____ 23
   A. Historical Survey (excerpts from: *Music in Ancient Israel/Palestine* [=Series *The Bible in Its World*, gen. ed. D. N. Freedman] tr. by Douglas W. Stott, Grand Rapids, Mich./Cambridge, U. K., 2002 _____ 23
   B. Biblical Terminology of Music Instruments (excerpts from: *Eerdmans Dictionary of the Bible*, ed. D. N. Freedman, Grand Rapids/Cambridge, 2000, pp. 927-929) _____ 42
   C. The Near Eastern Context (from "Musical Instruments," in: *The Oxford Encyclopedia of Archaeology in the Near East*, ed. in chief E. M. Meyers, New York/Oxford, 1997, vol. 4:70-79). _____ 51

II. Some Remarks on the Music History of Ancient Israel/Palestine: Written or Archaeological Evidence (from: *Orient-Archäologie: Musikarchäologie*, vol. 7/II, ed. E. Hickmann et al., Rahden/Wetf., 2000, pp. 135-140). _____ 73

III. Music in Ancient Israel/Palestine and Ethnicity (based on papers at the ICTM /Rio de Janeiro 2002/ and IMS /Leuven 2003/ congresses). _____ 83

IV. The Lute in Ancient Israeli and Jewish Iconography (from: *Festschrift Christoph-Hellmut Mahling*, ed. A. Beer et alii., vol. 2 =*Mainzer Studien zur Musikwissenschaft* 37/2. Tutzing, 1997, pp. 163-188). _____ 127

V. The Iconography of the Organ: Change in Jewish Thought and Musical Life (from: *Music in Art*, 2004, 27: 55-69). _____ 143

The Diaspora: East Europe – Russia – Soviet Union _____ 157

VI. The Unpublished Volumes of Moshe Beregovski's *Jewish Musical Folklore* (from: *Israel Studies in Musicology* IV, 1987, 125-143). _____ 159

VII. The Large Forms of Klezmer Music: The "Missing Link" (based on paper at the 3ed Congress on Jewish Music, London University 2000). _____ 181

VIII. The Jewish National School of Music in Russia (from: *Proceedings of the World Congress on Jewish Music*, Jerusalem 1978, ed. J. Cohen, Tel-Aviv: The Institute of Translation of Hebrew Literature, 1982, pp. 198-204). _____ 195

IX. Jews in Soviet Music (updated version of *Research Paper No. 22*, The Hebrew University of Jerusalem, The Soviet and East European Research Centre, and *Jews in Soviet Culture*, ed. Jack Miller, London, Institute of Jewish Affairs, 1984, pp. 65-106). _____ 203

X. Die Bekämpfung der Moderne und der Antisemitismus (from: *Die Musik des osteuropäischen Judentums: totalitäre Systeme – Nachklaenge*, ed. F. Geisler, Leipzig/Dresden 1997, pp. 21-26). _____ 257

XI. On the Double Meaning of Jewish Elements in Dimitri Shostakovich's Music _____ 265
    A. The Double Meaning (from: *The Musical Quarterly*, LXXI/1, 1985, pp. 68-80) _____ 265

B. The Song Cycle *From Jewish Folk Poetry: Aspects of Style and Meaning* (from: M.H. Brown, ed., *Russian and Soviet Music: Essays for Boris Schwarz*, Ann Arbor, Mich., 1984, pp. 259-286) _____ 277

C. The Present Shostakovich Discourse (based on paper at the International Shostakovich Symposium, Glazgow, November 2000). _____ 309

XII. Christian and Jewish Religious Elements in Music: A Hidden Language of Resistance in Soviet Riga (from: *Musikgeschichte zwischen Ost- und Westeuropa: Kirchenmusik – geistliche Musik – religiöse Musik.* Ed. H. Loos/Kl.-P. Koch, Sinzig, 2002, pp. 77-82). _____ 323

XIII. Music – Survival – Resistance (based on paper at the conference *Collaboration and Resistance During the Holocaust*, Uppsala University, April 2002). _____ 331

Israel Today _____ 341

XIV. Aspekte der Musiksoziologie in Israel (from: *Studien zur systematischen Musikwissenschaft =Hamburger Jahrbuch für Musikwissenshaft* 9, ed. P. Petersen, Hamburg, 1986, pp. 85-104). _____ 343

XV. Towards a Study of Israeli Musical Culture: The Case of Kiryat Ono (with T. Bensky and U. Sharvit, from: *Asian Music*, XVII/2, 1986, pp. 186-209; abridged version). _____ 369

Conclusion _____ 395

XVI. The Musical Landscape in Israel/Palestine: 3,000 Years Ago and Today (from: K. Eberle, et al., *Musikkonzepte – Konzepte der Musikwissencahft: Bericht über den Internationalen Kongress der Gesellschaft fuer Musikforschung, Halle-Saale, 1998*, vol. 2., 2000, pp. 52-61). _____ 397

Figures _____ 409

List of Figures

Figures Ch. I-A

Fig. IA-1. Pelvic bone withh fox teeth string rattle, Hayonim Cave (10th mill. B. C.), IAA 79.536

Fig. IA-2. Ivory plaque, Megiddo, lyre player at symposium of ruler (12th-13th cent. B. C.), IAA 38.780

Fig. IA-3. Terracotta plaque relief, Dan (15th cent. B. C.), Hebrew Union College (Jerusalem), No. 23.095

Fig. IA-4. Drawing, tomb of Khnumhotem II, Beni Hassan, lyre player with a group of Semitic nomads (20th cent. B. C.), fragment (from Newberry, 1893, pl. XXXI)

Fig. IA-5. Alabaster relief, captured Jewish lyre players, Nineveh (8th cent B.C.), BM 12497

Fig. IA-6. Clay stand with five musicians, Ashdod (11th cent. B. C.), IAA 68.1182

Fig. IA-7. Mosaic floor, Sheikh Zouede, Gaza, Dionysian procession (3ed-4th century C. E.), Ismailia Historical Museum, (a) relief drawing from Hickmann 1949, (b) fragment (photo by Prof. A. Ovadia)

Fig. IA-8. Mosaic floor, Sepphoris, Dionysian POMPI, in situ (3ed century C. E.)

Figures Ch. I-B

Fig. IB-1. Wall drawing, Idumaean Necropolis, hunting scene with trumpeter, in situ (3ed cent.)

Fig. IB-2. Bar-Kokhba coin (132-135 C. E.), lyre – probably, kinnor, EIM K- 4676

Fig. IB-3. Bar-Kokhba coin (132-135 C. E.), lyre – probably, nebel, EIM K- 4649

Fig. IB-4. Terra-cotta figurine with double-pipe, Achziv (8th-7th cent. B. C.), IAA 44.56

Fig. IB-5. Mosaic floor, synagogue, Hamat Tiberias (3ed cent. C. E.), shofar with *menorah* (seven-branch lampstand), *mahta* (incense pan), *etrog* (cirus fruit), and *lulav* (palm frond), in situ.

Figures Ch. I-C

Fig. IC-1. Sistrum, (a) Egyptian (from Hickmann 1961, MGB II/1, fig. 25, 11th -8th cent. B. C.), (b) Sumerian (from Rashid 1984, fig. 42, first half of 3ed mill. B. C.)

Fig. IC-2. Rock etching, Negev, drawing of (a) lyre players and (b) drummer and dancers (from Anati 1963), in situ (first half of 2nd mill. B. C.)

Fig. IC-3. Mesopotamia, chordophone-membranaphone duet lyre with drummer (from Rashid 1984, fig. 59)

Fig. IC-4. (a) Basalt etching, Harra Desert (1st-4th century C. E.) *arghul* player with dancer, AM J1886, (b) Terra-cotta figurine, double *zurna* player, Tel Malhata, IAA 94.3394 (7th cent. B. C.), (c) Beth-Shean, mosaic floor, (6th century C. E) Convent of St. Mary, mono *zurna* player

Fig. IC-5. Wall painting, Thebian necropolis No. 52 (15th century B.C.), harp, lute, and double-pipe players (from Hickmann 1961, MGB II/1, Fig. 61)

Fig. IC-6. Mesopotamia, vertical harp (from Rashid 1984, Fig. 152, Ninive, 8th-7th cent. B. C.)

Fig. IC-7. Mesopotamia, Ur King Burial (mid. 3ed mill. B. C.), Silver Bull-head lyre (from Rashid 1984, Fig. 4)

Figures Ch. III

Fig. III-1a. Clay rattle, spool form, Hazor, IAA 67.1160.
Fig. III-1b. Clay rattle with handle, Tell el 'Agul, IAA 35.4157.
Fig. III-1c. Clay rattle, anthropomorphic form, Tell el Far'a South, IAA 16936.
Fig. III-1d. Clay rattle, bird form, Ashdod, IAA 60.1031.
Fig. III-1e. Fruit form, Megiddo, OI A18362.
Fig. III-1f. Bell form (x-ray), Hazor, HUIA 45288.

Fig. III-1g. Terracotta figurine, idol with rattle on his head, Qitmit, IAA 87.117.

Fig. III-2a. Symmetrical lyre with rounded resonance body, Ashdod (original lost).

Fig. III-2b. Symmetrical *kithara* type-"concert" lyre, Gaza (copy in IM).

Fig. III-3a. Bell-shaped figurine of female drummer, Achziv (from Mazar 1996, fig. 53:8).

Fig. III-3b. Plaque relief of female drummer, Tell el-Fara'a N., EB F3426.

Fig. III-3c. Plaque relief of female with disk and hands in a symmetrical position, Taanach, AAM J.7285.

Fig. III-3d. Bell shaped figurine of female drummer, Nebo, SBF M1072.

Fig. III-3e. Broken drums from terra-cotta plaque figurines, Amman, AAM ATH 66-3/4

Figures Ch. IV

Fig. IV-1. Dura-Europos Synagogue, (a) wall painting, 2nd-3ed century (From E. R. Goodenough, *Jewish Symbolism...*, vol. XI, pl. xiii); (b) idem., drawing of destroyed.objects, among others two lutes

Fig. IV-2. Parma City Library, Ms. 1870, (a) fol. 105r/ Ps. 76, (b) fol. 89r/Ps. 67, (c) fol. 198r/Ps. 137.

Fig. IV-3. Farhi Bible, fol. 186r, 1366-1382, Sasson Collection, Jerusalem.

Fig. IV-4. Golden Haggadah, fol. 15r, British Library, BL-Add. 27210 .

Fig. IV-5. Barcelona Haggadah, fol. 61r, British Library, BL-Ad 14761fol.

Fig. IV-6. Arba'a Turim, Vatican Library, 1435, Cod. Rossiana-555, fol. 292/293, frame with (a) lute and (b) organ player.

Fig. IV-7. Miscellany, Ms. Rothshild-24, fol. 322v, IM Jerusalem.

Fig. IV-8. Miscellany, Ms. Rothshild-24, fol. 464v, IM Jerusalem.

Fig. IV-9. Siddur, Bodleian Library, Ms. Opp. 776, fol. 79v.

Fig. IV-10. Bible, 1411, British Library, Royal 19.D.iii, fol. 458.

Fig. IV-11. Hagaddah Yahudd, Israel Museum, Jerusalem, Ms. 180/50, fol. 17r.

Figures Ch. V

Fig. V-1. Terra-cotta oil lamp, 3ed-4th century, Ein Hashofet, Israel, IAA 71.5080.
Fig. V-2. From Abdul Rizaq Zaqzyq and Marcelle Duchesne-Gullemin, "La mosaique de Mariamin," in: *Annales Arabes Syriennes*, XX/1 (1970), pp. 93-125, Pl. 1-2.
Fig. V-3. Drawing, representation of the Talmudic *magrepha*, Second Kennicot Bible, 1366-1382, Bodleian Library, Ms. Kenn.2, fol. 1v.
Fig. V-4. Kaufmann Haggadah, late 14th century, Budapest City Library, Kaufmann Collection, Ms. A 422, fol. 3v.
Fig. V-5. Lobkovitz Prayer Book, 1494, Prague, Klementinium-Universitni Knihovna, Ms. XXIII F202.

Abbreviations

AAM, AM	Amman Archaeological Museum
BM	British Museum
EIM	Eretz Israel Museum, Tel-Aviv
EB	Ecole Biblique Jerusalem
HUIA	Hebrew University Jerusalem Institute of Archaeology
IAA	Israel Antiquity Authorities
IM	Israel Museum Jerusalem
OI	Chicago University Oriental Institute
SBF	Studia Biblicum Franciscanum, Jerusalem

Anati, Emmanuel 1963. *Palestine before the Hebrews*. New York.
Hickmann, Hans 1949. *Cymbals et Crotale dans l'Égypte Ancienne*. Cairo.
Hickmann, Hans 1961. *Ägypten*. Leipzig.
Mazar, Eilat 1996. *The Achziv burials*. Jerusalem.
MGG. *Musik in Geschichte und Gegenwart*. Ed. F. Blume, vol. 1-14, Kassel-Basel, 1949-79.
Newberry, P. Edward et al.1893. *Beni Hasan, vol. 1 – 4*. London.
Rashid, Sbhi Anwar 1984. *Mesopotamien*. Leipzig.

Musical Examples

Mus. ex. VI-1: Beregovski Ms., No. 20, *Taksim*.
Mus. ex. VII-1: (a) Beregovski Ms., Add. No.1, Pedhatsur, *Viglid*; (b) Goizman, *Yiddišer Koncert*.
Mus. ex. VII-2: (a) Beregovski, Ms. No. 21, *Doina*; (b) Kotlyarov No. 4, *Doina*.
Mus. ex. XIA-1: (a) Shostakovich op. 79/2, and Skoletz, *S'loyfen, s'yogn*; (b) Shostakovich op.79/5, Beregovski 1962, no. 111 and 113, Gnessin, op. 41/33.
Mus. ex. XIA-2: Shostakovich, op. 107.
Mus. ex. XIA-3: (a) Shostakovich, op. 87/8; (b) weekday morning service (Eisenstein); (c) Lebele Alukster's chanting (Ephros).
Mus. ex. XIB-4: (a) Shostakovich, op. 79/6; (b) Idelsohn, *Thesaurus*, vol. 9/581.
Mus. ex. XIB-5: (a) Shostakovich, op. 79/11; (b) Idelsohn, *Thesaurus*, vol. 10/52; (c) ib., 10/73.
Mus. ex. XIB-6: Freigish mode.
Mus. ex. XIB-7: Shostakovich, op. 79/1. Modal ambiguity.
Mus. ex. XIB-8: Shostakovich, op. 79/3 Simultaneous use of minor and major third.
Mus. ex. XIB-9: Shostakovich, op. 79/2, 3, 4, 5, 6, 9, 10, and 11. Leitmotive.
Mus. ex. XIB-10: Iambic prime.
Mus. ex. XIB-11: Altered Phrygian or *freigish* and altered Dorian modes.
Mus. ex. XIB-12: Study-*shteiger*, Idelsohn, *Jewish Music*, p. 189.

Past

I. Music in Ancient Israel/Palestine, the Biblical Terminology of Music Instruments and the Near Eastern Context*

A. Historical Survey

Preface

Neither sound nor any musical notation remains of the music of the ancient world or of ancient Israel/Palestine. Apart from the sparse written records, the only information we have is that provided by the stone, bone, or metal unearthed by archaeologists.

Yet even musical periods documented much more richly than of the ancient world can leave us in uncertainty. How were Beethoven's works actually performed? How were the harmony and melody of Correli's *continuo* realized? What was the correct interpretation of neumatic notation symbols? What about the Jewish *ta'amei hamikra*? With even less information at our disposal, what can we possibly say about the music of the ancient world? This music, the music of ancient Israel/Palestine, is still passed on orally and from father to son. Beginning in this small strip on the eastern edge of the Mediterranean, it has over the course of two and a half millennia spread over the entire globe and assimilated literally hundreds of musical styles.

The only way to deal with this situation is to assemble a portrait of this past musical world from many small *tesserae*. Because the music itself has probably disappeared forever, the goal obviously cannot be total restoration; we can, however, certainly hope to gain insight into the char-

---

* (A) Music in Ancient Israel/Palestine: Historical Survey (excerpts from: *Music in Ancient Israel/Palestine* (=Series *The Bible in Its World*, Gen. Ed. D. N. Freedman), tr. by Douglas W. Stott, Grand Rapids, Mich./Cambridge, U. K., 2002; (B) Biblical Terminology of Music Instruments (excerpts from: Eerdmans Dictionary of the Bible, ed. D. N. Freedman, Grand Rapids/Cambridge, 2000, pp. 927-929; and (C) The Near Eastern Context (in: "Musical Instruments," *The Oxford Encyclopedia of Archaeology in the Near East*, ed. Eric Meyers, New York/Oxford, 1997, vol. 4:70-79).

acter of that music, into its "setting in life" and symbolism. Even at best, though, such a mosaic can offer no more than a fragmented, vague imitation of this past world of sound. Given the nature of our sources, we must simply accept that parts of the mosaic will have faded with time; others will have been destroyed entirely. Similarly, even the relationships between what tiny pieces of the mosaic we do have at our disposal may not always be what we think.

The acoustic restoration of musical events is impossible not only because the source material is absent in the first place, but primarily because the historical situation, the social circumstances, and the listeners' psychological disposition and corresponding reaction to this music are forever beyond our reach. The acoustic ecology of this millennial past was radically different from our own. We today can hardly imagine how in the relative stillness of the ancient world, the rustling of the ornamentation women wore on their arms, feet, and hips was a significant experience of sound, or how the sound of an animal horn or of a trumpet was perceived as a supernatural rumbling.

Although the present study draws from both archaeological and written and comparative ethnological sources, the focus is on archaeological findings. The only real witnesses to this acoustic past are the musical instruments, terracotta and metal figures, etched stone illustrations, and mosaics unearthed by archaeologists. And yet even this evidence is often a matter of dispute, or even deceptive.

Of all pre-Christian cultures, none has a music history as burdened by one-sided and subjective perspectives and prejudices as that of ancient Israel/Palestine. Research into other high cultures of the ancient world has never been as plagued by a neglect of scientific principles or by unscientific arguments as is the case of this region. Indeed, until the mid-twentieth century, the entire assessment of the music of ancient Israel/Palestine was based on a single source, namely, the Bible; although this source was clearly of a mythological nature, its theological significance elevated it to the status of a historical document. This one-sided focus prompted an attitude of fetishism with regard to what the Bible actually recounts about instruments, musical events, and music in the larger sense, and led scholars to disregard completely all cultural entities and tendencies within ancient Israel/Palestine besides the specifically Israelite.

Not surprisingly, then, the genuinely new character of the history of music in this region is emerging only now, at the end of the twentieth century. This new assessment has been made possible by an examination of the only sources capable of ensuring an objective discussion based on factual material, namely, archaeological and iconographical evidence from ancient Israel/Palestine itself.

The history of music in ancient Israel/Palestine easily transcends the boundaries of purely musical interest. Musical findings illuminate for the historian certain social processes that otherwise cannot be perceived in quite the same way, or allow the historian to clarify misunderstandings that neither the natural nor the social sciences can really articulate.

Scholars today generally accept that music is an expression of certain socially shaped aspects of human behavior. Because the ancient civilizations of the Mediterranean always viewed music this way themselves, the history of ancient music invariably reveals much about these civilizations that we otherwise might miss entirely.

Interest in the history of music in ancient Israel, often erroneously called "music in the Bible" began during the period immediately following the conclusion of the Greek version of the Old Testament (the Septuagint; third/second century B. C. E.). Because for centuries musicologists viewed the Bible as the only primary source, it became by default the only material actually studied; even though the Septuagint itself also qualified as such alongside the Hebrew version, in reality it represented the first interpretation of the original biblical texts. Even at that early stage, though, translators interpreted the text differently and were otherwise often insecure about the various terms; the confusing result was that they translated the names of musical instruments quite inconsistently. This insecurity becomes even more pronounced in another pre-Latin translation, namely, the Syrian Peshitta. By contrast, and despite many deviations, the Latin Vulgate is much more consistent in this regard, though this consistency probably derives more from the disciplined system of translation itself than from a more accurate understanding of the material.

Although Roman authors do indeed add certain secondary details, their discussions do not contribute much to clarifying hard facts. Flavius Josephus, Philo of Alexandria, Plutarch, and Tacitus function as more or less reliable eyewitnesses who provide various tangential comments concerning Jewish music during the Roman period.

The tractates of the Mishnah and Talmud (second to sixth centuries) function as both sources and interpretative attempts, the former primarily for contemporary circumstances, the latter on the basis of a lengthy oral tradition. Although both works sometimes provide excellent descriptions of musical reality, some of their traditions cannot really be taken seriously. Care must be taken, for example, when considering the tradition of the Jerusalemite magraephah, an instrument allegedly capable of producing one thousand tones (b. *Sukk.* 5:6) and whose sound could be heard as far away from Jerusalem as Jericho (m. *Tamid* 3:8).

Because the influence of Augustinian thought and its permutations was so pervasive, the *scientia musicae* of the Middle Ages tended to view the music of ancient Israel from a primarily allegorical perspective, ignoring the *musicae practica* of the Bible and focusing instead on the spiritual symbolism of the biblical musical instruments themselves. Focus on the instruments produced the equivalent of an inventory of ancient Israelite/Palestinian instruments, and focus on the symbolism became the central area of research. Neither, however, contributed anything of substance to genuine research into the music of ancient Israel; the discussion centered mainly on daily circumstances involving admissible or forbidden instrumental performance.

The Stone Age (12th Millennium-3200 B. C)

The Stone Age encompasses a rather broad temporal span, extending from the time when ancient Israel/Palestine was first settled by what we now call modern human beings about 700,000 years ago up to the Bronze Age.

Unfortunately, we have uncovered no direct evidence of any acoustic activity from the more distant cultures such as those of the cave dwellers of Tabun or Yabrud from the middle to late recent Acheulean Age (ca. 6th-1st millennium B. C.). One can assume, however, that people did engage in organized musical activity during this extended period now known as the "pebble-tool" culture. In lieu of musical instruments in the strict sense, people probably used various objects, both natural and manmade, including tools and even their own bodies, to produce music.

This assumption is plausible enough considering the basic forms of music-making or even noise-production familiar even today from many parts of the world, including the clapping of hands, stamping of feet, beating on one's chest, or slapping one's thigh. As effective as such activity is for producing primitive rhythms, it still leaves behind no tangible material witness. Hence the comparative method offers us the best hypothesis to date for describing the beginnings of music production, an activity that for millennia was a basic component of human culture. Such activity was doubtless also part of the Stone Age culture.

The Natufian Culture occurs considerably later, ca. 12,000-8500 B. C., and it was during this period that the hunter-gatherer culture was replaced by the beginnings of agriculture and animal husbandry. These developments were part of long-term processes that included what is now known as the "Neolithic revolution" or, by another designation, the "agricultural revolution," depending on one's focus. Microlithic production developed in this context, and for the first time we find material witnesses to emergent music- or noise-production as well as to an understanding of faith and art associated with intentional acoustic effects as, for example, the first discovered sound-producing artifact – a string rattle (**Fig. IA-1**). It is during the "Neolithic revolution" that at the time of basic changes in human lifestyle, during increasing sedentary, first actual steps towards domestication of plants and animals, also for the first time signs of a new instrumental quality of acoustic activity may be confirmed. It accentuates the place of sound in a society of new patterns – the crystallization of craft specialization and emergence of a social elite. Indeed, these changes were radical enough to be called revolutionary.

The historian is handicapped with regard to the Stone Age insofar as source material is still accumulating only very slowly. Isolated examples must suffice for assembling an admittedly incomplete survey of the period as a whole, and even such a survey is hampered by the difficulty in assessing the often virtually indiscernible changes that took place in Stone Age musical culture over extremely long periods of time. An analogy to such changes might be the hand-axe, which some believe represented the main object of human production for hundreds of thousands of years. So also did the main noisemaker remain the same for millennia.

Especially with regard to the most conservative area of cultural and artistic activity during the Stone Age, namely, cultic music, scholars universally concur that no real changes, or only quite minor ones, took place during this period. Millennia passed before the basic methods of producing noise or sounds changed.

The peculiar chronological heterogeneity described by Helga Weippert[1] as "non-simultaneity within simultaneity" endured for millennia and with unusual tenacity in the musical culture of the Stone Age. Certain music-related objects of the Natufian culture persisted in various forms for millennia without leaving behind any discernible traces, though the first idiophones (pendant rattle ornaments) did make their appearance during the Natufian culture. One characteristic change during this period is that new materials were now used, such as mussels and stone, and even new methods of production and new combinations. Materials were now linked together, given a polished finish, or even adorned with carvings. Indeed, what we seem to have are syncretistic decorative objects such as necklaces of bone or stone whose musical effects resulted from various body movements and emotional expressions; such could include spirited movements during dances, while worshiping the deity, or even during work. Such objects functioned on at least two different levels. They were not only noisemakers in the narrower sense, but also broadly accepted cultic objects, personal valuables, or even implements of work attesting a polyaesthetic culture dominated by functional audio-visual values. Several millennia pass before we find evidence from the 7th millenium B. C. – the mystical "whirring sticks," known as bullroarers, normally associated with ancestral cults.

The Bronze Age (3200-1200 B. C.)

A new, different revolution takes place in the world of sound during the Chalcolithic period, the period straddling the transition between the Stone Age and Bronze Age in the 4th millennium B. C. This change should be called revolutionary and qualified as a genuine "organological" or "acoustic revolution" in the sense that qualitative new type of musical in-

---

1   H. Weippert, *Palaestina in vorhellenistischer Zeit* (Muenchen, 1988), pp. 26-27.

struments emerge. It is during this period that the first evidence for the hourglass drum and for a new generation of stringed instruments, namely, the harp appear.

Several factors prompted the musical culture of ancient Israel/Palestine to move on to the next stage. The socioeconomic situation changed, with urban culture replacing the Stone Age village culture in many parts of the country. As a result of this development, more and more inhabitants moved into the new urban centers, and rapid demographic changes took place. Because the smaller cities now had up to a thousand citizens, and the larger ones between six and eight thousand, musical life in them required more differentiated and more sophisticated sound production than was earlier the case. Earlier instruments no longer served the needs of the inhabitants of these emergent cities, and so the instruments themselves were subjected to change and further development. By and large, these changes prompted the development of musical instruments capable of producing a higher volume of sound.

The musical culture of Canaan reached an astonishingly advanced stage of development during the Bronze Age. Moreover, like its two larger neighbors, Egypt and Babylonia and Assyria, it did so at a unified autochthonous level. Scholars have often asserted that the musical culture in Canaan or ancient Israel/Palestine was only a receptive one, situated propitiously at the crossroads of the ancient Near East but possessing "no civilization of its own." Recent research, however, has taken a harder look at comparative archaeological materials and found that this musical culture in its own turn exerted considerable influence on its surroundings. It is no accident that virtually all written witnesses that mention ancient Israelite/Palestinian music in the neighboring regions of the Near East date to the Bronze Age.

One of the most intriguing aspects of Canaanite musical culture during this period concerns the instruments themselves, which are, of course, the most tangible witnesses to that culture. The Canaanites were familiar with virtually every instrument type already in use in the ancient Near East. At the same time, however, they imprinted upon each of those instruments specifically Canaanite features or altered each in a specifically Canaanite way, affecting such aspects as form, performance, and function. For example, the lyre, already known as the *knr* during the Bronze Age, is attested in Canaan only as a solo instrument **(Fig. IA-2)**. Commensurately, it is played in Canaan in a new position, one more conducive to virtuoso performance in the hands of a soloist. Similarly, the lute seems to have been played in a hitherto unknown way. The features now accompanying its performance suggest a more popular, informal, syncretistic style that combined music together with dance and farce (**Fig. IA-1, 2 and 3**). Prior to this period, the double pipe, a reed instrument, was never portrayed as a solo instrument accompanying erotic dance. The small, round frame drum (*toph*) appears quite early, at the beginning of the second millennium B. C., on a rock drawing in the Negev as an instrument accompanying a round dance of male figures, attesting thus a Near Eastern tradition thousands of years old. Many bronze cymbals (*msltm*) have been found along the entire length of the Levant coast from Ashkelon to Ugarit. Independent forms of other idiophones, including especially clay rattles, have been found in great numbers in excavations, confirming further the autochthonous nature of the musical culture of ancient Israel/Palestine.

A whole range of historical factors invites us to reassess the musical culture during this period. The understanding of Israel's origins has been revised during the past few years. Scholars no longer believe the country was taken by means of conquest, and believe rather that Israel emerged during the eleventh century BCE as a result of complicated and radical socioeconomic developments accompanying a process of migration involving the entire Near East during the Late Bronze Age. A dichotomy of highland and lowland cultures developed from the region's demographic dichotomy, which included both nomadic populations and, in greater numbers, sedentary populations. At the same time, the earlier Canaanite city-states were clearly in demise, and the resulting vacuum was filled at least in part by an influx of sea-peoples and other groups, Semitic and non-Semitic alike. The resulting historical situation was characterized by two features that would decisively affect the development of music in the region: the strong indigenous Canaanite cultural heritage, and a remarkably heterogenous local cultural tradition partially influenced by immigrants.

At this time, Canaan possessed a rich indigenous musical tradition. Ugaritic sources from the Late Bronze Age (1400-1300 B. C) attest the names of numerous instruments (*knr*, *tp*, *msltm*, also the word *sr*, song) that show up only much later in the Old Testament.

Various comparative attempts have been made to understand the music itself more precisely. One possible bit of evidence in this regard, albeit one that must be approached with caution, is the well-known collection of Ugaritic cuneiform writings (1500-1300 BCE), which have generally been understood as representing musical notation. Scholars have suggested such notation might also apply to contemporaneous Canaanite music as well. Given the similarity between the instrument inventory at least based on the names enumerated in those writings, and the presumed similarity regarding how they were actually played, one might assume that the musical styles and probably the overall results were also similar. It is also possible, of course, that melodies were fixed using a different system during this period in Canaan, perhaps even a non-written one. Chironomy is one of the oldest traditions associated with Israelite liturgical singing, being documented at least since the beginning of the Christian age (b.*Ber.* 62a), and is still in use in some East African congregations.

What we do know about the instruments used in Canaan during this period and about musical performance suggests that the resulting music was extremely emotional and perhaps even orgiastic. The large number of rattles and cymbals excavated from this period certainly points in that direction. Similarly, the functional incorporation of aerophones and chordophones into this music would have enhanced such an effect; nor should one forget that certain finds from Iron Age I derive from a Canaanite musical heritage. Moving from one local center of urban culture to the next with their accompanying profusion of deities during the Bronze Age, one would probably find that the musical styles differed primarily as regards the fullness of sound and the resulting volume, but not significantly as regards the instruments themselves.

The Iron Age (1200-586 B. C.)

The balance of power shifted dramatically in ancient Israel/Palestine in the thirteenth-twelfth centuries BCE. The golden age of the Egyptians and the Hittites came to an end, and peripheral tribes penetrated into Egypt and the Levant to the fill the vacuum these two high powers left behind. This was also the time of the emergent "sea peoples," the Philistines in the South and the Phoenicians in the North, who created not only a progressive, technologically mobile culture in the larger sense, but also an extraordinarily rich artistic tradition. Unfortunately, the history of these cultures still remains to be written. A similar situation applies to the emergent kingdoms of the Edomites, Moabites, and Ammonites in Transjordan, whose cultural tradition in many respects was quite independent and about which still little is known. Only recently have the material and musical cultures of this group come under more detailed study, a situation all the more regrettable because they quite possibly represent one of the most striking examples of the aforementioned "heterogeneity within homogeneity" within the region. Easily the most important development during this period was the gradual emergence of monotheism, which the Hebrew tribes cultivated until it finally established an enduring position for itself in Judea toward the end of this period. The first entities within which the Hebrew tribes finally consolidated themselves politically were the kingdom of Israel in the Judean-Israelite mountains (ca. 1020-928 BCE) and then later the divided kingdoms of Israel (until 721 BCE) and Judah (until 587 BCE). This emergence of the national political entity in the form of the state was the dominant characteristic of Iron Age Israel/Palestine. Not surprisingly, this political consolidation in its own turn profoundly affected the development of the region's musical culture.

Considering what the Old Testament says about music among the various peoples in ancient Israel/Palestine, we find that music during this period played a significant part in a wide variety of situations within the life of these nations. Music was engaged in connection with cultic activities, victory celebrations, secular rejoicing, communication, situations involving ecstasy and rapture, and mourning or grief. In a more abstract sense, music or the musical instruments themselves could even be used as symbols.

The Old Testament offers a plethora of examples demonstrating not only how music functioned in society, but also how it was understood or perceived. The sound of the *shofar* was so powerful that it was perceived as being supernatural (Ex. 19:13; Josh. 6:4-9). The famous scene in which David plays for Saul shows how the *kinnor* was also engaged for its therapeutic effects (1 S. 16:16). Certain kinds of music or musical instruments were perceived to be so powerful that they were used to stimulate or enhance moods of ecstasy or prophecy (1 S 10:5; 2 K. 3:15). Indeed, the importance of certain instruments derived from their association with God himself, such as the two silver trumpets Moses was ordered to make in the wilderness (Nu. 10:1-10). The Old Testament offers especially detailed information about the significance of music during the waning years of David's rule (1 Ch. 23-25), and later in connection with the central rite of worship in the temple, namely, the sacrifice (2 Ch. 5:6-14) and burnt offering, "according to the commandment of David" (2 Ch. 29:25), during the reign of King Hezekiah of Judah (2 Ch. 20-30). As is well known, tradition has it that King David himself organized the musical liturgy to be used in worship, and that this music played an especially important role in connection with the burnt offering. Peculiarly, however, neither of the original descriptions of the Davidic liturgy and sacrificial ritual, that is, neither 2 S. 20-24 nor 1 K. 8:62-64, mention this musical liturgy at all. It is only much later, in the parallel verses from Chronicles, that it appears in this connection. This situation may reflect the imposition of an idealized notion onto later texts. At this time also the first indirect libel concerning instrumental music is issued: "Take the *kinnor*, go about the city, you forgotten prostitute! Make sweet melody, sing many songs, that you may be remembered" (Isa. 23:16-17).

The early parts of the Old Testament contain various texts that were sung or that themselves mention different song forms performed in connection with victory, rejoicing, praise, veneration of heroes, or even lament (Ex. 15:1-19; Nu. 21:16-18; Dt. 32:1-43; 1 S. 18:6-7; 28:3; 2 S. 1:17-27; Jgs. 5: 1 K. 13:30). Structural or rhythmic forms can often be discerned in these song texts, including refrains (e.g., Ex. 15:2,21; 2 S. 1:19,25,27), or the familiar device *parallelismus membrorum*, in which a poetic motif is repeated two or more times in varying forms, e.g., "Tell it not in Gath, proclaim it not in the streets of Ashkelon; or the daughters of the Philistines will rejoice, the daughters of the uncircumcised will exult" (2 S. 1:20), or "Oh, may your breasts be like clusters of the vine, and the scent of your breath like apples," (Cant. 7:9). Such structural features within the texts themselves probably reflect parallel, slightly varying musical structures that unfortunately cannot be reconstructed given the presence status of scholarship.

Unfortunately, no iconographic evidence has come to light corresponding to these cultic and secular musical performances in the Old

Testament. One might perhaps adduce the grave mural from Beni-hasan as an indirect allusion to the original myth of the three initial and most important activities, namely, shepherding, metallurgy, and music (Gen. 4:19-23; comp. **Fig. IA-4**). Of course, the absence of any significant archaeological correlation for the biblical texts makes it all the more difficult to derive more from Old Testament musical texts as historical documents.

Ultimately, the effect of Canaan's musical culture is essentially the same as that of its mythology. It is not just the Ugaritic texts that exhibit a relationship with the later biblical books; elements of the Canaanite musical tradition are also discernible in the Old Testament. One need only compare the two parallel verses 2 S. 6:5 and 1 Ch. 13:8, both of which describe a cultic act that for the first time is also accompanied by music. The second, later text clearly has repressed elements of the older Canaanite tradition. The first text describes a loud, orgiastic orchestra consisting largely of idiophones and membranophones, including the *ase beroshim, tupim, mena'an'im, selselim, kinnorot and n'balim*. The second, later text, after being subjected to revision and even possibly after the musical ritual itself had undergone some change, describes a well-organized ritual featuring liturgical, vocal-instrumental music that including *sirim* (singing), as well as *kinnorot, nebalim, tupim, mesaltayim and hasosarot.*

During the late Canaanite period, local female musicians were admired throughout the entire Near East. At the time of the Judean king Hezekiah (ca. 727-698 B. C.) the lyre players and female Judean minstrels were viewed as the highest tribute for the Assyrian king Sennacherib (see **Fig. IA-5**, Sennacherib relief, ca. 701 B. C. and 2 K. 18:14-16).

Although many elements of tradition did indeed continue forward during the Iron Age, distinct changes become discernible which were probably part of a lengthy cyclical process. On the one hand, many instruments and noisemakers clung tenaciously to their previous forms and functions. Mass devices such as clay rattles continued to be used, and indeed it was not until the Babylonian-Persian period that iron bells replaced them for good. Similarly, drums changed only slightly during this period, and like the rattles, became to a certain extent a mass fetish instrument. On the other hand, several instruments either disappeared entirely or underwent changes. Archaeological evidence for certain idiophones such as cymbals disappears entirely during this period, instruments originally used only by the upper classes or by those familiar or involved with the cult. These particular instruments do not reappear until much later, during the Roman period. The lyre, originally in use among a wide variety of population groups, especially among priests, remained the most commonly played instrument, but now acquired a more convenient, simplified form. These structural changes in the lyre resulted from a reduction in the number of strings and accordingly probably also from a change in the music itself. The lute and the harp also disappeared entirely from musical life in ancient Israel/Palestine during this period, and did not reappear before the Roman period. Still other instruments continued to be as popular as ever, such as the double-reed wind instruments, which maintained their dominant status and yet in certain areas, such as Edom, underwent revolutionary changes, metamorphosing into the conical Edomite mono-pipe of the *zmra*-type **(see Fig. IC-4b)**. At this time clear evidence of the emergence of an autochthon musical instrumentary in Judean, Edomite and Philistine population centers is attested.

If we are to believe the archaeological record, a great many changes occurred within the musical culture of ancient Israel/Palestine when the Israelite monarchy and other national states first became established. Certain musical instruments simply vanished. Others were now played in a different way and even changed their form. Still others simply continued on as before. Finally, completely new instruments appeared. One of the most important changes within instrumental music proper was the emergence of the chordo-aero-membranophone ensemble, familiar as the "Phoenician orchestra"; in this form, the ensemble dates to the eleventh-tenth century B. C. and can be seen on a cult stand from Ashdod with its five musicians. More recent analysis, however, suggests that precisely this ensemble should probably be reinterpreted as an early form associated with the Cybele cult. That is, what we have hitherto called a "Phoenician orchestra" derives in fact from a Canannite-Philistine-Israelite tradition **(see Fig. IA-6)**.

The Babylonian-Persian Period (586 B. C. – 332 B. C.)

The purely objective circumstances that developed following the catastrophe of 586 B. C. after Cyrus finally came to power were quite favorable, especially for Judea/Israel. The liberal attitude and tolerance this ruler showed toward the region did much to encourage both ethnic-cultural and religious developments, the most obvious sign of such renewal being the reconstruction of the second temple during the waning years of the fourth century B. C. Because the temple genuinely was rebuilt, one can legitimately conclude that both religious and cultural life, including music, blossomed anew. And indeed, the picture painted by written sources for this period, namely, the books of Ezra and Nehemiah, is glorious and radiant (see pp. 78-81). This evaluation of musical life for the Babylonian-Persian period was accepted by general historians as well as by musicologists, and in some cases even enriched by personal fantasy.

The unfortunate truth is that archaeology has confronted us with a gap of approximately three hundred years with respect to precisely this period. This complete lack of archaeological information is still extremely difficult to explain, even when we consider various contributing factors and circumstances. It is possible that at least part of the absence of iconographic materials in Israel/Palestine may well have its roots in the influence exerted by iconoclastic powers within the Israelite-Judaic religious hierarchy. Given the present status of scholarship and resources available at present, the question of the musical culture during this period must remain open.

The Hellenistic-Roman Period (4th Cent. B. C. – 4th Cent. A. D.)

By and large, the musical culture in ancient Israel/Palestine during the Hellenistic-Roman period does not escape the multi-layered complexity and contradictory nature otherwise generally attaching to the term "Hellenization." The collapse of the traditional pagan religious canon is now less an issue than the confrontation between the Greek enlightenment on the one hand, and Judaeo-Christian religious thinking on the other. This polymorphous cultural situation is also responsible for the multifaceted nature of music and musical life during the age. Pagan, Judaic, Samaritan, and early-Christian religious rituals all flourished in close proximity, and all made use of music. The very notion of such cosmopolitanism, of "world citizenship," and of "biological equality" was fostered at every quarter by the overwhelming influence of Greek Stoicism. After the period when musical culture was largely specific to a certain city or nation, the setting created by the emergence of a genuine world power could hardly have been more propitious for the development of a rich, multifaceted, even comprehensive musical culture that would produce commensurately syncretistic, comprehensively cosmopolitan musical styles. The Syrian poet Meleager of Gadara proclaimed in an epigram his cosmopolitan belonging to Tyre, Gadara and Athens, and during this period actors, artists, jockeys, and musicians in ancient Israel/Palestine were not identified according to any ethnic or national group, but solely according to where they lived. After the preceding disparity, archaeological and written materials complement one another and show that there was a break in the development of the musical culture. A rich, syncretistic style of music emerged especially within the sphere of purely artistic music, indicating that apparently musical life itself had now become stratified differently than during preceding period.

Archaeological finds now include the entire spectrum of contemporary musical instruments. Bronze- and Iron-Age idiophones such as bells, cymbals, and rattles emerge anew as instruments of the masses, exhibiting both their old forms as well as new ones such as those exhibited by slap cymbals (often known as forked *crotala*, *crotalum*) and castanets. We now encounter the first archaeological evidence for several Old Testament versions of otherwise widespread Near Eastern traditions, such as attaching small bells to a priest's garment (Ex. 28:33f.). The vigorous cultural exchange characterizing this period also included the introduction of foreign musical instruments; for example, the much larger, semispherical Greek *tympanon* replaced the traditional, smaller, round frame drum.

Chordophones and aerophones now undergo dramatic changes. After a long absence, lutes are reintroduced. Harps, primarily in the form of the small angular harp, are now also incorporated into musical life, possibly by way of Sidonian and other immigrants. On the other hand, the lyre now loses its dominant role in musical life and is often used merely as a symbol, the first known example being found on Ptolemaic coins from Acco dating to the second century B. C. Oddly, even though zithers are often thought to have originated during the eighth century B. C. in the Phoenician sphere, and to have played a not insignificant role in later Islamic culture, there is still no evidence attesting their presence during this period in ancient Israel/Palestine.

New wind instruments now appear with a technologically more advanced form likely reflecting a more highly developed level of artistic virtuosity. Such is the case with the double aulos; its new construction included bones overlaid with copper or some other metal and was innovative enough to prompt a critical comment in the Talmud (*Arak.*10:2). In a typical confrontation between traditional aesthetics and innovative production technology, the Talmud declared that the innovation made if difficult to produce the instrument's traditional, ideal sound. Archaeological finds also clearly confirms that aulos players were now divided socially into professional virtuosos, semiprofessional musicians, and dilettantes. It is also during this period that we have the first witness to the cross flute in the Near East, depicted in this case on coins from Baniyas (Paneas or Caesarea Philippi, A. D. 169-222). Although the panpipe appears often in iconography, it seems it was used more as a symbol than as an actual instrument. Shofars also appear in illustrations from the second-third century B. C. on; the first one, in fact, appears exclusively as part of a symbolic grouping consisting of Jewish cultic accoutrements. Although the trumpet is attested in Idumaic iconography for the first time in music history as a hunting instrument, it is still not unequivocally attested in any function associated with the temple, since the authenticity of the popular portrayal on the Arch of Titus is questionable. Finally, the Samaritan oil lamps with representations of portable pneumatic table organs represent some of the most important archaeological finds of this period. The organ always is accompanied by two pairs of slap cymbals (see **Fig. V-1**). These illustrations can certainly illuminate further the musical culture of the Samaritan community specifically and of Hellenistic Judaism in the larger sense.

For the first time we encounter a Jewish musician by name, an actual Hellenistic *klezmer*. The aulos player Jacobius ben Jacobius is listed among cattle owners (144-155 B. C., Samaria, Egypt[2]). Hygros ben Levi, a singer mentioned several times in the Talmud (*Šeqal.* 5:1;*Yoma* 3:11) seems to have been an actual person as well judging by these accounts, which sound realistic and credible enough. He seems to have had an extraordinarily artistic vocal technique that involved varying his singing style by placing his thumbs in his mouth (*Šeqal.* 5:1), but was criticized for refusing to teach this special art to any other singers (*Yoma* 3:11). Finally, we now have the first iconographic evidence with an inscription portraying a female Nabataean *arghul* player (see **Fig. IC-4a**).

The mutual interweaving and inter-penetration of the various musical cultures in Hellenistic-Roman Palestine makes it virtually impossible to determine to which ethnic group or ritual association one should assign various instruments. On the one hand, the same instruments might be used in widely differing social situations and widely differing musical purposes in the same community. For example, Isa. 5:11-12 associates the *halil* with revelry, while Jer. 48:36 associates it with mourning. The book of Job associates the *kinnor* and the *'ugab* with both joy and sadness (21:12 and 30:31). On the other hand, the same or similar musical practices and instruments could be present in extremely diverse ethnic and religious groups where they nonetheless addressed similar psychological and emotional needs and accompanied similar socio-functional events. When comparing the various ritual customs of the time, contemporary authors emphasize precisely this similarity between the accompanying musical practices. Plutarch, Tacitus, Philo of Alexandria, and other sources such as the books of the Maccabees all point out that the same music ceremony accompanied the rituals associated with the Nabataean and Jewish communities, and this ceremony was in its own turn quite similar to that associated with the cult of Dionysus.

Naturally enough, similar music ceremonies of this sort also fostered similar musical styles. Psalms were sung not only in Jewish worship and in a modified form at the Dionysian cultic festivals, but also in secular situations such as drinking bouts accompanied by musical entertainment. Clement of Alexandria tells in his *Paedagogus* (II: 4) that the Greek *skolion* with lyre accompaniment was actually quite similar to the singing of

---

2   V. A. Tcherikover, *Corpus Papyrorum Judaicarum*, vol. I (Cambridge, Mass., 1957), p. 171.

Jewish psalms, while Erik Werner[3] believes he has determined the mode of these songs, the *tropos spondeicus*, that is, the Dorian mode with avoided second and fourth degree.

The Hellenization of musical life in ancient Israel/Palestine also drew considerable impetus from specifically Greek musical institutions and cultic events such as the gymnasium, public sporting events, and the theater wherever these were found, including in urban centers such as Jerusalem, Tiberias, and Caesarea. This development was especially strong during the reign of Herod the Great (37 B. C. – 4 A. D.), when "there were very great rewards for victory proposed to those that were musicians also, and were called thymelici and he spared no pains to induce all persons, the most famous for such exercises, to come to this contest for victory."[4] Such Hellenistic cultural influence was not, of course, limited to public life; it also found its way into private life. In Jerusalem, Gaza, Ashkelon, and Sepphoris, the private homes of pagans, Christians, and Jews alike could be decorated with mosaic floors and wall murals depicting a variety of musical themes.

Another source giving clear expression to the Jewish-Hellenistic syncretism characterizing this musical disposition is the apocryphal work of Ben Sira (second century A. D.): "Where there is singing, do not pour out talk; do not display your cleverness at the wrong time. A ruby seal in a setting of gold is a concert of music at a banquet of wine" (32:4-5); "the flute and the harp make sweet melody, but a pleasant voice is better than either" (40:21).

The relationship of the Romans (basically cosmopolitan) and the Jews (basically separatist) was not always harmonious. On the contrary, after the destruction of the Jerusalem Temple in A. D. 70 mutual enmity grew stronger, on one side, the Jews gladly attended and participated in public social events, although the Roman mimes and pantomimes frequently mocked Jewish habits and rules. On the other hand, the Jewish religious establishment increasingly prohibited Jews from attending the theater and other public events, and the Jewish communities became even more isolated, which continued into next two millennia.

---

3 E. Werner, *The Sacred Bridge* (London-New York, 1959), pp. 442 and 591.
4 Flavius Josephus, *Antiquities of the Jews*, xv.8.1

The Talmud gives a colorful story about a Jewish musician and mime from Caesarea who appeared to Rabbi Abbahu in a dream, was asked by him to pray for rain, and, indeed, rain came. When asked by the Rabbi what his occupation was, the man, named Pentakaka referring to himself, replied: "This man commits five sins (Gk. *pentakakos*) – he adorns the theater, engages the *hetaerae*, brings their cloth to the bath house, claps hands and dances before them, and beats the *babuia* (aulos – JB)" (y. *Ta'an.* 1.4). This Talmudic passage no only tells us that the theater was syncretistic art and included drama, pantomime, dance, and instrumental music; it also confirms the existence of Jewish performing artists. Although this occupation was condemned by Jewish religious rules as a grave sin, it did not prevent Pentakaka's prayer from being accepted.

These syncretistic inclinations of local musical culture ran directly counter to both the Jewish and the Christian theocracy. One intimation of just how severe this conflict was is found in the book of Daniel, which obstinately repeats the same verse (3:5,7,10,15) reminding the reader that foreign music and foreign instruments always announce the worship of the golden statue King Nebuchadnezzar had set up. Although the content of the verses refers to the time of Nebuchadnezzar, the text itself was composed around 167-164 B. C. when the real reference was probably to Hellenistic-Roman temptations. Clement of Alexandria (150-215) composed a whole series of equally condemnatory passages against pagan music.

Amid all the animated cultural syncretism during the Hellenistic-Roman period, however, the most important development seems to be in at least one sense one of divergence rather than of fusion. Closer examination reveals traces of what will later become two different worlds of contemporary music, one western, and one eastern. The most tangible reflection of this development is found perhaps in two mosaics both from the cult of Dionysus. The first, from the house of Sheikh Zouede (in Gaza), is a kaleidoscopic, pluralistic musical world bursting with color and orgiastic, pagan sentiment. The second, from Sepphoris (in the Galil), is an organized, mono-thematic musical world of Judeo-Christian disposition **(Fig. IA-7** and **IA-8)**. A change, which reminds the change in the music entourage of King David as depicted in 2 Sam. 6:5 and centuries later in 1 Chr.13:8.

Related bibliography

Bathia Bayer, Music, in: *Encyclopedia Judaica* (Jerusalem, 1971), vol. 12:554-574.
Joachim Braun: "Biblical Instruments" and "Jewish Music," in: *The New Grove of Music and Musicians*, 2nd ed. (Macmillan, 2001), vol. 3:524-535 and vol.13: 24-37.
Joachim Braun & Judith Cohen, "Jüdische Musik", in: *Die Musik in Geschichte und Gegenwart*, 2. Neubearbeitete Ausgabe (Bärenreiter, 1994), Sachteil Bd. 4:1511-1569.
Abraham Partaleone: *Shilte ha-giborim*, Mantua 1612.
Michael Praetorius: *Syntagma musicum*, Wittenberg 1614/18.
Alfred Sendrey, *Music in Ancient Israel*, New York, 1969.
Amnon Shiloah: *Jewish Musical Tradition*, Detroit, 1992.
Helga Weippert: *Palästina in vorhellenistischer Zeit*, München, 1988.
Eric Werner et al., *Jewish Music*, in: *The New Grove of Music and Musicians*, Macmillan PL, 1980:614-644.

B. Biblical Terminology of Music Instruments

Music and its tools of production, musical instruments, as mentioned in the Bible are among the most perplexing phenomena of the past. This stems from both the ephemeral nature of music itself and the indirect sources of study – written, archaeological-iconographical, comparative – and the fact that only a few musical instruments discovered in excavations (e.g., cymbals, rattles) are still able to produce sound.

The Bible, considered the main source for the study of music in ancient Israel, may be helpful only for the study of the social context of instrumental performance, e.g., at the sacred service (1 Chr. 23; 2 Chr. 29:25) and praise of God (Isa. 12:5-6; Ps. 150); the apotropaic-prophylactic (Exod. 28:33; 1 Sam. 16:16), ecstatic-prophetic (10:5), or supernatural (Exod. 19:19) media; communication (Num. 10:1-9); war (2 Chr. 20:28); events of joy (Exod. 15:20) and sorrow (2 Sam. 1:17-27); or as symbol of sin and prostitution (Isa. 5:12; 14:11). The accounts are sometimes ambiguous: e.g., the advance of David with the ark as a kind of orgy, with dominant percussion instruments of a Dionysiac character

(2 Sam. 6:5), or a somewhat ceremonial occasion with singing and trumpet fanfare (2 Chr. 13:8).

The greatest potential for information concerning music as described in the Bible is the study of the instruments recorded, but this information is similarly limited. The precise character of the music is never described, except for some general terms regarding the shophar and trumpet signals (Num. 10:2-10). Only three verses mention the material of which a musical instrument is made (Num. 10:2; 1 Kgs. 10:12; 1 Chr. 15:19), and seldom is the performance technique mentioned (1 Sam. 16:23).

The names of musical instruments are not entirely clear. The LXX, Peshitta, and Vulgate translate them with no precise understanding of their meaning. One version may render the same word in several different ways: e.g., the LXX translates Heb. *kinnor* as *kithara, kinara, psalterion, organon,* and *nabla;* '*ugab* as *kithara, psalmos,* and *organon*. Ambiguous information is available from post-biblical sources: the writings of Josephus Flavius and Philo from Alexandria, the Talmud, and the Qumran scrolls.

For these reasons, and particularly the historical and chronological uncertainty of the biblical record, archaeology must be regarded the primary source for the study of the musical cultures of the biblical world. At present some 700 artifacts – actual remains of musical instruments and artistic depictions – have been excavated. Statistical analysis of these artifacts provides an important indication of musical instruments present in ancient Israel/Palestine. For instance, harps are not attested, so consequently there is no reason to interpret the Heb. *nebel* as "harp", the instrument King David is commonly depicted as playing. From the Babylonian-Persian period, which the books of Ezra, Nehemiah, and Chronicles report as having developed an exceptionally rich musical liturgy and musical life, no significant musical evidence has survived.

The most common instruments in Iron Age Israel were derived from Canaanite culture. They seem to have been of modest construction, yet of great variety and capable of relatively sophisticated performance technique. Among those instruments available to the masses were clay rattles (probably *měna'an'im),* round frame drums *(tof),* and double pipes similar to the oboe and clarinet (probably *ḥalil).* The elaborate Egyptian lyres with eight or more strings gave way to the smaller *kinnor* and *nebel* with fewer strings, mainly used in cultic and court music. During the Babylonian-Persian period, a decline in musical life was apparent, perhaps reflective of local religious and social constraints (cf. Isa. 5:12; 24:8-9; Hos. 9:1). The Hellenistic-Roman period brought a blossoming of all kinds of musical activities and the introduction of many new types of instruments (e.g., new varieties of harps and lutes, aulos type bone pipes with bronze overlay). This was met with resistance in orthodox circles, who cited biblical admonishments regarding licentious activities associated with musical instruments (m. Sota 9:11; b. Sota 48a-b; Git. 7a-b).

(i) *'aṣey beroshim* (2 Sam 6:5)

Instruments made of various kinds of wood, used as double-clappers (2 Sam. 6:5) by the masse (in contrast to the Egyptian-type ivory or bon Hathor-clappers of the wealthy). Only once mentioned in the Bible (*běkol 'aṣey beroshim*, "all manner of instruments made of fire wood"); in the parallel passage (1 Chr. 13:8) it is replaced by the phrase *bekol 'oz uvshirim* ("with all their might and with songs"), apparently to evade the instrument's secular and orgiastic aspect.

(ii) *ḥalil* (1 Sam 10:5; 1 Kgs 1:40; Isa 5:12; 30:29; Jer 48:36)

Single or double-pipe reed instrument similar to the clarinet or oboe (from *hll*, "hollow, empty," also "profane"). It accompanied ecstatic prophecy (1 Sam. 10:5), and was used in both joyful revelry (1 Kgs. 1:40) and mourning (Jer. 48:36) as well a secular debaucheries (Isa. 5:12). Simple bone instruments as well as elaborate ones dressed in bronze have been found from the Hellenistic-Roman period, and numerous artistic representations from a strata as early as the 14th century B.C.E. portray goddesses and erotic dancers, priests and satyrs, mourners and the joyful playing double-pipes (see **Fig. IA-6, IA-7, IA-8 and IB-4**).

(iii) *ḥaṣoṣ'rah* (Num 10:2, 8-10; 31:6; 2 Kgs 11:14; 12:14; Hos 5:8; Ps 98:6; Esra 3:10; Neh 12:35 u. 41; 1 Chr 13:8; 15:24 u. 28; 16:6 u. 42; 2 Chr 5:12 u. 13; 13:12 u. 14; 15:14; 20:28; 23:13; 29:26-28).

The trumpet, made of hammered silver (Num. 10:2) or bronze. It was originally to be blown only by the priests for communication (to assemble the congregation and leaders) or alarm, in times of war, celebration, or on solemn days, at the beginning of the month and for the burnt offering (Num. 10:2-10). In the Babylonian-Persian period the trumpet was blown at the temple service (2 Kgs. 12:13), at coronations (11:14; 2 Chr. 23:13), construction of the temple (Ezra 3:10), and in connection with vows to God (2 Chr. 15:14). Some passages describing trumpet blowing should be considered later additions reflecting liturgical practices (cf. 2 Sam. 6:5; 1 Ch. 13:8). Depictions believed to represent the temple trumpets on the Bar Kokhba coins and the arch of Titus are now questioned. A local depiction of the instrument similar to the trumpet from the tomb of Tutankhamen and from the same time (14th cent. B.C.E.) was recently discovered at the Beth-Shean excavations by Prof. A. Mazar. From a later period (3ed cent. B. C. E.) a drawing from an Idumean Necropolis at Beit-Govrin depicts a trumpeter at a hunting scene **(Fig. IB-1)**. Early Byzantine iconography suggests that the trumpet-*haṣoṣ'rah* and horn-*shofar* where confused by the artists depicting the instruments (comp. the mosaic floors from the El-Chirba Samaritan and Sepphoris Jewish synagogues). Num. 10:4-5 and especially the Qumran scrolls (1QM2:15; 3:1; 7:9; 9:9) contain general descriptions of techniques for playing the trumpet (sustained sound, short blast, quavering blast, sharp sound, battle alarm).

(iv) *kinnor* (Gen 4:21; 31,27; 1 Sam 10:5; 16:16 and 23; 2 Sam 6:5; 1 Kgs 10:12; Jes 5:2; 16:11; 23:16; 24:8; 30:32; Ezra 26:13; Ps. 33:2; 43:4; 49:5; 57:9; 71:22; 81:3; 92:4; 98:5; 108:3; 137:2; 147:7; 149:3; 150:3; Job 21:12; 30:31; Neh 12:27; 1 Chr 13:8; 15:16, 21 u.28; 16:5; 25:1,3 u. 6; 2 Chr 5:12; 9:11; 20:28; 29:25.

The lyre, a popular instrument attested in various ancient Near Eastern texts, as well as in the name of gods and place names, and in Syro-Palestinian iconography. It was a symbol of early professional musical activities (Gen. 4:21) and associated with nearly every type of musical occasion, from praise of God (Ps. 150:3) and prophecy (1 Sam. 10:5) to grief (Job 30:31), secular celebrations (Gen. 31:27) and debauchery (Jes 23:16). The *kinnor* was made of almug wood (1 Kgs. 10:11-12), with 10 (Josephus *Ant.* 8.3.8) or seven (m. Qinnim 3:6) thin gut strings, and usually played with a plectrum but also plucked by hand in special situations (1 Sam. 16:16). The most reliable depictions of the instrument seem to be from the Bar-Kokhba and Acco coins (see **Fig. IB-2**), while the well-known lyre from the "Ma'adana" seal (depicted also on the modern Israeli half shekel coin) should be rather considered a fake. The *kinnor* changed form over time, although regional differences were less apparent in the multicultural biblical society.

(v) *m'na'anim* (2 Sam 6,5).

An idiophone, probably a clay rattle (from *noa'*, "shake") of various shapes (geometric, zoo- and anthropomorphic; 5-12 cm. [2-5 in.] long), as suggested by more than 120 archaeological finds from the Bronze to Babylonian periods (**Fig. III-1a-f**). It was a popular instrument used in orgiastic cultic activities (2 Sam. 6:5), and so not favored by the theocratic establishment (similar to *'aṣey beroshim* avoided by the Bible in the parallel description cf. 1 Chr. 13:8). Mostly discovered in graves, and probably, was serving as cult instrument in neighboring Edom, were the rattle is placed on the head of some kind of godhood (**Fig. III-1g**).

(vi) *m'ṣiltayim* and *ṣelṣelim* (Ezra 3:10; Neh 12:27; 1 Chr 13:8; 15:16, 19 and 28; 16:5 and 42; 25:1 and 6; 2 Chr 5:12 and 13; 29:25;.: 2 Sam 6:5; Ps 150:6).

Cymbals (occurs only in the dual form), mentioned as early as the 14th century. Examples have been recovered ranging from Canaanite occupations to Hellenistic-Roman sites nearly a thousand years later. Two types have been found: slightly vaulted discs (7-12 cm. [3-5 in.]) held by hand loops, beaten mainly in a vertical position, and smaller discs (3-7 cm. [1-3 in.]), probably fastened to two fingers of one hand or used as clappers of forked cymbals. Cymbals "of brass" are mentioned only in postexilic texts (1 Chr. 15:19; cf. Ezra 3:10; Neh. 12:27); they are to be played by the Levites (1 Chr. 15:16) and at cultic events (2 Chr. 5:13). The *ṣelṣelim* mentioned at 2 Sam. 6:5 may have been simply small noise-making instruments, a kind of metal rattle, while the *m'ṣiltayim* in 1 Chr. 13:8 are larger and so better suited to temple worship. Ps.150:5 mentions *ṣelṣelim-shama* ("clanging *ṣelṣelim*") and *ṣelṣelim teru'ah* ("loud, crashing *ṣelṣelim*"), perhaps the two types attested by archaeology.

(vii) *nebel* (1 Sam 10:5; 2 Sam 6:5; 1 Kön 10:12; Jes 5:12; 14:11; Am 5:23; 6:5; Ps 57:9; 71:22; 81:3; 108:3; 150:3; Neh 12:27; 1 Chr 13:8; 15:16, 20 u. 28; 16:5; 25:1 u. 6; 2 Chr 5:12; 9:11; 20:28; 29:25); and *nevel 'asor* (Ps 33:2, 92:4; 144:9).

The root *nbl* can be vocalized in two ways, *nabal* and *nevel*, and thus may indicate 'ritually unclean', 'godless,' in the first case, and 'leather bag', 'pitcher', in the second. The function of the *nebel* was similar to the *kinnor*; like the *kinnor*, with which it is generally mentioned, the *nebel* was made of almug wood (1 Kgs. 10:12), but it had 12 thick strings (m. Qinnim 3:6) and was always, probably, plucked with a *plectrum* (Josephus *Ant.* 7.12.3). Archaeological evidence discounts its identification as a harp (NRSV), suggesting instead that the *nebel* was a large, lower-pitched bass lyre (see **Fig. IB-3).** The *nebel 'asor* (Ps 33:2; xcii:3) was, probably, a ten-stringed lyre (Ps. 44:9). The *nebel* was played by Levites (1 Chr. 15:16; 25:1) at cultic events (1 Chr 13:8; Ps. 150:3), victory celebrations (2 Chr. 20:28), and accompanying ecstatic prophecies (1 Sam. 10:5), as well as orgiastic revels (Isa. 5:12). Recently, a crucial proof of interpretation of the biblical *nebel* has come to light: a stone carving of the Roman period was discovered in Dion (Greece) by Dimitrios Pandermalis, showing the first instance of text and image side by side – a relief of a lyre next to the carved wording of a hymn of praise on the *nabla*.

(viii) *pa'amon* (Ex 28:33 and 34; 39:25 and 26).

Bell (from Heb. *p'm*, "beat"). "Bells of gold," placed, between pomegranates, were attached to the lower hem of the high priest's robe (Exod. 28:33,34) and had apotropaic-prophylactic significance. Attested in the Near East as early as the 15th century, bells appear in ancient Israel from the 9th-8th centuries on. Finds from the Hellenistic-Roman period include bells accompanied by remnants of fabric which may indicate their placement on a garment. The recently discovered mosaic from the Sepphoris synagogue (early 5th century) depicts Aaron with bells fastened to his robe. A dancer with a bell is depicted at a Dionysian procession (see **Fig. IA-7b).**

(x) *šofar* (Ex 19:16 and 19; 20:18; Lev 25:9; Jos 6:4, 5, 8, 9, 13, 16 and 20; Judges 3:27; 6:34; 7:8, 16, 18-20 and 22; 1 Sam 13:3; 2 Sam 2:28; 6:15; 15:10; 18:16; 20:1 and 22; 1 Kgs 1:34, 39 and 41; 2 Kgs 9:13; Is 18:3; 27:13; 58:1; Jer 4:5, 19 and 21; 6:1 and 17; 42:14; 51:27; Ez 33:3-6; Hos 5:8; 8:1; Joel 2:1 and 15; Am 2:2; 3:6; Zef 1:16; Sach 9:14; Ps. 47:6; 81:4; 98:6; 150:3; Job 39:24 and 25; Neh 4:12 and 14; 1 Chr 15:28; 2 Chr 15:14); *šofrot hayov'lim* (Jos 6:4, 6, 8 and 13); *qeren hayovel* (Jos. 6:5).

Ram's horn (cf. Akk. *šapparu*, "wild goat"). The most frequently mentioned musical instrument in the Bible, used from at least the Iron Age until today. It is capable of producing two or three sounds of different pitch and alarming nature, characterized as qol ('voice'), *teqi'ah* 'blast'), *těru'ah* ('rejoicing'), and *yevavah* ('sobbing, groaning, trembling'). Details of the instrumnt's construction are known only from post biblical writings, mainly the tracts of the Mishnah and Talmud (*Rosh ha-*

shanah, Sabbath), The earliest known musical notation for the *šofar* is recorded in Sa'adia Gaon's *Siddur* (10th century C.E.). The *šofar* was a solo instrument at significant cultic and national events: theophanies (Exod. 19:13, 16); the Day of Atonement (Lev. 25:9), the New Moon feast (Ps. 81:3]), the day of judgment (Joel 2:1), transporting the ark (2 Sam. 6:5), during battle (Judg. 3:27), and in victory celebrations (1 Sam. 13:3). Iconographical evidence of natural horns in the Middle East dates back to the 2nd millenium B.C.E. In the Israelite and Judean context, depictions of the *šofar* do not appear before the 2nd- 3rd century C.E., and then only in a group of Jewish symbols (**Fig. IB-5**), supplemented first by the *menorah* (seven-branched candelabrum) and the *maḥtah* (a small incense scoop), and later by the *lulav* and *etrog* (palm branch and citrus fruit). A survey of archaeological finds (synagogue mosaics, pedestals, tombstones, sarcophagi, oil lamps, seals and amulets) shows that it was a symbol of ethnic and national identity used in both sacred and secular context. Both *šofrot hayov'lim* and *qeren hayovel*, indistinguishable in practice, appear only once in the mythical tale of the destruction of the walls of Jericho. The semantic field of the instrument is here amplified by the term *yovel* ('jubilee', 'leader').

(xi) *tof* (Gen 31:27; Ex 15:20; Judges 11:34; 1 Sam 10:5; 18:6; 2. Sam 6:5; Is 5:12; 24:8; 30:32; Jer 31:4; Ps 68:26; 81:3; 149:3; 150:4; Job 21:12; 1 Chr 13:8.

Round frame drum (see **Fig. IC-2b, III-3a-e**) – an instrument widely attested throughout the ancient Near East. Its most common form in Syria-Palestine was a 25-40 cm. (8-16 in.) frame over which was stretched a skin or membrane. It had both cultic and secular use, accompanying singing and dancing (Ps. 149:3) and prophetic ecstasy (1 Sam. 10:5). Drums were played for feasts (Ps. 81:2), processions (2 Sam. 6:5; Ps. 68:25), and other celebrations (Gen. 31:27), but apparently not for temple worship. The *tof* seems to have been played most often by women, frequently as a solo instrument and in connection with dancing, also a female activity. Numerous terracotta figurines of female drummers have been found from the Iron Age on; two types are common, seemingly reflecting the synthesis of sacral and secular in the musical culture of ancient Israel: women in long bell-form dresses, without jewelry, or partly unclad and wearing rich jewelry.

(xii) *'ugav* (Gen 4:21; Ps 150:4; Job 21:12; 30:31).

The name of this instrument is controversial, and its etymology has not been entirely explained. The root *'gv* is related to *'agava* ('ecstasy of love,' 'sensuality,' desire'). The translations are very inconsistent (see above)/In modern musicology identified as a vertical flute (cf. Egyptian *ma't)*, although the LXX and Josephus consider it a stringed instrument. The *'ugav* occurs as one of the first two instruments mentioned in the Bible (Gen 4:21), and only three times after it as instrument of praise (Ps. 150:4), joy (Job 21:12) and mourning (Job 30:31). In the Aramaic of the Targum, the *'ugav* is equated with the *abuva*, the instrument of the Roman *ambubiae* – prostitutes who blow a kind of aulos. In the Mishnah (*'Aarkhin* ii.3) the *abuva* is identified as *halil* (see **Fig. IA-7, IB-4**).

The Instruments in the Book of *Daniel* (Dan 3:5,7, 10 u. 15).

The names of the six musical instruments, called the 'Nabuchadnezzar orchestra' listed in Dan. 3:5, 7, 10, 15 are of Aramaic or Greek origin: *qarna'* (cf. Heb. *qeren*, "animal horn"), here a brass trumpet known from Neo-Babylonian sources; *mashroqita* (from *shrq* 'to whistle'), probably a kind of reed instrument; *qaytras* (Gk. *kithara)*, a Greco-Roman lyre; *sabbekka*, Greek or Phoenician angular harp, attested in the Seleucid period; *pĕsanterin* (cf. Gk. *psalterion)*, a large, angular horizontally-held harp, beaten with two sticks; *sumponyah*, variously understood as the bagpipe or kettledrum is now mostly understood as designation for "the entire ensemble" ("*ve-kol zenei zamara*), which occurs at the end of the recurring passage ('all kinds of music') to a great degree confuses. In *Daniel* are described instruments of a Seleucid group of musicians. Although the author of *Daniel* was describing events of the 6th cent. B. C. E. the text seems to reflect the ideological situation of the time when Jewish and Hellenistic confrontation was becoming more acute during the 2nd cent. B. C. E., the time when *Daniel* was written. The recurring four times ominous ostinato of the text seems to symbolize an alien and hostile musical culture.

Collective Terms

These occur designating classes or varieties of instruments, mostly string instruments: *kelim,* lit., "vessels, implements," a generic term for string instruments (1 Chr. 23:5); *kley-David,* "instruments of David," probably, lyre or harp (2 Chr. 29:26); *kli-nebel,* lyre instruments (Ps. 71:22; 1 Chr. 16:5); *kley oz,* "loud instruments" (2 Chr. 30:21);, *kley šir* "instruments of song" (e.g., Amos 6:5); *minnîm,* "strings" (Ps. 150:4).

Superscriptions to the Psalms

Musical terms in the headings of the Psalms are among the most difficult problems in translating the Bible. Modern musicologists consider many to be notations regarding performance techniques or perhaps catchwords for popular melodies. It is possible that there is a parallel with the Arabic *maqam* or Indian *raga* names. The diversity of variants given in the earliest translations shows that the meaning if these texts had already been lost in antiquity. Even the most frequently mentioned words are not consistently interpreted: the Heb. *lamenaṣeaḥ* (from *niṣṣaḥon,* 'victory'), which occurs 54 times, is translated as 'to the end' (Aquila), 'to sing publicly' (Luther), 'for the choirmaster' or "master of victory" (*Jerusalem Bible*) etc. The Heb. *mizmor,* which occurs in 57 Psalms, may specify singing with instrumental accompaniment. Many of the notations remain highly uncertain. For example, *bi-nabalim 'al-'alamot* (1. Chr. 15:20) may mean "high pitched string instrument in soprano register" or "drum" (cf. Ps. 68:25) or perhaps the combination *bi-nebalim 'al-alamot* may indicate "on the eighth tone or mode (in octaves)." The Heb. *'al-haggittit* (Pss. 8, 81, 84) may specify "in the style of Gath" or "on the instrument of Gath."

Related bibliography

B. Bayer, "The Titles of the Psalms...," in: *Yuval,* 4: 92-123 (1982); J. Braun, *Music in Ancient Israel/Palestine,* ch. i (Grand Rapids, 2002); D. A. Foxvog and A. D. Kilmer "Music," in: *Internatonal Standard*

Bible Encyclopedia, vol. iii:436-449 (Grand Rapids, 1980); C. Sachs, *The History of Musical Instruments*, ch. 5 (New York, 1940); A. Sendrey, *Music in Ancient Israel*, sect. iv and vi (New York, 1969).

C. The Near Eastern Context

The understanding, socio-historical interpretation and research of musical instruments (sound tools) as part of human culture is a *conditio sine que non* of modern scholarship, Modern musicologists define music as a pattern of human behavior in a relevant cultural context, in which sound-producing tools undergo changes based on changes in culture. Musical instruments and their iconography represent the only available material evidence from preliterate societies and are the primary source of investigation for societies that have an oral musical tradition. An interdisciplinary approach, combining archaeological, socio-historical, musicological, and ethnographic-comparative analysis, has turned archaeo-musicology (a field established as an independent branch of scholarship only in the late 1970s-early 1980s) into a most effective tool of study of music in ancient cultures.

While archaeological finds of musical instruments may make it possible actually to hear "historical sound," and provide information on the audio ecology of the past, archaeological iconography is more helpful in studying socio-cultural matters, performance practices, the social performance environs, and the body language of performers. The central tool of organological research (typological analysis) raises the question of classification[5]. It is assumed that each culture has both its own "culture-emerging," or "natural," musical instrument classification (which scholarship does not necessarily always discover – e.g., Phoenician instruments) and an "observer-imposed," or "artificial," one created for a particular research scheme. Certain Near Eastern cultures (e.g., Sumerian) appear to tend to a natural model guided by the construction material of the musical instrument itself (e.g., determinatives are *giš*, "wood";

---

5 Kartomi, M. J., *On Concepts and Classifications of Musical Instruments* (Chicago, 1990), pp. 12-13.

gi, "cane"; *si*, "horn;"[6] some (e.g., Hittite) combine this with the method of sound production (*hazzik*, "strike," *pariparái*, "blow;"[7]); others (Israelite/Judean), divide instruments into sacred (horn, trumpet), levitic (lyre), and secular (reed pipes).[8] On the other hand, since the early days of organology, artificial classification systems have been used, although natural systems sometimes contribute more to understanding a certain culture. At present, Erich M. von Hornbostel and Curt Sachs's artificial classification[9] appears to be the most functional system for ancient cultures. It is based on the source of sound, or the nature of the vibrating body: idiophones, membraphones, aerophones, and chordophones (see below).

The names of the musical instruments are in most cases highly uncertain. Contrary to the conditions in Egypt, where music instrument iconography frequently is accompanied by texts bearing the name of the depicted instrument, other Near Eastern archaeological finds lack written comments, and the preserved texts with names of musical instruments include hardly any information on the type of instrument. Only as late as the third century BCE-third century CE do the first known parallels of iconography and written sources appear (*lilissu*, Akkadian, "kettle drum,"[10] *zmr*, clarinet-type double pipe with one long pipe and one short one[11]). Most names of musical instruments have to remain in the realm of suggestions (e.g., GIS *gu=di/de*, "lute"[12]), but there are several exceptions where the identification is nearly unanimous (Old Sumerian *balag*, "harp"; Bib. Heb, *hăsōsĕră*, "trumpet"). In certain cases one name is used for different instruments of one type (e.g., *tp*, different drums, most Semitic languages).

---

6   Sachs, C., *The History of Musical Instruments* (London, 1940), p.164.
7   Tumbull, H., "Anatolia." In: *The New Grove Dictionary of Music and Musicians* (=NGD, 1980), 1:391.
8   Braun, J., "Biblische Musikinstrumente," in: *Die Musik in Geschichte und Gegenwart* (=2MGG 1994), 1:1512.
9   *Zeitschrift für Ethnologie*, 46 (1914), 553-590.
10 Rashid, S. A., *Mesopotamien* (=MGB II/2), ed. W. Bachmann (Leipzig, 1984), p. 140.
11 Braun, J., "...die Schöne...," in: *Festschrift Wolfgang Suppan*, ed. B. Habla, (Tutzig, 1993), p. 176.
12 Kilmer A. /D. Collon, "Lute" and "Leier," in: *Reallexikon der Assyrologie...*, 6:512 (1980-1983).

The primary importance of ancient Egyptian, Hebrew, Greek, and Roman music cultures has been acknowledged since the beginnings of modern (eighteenth century) music historiography. Carl Engel's study of the music of ancient cultures was the first to focus on archaeological sources.[13] The first clear statement on the decisive significance of Near Eastern musical instruments for world music culture was made by the founder of contemporary organology Curt Sachs.[14] The linguistic approach, which dominated studies of ancient Near Eastern musical instruments, and proved to be insufficient, dominated the period following World War II but was more and more replaced by a combined interdisciplinary approach.

Since World War II, the study of ancient musical instruments has focused on three areas:

1. *Musical instrument types*. Based on a typological approach to musical instruments, the study of instrument types mostly strives for an organological-ergological and historical classification; the aim of this genre is to produce a "history" of the type (the classical examples of this type are Hans Hickmann entries in the 1st MGG edition).

2. *Musical instrumentarium of certain cultures or geographic areas*. Socio-anthropologically oriented studies of the particular instruments, which strive for the incorporation of archaeo-musicological research results into the general framework of historiography[15]

3. *Artifacts*. Nearly the broadest, in terms of quantity, and developed along with musicologists by archaeologists, historians, and art historians, the study of individual artifacts recovered in excavations stresses the organological-ergological and socio-anthropological, approach.

The few studies designed as comprehensive discussion on the Near Eastern music cultures continue the approach of Engel and Sachs. However, the discussions of the different Near Eastern areas and cultures are

---

13 Engel, C. *The Music of the Most Ancient Nations* (London, 1864).
14 Sachs, *History*...
15 For Egypt, Greece, Mesopotamia, Etrurien, Rome, Central Asia, and Islam, see the volumes of the series *Musikgeschichte in Bildern*, ed. H. Besseler, M. Schneider and W. Bachmann (Leipzig, 1961-1990); for other areas: M. Wegner, "Hethitische Musik", in: 1MGG 6:330-34; H. Turnbull., "Anatolien," in: 1NGD, 1:388-393; M. Duchesne-Guillemin, *Les instruments de musique dans l'art Sassanide* (Ghent, 1993); J. Braun, s. footnote 8, and "Jüdische Musik," in: 2MGG 4:1512-1527.

individual and not synthetic. Wegner defends the position that "the ancient Oriental world does not present a unity also in its musical culture,"[16] which was especially true, according to the author, of the opposed nature of Near Eastern and Hellenistic musical instruments: the former are changeable and irregular and the latter are stable and invariable. This disputable theory was developed based on Sachs's thesis on the "classical" and quite solemn character of Egyptian Old Middle Kingdom musical instruments, as opposed to the orgiastic, noisy, and savage character of the New Kingdom/Near Eastern sound tools.[17] This popular theory was proved wrong by Hickmann[18] on the basis of later archaeological discoveries.

The only attempt to discuss Near Eastern musical instruments comprehensively and comparatively was made by Hans Hickmann in 1957[19] and 1961, and his central conclusions are still unchallenged: in certain cases the Egyptian music instrumentarium (e.g., rattles, sistrum, concussion sticks, flute, trumpet) influenced Babylonian cultures; in others primacy belonged to the Sumerians (e.g., lyre, angular harp, cymbals, frame drums); and in still others the development was parallel but independent (e.g., the harp[20]). As regards the provenance of the Western instrumentarium, "certain is the Oriental provenance... of a number of musical instruments, which are adequate to the common sound-ideal of the Mediterranean countries."[21] The central Phoenician and Israel/Palestine area of the eastern Mediterranean coast from the Sinai desert to Anatolia was considered to be a transit channel only; its significance as a center with an indigenous culture was ignored, even though a number of musical in-

---

16 Wegner, M., *Die Musikinstremente des Alten Orients* (Munster, 1950), p. 50.
17 Sachs, *History...*, p. 98).
18 Hickmann H., "Vorderasien und Ägypten im musikalischen Austausch," in: *Zeitschrift der Deutschen Morganläaendischen Gesellschaft*, 111/1: 23-41 (1961).
19 Idem., "Die Rolle des Vorderen Orients...," in: *Cahiers d'Histoire Egyptienne* 9/1-2:19-37(1957).
20 Hickmann, "Vorderasien und Ägypten...," pp. 23, 35
21 Hickmann, "Die Rolle...," p. 35.

struments, and especially new instrumental performance traditions, originated there.[22]

Idiophones

Self-sounders, or sound produced by vibrations of the substance of the instrument itself (e.g., rattles, cymbals), are known as idiophones.

Natufian strung rattles

Rattles from modern Israel's Carmel range (11,000-9,000 BCE) are the earliest attested sound tools in the Near East (see **Fig. IA-1**). This type of syncretic jewelry/sound cult object, often disregarded by researchers, exists in various forms and was probably among the earliest artifacts of human culture.

Concussion sticks

Pictograms from Uruk (Uruk IV period, 3000-2900 BCE) and a carved shell from a burial (PG 789) at Ur show concussion sticks. A bronze sound tool also was found at Kish from the Jemdet Nasr period (2900-2800 BCE).[23] Egyptian ivory concussion sticks appear somewhat earlier (first dynasty, 3300-3000 BCE).

Sistrum

In the middle of the third millennium, the sistrum (a type of open rattle) appears in both Sumer and Egypt; the Sumerian examples are U-shaped and are open at the top,[24] and the Egyptian examples are rectangular, in the shape of a temple naos, a Hathor image, or a horseshoe[25] **(Fig. IC-1a**

---

22 Caubet, A. and J. Braun in: C. Homo-Lechner, ed., *La pluridisciplinarite en archeologie musicale*, 4th ICTM archaeology of music SG conference, Saint-Germain-en-Laye, Octobre 1990 (Paris, 1994), pp. 129-147).
23 Rashid, *Mesopotamien*, p. 48, ill. 16.
24 Idem., p. 40, ill. 8.
25 Hickmann, , *Aegypten* (=MGB, II/1, Leipzig, 1961), p. 160, ills. 26-27.

and **b)**. Only two or three centuries later, rectangular metal sistra, ornamented with animal figurines, appeared at the Anatolian sites of Horoztepe, and Alaca Hujuyuek.[26] In all cultures, sistra were cult instruments.

Clay rattles

The most popular Near Eastern idiophones are clay rattles (see **Fig. III-1a-g)**. Among those preserved are egg-shaped examples from the fifth-millennium Lower Egyptian Merimde culture[27]; these are the oldest examples and were in use at least until the eighteenth dynasty. Zoomorphic and piecrust shaped clay rattles from the Old Babylonian period (1950-1530 BCE) have been found at nearly every Mesopotamian site,[28] and from the Middle Bronze Age IA-II in ancient Israel/Palestine, some one hundred items in zoomorphic, anthropomorphic, and geometric forms are preserved – the spool shape being the most popular (see **Fig. III-1a)**. On Cyprus, the Late Bronze zoomorphic forms, especially of birds, are found frequently (Cyprus Museum, no. A-990). The quantity, dispersion, and archaeological context of the Near Eastern clay rattles, which preserve an indigenous artistic form in every local culture, confirm their plural function as cult implement, amulet, sound tool, and game – rather than solely as a child's toy, and substantiates it as mass-music, -cult, and -culture commodity.

Bells

From the early first millennium BCE, bronze bells appear – mostly the sound tool itself (from Nimrud alone there are some one hundred bells that are the property of the British Museum) – that are rarely represented iconographically: the first representations are horse bells on Assyrian bas-reliefs.[29] Bells are first attested in the tenth century BCE in northern

---

26 Turnbull, "Anatolia…," p. 388.
27 Hickmann, H. *Catalogue général des antiqutés é gyptiens du Musée du Caire* (Caire, 1949), p. 70, pl. XLIII.
28 Rimmer, J. *Ancient Musical Instruments of Western Asia in the British Museum* (Londion, 1969), pl. III.
29 Rimmer, idem., pls. XVII and XVIII.

Persia, at Amlash[30] and a century later in Assyria, at Nimrud,[31] and in Israel/Phoenicia, at Megiddo (Oriental Institute, no. M936); two centuries later they are found on Cyprus and in twenty-third-dynasty Egypt at Tell Basta.[32] A dispersion from east to west and a Caucasian or Asian provenience are thus plausible. Bells in various sizes (2.5-12 cm) and forms were designed for animals and humans, mostly probably with an apotropaic function (a supposition based on Ex. 28:35 and questioned for its uniform interpretation by Peter Calmeyer).[33] Bell-shaped clay rattles and clay bells[34] may indicate a continuity of the social and acoustic function of the two idiophones.

Scrapers

Notched implements, such as scapulae, were scraped with a rigid object to produce sound. Scrapers are known throughout the world from prehistoric times. While they do not appear with any frequency in the Near East, there are examples from Ugarit, thirteenth century BCE.[35] and eleventh century BCE Ekron.[36] A concentration of some ten items was discovered at Kiton, from the twelfth-fifth centuries BCE.[37] The identification of these artifacts, however, as sound tools, based on the presence of trails of erased patina, is doubtful.[38]

---

30 Rimmer, idem., pl. XIXc-d.
31 Rimmer, idem., pl. XIXa.
32 Hickmann, *Catalogue...*, pl. XXIIIA).
33 "Glocke," in: *Reallexikon der Assyrologie und vorderasiatischen Archaeologie*, 3:427-31.
34 Rashid, *Mesopotamien...*, ill. 131; see also at Hebrew University, no. 9245 and Cyprus: Limassol District Museum, no. T474.
35 Caubet, "La musique à Ougarit," in: *Comptes Rendus de l'Academie des Inscriptions et Belles-Lettres* (1987), figs. I, 2
36 Dothan T. /S. Gitin, "Tel Miqne (Ekron) 1982," in: *Israel Exploration Journal* 33 [1983]: 127-129.
37 Karageorghis, V., *Excavations at Kiton*, vol. 5.2, 1985, p. 317.
38 Idem., pp. 327-328.

Bronze cymbals

Among the best-attested musical instruments for the entire Near East are bronze cymbals. The earliest representations are on bas-reliefs from southern Babylonia at the end of the third millennium.[39] These rather large (some are 20 cm in diameter) cymbals, however, disappeared in Neo-Assyrian times; at Nimrud (ninth century BCE) original cymbals (some 10 cm in diameter) were discovered.[40] More than twenty pairs of cymbals (12-8 and 6-4 cm in diameter) dated at least four hundred years earlier have been found at Late Bronze Canaanite/Phoenician sites (Tell Abu Hawam, Hazor, Megiddo). Already mentioned in fourteenth-century BCE sources from Ugarit,[41] and frequently encountered in the Hebrew Bible (*měsiltayim*), cymbals disappear from the archaeological finds of Israel/Palestine between the Early Iron Age and the Hellenistic period. Figurines of cymbal players were popular in the Neo-Babylonian kingdom,[42] and on Cyprus;[43] cymbals appear in Anatolia[44] and Egypt[45] from the seventh century BCE onward. Cymbals and forked crotala (see below) were widely used at Cybele and Dionysian cult events in Palestine, Anatolia, and Syria, as well as in the Sasanian kingdom.

Forked crotala

Small cymbals attached to a forked handle and larger cymbals were among the most popular instruments in the Hellenistic-Roman Near East. A frequent combination of instruments seems to be the *crotala* and the organ (see **Fig. IA-7** and **V-1**).[46]

---

39 Rashid, *Mesopoptamien...*, pp. 70-73.
40 Idem., p. 110.
41 Caubet, "La musique à Ougarit"..., p. 734.
42 Rashid, *Mesopotamia...*, p. 134.
43 Hickmann, *Catalogue...*, fig. 29; see also at Israel Antiquities Authorities, no. P1823.
44 Bittel, K., "Cymbeln für Kybele," in: *Günter Wasmuth zum 80. Geburtstag...*, pp. 79-82 (1968).
45 Marcuse, S., *A Survey of Musical Instruments* (NY 1975), p. 10.
46 Fleischhauer, G. *Etrurien und Rom* (=MGB II/5), Leipzig, 1964, fig. 46 and 53; Braun, J., *Alt-Israel/Palästina: Studien zu den archäologischen, schriftlichen und vergleichenden Quellen* (Freiburg, 1999), pp. 198-200, and fig. V/5-2d.

Membranophones

Instruments that produce vibrations from a tightly stretched membrane, such as the drum, are known as membranophones. Drums belong to the most ancient and popular category of musical instruments attested in the Near East, where they are the main membranophone. They were made with one or two membranes and in various size (20-150 cm) and forms (round and square frame, cylindrical, hourglass, kettle, goblet, and bowl shaped). They were held in several positions (in front of the chest, above the head, under the arm) or placed on the ground. Wall paintings of hunting scenes at Çatal Hueyuek in Anatolia (seventh millennium B. C.) show men dancing and beating small round-frame drums with a stick.[47] This drum (with one or two skins?) appears again at the beginning of the second millennium BCE in a scene of dancing etched on a rock in Israel's Negev desert[48] and remains the main membranophone of the Near East (see **Fig. IC-2b**). It seems that beginning in the Chalcolithic/EB terra-cotta goblet-, cornet-, chalice- (Ghassulian culture: e.g., IAA, no. 36.66 and 36.97) and hour-glass-forms (Gilat, in the Negev: IAA, no. 76.54) were used. In the late third millennium the Mesopotamian giant drum, probably in bronze, or with a bronze frame,[49] and in the early second millennium BCE the bronze goblet form, *lilissu*,[50] appeared. A barrel-shaped drum with two skins and a rectangular drum are attested in Middle Kingdom Egypt.[51] With rare exceptions, the entire corpus of pre-Iron Age drum iconography shows the instrument in a cultic context.

In the first half of the second millennium BCE in Old Babylonia and later, but especially in the Iron Age, in other Near Eastern areas, two forms of the female drum player, the most notable indigenous type, appear on terracotta figurines (see **III-3a-e**). One type – deep-relief terracotta plaques depicting naked but adorned with jewelry and wig or head-

---

[47] Stockmann D., "On the Early History of the Drums...," in: Lund, C., ed., *Second Conference of the ICTM Study Group of Music Arcaheology,* vol. 1(Stockholm,1986), pp. 12-14.
[48] Anati, E., *Palestine Before the Hebrews* (New York, 1963), p. 211.
[49] Schmidt-Colinet, C., *Die Musikinstrumente in der Kunst des Alten Orients* (Bonn, 1981), ills. 71-75.
[50] Idem., ill. 76 and 77.
[51] Hickmann, *Ägypten...*, pp. 28, 106.

cover females with a disk (frequently, drum) pressed against the chest with both hands;[52] and, the other type – bell-shaped figures dressed in a long gown, beating a drum, which is in a position perpendicular to the body.[53] Preserved only in Israel/Palestine, there are more than forty items of the first type and some fifteen of the second extant. Mixed types appear on Cyprus and in Syria: pillar figurines with a disk pressed against the chest and figurines on votive stands. It is probably at this time that the drum (*toph* in the Hebrew Bible) acquired a function in both the cultic and everyday life of the lower strata of the population. The function of this type – homogeneous in its Near Eastern unity and autochthonous – is not yet clear: the range of use is from *dea nutrix* and amulet to apotropaic object and toy; even the identification of the disk type is questioned (drum, solar disk, bread?). The hourglass drum (*darabbuka*, also a popular drum among modern Arabs and Druze), characteristically held under the arm, appears once in the Negev and more frequently in finds from Old Babylonia between the Iron Age and Hellenistic periods. Excavations from the Hellenistic-Roman period confirm the appearance of the Greco-Roman frame drum (mostly on mosaics – e.g., at Sepphoris in Israel).[54] In the earliest drum iconography, the membranophone-chordophone duet may be considered to be a typical Near Eastern ensemble (**Fig. IC-3**).[55]

Aerophones

Vibrations of air enclosed in an instrument, produced by wind or breath across its edge (flute), via a reed (clarinet), a double reed (oboe), or the performer's lips (trumpet) distinguish the category of instruments known as aerophones.

---

52 Rashid, *Mesopotamia...*, ills. 91-95.
53 Meyers, C., "A Terracotta in the Harvard Semitic Museum and Disc-Holding Female Figures Reconsidered," in: *Israel Exploration Journal* 37/2-3:116-122 (1987).
54 Meyers, E., et al., *Sepphoris* (Winona Lake, Ind., 1992), p. 49.
55 Anati, *Palestine Before...*, p. 211; Rashid, *Mesopotamia...*, p. 76.

Bullroarer

A slab of wood 10-20 cm long, rhomboid in form and frequently carved and ornamented, with a small hole at the end for a cord, is a bullroarer. It is a noisemaker used at ritual and magic events that produces a roaring sound through circular movement. Probably one of the earliest aerophones, it is attested by the finds from the Natufian Kebara cave in Israel's Carmel hills (IAA, no. 13.85) and the Neolithic Nahal Hemar cave.[56] In Egypt, the bullroarer appears in predynastic times.[57]

Flute

The first archaeological evidence for flutes is not earlier than the late fourth millennium in Egypt;[58] this flute type, the *nay* (60-90 cm long) is still in use and is usually held at an oblique angle. The flute is also attested in third millennium-Mesopotamia.[59] The single flute, however, either was not popular in the ancient Near East, or was not frequently depicted in the Bronze and Iron Ages because of its low status. A corpus of some ten short (7-12 cm) whistles with a single side opening has appeared in areas of Canaan/Israel, the earliest dated to the third millennium (Megiddo: IAA, no. 39.680) and the latest to the seventh century BCE. In the first-dynasty royal cemetery at Ur, fragments of silver tubes were discovered that have been interpreted as flutes. The early cross-flute iconography appears on the unusually rich in musical wind instrument depictions on the 2nd-early 3ed century city-coins of Paneas, a Selecuid city in northern Palestine.

Double pipe

The most typical aerophone in the ancient Near East was the double pipe (two tubes) with a single or double reed (i.e., a clarinet or an oboe type, not to be confused with the flute, **Fig. IB-4** and **IC-4**). The double pipes

---

56 *Treasures of the Holy Land: The Metropolitan Museum of Art (New York, 1986)*, fig. 17.
57 Hickmann, *Ägypten...*, 1961a, p. 157.
58 Idem., Ill. 1.
59 Rashid, *Mesopotamia...*, p. 50.

produce a rich, harsh, penetrating, and sensual timbre. While the single flute was still in use during the Old Babylonian period,[60] the divergent double pipe with cylindrical tubes, of Cycladian provenance,[61] permeated musical life. The double pipe has been discovered in excavations in contexts from the middle of the second millennium B. C. E. up to Byzantine times; mostly, however, it appears in iconographic material both as a single instrument and in ensembles. The differences in representations are mainly in the degree of divergence of the pipes: length of pipes (the longer one, possibly a drone), the way how the pipes are held (horizontally or vertically, together or apart), performance style (position of the hands), and type of reed (single or double). Finds from the ninth-seventh centuries BCE (e.g., from Achziv[62] and Karatepe[63]) show that the double-pipe performer – mostly female – has become a popular Near Eastern terracotta figurine topos, along with the drum player.

The instrument acquired all the signs of the classic aulos; in Greece itself, however, the instrument does not appear prior to 700 BCE. After the seventh century BCE, the *phorbeia* (a leather band passed over the lips and cheeks to secure stability while blowing) appears on Cypriot and Anatolian figurines,[64] but is absent from Neo-Assyrian examples and on finds from Israel/Palestine. The double pipe is frequently part of the Neo-Assyrian orchestra (e.g., the Elamite orchestra, Niniveh, seventh century BCE);[65] or the membraphone-aerophone-chordophone "Phoenician orchestra" (ninth-seventh centuries BCE).[66] This ensemble can be traced back to Philistian/Judaean ensembles, probably connected to the Cybele cult (11th – 10th cent., B. C., see **Fig. IA-6**).[67] In Hellenistic-Roman contexts, finds of actual *aulos* instruments are frequent and seem to indicate microtone scales. In that period, also for the first time, the double pipe

---

60 Rashid, *Mesopotamien*..., ills. 85, 86.
61 Aign, B., *Die Geschichte der Musikinstrumente des griechischen Raums bis zum 700 v. Chr.* (Frankfurt am Main, 1963), ill. I/5.
62 IAA, no. 44.56.
63 Schmidt-Colinet, *Die Musikinstrumente*..., no. 89.
64 Idem., no. 90; Hermary A. et al., *Catalogue des antiquités de Chypre* (Paris, 1989), no. 578-579.
65 Rashid, *Mesopotamien*..., ill. 151.,
66 Aign, *Die Geschichte*..., figs, 89, 90, 91.
67 Ashdod: IAA, no. 68.1182.

with a short melody pipe and long drone (*arghul* type) can be attested with certainty (**Fig. IC-4a**). Mosaics and other artifacts from the Hellenistic-Roman period show the double pipe both as a musical instrument of lament (e.g., in a wall painting in the Idumean necropolis at Marisa/Mareshah, (in situ) and of orgiastic joy (in a Dionysian context, see **Fig. IA-7 and 8**).[68]

Zamr

A new period in the history of the double pipes, and especially single pipes, began with the use of conoid double-reed pipes. The *zamr* type of double pipe from the seventh century BCE is still dominant in the Near East. Among the first examples to attest this aerophone is one from Tel Malhata, in southern Israel: a terra-cotta figurine of a man blowing a divergent conical double pipe (IAA, no. 94.3393, **Fig. IC-4b**); bronze figurines from Anatolia should be associated with this type of aerophone rather than with trumpets.[69] Representations of *zamr* instruments appear on the city-coins from Paneas (Israel). In early Byzantine iconography a new topos of the *zamr* blower in pastoral surroundings appear (**Fig. IC-4c**).[70]

Panpipe

The earliest evidence of the panpipe (*syrinx*) in the region is probably from Anatolia (seventh century BCE.)[71] It has been one of the most popular instruments in Near East since Seleucid times[72] and has kept its autochthonous peculiarities in every area. In the second century CE the panpipe was accepted a symbol on the city coins of Paneas/Banias in

---

68 Braun, *Altisrael/Palästina...*, Ch. V/2 and V/5.
69 Turnbull, H., "Anatolia", in: 2NGD, 1:388-1980, fig. 8.
70 This topos is depicted also on Medeba, Khirbet Shema, and Caesarea mosaic floors (Jordan and Israel); see also, Farmer, H. G., *Islam*, ed., (=MGB III/2, Leipzig, 1966), ill. 7 ec.
71 Turnbull, "Anatolia"..., fig. 7.
72 Rashid, *Mesopotamia...*, p. 142

northern Palestine (in the second-third centuries called Caesarea Philippi).[73]

Organ

In the third century BCE the organ, based on the panpipe (*hydraulus*), was invented in Alexandria, Egypt. The first iconographic evidence of this instrument are terracotta from Alexandria (second-first centuries BCE,[74] pre-Christian Tarsus and second century Carthage).[75] The most significant example has come to light in a Hamath (Syria) mosaic that depicts a third-century ensemble performance (organ, *crotals*, lyre, double-aulos, bells, sounding bowls, see **Fig. V-2**). Attention has been drawn to the Samaritan terra-cotta oil lamps that depict an organ (again with *crotal*);[76] it seems that this instrument was used in both liturgical and secular life.

Animal horns

Comparatively scarcely attested, animal horns may have been used in Anatolian Neolithic cultures,[77] but they undoubtedly appear in only two finds: in an early second-millennium BCE drawing from Mari and in a ninth-eighth century BCE stone relief from Carchemish.[78] There is evidence as well of the use of oxhorns in fifteenth-century BCE Egypt during the reign of Amenhotep IV.[79]

---

73 See Meshorer, Y. "The coins of Caesarea Paneas", in: *Israel Numismatic Journal* 8 (1984-1985).
74 Perrot, J., *The Organ from its Invention in the Hellenistic period to the End of the Thirteenth Century* (London, 1971), pl. V.
75 Idem., pl. XII and XVI.
76 Homo-Lechner, C., *La Pluridisciplinarité en archaéologie musicale...*, (Paris,1994), p. 142.
77 Lund, *Second Conference...*, p. 20.
78 Schmidt-Colinet, *Die Musikinstrumente...*, ill. 75.
79 Marcuse, *A Survay...* p. 747.

Shofar

The ram's horn, or šofar, is the most frequently mentioned music instrument (seventy-two times) in the Hebrew Bible. However, it does not appear in archaeological contexts until the third century (among the earliest appearances is the Hammath Tiberias synagogue mosaic, in situ, see **Fig. IB-5**);[80] the šofar is always depicted as part of a cultic symbol accouterment group which include *menorah, šofar, lulav,* and *etrog.*

Shell horn

A different type of horn, the shell horn, was used in Israel/Palestine beginning at least in the late second millennium BCE (Tell Qasile: Hebrew University no. 2968:227).

Trumpet

The elite music instrument the trumpet descends from the animal horn and is similar to it. It appears rarely, however. Besides the two famous Tutankhamun trumpets (one silver, 58.2 cm, and the other bronze, 49.4 cm), there are only some fifteen representations of the trumpet from Egypt. Among them, the first certain depiction (sixteenth-fifteenth centuries BCE), shows a clear cultic and military affiliation.[81] Mesopotamian cultures show extremely little evidence for this instrument: there are only two between the Mesalim and Neo-Babylonian periods.[82] The situation is similar in Israel/Palestine, where, contrary to its significance in the Hebrew Bible (e.g., Nu. 10:2-10), and in the Dead Sea Scrolls from Qumran (IQM II. 15 and V11.9), the only iconographic evidence for the trumpet is on the wall paintings in the Idumean necropolis near Beth-Guvrin (in situ, third-second centuries BCE). There, for the first time in trumpet iconography, the instrument – an early example of the Roman tuba – is part of a hunting scene.[83] The aerophone depicted on the coins minted by Bar

---

80 Dothan, M. "Th Muscians of Ashdod", in: *Archaeology* 23/4:310-311.
81 Manniche, L., *Ancient Egyptian Musical Instruments* (Munich, 1975), pp. 33-35; Hickmann, *Ägypten...,* p. 74.
82 Rashid, *Mesopotamien...,* ills. 37, 143.
83 Peters,J. P./H. Thirsch, *Paintd Tombs in the Necropolis of Marissa* (London, 1905).

Kokhba in 132-135, frequently defined as trumpets, can hardly be considered as such,[84] and the two trumpets depicted among the booty from the Jerusalem Temple on the Arch of Titus in Rome may not necessarily be the Temple instruments but, rather, copies of the Roman tuba. There are only isolated instances of trumpet representations from later periods, such as the pair of trumpets on the rock carving at Tak-i-Bostan from the Sasanian period.[85] In spite of the early appearance and significance of the trumpet in Egypt, and the importance attached to it in Near Eastern written sources, this instrument may actually have been used very little in the Levant.

Chordophones

An instrument in which a stretched string vibrates is known as a chordophone. Its subgroups are the zither, lyre, harp, and lute. The phenomenon of appearance of sophisticated string instruments at early stages in the history of music without evidence of earlier rudimentary forms is clearly manifested in the Near East.

Harp

The oldest archaeological document of a chordophone is a stone etching from Megiddo, strata XIX (late 4th mill. B. C.) depicting a female figure with a triangular, fully developed harp. The instrument appears again in Cycladic culture[86] but was not witnessed again in the Near East. While other forms of the harp have been attested since the early third millennium in Mesopotamia and the fourth dynasty in Egypt (see **Fig. IC-5** and **6**), the harp itself is absent from the central areas along the eastern Mediterranean coast from the Sinai to Anatolia. This strongly questions the popular interpretation of *nēbel* in the Hebrew Bible as the "harp" of ancient Israel.

The early Sumerian harp (Uruk IV and Mesalim periods), a small (50-70 cm), arched instrument, is depicted mainly on seals in a cultic context,

---

84 Sachs, *The History...*, p. 120.
85 Behn, Fr., *Musikleben im Altertum und frühen Mittelalter* (Stuttgart, 1954), p. 77.
86 Aign, *Die Geschichte...*, figs. 1-3.

frequently being played by animals.[87] At the beginning of the second millennium BCE, the arched harp was replaced by the angular harp, which was held vertically or horizontally;[88] while the horizontal harp was known only in Mesopotamia, the vertical one was used to the West, especially on Cyprus.[89] Toward the first millennium BCE the size of the instrument and the number of strings increased. The horizontal harp (eight-twelve strings) was plucked with a plectrum and the vertical harp (eighteen-twenty-two strings) with the hand, which suggests a bass function for the first and a melodic function for the second (**Fig. IC-6**). The placement of the hands on the strings allows some conclusions about the style of the music being played.[90] A new small rectangular vertical harp with upright resonator on the side of the frame appeared during the Seleucid period;[91] in Roman times this type became popular throughout the Near East, Greece, and Rome. The first Egyptian harps, also arched, are dated somewhat later, at the time of the fourth dynasty,[92] and only then appear the much larger (150-180 cm) instruments, richly ornamented in sophisticated forms, some with a developed tuning system up to thirty-six pegs (e.g., the harp from the tomb of Rameses III.)[93] There are representations since the eighteenth dynasty of the vertical angular harp, which is considered an import from elsewhere into the Near East;[94] smaller harps are depicted as well – the portable "shoulder harp" and the "ladle harp."[95] All of these instruments, mostly built from expensive wood from Lebanon and designed as works of art, seem to have been used only in the highest circles of society. In terms of chronology, the Egyptian harps followed in the footsteps of the Mesopotamian harps but developed greater sophistication in construction. In Hellenistic-Roman times, in both the Ptolemaic

---

87 Rashid, *Mesopotamien...*, pp. 52-59.
88 Idem., figs. 69-75.
89 Idem., fig. 152.
90 Sachs, *The history...*, p. 82.
91 Rashid, *Mesopotamien...*, p. 150; Behn, *Musikleben...*, pl. 55.
92 Hickmann, *Ägypten...*, pp. 20-27.
93 Idem., pp. 44, 64, 128.
94 Idem., pp. 30, 130.
95 Idem., ill. 93, 94 and 95.

and Seleucid Empires, the smaller, simply worked, angular harp was played.[96]

Lyre

The primary musical instrument in the Near East was the lyre. From its first appearance on Sumerian seals in the first half of the third millennium, where it is depicted as a perfect chordophone,[97] the lyre dominates the musical scene of the region until the Early Byzantine period. The elaborate Sumerian asymmetrical lyres have a resonator in the form of a bull (upright it is some 150 cm high, **Fig. IC-7**) or are ornamented with a bull's head (portable, 100-120 cm), and have eight-twelve strings. The instruments recovered in excavation and supplemented by iconographic material[98] show a royal context for lyre music. The smaller, vertically held, asymmetrical lyre with two unequal side-arms appeared in Akkad and was played also in Carchemish and Babylon.[99] In the late third-early second millennium BCE, when large standing lyres were still in use in Babylon and Anatolia,[100] and the first modified forms appeared in the hands of naked dancing women (Negev rock etching, nineteenth century BCE **Fig. IC-2a**),[101] dramatic changes took place nearly simultaneously in several places of the Near East. The Sumerian grand royal lyre was replaced by a simply built, small (40-50 cm), portable, symmetrical, and sometimes asymmetrical, instrument. For the first time it was held horizontally, in front of the musician; it was played mostly by musicians low social status, Semitic traveling merchants, and women – the latter often depicted naked.[102] The new lyre type entered Egypt from Syria and Canaan. It took root there in its horizontal asymmetrical form and was played mostly by women. In Late Bronze Age Canaan, a new way to hold the asymmetrical lyre, with the sound box under the arm, can be seen on

---

96 Idem., ill. 109.
97 Rashid, *Mesopotamien...*, p. 50.,
98 Hickmann, *Ägypten...*, ills. 11, 28-39.
99 Idem., ill. 43; Aign, *Die Geschichte...*,figs, 78, 79.
100 Rashid, *Mesopotamien...*, ills. 79, 80; in: Turnbull, Anatolia..., p. 388.
101 Anati, *Palestine Before...*, p. 210.
102 Rashid, *Mesopotamien..*, ills. 47, 59, 76, 80; Behn, *Musikleben...*, pl. 85; Porada, E., "A Lyre Player from Tarsus and His Relations," in: *The Aegean and the Near East...*, ed. S. Weinberger et al., pp. 185-211 (New York, 1956), figs. g-j.

a Megiddo ivory tablet (see **Fig. IA-2**). This change significantly increased performance possibilities, and in its new capacity the lyre became the main instrument of priests and musicians in holy places, courts, and elite military orchestras.[103] This new playing technique migrated to Assyria, partly with musicians-prisoners from Judah.[104] The first half of the first millennium BCE is marked by a multitude of lyre forms, demonstrating both the autochthonous creativity of different groups and certain common Near Eastern tendencies. The most common lyre-forms are the following:

Large asymmetrical with diverging arms and rectangular sound body (70-120cm)

Examples appear with differently arranged strings throughout the Near East, including Mesopotamia and Israel/Palestine (see **IC-2a** and **7**).[105] While the Mesopotamian famous lyres with bull-head belong to a purely royal context, the Israel/Palestine examples are instruments of some kind of nomadic tribes.

Smaller asymmtrical with parallel arms and rectangular sound body (40-70cm)

A very popular type in the entire Near East during the 2nd and 1st millenium B. C. (**Fig. IA-5**). In Egypt and Mesopotamia known from the early 2nd millenium it penetrated Palestine/Israel at the end of the millenium (see **Fig. IC-3**).

Symmetrical with rectangular sound-body (40-90cm)

Early attested in Mesopotamia (middle 3ed mill. B. C.), they reached the peak of popularity in Syria, Israel/Palestine, but especially in Greece towards the first millenium (**Fig. IA-4** and **IB-2**).[106]

---

103 Rashid, *Mesopotamien...*, ills. 120, 142, 145, 148 and 150.
104 Idem., ill. 142.
105 Rashid, *Mesopotamien...*, pp. 31-35: Anati, *Palestine Before...*, pp. 203-214.
106 Behn, *Musikleben...*, fig. 19; Kamid el-Loz excavations, no. 78:504.

Symmetrical with parallel side-arms and rounded sound-body (U-form)

Early examples of this type appear from the 10th century on the Palestinian Philistine coast, in particular in the Ashdod area (see **Fig. IA-6, IB-3 and III-2a**). Together with the symmetrical lyre with rectangular sound-body, this lyre-form became the dominant chordophone of the Hellenistic-Roman Near East. This instrument appears in nearly every social context, and is now often represented in a stylized form, which may indicate symbolic meaning.[107] Similarly the large *kithara* "concert" form (symmetrical lyre with rectangular body) became in the late Roman-early Byzantine time rather a symbol than live instrument **(Fig. III-2b)**.

Lute

Instruments of the lute type are the most mobile, dynamic, and subject to local adoption among all chordophones. By permitting the performance of a nearly unrestricted number of sounds from one string, they can be adjusted to any kind of tonal system and music style. Their inexpensive and simple construction, as compared to harps and lyres, and their rustic, entertaining, and erotic performance context made them popular among the common people and seems to explain the comparatively rare depictions of the instrument. The question of the origin of the lute remains unanswered – theory suggestions range from the Caucasus and Central Asia,[108] to Syria and Babylon.[109] The first iconographic evidence for the long-necked lute appears on seals from Akkad, probably in a cultic context.[110] In the Old Babylonian period, the musicians are often naked men and women;[111] the lute rarely appears then in connection with a cult or temple service, although later it does, in Anatolia.[112] In the middle of the

---

107 Hickmann, *Ägypten...*, ills. 110 and 111; Braun, "Biblische..." cols. 1509-10; Rashid, *Mesopotamen...*, pp. 152-153.
108 Marcuse, *Survey...*, p. 406.
109 Turnbull, H., "The Origin of the Long-necked Lute," in: *Galpin SocietyJournal*, 25:56-66 (1972); Rashid, *Mesopotamien...*, p. 92.
110 Idem., ills. 38 and 39.
111 Rashid, *Mesopotamien...*, pp. 75-76, 81-84.
112 Schmidt-Colinet, *Die Musikinstrumente...*, figs. 60 and 62.

second millennium BCE, probably via Canaan (a male terra-cotta figurine, sixteenth century BCE, was discovered in Tell el-Ajjul, IAA, no. 33.1567) the lute reached Egypt. While attested in Canaan in two more finds (see **Fig. IA-3**), the lute does not appear in Israel/Palestine again until the Hellenistic period. In Egypt the instrument became very popular and was played by undressed females (**Fig. IC-5**) and on some occasions by men, possibly in a cultic context.[113] In the earliest depictions, lutes are generally shown with two-three strings marked with decorative tassels at the tuning box. A long, frequently fretted neck emerges from a small, resonator out of wood or tortoise shell covered with animal hide. Mostly plucked with a plectrum, fastened by a cord to the body of the instrument, the form of the lute has not changed significantly over the centuries. The way to held it, however, has changed constantly, and there have been attempts to create a lute chronology according to the performance position: a) in the Old-Babylonian period – horizontal holding; b) in the Kassite-Neo-Assyrian period – lute neck at an oblique angle, pointing upward; and c) in the Seleucid period – lute neck at an oblique angle, pointing downward.[114] The short-necked lute with a broad, pear-shaped body, perhaps of Central Asian origins, appeared only rarely in the ancient Near East (for the first time attested in the Egyptian nineteenth dynasty).[115] In Hellenistic times the instrument is represented on terra-cotta from Egypt and Palestine,[116] and it acquired great popularity in the Sasanian period,[117] when it developed into one of the most popular traditional instruments of Islamic countries, the *'ud*, predecessor of the European lute.

Zither

The zither type is actually nonexistent in the Near East, and information on this chordophone type, often also called psaltery (*psalteria*, from Gk., *psalmos*, "finger;" in antiquity their strings were plucked with bare fingers) is scarce and confused. One of the rare examples, also interpreted

---

113 Hickmann, *Ägypten...*, p. 98, ill. 101.
114 Rashid, *Mesopotamien...*, p. 146).
115 Hickmann, *Ägypten...*, ill. 104.
116 Hickmann, *Ägypten...*, ill. 105; Marisa/Mareshah excavation (Israel), no. 1386.
117 Farmer, *Islam*, ill. 4; Duchesne-Guillemin, *Sassanide...* (footnote 11).

as xylophone, is a beautiful carving on an ivory pyxis (BM, no. 118179, ninth-eighth century BCE), where as part of a probably Phoenician ensemble two persons are plucking (?) square stringed frames or boxes with nine and ten strings.[118]

---

118 Aign, *Die Geschichte...*, pp. 158-159; and Sachs, *History...*, p. 118.

II. Some Remarks on the Music Hisotry of Ancient Israel/ Palestine: Written or Archaeological Evidence*

I am using this occasion to put to your attention a case of far reaching contradictions between written and factual archaeological evidence. We are talking about the archaeological evidence from Ancient Israel/Palestine, and the written evidence from the Old Testament.

I am glad that I can base my statement to Professor Schumacher's paper on archaeological evidence and *Geschichtsbewusstsein* in Indonisian music history – as we see, the problem is universal. "Wurde Geschichte in mündlicher Tradition, oder vielleicht in schriftlichen Quellen erfunden?" asked Professor Schumacher. Now, in regard to the Bible: was history or, I should say, music history, invented by the authors of the Holy Scripture, or was it a process of myth-making in the centuries of oral tradition, as it happens in any folk epic?

While in other fields scholars years ago surmounted the reverential regard for the Holy Scripture and it became quite clear, that the primary source for the *Geschichtsschreibung* of the Ancient World is archaeology and that as any other written source, the Holy Book should be checked over and over again by archaeological evidence (cmp. studies by D. W. Dever, D.V. Edelman, I. Finkelstein M. Görg, O. Keel, E. A. Knauf, N. Na'aman, H. Weippert etc.), musicologist and adjacent scholars in regard to music history continued to be strong believers and remained *päpstlicher als der Papst* far to long. The canonical holy source was never called in question in the field of musicology and was never confronted with archaeological finds.

From the early days of modern historiography of music both Jewish and Christian historians relied on one central and mostly single source, the Holy Scripture This source dominated the writing of the history of

---

* Paper at the Archaeology of Music ICTM Study Group, Michaelstein, 1998; published in: *Orient-Archäologie: Musikarchäologie*, vol. 7/II, ed. E. Hickmann et al., Rahden/Westf., 2000, pp. 135-140.

music from Abraham Partaleone[1] and Michael Praetorius[2] till our days. In 1980 the *New Grove Dictionary of Music and Musicians* in the section "Sources" mentions the importance of archaeological evidence, and presents after this an entry of some seven pages on the music of ancient Israel titled, however, "3. Survey of the Biblical Period," "4. The Instruments of the Temple," "5. Repertory and musical practice of the Temple," and "6. The Second Temple" (vol 9, pp. 616-623). This entry by the foremost musicologist of Israeli music is based *in toto* on Biblical quotations, and among the eleven illustrations only six are directly related to the text. Even recently there appeared a book under the title "Musik in Altisrael,"[3] where the author is drawing a historical picture of the musical life in Ancient Israel, entirely following the biblical descriptions; and some years ago Amnon Shiloah still wrote in his *Jewish Musical Traditions* that "the Bible is the principal and indeed the richest source of knowledge about Israel's music in ancient times."[4] The existence of archaeological-iconographical sources was often denied on grounds of the Second Commandment (Exodus 20:2-6), as in Praetorius' times nearly 400 years ago, or, if some of those sources were used, it was done only in passing for general illustration and in no relation to geographical or chronological context. Even if the significance of archaeological findings as source for the music history of ancient Israel is sometimes acknowledged, it still is applied only to the lyres and pipes from Ur, the trumpets from Egypt, and the *aulos* from Greece which should be studied for this purpose.[5]

Sixty years ago Curt Sachs wrote in his classical study on musical instruments: "As the Bible was opposed to depicting men and objects of any kind, we have no reliefs or paintings to consult concerning the nature of the few instruments named in the Holy Script."[6] Alfred Sendrey's *Music in Ancient Israel*[7] presents 62 illustrations without any discussion and only ten are relevant for Ancient Israel/Palestine; just ten years ago in Carl Dahlhaus' edited *Neues Handbuch der Musikgeschichte* Eric

---

1 Abraham Portaleone, *Shilte ha-giborim*, Mantua, 1612.
2 Michael Praetorius, *Synagma musicum*, vol. 1-3, Wittenberg, 1614/19.
3 Hans Seidel, *Musik in Altisrael*. Frankfurt/Main, 1989.
4 Amnon Shiloa, *Jewish Musical Traditions*, Detroit, 1992, p. 38.
5 Idem., p. 39.
6 Curt Sachs, *History of Musical Instruments*, New York, 1940, p. 105.
7 Alfred Sendrey, *Music in Ancient Israel*, New York, 1969.

Werner[8] hardly mentions archaeological finds and shows only two from five illustrations related to the subject. Early examples of a modern interdisciplinary scholarly attitude in studies on the musical archaeology/iconography of Ancient Israel/Palestine were ignored or were mentioned without deeper consideration (this was the fate of most Othmar Keel's or Bathja Bayer's studies).[9]

Modern research has already some time ago disclosed the many dubious and spurious passages of the Bible, not to mention the chronological perplexity of the entire opus. As researchers of the past in a certain field of human activity we are interested in the history of music of Ancient Israel/Palestine rather than in the music theology or music philosophy of the Old Testament which itself is a relatively late creation (not before the Babylonian/Persian Period, 5.-4. cent. BCE, and in many of its aspects later). What part of the oral tradition was delivered unchanged and what was changed, or what was written down and later changed or subject to censorship – all this is mainly a question of future research. We have only few examples from the Old Testament to get hold of the changes in a sense of the historical reality; for example, the two parallel passages in 2. Sam 6:5 and 1. Chr 13:8: an orgiastic musical instrumentary in the first passage (wood clappers, lyres, drums, rattles and metal clappers) was changed or censored to a regular liturgical music performance – in the second (songs, lyres, trumpets, drums and cymbals).

I do not intend here to contradict the Biblical evidence on music as a totality; there, certainly, are cases where we may see a mutual conformation of sources, at least on the surface: the absence of the lute, for example, in archaeological excavations of Iron Age to Hellenistic/Roman Age layers coincides with the Biblical text; the social context in the use of the *kinnor* (lyre) in text and archaeological iconography do not contradict.

Time has come, however, to disclose the undeniable deep conflict, which in many cases surfaces and seems to allow now a unequivocal *entweder-oder* judgement. It was like this with the interpretation of both the *kinnor* and *nebel* as lyres on the basis of archaeological evidence,

---

8 "Die Musik im alten Israel", vol. I, pp. 76-112 (1989)
9 Such as Keel's *Die Welt der altorientalischen Bildsymbolik...* (Zurich, 1972) or "Musikinstrumnte, Figuren und Siegel im judaischen Haus der Eisenzeit II," in: *Heiliges Land* 4:35-43; see a list of Bathja Bayer's publications in: Irael Adler, *The Study of Jewish Music: A Bibliographical Gide* (Jerualem,1995).

which seems now to be unanimously accepted and will put an end to the legend of "King David's harp".

When in 1990 at the Saint-Germain-en-Laye-meeting of the ICTM Study Group for Archaeology of Music I mentioned some aspects of this inconsistency between written and archeological evidence, this concept was strongly opposed. Now, nearly ten years later, we should again consider this situation, especially if we recall, that from the territory of Ancient Israel/Palestine there are at present at our disposal some 650 finds with musicological meaning, on the one hand, and that modern archaeological work on the territory of Israel and Jordan has reached a level which hardly allows to expect basic changes in the general picture of Israel/Palestine's musical scenery – on the other.

It is my intention to present to your attention some examples of Biblical text contra the state of archaeological research.

The clay rattle

The archaeological clay-rattle is the most verified musical instrument in our region and appears more then 70 times in excavations on the territory of Israel and Jordan (see **Fig. III-1a-g**). In spite of this, the instrument is not mentioned in the Bible, and no depictions of the clay-rattle were found, although we have from the same area and for a much shorter time more than thirty depictions of the lyre, the instrument of the higher classes, the priests and court musicians. The clay-rattle, usually a robust, by non-professional hand simply mastered cult-tool, mostly discovered in burials, was a broadly used mass-instrument by people of low standing of all or most ethnic groups. This instrument had no place in the written history of the "chosen" people, neither in picture nor in text. *mena'anim*, the name of a musical instrument in the Old Testament commonly identified today as clay rattle[10] is mentioned only once in the entire Old Testament, and, curious enough, in 2. Sam 6:5 in the context of the mentioned above orgiastic orchestra. The word never appeared again in the Old Testament, and not in the parallel passage 1. Chr 13:8 from where it was removed. The absence of a word from the Old Testament is not less indicative as its presence. The clay-rattle, regardless of its broad use in the

---

10 Bathja Baier, "*m'na'anim* – clay rattles?" in: *Tatzlil*, 4 (1964), 19-22.

musical reality of ancient Israel, was not a musical tool to be accepted in the written imaginative world of the holy text.

The cymbals

The archaeological information on cymbals[11] is as follows:

some 30 items (11 of them in pairs) are preserved; twelve have a diameter of 7,2 to 10,5 cm, and fourteen – 2,0 to 6,0 cm. Geographically they are distributed from Akko to Ashkelon along the entire shore and from Hazor to Jerusalem in the inland. Chronologically – and this is in the center of our attention – 14 belong to the Late Brone Age, some four, probably, to the early Iron Age, four to the Hellenistic/Roman time, and the rest is of uncertain date. All the items from the Hellenistic-Roman times are of the small type, which means that they were used as finger or forked cymbals, and had hardly access to holy places or temples. To conclude – we have no cymbals from nearly the entire Iron Age (1200-586 BCE), no from the Babylonian/Persian period (586-332 BCE), and, in fact, no for liturgical performance of the Hellenistic-Roman time (332 BCE-200 CE).

The text of the Old Testament mentions the *meşiltayim* (in *consensus omnium* interpreted as cymbals) thirteen times and only in post-exile books, which are dated from the late 4th – 2nd cent BCE: once in Esra, once in Nehemia, and eleven times in the Chronicles. The text itself, however, mentions also events of earlier times, the reign of David and Salomon. (We may disregard the term *şelşelim*, which are not necessarily cymbals, on the one hand, and are mentioned only twice /2. Samuel 6:5 and Ps 150/, from which we consider the first a half pagan/half Jewish ritual, and the second – a very late theological doxology – on the other).

We have to explain the total absence of any finds of liturgical cymbals (which, by the way, are made from durable material) for a period of nearly 1,000 years, when according to the chroniclers the cymbals, a guild-instrument of the Asaphites, Hemenites, Etanites or Jedutuns were supposedly beaten in great quantities at the most significant events of Jewish life: see 1. Chr 15:16, 19 and 28; 16:5 and 42; 25:1 and 6; 2. Chr 5:12 and 13; 29:25. Cymbals are described to be a significant part of the

---

11 2MGG, 1:1518-19.

orchestra at David's second ascent to Jerusalem, in the musical accompaniment at the placement of the Ark and the following musical order, at the dedication of Salomon's Temple and in Hezekijah's reformed musical liturgy. In the time of Esra and Nehemia the cymbals were supposed to be part of huge musical events during the offerings, the placing of the cornerstone at the building of the Second Temple and dedication of the city-wall of Jerusalem (Esra 3:10 and Neh 12:27). And still – no archeological evidence of cymbals for this whole period! With this contradiction not explained, we can hardly rely on the books Esra, Nehemia and the Chronicles as a source for confirming the active use of cymbals.

We may suppose that as in the already mentioned 1. Chr 13:8, where the *meşiltayim* appeared as result of "improvement" or censorship, cymbals were included in the following parts of the First Book of Chronicles both to improve the effect and embellish the musical liturgy of David's court. Later the cymbals in the pompous orchestra of king Solomon where to impress the reader as part of the glory of Solomon's kingdom, and during the liturgical reforms of Hesikiyah – of the majestic ceremony "as ordered by David." In Esra and Nehemia the cymbals are already not only part of the liturgical pomp of the Second Temple but should also be a bond to the great kingdoms of the first Temple.

What is the real reason for the archaeological absence of cymbals during this entire period – is it economical, industrial, political or theological? Was there behind this an act of total destruction by the enemy, or by the condemned to death priests? Or are the texts on the *meşiltayim* just wishful thinking on the part of the chroniclers, an imaginative picture of the glory of earlier heroic times?

The musical splendor of the Second Temple

The contradiction of biblical imaginative reality and historical facts reaches it's heights in the case of the musical culture of the Babylonian/Persian (586-333) and early Hellenistic I Period (333- 168 B.C.E.), which also constitutes a great part of the so called Period of the Second Temple (586 B.C.E. – 70 AD). For some reasons this conflict was never mentioned before. Moreover, we know from general historians that for this period the situation of sources is *ausgesprochen gut*[12] and that with the rebuilding of the Temple after the decree of Kyros the historical circumstances for cultural and economical developments were especially favorable.[13] Historians of music gladly accepted this general situation for their particular field. We may expect now rich developments for the musical culture. And indeed, such a picture of musical splendor and grandeur, liturgical and ceremonial parade emerges from written sources – the Books of Esra and Nehamia (dated into the 4.-3. Cent. BCE). These books tell us about a surprising number of cult-musicians which returned from the exile – 4, 289 *kohanim* (priests who blew the trumpets), 74 *levites* (musicians who played the cymbals, lyres and other instruments), 128 or 148 *mešorerim* (Temple singers and, possible poets/composers) and some 200 to 245 singers of lower status, who participated in two large chorus; huge orchestras and chorus, performing at such events as the laying of the cornerstone of the Temple and the building of the city walls in Jerusalem. According to the text, huge processions of singers and musicians under the guidance of Esra and Nehemia marched through the entire city to celebrate the important events,[14] and on other, probably more regular occasions, different processions were arranged: first the singers, then the maidens with the drums and at the end the musicians were passing, as described by Ps 68:26. Joseph Flavius, more or less, matches the descriptions of the Bible. The later canonical sources – the Mishna (2.-3. cent.) and Talmud (5.-6. cent.) – already add in detail some particularities: the Temple orchestra should include not less then two and not more then six *nebalim*, not less then two and not more then twelve *ḥalilim*, not less then nine *kinnorot* and two trumpets; the number of the last two instruments, however, may be increased till the endless, and, in general, all musical instruments should be included without restriction (!?) of type and number (Mishna, Arakhin 2:3, 5; Sukkah 5:4).

It is not surprising that, with this rich written information on hand and relying on these sources only, musicologists decided, that about the music of the Second Temple "we are remarkably well informed."[15] Further-

---

12 Weippert, Helga, *Palästina in vorhellenistischer Zeit* (München, 1988), p. 693.
13 Israel Finkelstein/N.A. Silberman, *The Bible Unhearthed*...(New York, 2000).
14 Cmp. Esra 2:36-41, 65; 3:10; Neh 7:39-44, 67; 12:27, 31, 35-38; 40-42.
15 McKinnon, James, "The Exclusion of Musical Instruments from the Ancient Synagogues", in: *Proceedings of the Royal Musical Association*, 106 (1979/80), p. 77.

more, the story was improved and enriched, gained musicological respect and strength: according to Eric Werner and Hans Seidel, who, probably relied on the first,[16] in the Second Temple string instruments have dominated the orchestra, the ten-string harp was newly introduced into the orchestra and the cymbals were beaten in and outside the Temple. Historical reality, however, looks different.

We are confronted with a surprising lacuna of at least 300 years in archaeological evidence as regards the musical culture in general, and, especially, the musical liturgy. Between the rich finds of the Iron Age (at least 150) and the Hellenistic/Roman Age (more then 200) we may hardly consider a handful of finds relevant for the musical culture of the Babylonian/Persian and Early Hellenistic Period. The bronze items (two bells, IAA S-215 and HU without number, and a figurine, IAA 33.2771) belong to the earlier Egyptian culture, the archaeological musical instruments (a conch trumpet and whistle, IAA 67-487, EB K-8058) are divided between the Iron Age and Roman Age, and the coin with a bare lyre-player is of uncertain provenience (IAA 1442.1). The only sure artifacts are a clay figurine and a drawing on a terracotta shard with the depiction of female drum players/dancers,[17] which may be attributed to the local popular folk tradition of female folk dance with drum rhythm. And nothing more.

Even if we take into consideration the comparatively short time of this period, the increasing iconoclastic tendencies of the period and seemingly feeble interest of scholars for this period – even than it is difficult to explain this contradiction of the Biblical splendor of musical activities and this total lack of archaeological evidence. Until this explanation is not provided we can not rely on the descriptions of musical activities by the Books of Esra and Nehemia, and because of that, even less should we consider as historical reality the enriched interpretations of the mentioned books of the Mishna and Talmud.

---

16 Eric Werner, "Die Musik im alten Israel", in: *Neues Handbuch der Musikwissenschaft*, Ed. C. Dahlhaus, I:90; Hans Seidel, *Musik in Altisrael...* (Frankfurt/Main, 1989), pp. 159, 167 and 193.
17 MacAlister, R. A. Stevart, *The Excavations at Gezer* (London, 1912) pl. 177:6 and 10; Ephraim Stern, *The Material Culture of the Land of the Bible in the Persian Period: 538-332 B.C.E.* (Jerusalem, 1982).

It is the only and one conclusion to which we may move at this stage of the art: we have here a case of mythologisation, heroisation and beautification of the past, necessary at that time (4.-3. cent. BCE) for the rising to power theocracy. To achieve this, everything was set in motion – from censorship on earlier descriptions of musical activities to the invention of a fictitious subordinated musical culture.

III. Music in Ancient Israel/Palestine and Ethnicity[*]

Years ago, Benjamin Mazar, the patriarch of Israeli archaeology predicted that the next generation of archaeologists would react away from technical archaeology and turn to texts. In response, I than expressed the wish that "Biblical musicologists" would react away from texts and turn to archaeology and iconography.[1] To some degree both statements became true. I am using the expression "biblical musicologists" rather loosely because I should say "historians of the music of ancient Israel/Palestine."

It would not be an overstatement to claim that of all pre-Christian cultures none has a historiography of music as burdened by prejudice as that of ancient Israel/Palestine. Until the mid-twentieth century, and quite beyond, the entire assessment of ancient Israel's music was based on one single source only – the Bible. We must not forget that for a long time the majority of professional musicians, and among them the writers on history of music, were in the service of the church or synagogue.

The historiography of ancient Israel's music in a modern sense was born nearly simultaneously both in Jewish and Christian circles. In 1612 the Rabbi Avraham ben David da Portaleone (c. 1540-1612) from Mantua, a physician and man of incredible versatility and encyclopedic knowledge, published his book *Shiltey ha-gibborim* (The shields of the mighty). Among discussions on architecture, archaeology, medicine etc., he presented a treatise on the music of the ancient Hebrews, where Biblical quotations mingle with fantasy, and musical instruments mentioned in the Bible often are interpreted as 17th century instruments. In the years 1614-18 Michael Praetorius (1569/73-1621), the well-known German or-

---

[*] This chapter is based on the papers presented at the 36th Congress of the International Council of Traditional Music (Rio de Janeiro, July 2001) and 17th Congress of the International Musicological Society (Leuven, August 2002).

[1] Joachim Braun, "Considerations on archaeo-musicology and the state of the art in Israel," in: *La pluridisciplinarite en arhaeologie musicale*, IVe recontres internationales d'archaeologie musicale de l'ICTM Saint-Germain-en-Laye, October 1990, p. 143.

ganist, composer, theorist, "son and grandson of theologians"[2] and author of theological tracts published his classical three volume *Syntagama musicum*, where he attempts the rendering of the names of ancient Hebrew musical instruments. Praetorius, entirely in accord with the knowledge of the early 17th century, wrote: "In Palaestina, Asia minore und Graecia sind keine Vestigia mehr vorhanden irgend alter instrumente" (vol. 2, fol. 4). Both the renaissance-type Rabbi dilettante and the professional theologian scholar were in their writings relying solely on Biblical texts. Unfortunately, this unbalanced attitude to historical sources continues into our days.

It is clear now, that an exegetic approach can not be the only basis for the study of Israel's musical past. The primary source of investigation should be archaeology, confronted with written (Biblical, post-Biblical or any other) and comparative sources (ethnological, geographical, traditional, oral etc.). Only from a more or less firm archaeological starting point we may approach the written and comparative evidence, regardless of what method of reasoning we are using. To point out the complexity of the study of ancient Israel/Palestine's history of musical cultures, it is enough to mention the unexplained phenomenon (never discussed before) of the musical culture of the Babylonian/Persian and early Hellenistic Periods (586-168 BC) – most part of the time of the Second Temple. The flagrant discrepancy between the biblical descriptions and the surprising lacuna in archaeological evidence creates one of the most perplexed problems of research.

After this somewhat extensive preamble on the general complexity of recreating musical cultures of antiquity, we may turn to another, even more complicated subject, in general, and ancient Israel/Palestine, in particular – the problem of music in ancient cultures and ethnicity.

The music of Ancient Israel/Palestine, this multi-cultural and multi-ethnical land, can not be studied without considering the micro-cultures of the Philistines, Phoenicians, Edomites, Ammonites, Moabites and other local ethnic groups, which inhabited this area. Unfortunately, this indeed was how the history of music of ancient Israel/Palestine was studied and depicted in standard reference works up to our days – the *MGG* (1958), *The New Oxford History of Music* (1960), the *New Grove*

---

2 The *New Grove Dictionary of Music and Musicians*, 2nd edition, 2001, vol. 20: 262.

(1980) and others[3] – all of which considered solely Jewish music. On the other hand, there are recent attempts of the post-modernism or deconstructionist trend to re-create this history, ignoring the cultures of Judah and Israel.[4] Although this trend has not yet produced any specialized studies on music or music culture, it is of interest in our case so far as it can be marked out by the total denial of ethnical aspects of archaeological research. As Lester L. Grabbe notes: "Markers of ethnicity are simply not present in the artifact finds...."[5] This statement can be especially destructive in research of the music culture of the ancient world that has irretrievably lost its central facet – sound. Artifacts are the only source for our research of the focal problem of modern archeo-musicology – the ethnic genesis and the ethnicity of remote musical cultures.

In our field – the musical culture of ancient Israel/Palestine – the very subject of ethnicity has been neglected for centuries.[6] The first chapter on two musical cultures in ancient Palestine "Phoeniker und Hebraeer" appears in 1954 in Friedrich Behn's *Musikleben im Altertum*. A certain interest in this problem may be found in the early 60s of the previous century. The founder of Israeli archaeo-musicology, Bathya Bayer turns to this question in the *Postscript* of her *Material Relics of Music in Ancient Palestine* (1963). In a short discussion, speaking rather about the Greater Canaan than Palestine, the authors judgement is, that "the overall archaeological record shows an essential unity of material culture in any period" (p. 41). This statement certainly asks for explanation. Strangely enough, Bayer acknowledges only two settlement types – Israelite and Philistine, the latter labeled as a "riddle." Bayer question: are there at all any "Jewish instruments," "national instrumental forms"? Her answer is

---

3 See *Handbuch der Musikwissenschaft*, vol. 1 (1989); see also on the ancient music of Israel/Palestine books and articles, such as the ones by Hugo Gressmann (1903), John Stainer (1914), Sol B. Finensinger (1926), Joseph L. Saalschuetz (1929), C. Krealing/L. Mowry (1960), Alfred Sendrey (1969), Eric Werner (1989, 1980), Hans Seidel (1989) and others.
4 Such as the writings by Keith W. Whitelam, Thomas L. Thomson, Philip R. Davies, Niels P.Lemche et al. See the criticism of these publications by William G. Dever, *What did the Biblical writers know*...(Grand Rapids/Cambridge, 2001), Ch. 2.
5 Grabbe, L., ed., *Can a 'History of Israel' be written?* (Sheffield, 1997), p. 17.
6 From Abraham Portaleone (1612) and Michael Praetorius (1618) to the 2MGG and NGD 2001.

a short: "No. There do not seem to have existed any instrumental forms peculiar to ancient Israelite culture alone, not even as dialects" (p. 42). Since that time much has changed in our knowledge of the Israeli/Palestine scene, and Bayer's statements now may seem somewhat obsolete. Nonetheless, she has put the cornerstone for the question on musical ethnicity in ancient Israel/Palestine.

Unfortunately, this first discourse was not continued for some 40 years. For a long time the notion of a general, hardly distinctive "common iconographic vocabulary or belief system in all the various regions"[7] governed Israeli scholarship. In the 90s I have stressed the ethnic problem in the 2MGG entry "Biblische Musikinstrumente" without, however, really following up this line of inquiry neither in my book *Die Musikkultur Altisraels/Palästinas* (1999), nor in it's English version.[8]

During the last decade the topic of ethnicity in Israel/Palestine historiography – not without the influence of ideological factors – has become especially acute. The "ground-breaking publication" for me was the article "Archaeology, Ideology, and the Quest for an 'Ancient' or 'Biblical' Israel" by William G. Dever. "Ethnicity is the key issue," writes Dever, and "none is more critical or urgent than that of ethnicity."[9] The interdisciplinary approach, which can be clearly sensed in the title of Dever's paper, as well as the methodology of mapping of musical archaeological finds on which I was working, induced me to discuss some aspects of musical ethnicity at the recent 36th ICTM Conference (Rio de Janeiro 2001) and 17th IMS Congress (Leuven, August 2002). At these international musicology conferences for the first time special sessions were devoted to music in Ancient Israel/Palesine.

---

7 Levy, Th. E., ed., *The Archaeology of the Society in the Holy Land* (London, 1995), p.237.

8 Although I did consider separately the musical cultures of different ethnic groups, such as the Judaeans, Phoenicians, Philistians, Idumeans, Samaritans, Nabateans and Edomites, I was not sure if it is possible at all to discuss ethnicity of music at a distance of thousands years.

9 *Near Eastern Archaeology*, 61/1 (1998) p. 46; see also "Archaeology and Ethnicity: Peoples of Ancient Canaan/Israel", in: N. A. Silberman/D. Small, ed., *The Archaeology of Israel: Constructing the past, Interpreting the present* (Sheffield, 1997) pp. 216-287; I. Finkelstein , "Ethnicity and Origin of the Iron I Settlers...," in: *Biblical Archaeologist*, 59/4: 198--212 (1996).

The questions we are actually confronted with are the following: can we at all (and to what degree) distinguish the *ethnos* of musical artifacts? should we stick to culture, perhaps belief system, nation or state as superstructures of ethnicity? Can we ask: whose music was it? Palestinian, Judean, Israelite, Philistine, Phoenician, Edomite, Idumean, or Nabatean? Is it possible at all to discover ethnic parameters of an extinct music, known only by excavated archaeological instruments or iconography? And to what degree can the indirect methodology of mapping give us indications of musical ethnic affiliations in ancient Israel/Palestine? Whatever the answers to these questions are, it is quite clear that any approach has to be modified according to the particular historical setting and socio-cultural circumstances.

It is archaeology that provides us with primary evidence on any aspect of the music culture of the pre-literal past, and certainly the ethnic nature of music instruments and musical events of antiquity. The field of ethnoarchaeology, a heatedly disputed area of historical research, has embraced in the last years broad methodological approaches – from analogy in archaeological interpretation and hypothesis, to symbolic ethnoarchaeology, which builds on equating different assemblages of material cultures in the archaeological record with different subcultures.[10] The hybrid word "ethnoarchaeology," mostly used to define the method of comparing ethnographical and archaeological data in order to enhance the interpretations of the latter, in this restricted sense has outlived its usefulness. Ethnoarchaeology in fact, opens to us the possibility "within a diachronic contextual framework...to pick up the transformation of habitual material variation into active self-conscious ethnic symbolism...",[11] and on the basis of changes in the material styles involved, reveals something about the contexts in which ethnicity is generated, reproduced or transformed. In our case, intending to use ethnoarchaeology for the discussion of archaeological data pertinent to music, the correct term would probably be the somewhat clumsy expression archaeo-ethnomusicology, which comprises all theoretical and methodological aspects of the three arias and expresses the poly-disciplinarity of the approach.

---

10 See "Ethnoarhaeology," in: *Archaeological Method and Theory: An Encyclopedia* (New York & London, 2000), pp. 181-187.
11 Sian Jones, *The Archaeology of Ethnicity* (London & New York, 1997), p. 126.

As already said above, one can hardly make any deductions from written texts alone – Biblical or secular. The names of the instruments have to a great degree lost their distinctive local ethnic identification; their etymological and organological meaning has so often migrated both geographically and diachronically, that it is possible only in very general terms to arrive at any conclusions. Such is the case, for example, with the popular Biblical music instruments *nabal/nebel* or *'ugav*. In the Talmud, Apocrypha and in Greek-Roman secular literature, and from the time of the Septuagint until recently it has been the stumbling block of organology. The etymological dichotomy of the root of this word (*nabal* – degenerate, impure, obscene, or *nebel* – jar, vessel, string instrument) was the reason for a multitude of interpretations. Although in the last centuries the *nabal/nebel* mostly was identified as harp, archaeological evidence indicates now quite clearly that this instrument was a lyre.[12] Nevertheless, we can allege only that it was of general Near-Eastern ethnicity. For the present only few archaeological instruments and depictions of lyres are discovered that may be identified with some certainty as *nabal/nebel* (rather than *kinnorot*), and both their small number and chronological dispersion does not allow any conclusions as to their ethnic pertinence.

The floating term *'ugav*[13] is even more perplex. The Septuagint was already uncertain about the translation and used different words in the four passages where the instrument was mentioned: *kithara, organon,* and *psalmos*, and till today we are not sure about the organological identification of the instrument.

In our attempt to recover the ethnic affiliation of musical instruments on the territory of ancient Israel/Palestine, there is at this stage one first step to be taken – the mapping of the artifacts. I would suggest, that the minimal number of finds for an organological mapping on the territory of Israel/Palestine should be not less than five items for the Bronze Age, ten for the Iron Age, and at least 15 artifacts for the Hellenistic-Roman Age. For the discussed here case-studies I have chosen three examples – the

---

12 On the basis of archaeological finds on the territory of Israel/Palestine, and the lyre drawing with accompanying text from Dion (Greece), the *nebel* is now identified as a baritone/bass lyre (see J. Braun, *Music in* ..., pp. 22-24, and ch. IV/3).
13 The root of the word *'gb* stems from *agaba* – sensual desire, lust.

clay rattle, the lyre and the drum (or, to be more precise, female drummer terra-cotta) – to discuss the ethnic fate of the instruments.

The clay-rattle

This archaeological idiophone is the most verified sound tool in our region. From at least 120 items, listed on the territory of ancient Israel/Palestine, into the following discussion will be included seventy-four rattles discovered in controlled excavations and preserved to a degree, that their form – the central parameter of our analysis – can be determined (see **Tab. III-1).** This impressive amount of finds – by itself a significant manifestation of the wide spreading and use of this sound tool – is one of the reasons for choosing it for mapping. The discovered items, dated to the period from the Late Chalcolithic to the late Iron Age, usually are robust, mastered by hand or wheel-made closed clay containers measuring 10-15 cm filled with small clay balls (sometimes dry seeds), which produced sound by rattling the instrument.[14] During the centuries these clay rattles came in a multitude of forms and shapes – from spool form and rattles with handle to anthropomorphic, bird-shaped, fruit and bell form (see **Fig. III-1a-f)**, all of which had no parallels in neighboring cultures, and may be considered as rare autochthon topos of ancient Israel/Palestine. Mainly discovered at burial sites, the clay rattle may be defined as cult mass-instrument, broadly used by people of low social standing. Strange enough, no depiction of the clay-rattle, except one (**Fig. III-1g**), was ever discovered, although we have from the same area and for a much shorter time period more than thirty depictions of the lyre, in the Iron Age mostly an instrument of the higher classes, the priests and court musicians. The clay-rattle was, probably, not considered important enough to be depicted; at some point maybe even measures were taken to destroy the image of this pagan sound tool, and erase it's name – *mena'anim* – from folk-memory. The clay-rattle had also no place in the written history of the Jewish people: it is mentioned only once in the entire Old Testament under the now generally accepted for clay-rattles term *mena'anim* (from the root *nua'*, rattle, shake; first suggested by Curt

---

[14] The earliest known item is a small clay ball (Ø 2,9 cm, IAA 82-1630, not published) from the late 4th millenium discovered near Be'er Sheva (Tab. III-1:37).

Sachs[15]). In 2Sam 6:5 the *mena'anim* are mentioned in the context of an orgiastic orchestra, dominated by idiophones, which accompanied King David, dancing at the transfer of the Ark to Jerusalem. In 1Chr 13:8, where the same scene is described, the text is altered: most idiophones are eliminated, metal rattles replaced by cymbals, and trumpets as well as singing were added to the music performance. Now the impression of a proper liturgical music ceremony at a cult procession was created, appropriate for the imaginative reality of the holy text.[16]

Were *mena'anim* censored by the theocratic establishment? Did the centuries, that separate the two Bible books, bring this change into musical life, or did the *mena'anim* just fade in oblivion? By mapping the finds, we will make an attempt to find the answers to these questions and see what really happened to our clay-rattles during the nearly two millenium of its existence.

I. In the Bronze Age (from the late 4th Mill. – 1200 B. C.) the entire population of all ethnic groups where using this sound-tool (see **Map III-1**). From this period twenty rattles in a variety of forms dispersed over the country were discovered; six of them had handles, which may indicate the prolonged usage (by carrying or fastening the sound tool to some device), possibly in processions.[17] Only four rattles of this period are in the later so dominant spool-form.

II. In Iron Age A (12th cent. B. C. – 900 B. C.) the number of rattles decreased remarkably: only 12 items from this period are discovered, and all are from Judah (see **Map III-2**).[18] Certain rattle forms are mostly concentrated in restricted geographical areas: the bird-form rattles around

---

15 *History of Musical Instruments*, New York, 1940, p. 121; for the first time discussed by Bathya Bayer, "*M'na'anim* – Clay rattles?" (in Hebrew), *Tatzlil*, 4:19-22 (1864).

16 All writers on the ancient Israel/Palestine clay rattles, including the most recent (e.g., N. S. Fox/A. R. Roskop, "Of Rattles and Rituals," in: *Hebrew Union College Annual*, 70/71, 1999-2000: 5-26), avoid the discussion on the contradiction of the two Biblical passages.

17 Fox/Roskop, "Of Rattles and Rituals...," (pp. 25-26) convincing suggest that some rattles in the form of figurines, such as the one from the Cincinnati Art Museum were used as icons at ceremonial processions.

18 It is not possible to claim that the number of artifacts discovered is a indisputable index of geographical distribution density of the item in a certain culture. But it certainly is indicative enough to show the distribution tendency, especially if we deal with one type of artifact or event.

Philistine Ashdod, and the geometrical spool-form to the north along the line Gezer – Beth Shemesh – Beth Mirsim. In Gezer, close to Samaria, the anthropomorphic female-shaped rattle was found. We clearly can witness here local styles and probably local workshops in a particular geographical and chronological setting.

III. In the next period, the late Iron Age B (9th cent. B. C. – 6th cent. B. C.), Judah presents an entirely new picture (see **Map III-3**), compared not only to the late Bronze Age, but the Iron Age I as well. Now the number of discovered clay-rattles increased drastically (more than 40 items were discovered), but almost the one and only wheel made spool form is attested over the entire country (**Fig. III-1a**).[19] The area covered by spool-formed rattles stretches beyond Judah into neighboring Samaria and even to the North, up to the Kinneret See. In the South spool-form rattles appear in areas with strong Edomite culture influence such as Qitmit and Tel Malhata. In Judah, heavy populated by Jews, ruled by increasingly nationalistic and zealously pious kings (Hezekiah, Josiah), the geometrical non-pictorial spool-form became the dominant form used and, probably, permitted. Not able to eliminate completely the pagan sound-tool, the local religious establishment, guided by iconoclastic tendencies, could admit only the form of rattles which was in consonance with the Second Commandment – the spool-formed clay-rattle, thus clearly marking the Judean ethnic imprint of this sound-tool during the existence of the Kingdom Judah. This could be a clear indication of the "Judaisation" of this sound tool – the clay rattle became a Judean ethnic musical instrument. We, probably, should see this change of ethnic affiliation of the clay-rattle and/or the local musical culture as a result of a combined ethnic-theological drive against "the others." The increasing pressure of the surrounding non-Jewish world, on one hand, and the industrialization of the developing mass-production, on the other, were, probably the main factors which activated the manifestation of Jewish identity at the particular socio-historical setting of the late Iron Age. The 7th century B. C. Edomite idol (deity?) with the spool-formed rattle on his head **(see Fig. III-1g)**, recalling the Egyptian goddess Hathor with the

---

19 Only five other forms appear: one bird-form in Ashdod (probably, a relic of the Iron Age IA), three circular from Samaria and Kh. Uza, and two in bell-form (probably, a primitive copy of the new to expensive metal idiophone.

naos-sistrum, is a reliable indication for the holiness of the spool-formed rattle not only in Judah but also in the neighboring Edom, at this time partly under Judean control.[20]

Thus we may say, that the spool-formed rattle, this multiform, multi-ethnical sound-tool of Bronze Age Caanan became towards the late Iron Age a uniform instrument of restricted Judean ethnic utility.

The lyre

A very different picture emerges when we try to analyze the development and distribution of lyres in ancient Israel. Parallel to the vernacular clay-rattle, the aristocratic lyre was broadly in use from the Middle Bronze Age (early 2nd cent. B. C.) to the Hellenistic-Roman Period. Did this instrument also have a "ethnic history" in ancient Israel/Palestine?

Starting from the very appearance of the lyre in this area, three types (roughly classified) are to be found in Ancient Israel/Palestine: (A) the asymmetrical lyres with rectangular resonance body and diverged or parallel side arms (see **Fig. IA-2, IA-5, IC-2a, IC-3** and **IC-7**); (B) the symmetrical with rectangular resonance body (see **Fig. IA-4** and **IB-2**), and (C) symmetrical lyres with rounded resonance body (see **Fig. IA-6, IA-7, IB-3** and **III-2a**). The *kithara* type "concert" lyre, which can be seen on the early Byzantine David-Orpheus iconography may be considered a symbol of the mythological past rather than a current music instrument (**Fig. III-2b**).

The lyre appeared in this area in the early second millennium as instrument of the nomads and desert people. With certainty the symmetrical lyre (type B) was attested Southwest from Canaan in Beni Hassan (Egypt, **Fig. IA-4**) on the well-known fresco, portraying Canaanite artisan-nomads entering Egypt (**Tab. III-2: 3**).[21] Nearly at the same time a quite different type of the instrument (A) was discovered in the hands of dancing naked female figures, depicted on a rock etching in the Negev (**Tab. III-2: 1-2, Map III-4, and Fig. IC- 2a**).

At the end of the Bronze Age, probably under Egyptian influence, the asymmetrical lyre was turned into an instrument of the aristocracy and

---

20 "Edom", in *Eerdmans Dictionary*..., p. 372-373.
21 See Braun, *Music in*..., pp. 77-79.

priestly class, as can be observed from the famous Megiddo ivory (see **Fig. IA- 2)**; during the Iron Age (see **Map III-5**) this type nearly disappeared, remaining only in depictions on seals, as to symbolize the aristocratic character of the instrument (the only artifact which still confirms the existence of the asymmetrical lyre in Iron Age Israel/Judah is the one from Nineve, depicting three Israeli captive musicians with an asymmetrical lyre – a quite primitive instrument compared to other examples of this type (see **Tab. III 2: 13**; see **Fig. IA-5)**. The symmetrical lyres, on the contrary, were broadly used and achieved during this time social importance. Six depictions of local lyres are of the symmetrical type (B) and (C); they appear in different parts of the country, and seem to have existed side by side. We cannot help but notice, that the earliest finds of the new symmetrical lyre with round sound box **(Fig. IA-6)** are concentrated at one place – in Ashdod, which may suggest the birth of a local style **(Tab. III 2: 6, 7 and 9)**. It is possible, that this early Ashdod type was determinant for the dispersion and popularity of the symmetrical lyre with round sound box in ancient Israel.

Especially wide-spread adoption the lyre enjoyed during the Hellenistic-Roman Period **(Map. III- 6)**. Both symmetrical lyre types were current in various sections of the population – from inhabitants of the desert to urban aristocracy, and are attested in numerous artifacts, sometimes even (as on the terra cotta plaque from Petra) both lyres are depicted side by side in the same ensemble **(Tab. III 2: 15-16)**. Remarkably enough the lyre can be seen at the same time on Synagogue mosaics and among the instruments in Dionysian processions **(Tab. III 2: 24 and 25)**, and on both Roman and Judean (Acco and Bar-Kochba) coins, discovered on opposite poles of the country **(Tab. III 2:17, 18, 21 and 22)**. Of the obsolete *kithara*-type lyre we have at least four depictions, dating to the Early Byzantine time (4th-7th cent), but this instrument should be considered rather as mythological symbol than "live" contemporary instrument (see **Tab. III 2: 23, 26-28)**. The dubious lyre-representation on the Sepphoris Orpheus-mosaic is the best conformation for this **(Tab. III 2: 26)**.[22]

---

22 Several artifacts of UP with lyre can be accepted to the general picture (Tab. III-2:29-39).

The mapping presents a convincing picture of the dispersion of all three existing at the relevant time in the Near East lyres. There was never a period of neatly segregated Eastern and Western lyre shapes in the Levant, as sometimes claimed,[23] but rather a mixed distribution of all lyre types. The change of the lyre type was not necessarily the result of Eastern or Western impact on ethnic affiliation, but primarily a development in cohesion with historical changes. Starting its existence in ancient Israel/Palestine as an instrument of the nomads, the lyre became towards the Late Bronze Age the dominant chordophone of aristocratic circles and at cult activities; during the Iron Age the instrument spread in the upper classes, and by the Late Iron Age, but especially in Hellenistic-Roman times reached a broad non-ethnic dispersion nearly on all social levels.

It would be, however, wrong to deprive totally the art of lyre music and the lyre instrumentarium of any local coloring. We may assert that one Iron Age lyre type – the symmetrical lyre with rounded sound box, the so-called Ashdod-type (11th-8th cent. B. C., **Fig. III-2a)**, at the same time also attested in Cyprus, is a preferably Philistian ethnic instrument. The Ashdod lyre is a very early example of this type and may be considered an autochthon local Iron Age instrument. Ashdod was a center of intellectual and musical innovation, and lyre-music was part of this milieu. Here, in Ashdod, for the first time (11th-10th cent. B. C.) the musical setting of an incipient Cybele cult may have appeared and, with it, the Near Eastern, once defined as Phoenician, but in fact, Philistine orchestra (chordophone, aerophone and membrano- or idiophone players) was born.[24] The type of artifacts from the Iron Age that bear depictions of lyre players – individual professional art works and personal seals – confirms the status of the lyre as the musical instrument of the Iron Age upper classes,[25] a fact, which may explain the relatively large number of preserved lyre depictions in Israel. The way and style of performance, which decisively shape the style of music, had, however, its own autochthone character from the early time of lyre playing. The earliest example – the

---

23 See Bo Lowergreen, "Distinction among Canaanite, Philistine, and Israelite Lyres, and their Global Lyrical Contexts," in: *Bulletin of the American Schools of Oriental Research,* 1998, p. 42.
24 See Braun, *Music in...*, pp. 174-175.
25 Braun, *Music in...*, Ch. IV/3, 4 and V/3, 4, 5 and 7.

mentioned above famous 19th century B. C. Caanan musician from Beni-Hasan with the horizontal performance position of the lyre, and the somewhat later Megiddo lyre player with a tucked under the arm instrument – both confirm the soloist virtuoso style. In the Iron and early Hellenistic time the performance moved towards chamber-music performance with a pair of smaller lyres (a bass/tenor and discant instrument) mostly plucked with a plectrum. The character of lyre playing in Israel/Palestine manifested itself by performance and music, creating, as claimed by Bathya Bayer, musical ethnic identity by performance, rather than by the musical instrument *per se*. History of music knows many such examples, among others the case of the violin in the Western and Eastern world of music.[26]

These shortly discussed biographies of two musical instruments illustrate how different and rich in nuances the ethnic identity may become manifest in the ancient musical world.

Female drummer terracotta

For the third case-study I chose the popular in ancient Israel/Palestine female drummer image. It appears in two quantitatively unequal groups: a) bell-shaped figurines – 17 items, and b) relief terra-cotta plaques – nearly 50 items (**Fig. III-3a** and **b, Tab. III 3:11** and **4:34**). The figures of the first group are portrayed with longer garments and without any of the traditional adornments associated with women; on the terra-cotta relief plaques of the second group, the female figures are nude or half-nude with exposed right breast, and richly adorned. Our drummer figurines are only a small part of a large family of terra-cotta female images with exaggerated breasts supported by both hands, which date to the time of the Divided Monarchy (10th-7th cent. BC) and are considered to be connected to or represent the Judean fertility goddess, perhaps Asherah/Ashtoret.[27]

In the case of the first group, the identification of the instrument as drum is undisputed, while for the second group scholars have their doubts

---

[26] The modern violin of Western origin is played in our days both in a horizontal position in the Western concert halls, and in a vertical position in many Eastern countries performing Eastern ethnic music.

[27] Mazar, A., *Archaeology of the Land of the Bible* (New York, 1990), pp. 501-502.

and the interpretations vary from drum to holy solar disc, platter, or cake (offering cake or bread is attested in the Bible[28]). For this group I suggested a typological distinction according to the position of the hands on the disc: the drum identification may be assumed for the figurines showing the typical Near Eastern performance position (similarly to the bell-shaped figurines) – one hand holding the instrument from below, while the other hand strikes the center of the membrane. In the case of a more or less symmetrical position of the hands **(Fig. III-3c)** – I would say an essentially "anti-drummer" position – we should reject the drum interpretation. Furthermore, with the diameter of the disc some 10cm as can be seen on many plaque figurines, especially those from Cyprus,[29] the membrane could hardly produce any sound. After eliminating the "disqualified" figurines, as well as those of uncertain provenance, we remain with 14 bell-shaped figurines **(Tab. III-3)** and 42 relief plaques **(Tab. III-4)**, all from controlled excavations and dated to the Iron Age (12th to 6th BC).[30] These finds cover the Phoenician ruled north-eastern part of the Mediterranean coast and the Philistine ruled land along the south-eastern coast, as well as the central part, inland and highland, ruled by Israel and Judah. Some of the terra-cotta have also been found on the territories East from the Jordan River, such as Aram, Ammon, Moab, Edom and in later years Nabatea. The mapping of the artifacts reveal quite different pictures for the two groups of the female drummers:

The chronologically oldest finds of the *bell-shaped figurines* **(Map III-7)** are from Mt. Nebo 11th-10th century **(Fig. III-3d)**.[31] Somewhat later (10th-7th cent B. C.) this artifact type appears at several sites to the North-West: two in Samaria, and in remarkable numbers – (at least six figurines) on the Phoenician coast, in Acco and Shiqmona.[32] This impressive number of drummer artifacts (nowhere else in the Middle East con-

---

28 Jer 7:16-18).
29 See V. Karagheorgis and O. Picard, ed., *La necropole d'Amathonte Tombes 113-367* II (Nicosia, 1987), pl. iii-viii features
30 Some additional UP figurines are highly possibly of local provenance and may be included in the present discussion (Tab. III- 3: 12-14, and Tab. III-4: 43-45).
31 Sellers 1966, Fig. 28:1-2.
32 Crowfoot, J. W. et al., *The Objects from Samaria-Sebaste*, vol. III (London, 1957), pl. xi:8; Mazar, E., *The Achziv Burials...*, Ph. D., Thesis, Hebrew University (Jerusalem, 1996); Elgabish, J., "Shiqmona," in: *Israel Exploration Journal*, 25/4:257-8, (1975).

firmed) allows the assumption of a local workshop in this coastal area.[33] Farther to the Northwest near Tyre,[34] but especially on Cyprus, the Phoenician finds from the 7th-6th cent. B. C feature this type of figurines.[35]

As regards the origin of the bell-shaped figurines, the mapping data clearly refutes the theory of North/Northeastern genesis of the Palestinian female drummer. In this sense the described by Karageorghis line of migration can hardly be accepted: "the iconography of these terra-cotta is ultimately Mesopotamian in origin, passing through Syria and Palestine to Cyprus some time in the 7th century B. C."[36] Let us recall, that if in Old Babylonian areas relief figurines indeed were discovered in great quantities (as early as 1950 B. C.), the topos of bell-shaped drummer figurines with the drum perpendicular to the body is absent from Mesopotamian iconography.[37] Moreover, everything points to the opposite direction: the beginnings of this drummer figurine topos seem to have sprouted in the southeastern part of Israel/Judah, in the musically hardly researched area on the borderlines of the Judaean and Maob cultures. The archaeological finds of Judaean burials from the 10th century B. C. in the area of Mt. Nebo, where the earliest drummer figurines were discovered, confirm

---

33 The drum fragments discovered at Horvat Qitmit (P. Beck, *Catalogue*, in: I. Beit-Arieh, *Horvat Qitmit=Monograph Series of the Institute of Archaelogy*, Tel Aviv, 1995, pp. 162, and 164 – 166) are defined by Beck as "free-standing, i.e. not attached to the musician's body," or possibly "attached to stands." This puts them in the bell-shaped figurine group. Considering the difficulties of restoration of the fragments, this typology is questionable, and the fragments could not be included in the present discussion. Beck's division of the drums into "thick and thin" is obscure, and the term "tambourine" instead of frame-drums misleading.
34 Bikai, P. M., *The Pottery of Tyre* (Warminster, 1978), pl. 81:2.
35 Only the figurines from Tyre (Lebanon) and Amathus (Cyprus) may be considered as belonging to this drummer group. Other figurines, both bell-shaped and in plaque, can not be, as mentioned above, with certainty qualified us drummers. For this reason the division of the figurines in 'tambourine-holders' and 'tambourine-players' (Karagheorgis/Picard, ed., *La necropole*...pp. 17-18) does not seem convincing. Unfortunately, some Israeli archaeologists have accepted this misleading division (for ex., M. Dayagi, *The Achzive Cementeries*, Jerusalem, 2002, p., 146).
36 Idem, p. 18, and H. Weippert 1988, *Palästina in vorhellenistischer Zeit* (Munich, 1988), p. .630.
37 See S. A. Rashid, *Musikgeschichte in Bildern: Mesopotamia* (Leipzig, 1984).

evidence of Judean presence at the birth-place of this topos.[38] Moreover, only the Nebo figurines are designed with a nude upper half of the body, similar to the mentioned typical Judean terra-cotta, assumed to depict a fertility goddess. Consequently, the bell-shaped figurines migrated from 11th-10th century B. C. Maob/Judah to the central part of Israel (Samaria) and further North to the 8th-6th century B. C. Philistine Mediterranean coast (Achziv, Shikmona). This path of migration illustrates the Maobit-Judean-Israelitie-Phoenician acculturation process, typical for Iron Age Israel/Palestine. The archaeological indications (all the figurines were discovered in burial sites) and the iconography of the post-Mt-Nebo items (figurines completely dressed, with wig or head cover, and without any adornments) – all seems to suggest a cultic function of this female drummer figurine.[39]

In the second group of female drummers – *the terra-cotta relief plaques* – the development was quite a different one **(Map. III- 8)**. Dated to the same time as the pillar-figurines – mostly 10th to 7th century B. C., these artifacts were discovered over the entire territory of ancient Israel/Palestine with the majority in the northern part of the country: 27 items in Israel and 12 in Judah (partly east of Jordan). The origin of this female drummer type, indeed could be Mesopotamia, however, they probably became popular in the Near East at least two-three centuries earlier than the 7th century suggested by Karaghergis (see footnote 34).

At first sight this topos does not seem to communicate any typical Jewish symbolism. The mapping, however, confirms my previous opinion that we have here an indigenous Israeli/Judean group of artifacts.[40] The relief plaques with drummers were discovered, as mentioned, on the entire territory of Israel and Judah, refuting the obviously wrong statement by Paz/Bunimovitz (see **Tab. III-3 and 4**) about the exclusive allo-

---

38 Weippert, *Palästina...*, p. 490.
39 The latest study (S. Paz /Supervision of Sh. Bunimovitz/, *Drums, Women and Goddesses*, M. A. Thesis, Tel Aviv University, 2003) brings into the discussion several unknown till now new items; this, however, does not add to or change the interpretation of this artifact group, especially if the musical tradition of women is restricted to "drumming in fertility cults, for a while (?) as a part of the formal religion..., and victory songs" (p. viii). The statement that the "drum playing traditions...are missing from Judah," is certainly erroneous" (p. iv).
40 Braun, *Music in...*, pp. 131-133.

cation of the finds in the North, i. e. in Israel. The number of unearthed artifacts testify to a mass production, mass distribution and, probably, mass use of this terra-cotta type. The strong presence of this topos obviously confirms the audio-visual symbolism of the female drummer and of the art of drumming as well, something similar to the dual shape-sound function of the discussed above clay rattle.

We certainly may detect a relation of our relief plaques to Egyptian and Babylonian iconography material, as, for example, the ornamentation of the drum membrane similar to the 19th Dynasty Osiris drum, but no nude terra-cotta relief figurines have ever been found in Egypt. On the other hand, we have plenty examples of nude female drummers from Mesopotamia that might have served as models for the Judean reliefs.[41] It is obvious, that local Judean artists drew from both sources, Egyptian and Babylonian, and in a process of acculturation produced a new, indigenous and enduring Israeli/Judean ethnic topos, a process well known in ethnic music itself.

The fusion of sacral and profane elements, so characteristic for this age, has generated its own symbolic language in these relief figures. Nudity symbolizes fertility and sexuality, the adornment – prostitution, and the wig functions as an attribute of cult. Beyond this, the drum itself underscores the fusion of the sacred and profane symbolism even more emphatically. Although the drum accompanies religious ceremonies of praise (Ps. 81, 149 and 150), the instrument, with its sexual connotations, clearly did not belong to the accepted religious proceedings and was never used in the Temple. As such, the drum (and the female drummer) was bound to come into conflict with the official cult of Israel and Judah. Indeed, the broken and damaged drums (see **Fig. III-3e; Tab. III-4: 1 and 2**) frequently accompanying these terra-cotta may well betray the iconoclastic activity of the new ideologues. One can not rule out the possibility that the plaque female terracotta (with drum or with disc) did exist in Israelite/Judaean communities from the most early self-identification periods at the time of the immigration from Mesopotamia. We need only to recall here the *teraphim*, the small household gods Rachel stole from her father (Gen. 31:19, 34). This biblical scene, by the way, contains also the earliest mention of the drum in the Bible (Gen. 31:27),

---

41 Rashid, *Mesopotamien...*, Ill. 91-95 and 117

and the chronology of our finds coincides with the origin of these Biblical texts (approx. 900 B. C.). In this sense the female drummer terracotta can be identified as part of the "folk" or "popular" religion which is present in any society, and, certainly, in Iron Age Israel and Judah.[42]

The proto-Judean belief-symbolism could well persist in Iron Age Israel and Judah and act as a hidden belief-system, in certain situation even as latent dissent.[43] That such kind of dissent existed in Judah, and was persecuted, we know not only from Biblical sources (see the case of the *mena'anim*), but also from archaeological evidence of iconoclastic attacks, as the mentioned broken drum fragments from Amman and Horvat Qitmit but especially the spectacular Edomite finds.[44]

In conclusion, we may venture the suggestion, that although in conflict with the official cult, the female plaque terra-cotta with drum was a genuine Israeli/Judean ethnic work of mass art. The bell-shaped figurines depicting female drummers, on the other hand, belong to a chronologically and geographically rather mobile Israel/Palestinian multi-ethnic artistic style that in the 8th-6th centuries B. C. evolved into what we may call the classic Phoenician ethnic art expression.

This was an attempt to examine the possibility of discovering ethnic markers in musically relevant archaeological material of a definitive group, and (to quote Sian Jones) "within a diachronic contextual framework..., to pick up the transformation of habitual material variation into active self-conscious ethnic symbolism...."

---

[42] The archeological evidence on the phenomenon of "folk religion... as religious practice of the *majority* in ancient Israel an Judah" is discussed by W. G. Dever (*What did the Biblical Writers know & and when did they know it,* Grand Rapids, 2001, p.173).

[43] See Braun, *Music in...*, pp. 131-133.

[44] R. Cohen/Y. Yisrael, "Smashing the Idols", in: *Biblical Archaeological Review* (July/August 1998), pp. 41-51. A new aspect of the plaque figurine discussion is revealed in the latest publications by Beck (*Catalogue...*) and Paz (*Drums...*) stressing the element of gender, especially the dual hermaphrodite nature of several depicted images. If and how the dual gender is reflected in the drumming tradition of secular and religious cultic aspects remains to be proven.

Tables

Tab. III – 1. List of rattles discovered on the territory of Ancient Israel/Palestine
Tab. III – 2. List of lyre iconography discovered on the territory of Ancient Israel/Palestine
Tab. III – 3. List of bell-shaped terracotta figurines with drum discovered on the territory of Ancient Israel/Palestine, and
Tab. III – 4. List of relief plaques with drum or disk discovered on the territory of Ancient Israel/Palestine

Maps

Map. III. – 1. Bronze Age distribution of clay rattles (3200-1200 B. C.)
Map. III. – 2. Iron Age A distribution of clay rattles (1200-1000 B. C.)
Map. III. – 3. Iron Age B distribution of clay rattles (1000-586 B. C.)
Map. III. – 4. Bronze Age lyre iconography distribution (3200-1200 B. C.)
Map. III. – 5. Iron Age lyre iconography distribution (1200-586 B. C.)
Map. III. – 6. Hellenistic-Roman Age lyre iconography distribution (4th cent B. C.-6th cent C. E.)
Map. III. – 7. The distribution of bell shaped figurines with drum (11th-6th cent. B. C.)
Map. III. – 8. The distribution of relief plaques with drum or disc (10th-6th cent. B. C.)

Map Icons

spool form clay rattle

clay rattle with handle

anthropomorphic form clay rattle

bird form and zoomorphic clay rattle

asymmetrical lyre rectangular resonance body

symmetrical lyre with rectangular resonance body

symmetrical lyre with rounded resonance body

bell-shaped terracotta figurine with drum

plaque relief figurine with drum or disk

All pictures are by Courtesy of the indicated owner institution of the atifact:

AM	Archaeological Museum
AMJ/AAM	Archaeological Museum of Jordan
BM	British Museum
EB	Ecole Biblique, Jerusalem
EE	Excavation ownership
EIM	Eretz Israel Museum Tel Aviv
HM	Reuven Hecht Haifa University Museum
HSM	Harward University Semitic Museum
HUAI/HU	Hebrew University Archaeological Institute
IAA	Israel Antiquity Authority
IM	The Israel Museum Jerusalem
JAI	Jerusalem Albright Institute
JDA	Jordan Department of Antiquities
MMA	Mediterranean Museum of Archaeology

OIA	Oriental Institute Archaeological Collection, Chicago
SBF	Studium Biblicum Franciscanum, Jerusalem
TAUAI	Tel Aviv University Archaeological Institute
UP	Unknown provenience

Tab. III-1. Clay-Rattles Discovered on the Territory of AIP

Symbols: spool-form & related type: I; with handle: W; circular: o; bird form: B; anthropomorphic: H; bell-form: BL

No.	FUNDORT	CHRONOLOGY			COLLECTION	BIBLIOGRAPHY
		LB	I A	I B		
1.	Arad			I	IAA 64.2570	
2.	Arad		I		IAA 68-1674	
3.	Ashdod		B		IAA 60.1031	
4.	Ashdod		B		IAA 63.2166	Bahat 1971:170, fig. 96.5?????
5.	Ashdod			B	IAA 68.1090	
6.	Beth Shemesh			I	IAA P 440	
7.	Beth Shemesh			I	IAA P 441	
8.	Beth Shemesh			I	IAA P 447	MacKenzie 1912/3, pl. xxii: 16
9.	Beth Shemesh			I	IAA I 10560/37	MacKenzie 1912/3, pl. lvi: 17
10.	Beth Shean		B		IAA 89.1178	Yadin & Geva 1986, fig. 37:1
11.	Dalhamia			I	IAA 69.1531	
12.	El Khom			I	HUC 1720	
13.	Eshtemoa			I	HUAI 3969	
14.	Gath			I	IAA60.382	
15.	Gezer	W			IAA P214	Macalister 1912, II, fig.445: 1
16.	"	W			IAA P217	Idem, fig 2
17.	"	o			IAA P219	Idem., fig. 3
18.	"		I		MH P62460	Fig 4
19.	"		H		?	Fig. 5
20.	"		I		?	Fig. 6
21.	"	O*			?	Fig. 7

Continuation

22.	"	W		IAA 74.262	Fig. 8
23.	"	B			Ibid., III, pl. 66: 42.
24.	"	W			Ibid.,
25	Hatzor		I	IAA 67.1160;	Yadin 1960, pl. 88:19
26.	"		I	IAA 95.1570	Idem., pl.. 161:16
27.	"		BL	HUAI, inv. 9245	
28.	Jaffa	I		IAA 72.567	
29.	Jerusalem		I	IAA 68.201	Weill 1920, 156
30.	"		I	IAA 68.719	Saller 1964, 159
31.	"		I	IAA 64.1611	
32.	"	W		SBF 119	
33.	Khadid		I	IAA 99-3998	
34.	Kh.Ekev			IAA 90.801	Boaz 2000, pl. 3:12
35.	Kh. Uza		o	Kh. Uza coll. 2425	
36.	Kh. Za'k		W	IAA 76.347	
37.	Nah. BerSheva**	← o		IAA 82.1630	Ø 2,8 cm !!
38.	Lachish	W		IAA 33.2058;	Tufnell 1958, Pl. 28: 15
39.	Lachish		I	IAA 36.1601	
40.	Lachish		I	MMA 34.126.54	Ibid., Pl. 28:16
41.	Lachish		I	?	Tufnell 1953, Pl. 28:15
42.	Lachish		I	?	Ibid., 28: 24
43.	Lachish		I	?	Ibid., 27:69
44.	Lachisch		I	?	Ibid., 27:9
45.	Megiddo		I	OIA 18924	Loud 1948, Pl. 255:5
46.	"		I	OIA 18362	May 1935, Pl. 22: P3596

Continuation

47.	Miqne		I	JAI 13/1981	
48.	Pella	W		Irbid AM 2914	VR, 73
49.	Ramla		I	IAA 59.164	
50.	Samaria***		I	HUAI, 3532	Crowfoot 1957, fig. 27:12,
51.	Samaria		I	HU 3533	idem., 13,
52.	Samaria		I	HU 3536,	idem., 14
53.	Samaria		I	HU 4217,	idem., 15
54.	Samaria		o	?	idem., 16
55.	Samaria		o	?	idem., 17
56.	T. Einan		BL	IAA 95.8506	IAA mahsan H-299
57.	T. El 'Ajjul	o		32.2142	?
58.	T. El 'Ajjul	W		35.4157	Petrie, Gaza iv, 1934, pl. lvi
59.	T. Amal		I	75.5006	Mus. Med. Arch.
60.	T. Beit Mirsim		I	Albr. Inst. 10.1861	Albright 1943, pl. 32:8
61.	T. Beit Mirsim		I	Albr. Inst. 10.1862	Idem., pl. 32:11
62.	T. Far'ah S.	H		IAA I-6936	Macdonald et al.,1932: 23, pl. xlvii
63.	T. Far'ah S.	I		?	Ibid.: 24-25, pl. li
64.	T. Far'ah S.	H		IAA I-6996	Ibid.23, pl. liv
65.	T. Jerische		I	HUJAI, no. 3192	?
66.	T. El Hesi		B	EIM MHP-62460	Bliss 1902, fig. 241
67.	T. El Hesi		I	?	Bliss 1902: 86
68.	T. Kinarot		I	IAA 85.434	?
69.	T. En Nasbeh		I	M259	Bade/McCown 1947, Pl. 90:12
70.	"		I	?	Ibid, 13
71.	"		I	?	Ibid, 14

106

Continuation

				IAA 60.382	
72.	T. 'Erani				
73.	T. 'Ira			188112 pnimi	Beit-Arieh 1999, fig. 6.98:12
74.	"			307815 pnimi	?
75.	"			308991 pnimi	?
76.	T. Zafit		1	IAA 95.5457	?
77.	T. Zerur		1	IAA 66.314	?
78.	T. Zakaria		1	?	Bliss 1902, Pl. 45: 16
79.	T. Zippori		1	IAA 2001.1699	S-4571 Hiafa University
	In toto	19	12	43	
	In toto			74	8 not exmined	26 UP (in museums)
	In toto rattles known			82	108

* Some Gezer items are of dubious chronology; ** The Nahal Be'er Sheva rattle is from the Chalcolithic period; *** Not all Samaria items were *de facto* examined.

Tab. III-2. Lyre Iconography Discoverd on AIP Territory and Relevant Artifacts

No.	Site	Chronology	Type of artifact	Lyre type*	Supposed size of lyre	Collection	Bibliography
1	Negev	1900-1600 B. C.	rock etching	A	70-90 cm	In situ	Anati 1963, p. 203-214
2	Negev	"	rock etching	A	"	"	Ibid.
3	Beni Hassan**	1900 B. C.	drawing	B	50-60 cm	In situ	Newberry 1893, pl. xxxi
4	Megiddo	13th-12th cent. B. C.	ivory etching	A	50-70 cm	IAA 38.780	Loud 1939, pl. 4:2.
5	Megiddo	11th cent. B. C.	jar drawing	A	50-70 cm	IAA 36.1921	Seller 1941, Fig. 1
6	Ashdod	10th cent. B. C.	clay stand	C	40-45 cm	IAA 68.1182	DothanM 1970
7	Ashdod	10th-8th cent. B. C.	seal	C	50-60 cm	?	DothanM 1971, pl. 69:7
8	Nebo	10th-8th cent. B. C.	seal	A	40-50 cm	SBF-293	Saller 1966, fig.7
9	Ashdod	8th cent. B. C.	terracotta fig.	C	40-45 cm	IAA 63.924	DothanM 1971, fig. 62:1
10	Tell Batash	8th cent. B. C.	seal	B	40-50 cm	HU-3593	Kelm/Mazar 1982, fig.18
11	Kuntiller 'Ajrud	8th cent B. C.	jar drawing	B	40-45 cm	TAUIA S78.4	Beck 1982:3-68
12	Tell Keisan	9th-7th cent. B. C.	seal	A	40-50 cm	EB 3332	Briend/Humbert 1980, pl.89
13	Nineveh**	8th-7th cent. B. C.	alabaster relief	A	60-70cm	BM 124947	Rashid 1984, Ill. 142
14	Horvat Qitmit	7th cent. B. C.	terracotta fig.	B/C?	?	IAA 87.135	Beck 1995, p. 161
15	Petra	2nd-1st cent. B. C.	terracotta pl.	C	60-80 cm	AM J.5768	VR No. 232
16	Petra	2nd-1st cent. B. C.	terracotta pl.	B	40-50 cm	"	Ibid.
17	Acco***	125 -110 B. C.	coin	B	?	HAM 1156	Braun 1999, Ill. V/7-2a
18	Acco	125 -110 B. C.	coin	C	?	HAM 1205	Ibid., Ill. V/7-2c
19	Harra Desert	1st - 4th cent A. D.	basalt etching	B	50-60 dm	In situ	Harding 1969, Fig. 1
20	Caesarea	2nd-3ed cent. A. D.	tessarae	C	?	?	Hamburger 1986, pl. I:66-71
21	(Bar-Kokhba)	2nd cent. A. D.	coin	B	?	HUHM 049	Braun 1999, Ill. V/7-3a
22	(Bar-Kochba)	2nd cent. A. D.	coin	C	?	EIM K-4663	Idem., 3d

Continuation

23	Beth Govrin	2nd-3ed cent. A. D.	Terracotta fig.	K	50-60 cm	EE A. Kloner	Kloner 1996:56
24	Gaza	3ed-4th cent A. D.	mosaic	C	90-110 cm	Ismailia AM	Braun 1999, Ill. V/5-2
25	Sepphoris	5th cent. A. D.	mosaic	C	90-110 cm	In situ	Weiss/Netzer 1996:26
26	Sepphoris	6th cent A. D.	mosaic	K	70-90 cm	In situ	Weiss/Metzer, 113/1,pl.1
27	Gaza	6th cent. A. D.	mosaic	K	70-90 cm	?	Ovadia/Ovadia 1987
28	Jerusalem	4th-5th cent. A. D.	mosaic	K	70-90 cm	Istanbul AM	Ovadia/Mucznik 1981, pl. 1
POSSIBLY LOCAL ARTIFACTS OF UNKNOWN PROVENANCE FROM ISRAELI AND ABROAD COLLECTIONS								
30	PU (Galilee?)	10th-8th cent. B. C.	seal	B	70-90 cm	H-1870	Braun 1999, Ill. IV/3-6
31	" (Nebo?)	10th-8th cent. B. C.	seal	A	40-50 cm	TA-KhD3	Ibid., pp. 159
32	" (T. Keisan?)	9th-7th cent. B. C.	seal	A	40-50 cm	BIF nr. 135	Keel/Leu 1991, nr.
33	" (forgery?)	7th cent. B. C.	seal	C	?	IMJ-8O.16.57	Avigad 1878, 146
34	" (Samaria?)	4th cent. B. C.	coin	A	80-100 cm	IAA 1442.1	Braun 1999, Ill. V/6-1
35	" (Samaria?)	roman period?	terracotta	B	40-45 cm	HSM 907.64.474	Idem., Ill. V/6-9
36	" (Gadara?)	? 1st century A. D.	gem	C	80-90 cm	?	Idem., Ill. V/7-6d
37	" (Gadara?)	? 1 century A. D.	gem	C	50-60 cm	?	Henig/Whiting, ill. 181
38	" (Gadara?)	? 2nd century A. D.	gem	B	70-80 cm	?	Braun 1999, Ill. V/7a
39	" (Nabataean?)	? 2nd century A. D.	gem	C	?	?	Idem., Ill. V/7-7b
40	" (?)	Roman period	Lead sarcophagus	C	50-60 cm	?	Idem., Ill. V/5-3

* The multitude of lyre-forms requires a certain degree of approximation in the division of the lyre types. The following lyre types are distinguished:

A - asymmetrical lyres (40-90cm) with diverging or parallel arms and rectangular sound body;
B - symmetrical lyres (40-90cm) with rectangular sound body;

Continuation

C - symmetrical lyres (50-90cm) with parallel or horn-shaped side arms and rounded sound body.
K - *kithara* type - "concert" lyre (50-70cm).

** The Beni Hassan (3) and Nineveh (13) lyre iconography is here included, although they are not of Israel/Palestine provenance; the depiction of the instruments on the two drawings are generally acknowledged as very close to the Israel/Palestine reality. Into the mapping are included only items from controlled excavations.

*** The measurements of the lyre from coins and other artifacts without the possibility to compare the instrument with any other object will not be presented. The coins from Acco (16-17) and the Bar-Kochba uprising (19-20) depict two types of lyres: the smaller with 3-4 strings thought to be the discant/alt *kinnor* (type A), and the larger with 4-7 strings thought to be the bariton/bass *nebel*.

Tab. III-3. Bell-Shaped Terracotta Figurines with frame drum Discovered on the Territory of AIP

Symbols: (!) = intact; 1/2 = no head or lower part of body; 1/4 = only chest with drum; 1/8 = only drum; B = burial; G = building; C = cult place; D = approximate diameter of the drum in cm; . PU - provenance unknown; height in cm; all chronology - B. C.
* Because of the restitution difficulties of the Qitmit drum fragments their typology – bell-shaped or plaque figurine – is questionable; of the five fragments two are here included.

No.	SITE	CHRONOLOGY	HIGHT	Ø cm.	CONTEXT	COLLECTION	BIBLIOGRAPHY
1	Achsib	8-7 cent. B. C.	!20,5	20	B	IAA 44.264	MazarE 1996, pl. 53:14
2	Achsib	8-7 cent. B. C.	!17,4	22	B	IAA 44.53	Ibid., pl. 53:12
3	Achsib	8-7 cent. B. C.	!23,0	20	B	IAA 44.54	Ibid..., pl. 53: 13
4	Achsib	8-7	!18,5	35	B	?	Ibid., pl. 53: 8
5	Achsib	8-7	!19	30	B	?	Ibid., pl. 53: 9
6	Achsib	8-7	!18,5	?	B	IAA 61-563	Paz 2003, 5bet, p. 34
7	Nebo	11-10 cent. B. C.	!16,0	25	B	SBF M1072	Saller 1966, Fig. 28:1
8	Nebo	11-10 cent. B. C.	!14,0	25	B	SBF M2001	Idem., Fig. 28:2
9	Samaria	8-7 cent. B. C.	1/2, 10,5	25	G	?	Crowfoot 1957, pl. XI:8
10	Samaria	8-7 cent. B. C.	1/4, 10,5	?	G	?	Idem., p. 79
11	Samaria	8-7 cent. B. C.	1/4, 9,0	?	B	?	Idem., p. 79
12	Shiqmona	9-8 cent. B. C.	1/2 15,0	40	B	IAA 81.246	Braun 1999, ill. IV/1-4
13	Qitmit *	7 cent. B. C.	⅛	?	B	IAA 87.613	Beck 1995. pp. 162 -165.
14	Qitmit *	7 cent. B. C.	⅛	?	B	IAA 87.616	"
15	PU	9-6 cent. B. C.	!16,1	30	?	IM 82.2.7.	Ornan 1986, no. 10
16	PU	10-6 cent. B. C.	!25.0	20	?	HM MC875	---
17	PU	?10-7 cent. B. C.	!21,8	23	?	HSM 907.64.470	Meyers 1987, pl. 7

Tab. III-4. Terracotta Plaque Figurines with frame Drum or Disc Discoverd on the Territory of AIP*

No.	SITE	CHRONOLOGY Cent. B. C.	HEIGHT in cm	Ø in cm	COLLECTION	BIBLIOGRAPHY
1	Amman	??	3.5	35	AAM ATH 66-3.	Dornemann 1983, fig. 87:6-7
2	Amman	??	3.5	35	AAM ATH 66-24.	idem
3	Beth Schean	11	7.5	30	IAA I. 9684	James 1966, fig. 112:5
4	Beth Schean	11	7.9	20	PM. 29.103.883	James 1966, fig. 111:1
5	Beth Schean	11	9.4	25	PM. 29.103.882	idem fig. 111:4
6	Beth Schean	11	6.9	25	PM. 29.103.881	idem fig. 111:6
7	Deir 'Alla**	8-7	5.5	50	AAM J. 13746	VR, no. 159
8	Deir 'Alla**	11-90	9.0	20	AAM J. 12699	Franken 1960, pl. 13a
9	Deir 'Alla	8-7	9.0	25	AMM J.J. 13773	Paz 2003, no. 33a
10	Delhamiya	?	?	35	IAA 69-1538	Beck 1999, Fig. 7.7:6
11	Gerar	11	2.2	40	BM L285	Petrie 1928, Pl.35:14
12	Gezer	?8-7	7.5	25	?	Macalister 1912, II fig. 499
13	Gezer	?	7.0	20	?	idem. III Pl. 221:2
14	Hazor	9	7.5	30	?	Yadin 1980, Pl. 76:12
15	Hazor	10	4.0	40	?	idem. Pl. 76:13
16	Irbid	10-9	4.8	35	JDA T.A. 16	Dajani 1966, Pl. 33:16
17	Irbid	10-9	3.8	?35	JDA T.A 29	idem. Pl. 34:29
18	Jebel Qala**	11-9	5.5	35	AAM 68:17	Dornemann 1983, fig. 89:3
19	Kerak (near)	11-10	15,9	25	JDA J.5751	VR, no. 128.
20	Kerak (near)	9-8	6,7	20	JDA J.421	Harding 1937, pl. X:9
21	Kerak (near)	9-8	8,0	20	?	Glueck 1940 (1980), fig. 82.
22	Meggido	10-8	8.0	30	IAA 36.926	May 1935, Pl. 27:MI138
23	Meggido	11-10	12.1	30	IAA 36.958	Idem M5418
24	Meggido	10-9	8.9	30	IAA 36.944	Idem, M4365
25	Meggido	11-10	13.7	40	OI A18649	Idem. M65
26	Meggido	11-10	14.8	35	OI A18707	Idem, pl. 27:M810
26	Meggido**	8-7	8.2	25	OI A18705	Idem, pl. 27:M787
27	Meggido	11-10	12.0	30	?	Schumacher 1908, Fig. 156.

112

Continuation

28	Meggido	8-7	?	35	?	Schumacher 1908, fig. 71
29	T. 'Ira	8-7	13.8	25	IAA 84.62	Beit-Arieh 1985, 23.
30	Mt. Nebo	11-7	2.5	25	?	Henke 1959, Taf. 14:B
31	Samaria	10-7	?		?	Samaria I, 1924, pl. 75a
32	Samaria	10-7	?	25	?	Samaria I, 1924, pl. 75b
33	Ta'anach**	8-7	13.0	20	AAM J.7285	Lapp 1964, fig. 21
34	T. Amal	10	6.0	25	IAA 67.134	Levy/Edelstein 1972, fig. 17:7
35	T. Aphek**	13-12?		15		Kochavi 1975, II:C
36	T. El-Far'ah N.	9-8	4.8	40	EB F3031	Chambon 1984, Pl. 63:1
37	T. El-Far'ah N.	9-8	11.5	35	EB F3426	idem., pl. 63:2
38	T. Hadar				IA TAU	Paz 2003, pl. 3:5/9a
39	T. 'Ira	8-7	13.8	25	IAA 84.62	Beit-Arieh 1985, 23.
40	T. Malhata					Paz 2003, pl. 3:6/21a
41	Jet ???				Horovitz 2001	Paz 2003, pl. 3:11/ 50a/pl.4:1
42	UP	8-7				Zemer 1991, no. 37, p. 93
43	UP	8-6			IM, no. 82.2.14	
44	UP	8-7			IM, no. 82.2.17	

* The measurments of the frame drum/disc are given in proportion to the body or hand of the drummer, and should be taken relatively.
** The marked figurines can be considered as drummers only with great caution.

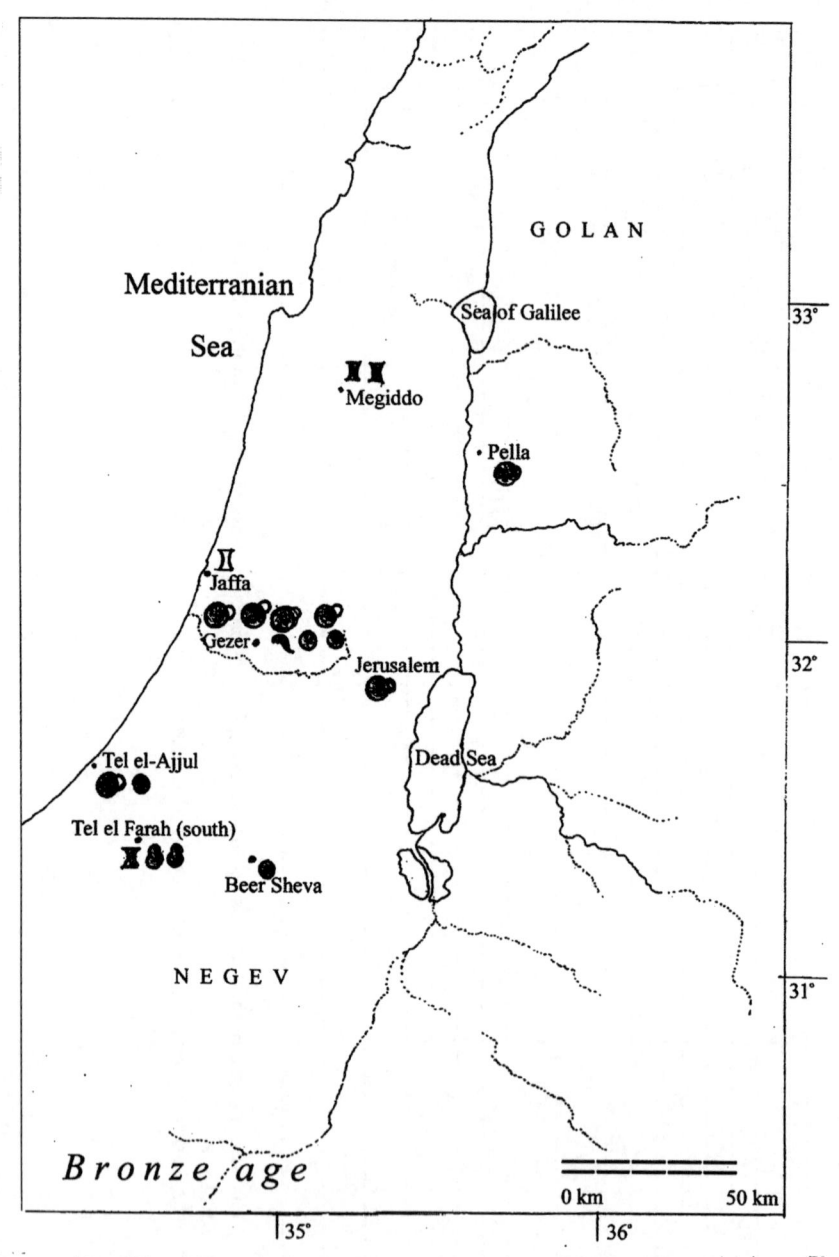

Map. III. – 1. Bronze Age distribution of clay rattles (3200-1200 B. C.)

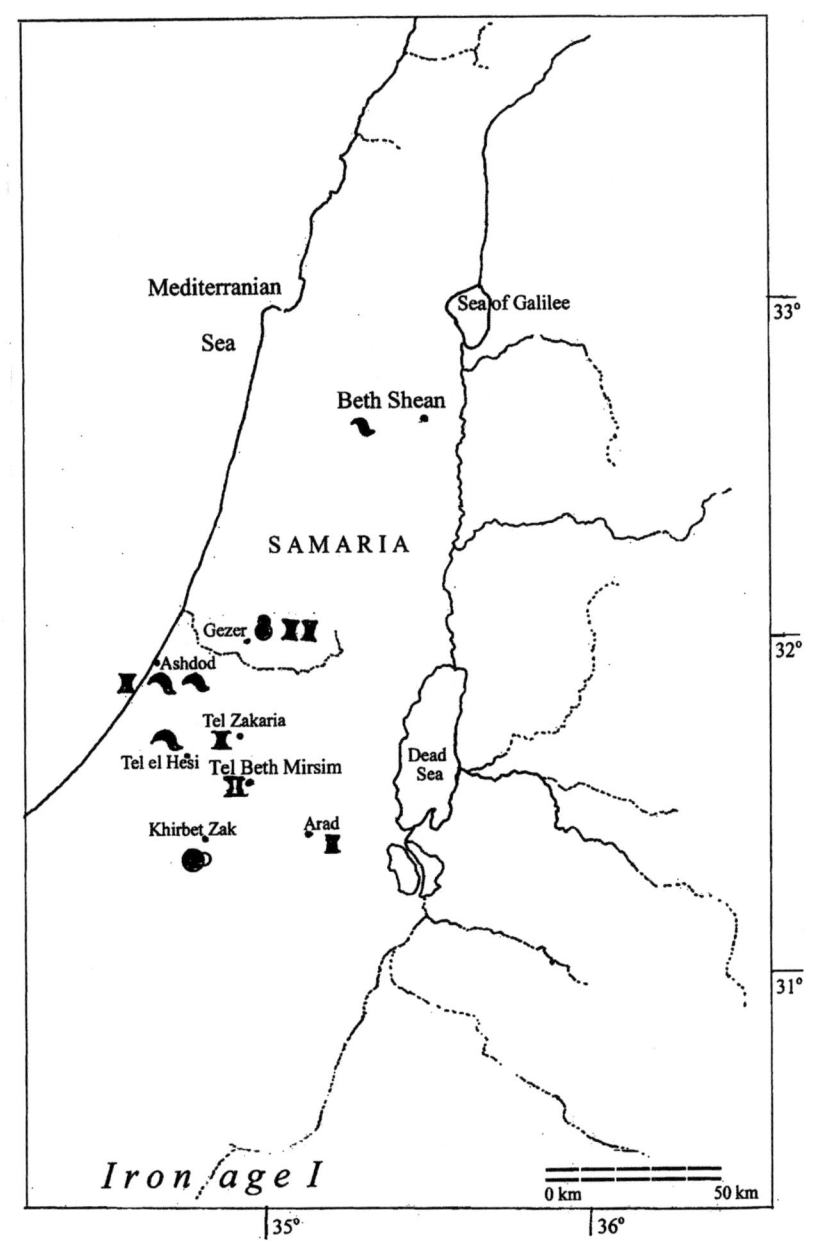

Map. III. – 2. Iron Age A distribution of clay rattles (1200-1000 B. C.)

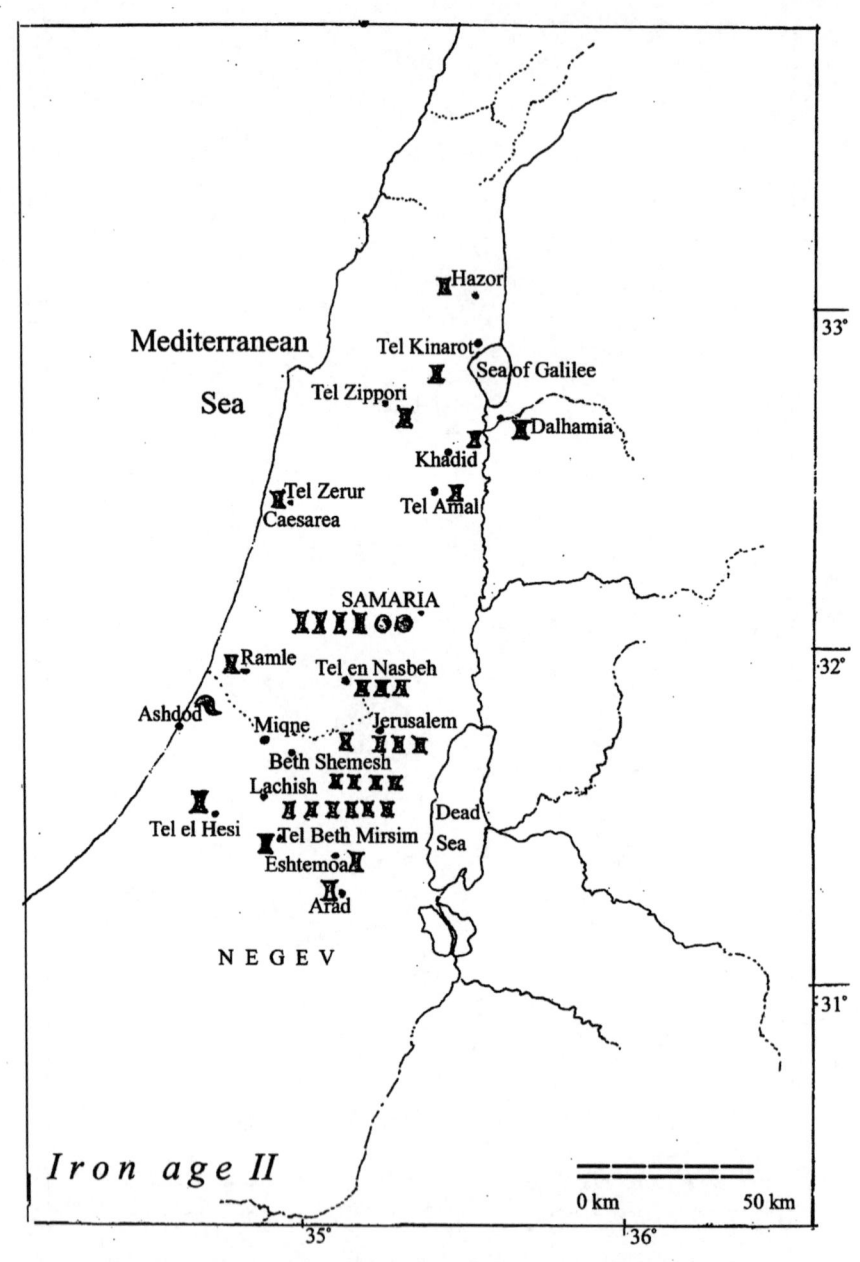

Map. III. – 3. Iron Age B distribution of clay rattles (1000-586 B. C.)

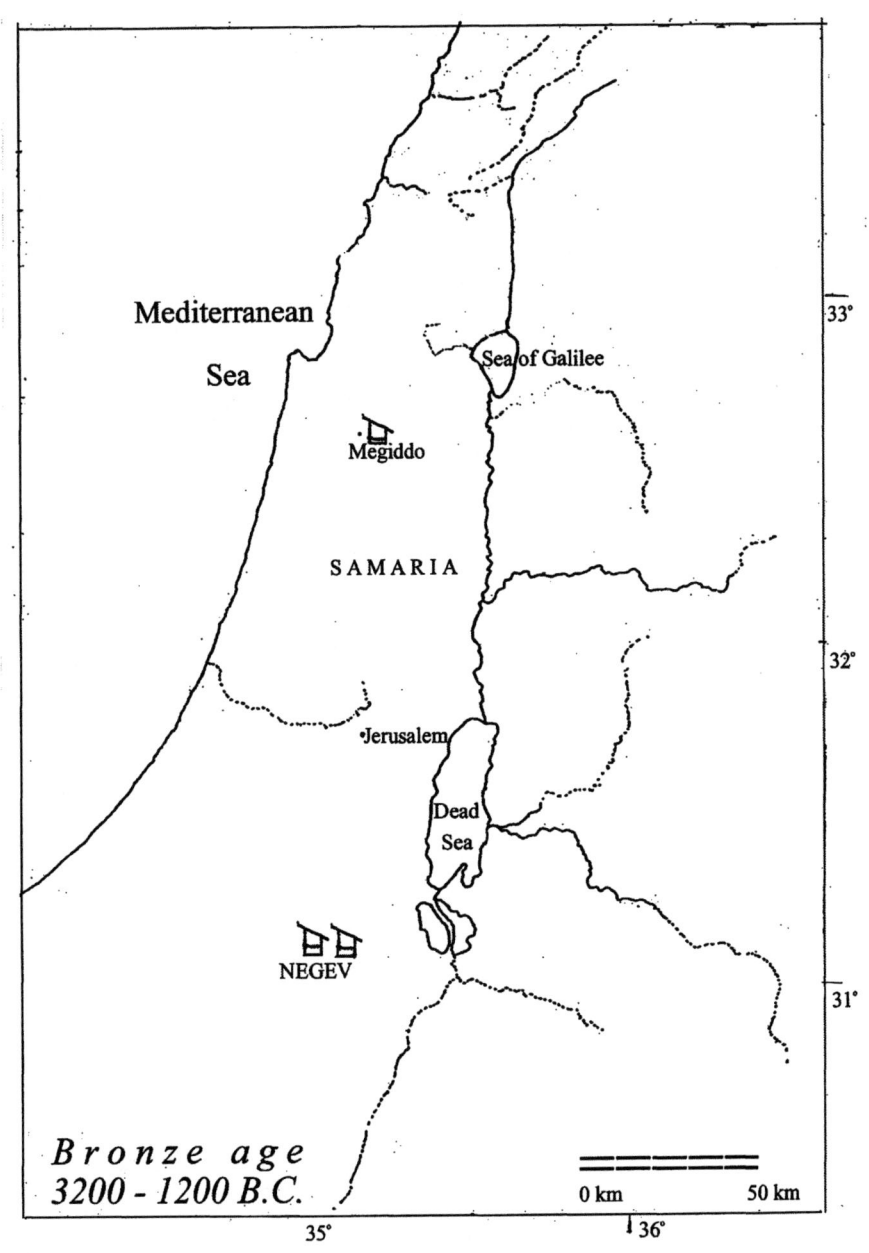

Map. III. – 4. Bronze Age lyre iconography distribution (3200-1200 B. C.)

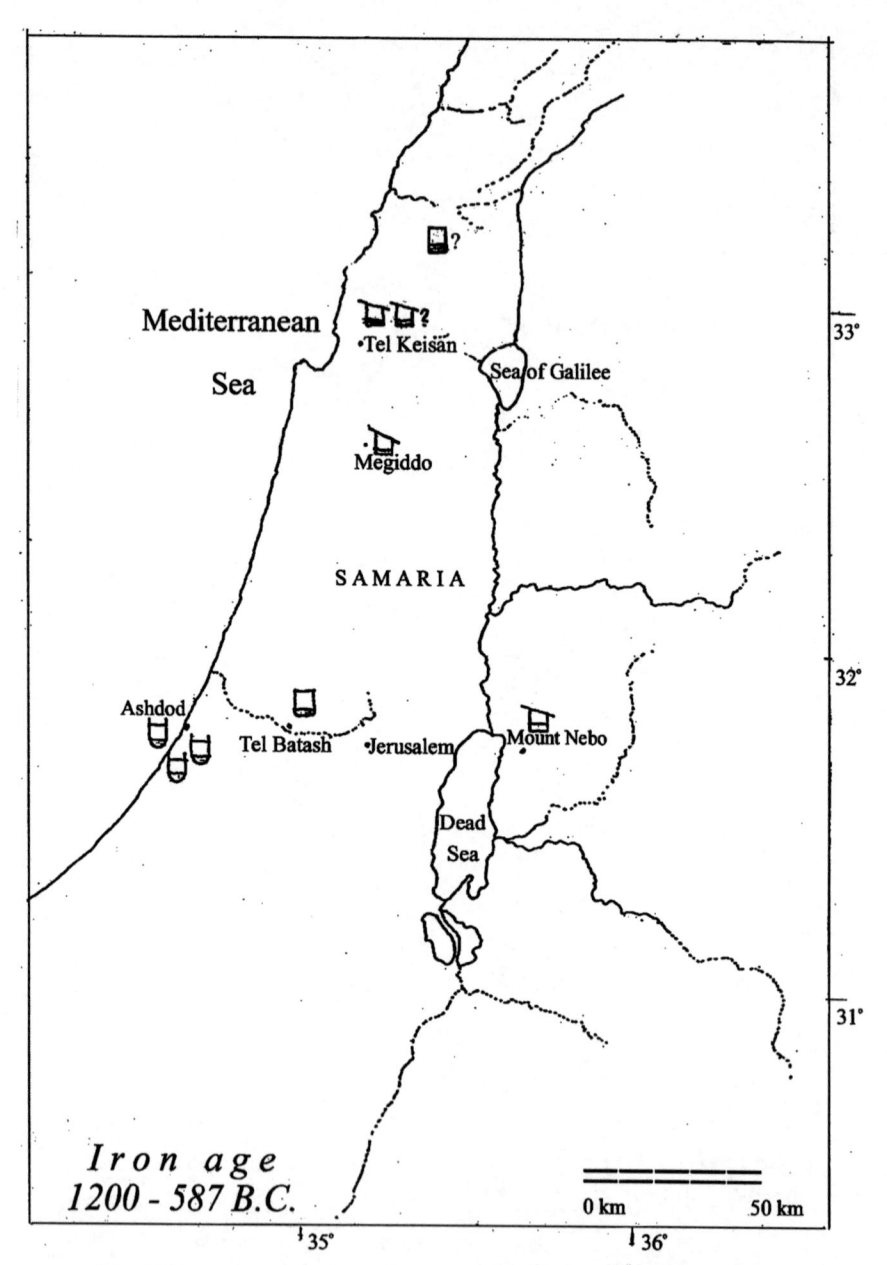

Map. III. – 5. Iron Age lyre iconography distribution (1200-586 B. C.)

118

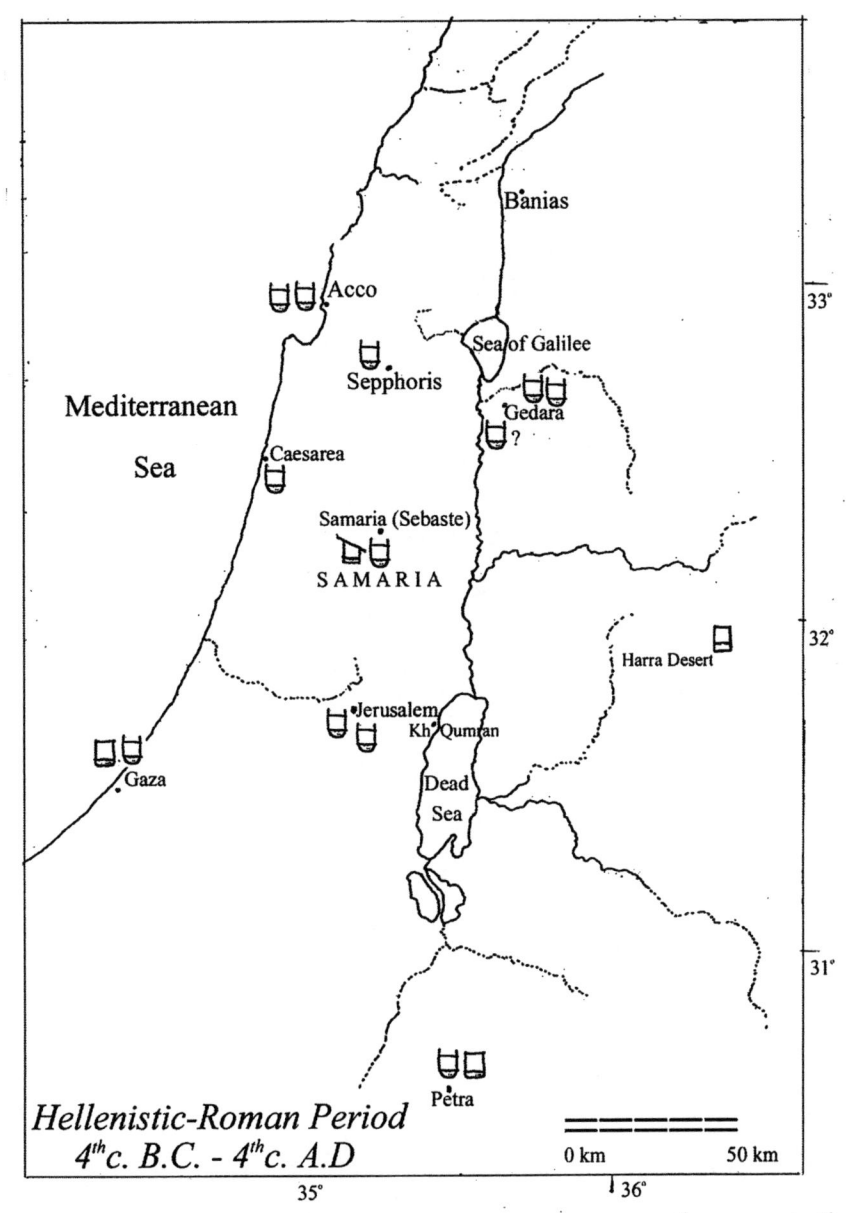

Map. III. – 6. Hellenistic-Roman Age lyre iconography distribution (4th cent B. C.-6th cent C. E.)

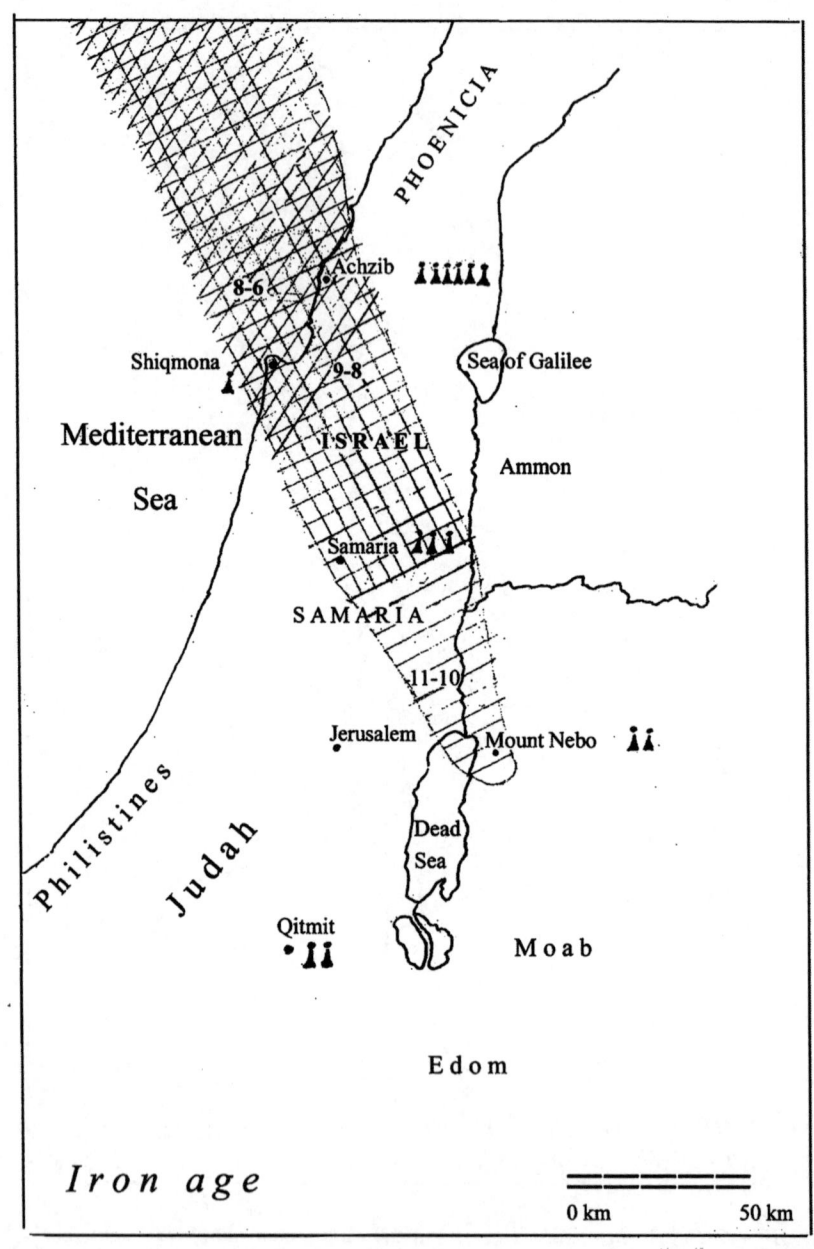

Map. III. – 7. The distribution of bell shaped figurines with drum (11th-6th cent. B. C.)

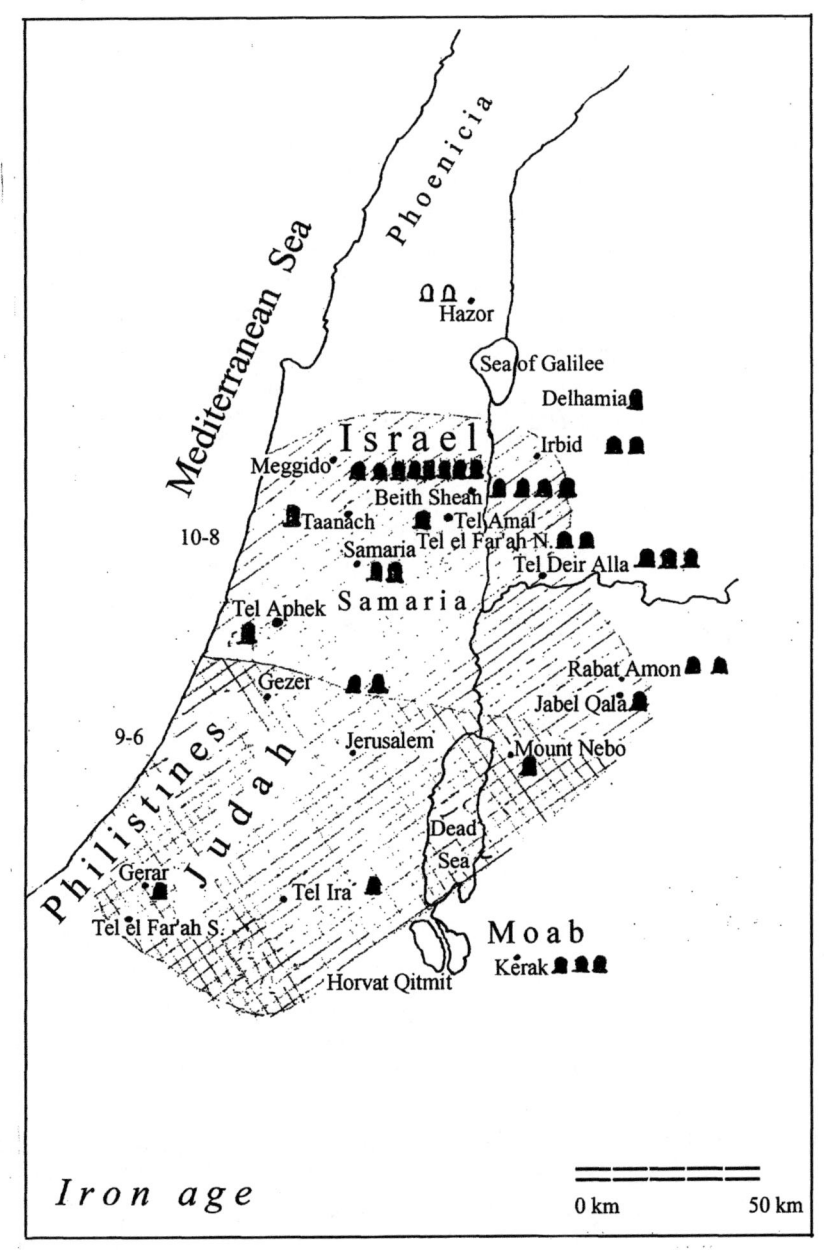

Map. III. – 8. The distribution of relief plaques with drum or disc (10th-6th cent. B. C.)

Ch. III. Bibliography

Albright W.F. 1943. *The Excavations of Tel Beit Mirsim III. The Iron Age. AASOR* XXI-XXII.

Anati E. 1963. *Palestine before the Hebrews: a history, from the earliest arrival of man to the conquest of Canaan.* New York.

Avigad N. 1978. The king's daughter and the lyre. In: *IEJ* 28: 146-151.

Balensi J. 1987. Mittlere Bronzezeit. In *Der Königs Weg. 9000 Jahre Kunst und Kultur in Jordanien und Palästina.* Köln: 93-103.

Bachi G. and Ben-Dov M. 1971. Area D. Stratigraphy and building remains. In: M. Dothan (ed.). *Ashdod II-III. The second and third seasons of excavations 1963, 1965: soundings in 1967. 'Atiqot* 9-10: 86-124.

Bade et al.1947

Bade W.F., McCown C. C. and Wampler J. C. 1947. *Tell en-Nasbeh* I: *archaeological and historical results.* II: *the pottery.* Berkeley-New Haven.

Bahat D. 1971. In: M. Dothan (ed.). *Ashdod II-III. Aria K. The second and third seasons of 1963, 1965, excavations: soundings in 1967.'Atiqot* 9-10: 168-180.

Beck P. 1982. The drawings frm Horvat Teiman (Kutillet Ajrud). In: *TA*, 9/1:3-68.

Beck P. 1995. Catalogue of cult objects and study of the iconography. In I. Beit-Arieh (ed.). *Horvat Qitmit: an edomite shrine in the Biblical Negev,* Tel Aviv: 7-197.

Beck P. 1999. Human figurine with tambourine. In: Beit-Arieh, I., ed. *Tel Ira: A stronghold in the Biblical Negev. Emery and Claire Yass publications in archaeology,* pp. 386-394. Tel Aviv.

Beit-Arieh I. 1999. *Tel 'Ira. A stronghold in the Biblical Negev.* Tel-Aviv.

Bliss F.J. and Macalister R.A.S. 1902. *Excavations in Palestine during the years 1898-1900.* London.

Boaz A. 2000. Pottery and small finds from the Late Ottoman village and the Early Zionist settlement. In: Y. Hirschfeld (ed.). *Ramat Hanadiv excavations. Final report of the 1984-1998 seasons.* Jerusalem: 547-582.

Braun J. 1999. *Die Musikkultur Altisraels/Palästinas: Studien zu archäologischen, schriftlichen und vergleichenden Quellen.* Freiburg. (abbreviations: 'Altisrael/Palästina' or 'Music in')

Briend J. and Humbert J.-B. 1980. *Tell Keisan (1971-1976): une cité phénicienne en Galilée.* Paris.

Chambon A. and Contenson H. de 1984. *Tell el-Far'ah I: l'age du fer.* Paris.

Crowfoot et al.1957

Crowfoot J.W., Crowfoot G.M. and Kenyon K.M. 1957. *Samaria-Sebaste III. The objects.* London.

Dajani R.W. 1966. Four Iron Age tombs from Irbed. In: *ADAJ* 11: 88-101.

Dornemann R.H. 1983. *The archaeology of the Transjordan in the Bronze and Iron Ages.* Milwaukee, Wisc.

Dothan M. 1970. The musicians of Ashdod. In: *Archaeology* 23: 310-311.

Elgavish J. 1975. Shiqmona, 1975. In: *IEJ* 25(4): 257-258.

Fortuna et al. 1971.

Fortuna M.T., Wallace B.L. and Yevin Z. 1971. Area G. In: M. Dothan (ed.) *Ashdod II-III: The second and third seasons of excavations, 1963, 1965: soundings in 1967, Atiqot 9-10:* 136-154.

Franken H. 1960. The Excavations at Deir 'Alla in Jordan. In: *Vetus Testamentus* 10: 386-391.

Fritz V. 1990. *Kinneret. Ergebnisse der Ausgrabungen auf dem Tell el 'Orēme am See Gennesaret 1982-1985.* Wiesbaden.

Gluek N. 1940. *The other side of the Jordan.* New Haven.

Hamburger A. 1986. Surface-finds from Caesarea Maritima-Tesserea. In: I. Levin and E. Netzer (ed.). *Excavations at Caesarea Maritima. Final Report. Qedem* 21. Jerusalem: 187-204.

Harding L 1937. Some objects from Transjordan. In: *PEQ*: 253-255.

Henig M. and Whiting M. 1987. *Engraved gems from Gadara in Jordan. The Sa'd Collection of intaglios and cameos.* Oxford.

James F.W. 1966. *The Iron Age at Beth Shan: a study of levels VI-IV.* Philadelphia, Pennsylvania.

Jones C. N. 1948. Discoveries in Palestine since 1939. In: *PEQ* 1948: 81-89.

Keel-Leu H. 1991. *Vorderasiatische Stempelsiegel: die Sammlung des Biblischen Instituts der Universitat.* Freiburg.

Kelm G. L. and Mazar A. 1982. Three seasons of excavations at Tel Batash – Biblical Timnah. *BASOR* 248: 1-36.

Kloner, A. *Marisha: An archaeological guide*. Jerusalem,1996 (in Hebrew).

Kochavi M. 1975. The First Two Seasons of Excavations at Aphek-Antipatris: Preliminary Report. *TA* 2: 17-43.

Lankenster-Harding G. 1969. A safaitic drawings and text. *Levant* 1: 68-72.

Lapp P.W. 1964. The 1963 Excavation at Ta'annek. *BASOR* 173: 4-44.

Levy S. and Edelstein G. 1972. Cinq saisons de fouilles à Tel 'Amal (Nir David). *RB* 79: 325-367.

Loud G. 1939. *The Megiddo ivories*. Chicago.

Loud G. 1948 *Megiddo* II: *seasons of 1935-39*. Chicago.

Macalister R.A.S. 1912. *The excavation of Gezer 1902-1905 and 1907-1909*. Vols. I-III. London.

Mackenzie D. 1912/13. Excavations at Ain Shems (Beth Shemesh). *PEFA* II.

MAW 1971. *Music in the ancient world*. Haifa. Museum of Ancient Art.

May H.G. 1935. *Material remains of the Megiddo Cult*. Chicago.

Mazar E. 1996. *The Achziv burials: a test-case for Phoenician-Punic burial customs*. Jerusalem.

Meshel Z. 1979. Kuntillat-Ajrud. *Le Monde de la Bible* 10: 33-36.

Meyers C. 1987. A Terracotta at the Harvard Semitic Museum and discholding female figures reconsidered. *IEJ* 37: 116-122.

Newberry et al. –

Newberry P.E., Griffith F.L. and Carter H. 1893. *Beni Hasan 1 – 4*. Archaeological survey of Egypt 1, 2, 3, 4. London.

Ornan T. 1986. *A man and his land: highlights from the Moshe Dayan Collection*. Jerusalem.

Ovadiah A. and Mucznik S. 1981. Orpheus from Jerusalem – pagan or Christian image?. In L.I. Levine (ed.). *The Jerusalem Cathedra* I: 152-166.

Ovadiah A. and Ovadiah R. 1987. *Hellenistic, Roman and Early Byzantine mosaic pavements in Israel*. Roma.

Paz S. 2003. *Drums, women and goddesses. Drumming and its meaning in Iron Age II Israel in light of the archaeological finds*. Tel Aviv (Hebrew).

Petrie W.M.F. 1928. *Gerar.* British School of Archaeology in Egypt. London.
Petrie W.M.F. 1934. *Ancient Gaza* IV: *Tell el-Ajjul.* London.
Rashid S.A. 1984. *Mesopotamien: Musik des Altertums.* Musikgeschichte in Bildern 2(2). Ed. W. Bachmann. Leipzig.
Reisner et al. –
Reisner G.A., Fisher C.S. and Lyon D.G. 1924. *Harvard excavations at Samaria: 1908-1910.* Cambridge.
Saller S.J. 1964. *The Excavations at Dominus Flevit* (*Mount Oliveto - Jerusalem*) II. *The Jebusite Burial Place.* Jerusalem.
Saller S.J. 1966. Iron Age tombs at Nebo, Jordan. *LA* 16: 165-298.
Schumacher G.1908. *Tell el-Mutesellim: Report of the excavations conducted from 1903 to 1905.* I-II. Leipzig.
Sellers O.R. 1941. Musical instruments of Israel. *BA* 4(3): 33-47.
Macdonald et al. –
Macdonald, E., Starkey, G. and Lancester-Harding, G. 1932. *Beth Pelet, vol. 2, Beth Pelet cemetery.* London.
Tufnell O. 1953. *Lachish (Tell ed-Duweir)* III: *The Iron Age.* London.
Tufnell O. 1958. *Lachish (Tell ed-Duweir) IV: The Bronze Age.* London.
VR – *La Voie Royale: 9000 ans d'art au Royaume de Jordanie,* Musée du Luxembourg 1987 (*Der Königsweg : 9000 Jahre Kunst und Kultur in Jordanien und Palästina.* Köln 1987).
Weill R. 1920. *La Cite de David. Compte rendu des fouilles executées à Jérusalem, sur le site de la ville primitive. Campagne de 1913-1914.* Paris.
Weiss Z. and Netzer E. 1996. *Promise and redemption. A synagogue Mosaic from Sepphoris.* Jerusalem.
Yadin Y. 1960. *Hazor III.* Jerusalem.
Yadin Y. and Geva S. 1986. *Investigations at Beth Shean. The early Iron Age strata. Qedem 23.* Jerusalem.
Zayadine F. 1987. in: *La Voie Royale. 9000 ans d'art au royaume de Jordanie.* Musée du Luxemburg.

BA   Biblical Archaeologist
BASOR   *Bulletin of the American Schools of Oriental Research*
IEJ   *Israel Exploration Journal*
LA   *Liber Annus*

PEFA   *Palestinian Exploration Foundation Annual*
PEQ   *Palestien Exploration Quarterly*
RB   *Revue Biblique*
TA   *Tel Aviv*

IV. The Lute in Ancient Israeli and Jewish Iconography [*]

Some remarks[1] on the state of art in Israeli/Jewish[2] archaeology and iconography of music are appropriate in this paper which is dedicated to our distinguished colleague and friend, who organized the seminal conference held in 1984 at the Johannes-Gutenberg-University Mainz, especially as this conference motivated me to become involved with iconography of music.

The phantom of the famous prohibition from Exodus 20:4 has had a lasting and destructive impact on the study of Israeli and Jewish history in general, and musicology, in particular. Assuming that, as a result of this prohibition, evidence from the visual arts did not exist, scholars, for years, did not search for or consider this type of evidence.[3] While both archaeological and icononographical sources[4] were neglected, we schould note, however, that the former have been used since Carl Engel's *The Music of the Most Ancient Nations* (1864), and during the last two

---

[*] Published in: *Festschrift Christoph-Hellmut Mahling,* ed. A. Beer et al., vol. 2 =*Mainzer Studien zur Musikwissenschaft* 37/2, Tutzing, 1997, pp. 163-188.

[1] This paper is based on a presentation at the First International Conference on Jewish Music at the City University of London (Tuesday 5 April – Thursday 7 April 1994).

[2] In this article, the term "Israel" refers to Ancient Israel (Bronze Age to Byzantine Period) which was located upon the territories of contemporary Israel/Palestine and part of Jordan. The term "Jewish" refers to the culture of the Diaspora (post-Roman times and extending up to our days).

[3] Even the *New Oxford History of Music* (vol. I, p. 295) still describes ancient Israeli music in the following way: "Of the instruments themselves not a single example has yet come to light, and from the pre-Hellenistic period no native representation of a Palestinian instrument survives". Curt Sachs (*The History of Musical Instruments*, New York, 1940, p. 105), and Eric Werner (*Grove Dictionary of Music and Musicians*, 5th ed., vol. IV, London, 1955, p. 618) directly point to the Second Commandment justifying this type of statements.

[4] As *terminus technicus* in this paper all sources from ancient Israel are designated as "archaeological," although, in fact, they are also often iconographical. Only the sources from the period of the Jewish Diaspora are designated as "iconographical."

decades have even become the central research material used in the study of ancient Israeli music culture ("Primärquellen...sind nicht in den biblischen Schriften zu finden, sondern nur von der Archaeologie zu erwarten").[5] Musicological publications used, and still use this material mainly for illustration, and at present hardly a dozen papers with an analytical approach have been produced.[6] Archaeological and historical literature is rather careless in the handling of archaeo-musical sources, and misinterpretations are frequent.

The latter, iconographical material from the "post-archaeological era" (mainly 12.-17. cent. illuminations from Hebrew manuscripts) is as well as completely ignored. To date only one musicological MA thesis on an iconographical subject has yet been written,[7] and to the best of my knowled several papers presented at the AIMCC-95 meeting are in print.[8] The only topos which involves iconographical sources is the image of the *klezmer*, the Jewish Spielmann.[9]

This short introduction was required in order to stress the urgent need for an extensive attack on Jewish iconographical sources by the musicological community. The study of this material may to a great extent change our assessment of many aspects of the history of Jewish music. Using as an example, the cases of the lute and the organ, I will attempt to

---

5 Othmar Keel, and Christoph Uehlinger, *Goettinnen, Goetter und Gottessymbole: Neue Erkenntnisse zur Religionsgeschichte Kanaans und Israels aufgrund bislang unerschlossener ikonographischer Quellen* (Freiburg-Wien, 1992), p. 4.
6 The main contributors to this field are Bathia Bayer (esp. her *Material Relics of Music in Ancient Palestine and its Environs*, Tel-Aviv, 1963), Yaacov Meshorer (papers on musical images on ancient coins), and the author of this paper. The book *Die Musik Alt-Israels/Palaestinas: Studien zu archaeologischen, schriftlichen und vergleischenden Quelen*, as a volume of the series *Orbis et biblicus et orientalis*, University Fribourg, Switzerland is in preparation.
7 Yaacov Snir, "Musical Instruments in the Illuminations of the 'Barcelona Haggadah' BM. Add. Ms. 14761," MA Thesis, Tel-Aviv University, Department of Musicology, Tel-Aviv, 1978.
8 Archaeology and Iconography of Music ICTM Study Group Conjoint Conference AIMCC-95: *Music Images and the Bible* (Bar-Ilan University, Israel, 30. Dec. 1994-3. Jan. 1995).
9 See Joachim Stutchevsky, *Haklesmorim* (in Hebrew, The klezmorim; Tel-Aviv, 1959); Moysey Beregovskiy, *Jevreyskaya narodnaya instrumental'naya muzika* (in Russian, Jewish instrumental folk music; Moscow, 1987); Walter Salmen, *Jüdische Musikanten und Tänzer vom 13. bis 20. Jahrhundert* (Innsbruck, 1991).

establish a continuity between the two bodies of visual sources – archaeoligical and iconographical, which are divided by a gap of at least one millenium, and show the interdependence of the musical cultures of Ancient Israel and the Western Jewish musical tradition.

The lute and the organ, two musical instruments with negative associations in the Jewish history of music, mainly due to their strong pagan, secular (the lute), and Christian (the organ) affiliations exemplify the processes of change in Jewish music.

Let us take a look at the socio-ethnic transformation of the semantics of lute-playing from ancient Israel to a modern Jewish context. The earliest archaeological source for the lute – a 15x10cm terracotta plaque (see **Fig. IA-3**) – comes from the 15th-14th cent. BC and was discovered at the Dan excavations (Galilee).[10] It probably served as the identification sign for either a private house, whose owner was a Late Bronze Age *Spielemann*, or as the identification sign for a building, where an entertainment establishment was located. The plaque shows a dancing musician playing a long-necked lute. The figure itself, the movement of the musician and the way the instrument is handled – evrything is without precedent we may say an autochthonous case. Moreover, the type of performance and the mask on the face indicate a syncretic artistic activity. There are two other finds which indicate that the lute of this period was the typical instrument of the pagan, pre-Israeli, Canaanite culture: a terracotta figurine of a male lute player, probably a warrior,[11] and a bronze figurine depicting a naked female musician.[12] Between the decline of the Canaanite culture, and arrival of the Hellenistic-Roman period the lute disappeared from Israel/Palestine, or, more precisely, no artifact which could prove its existence has been find. This *argumentum ex silentio*, which is also present in the history of other musical instruments (e.g., cymbals), has not yet been studied sufficiently. As to the present state of research, we may suggest that the lute was not commonly accepted in ancient Israeli culture (in contrast, for example, to the lyre, which is de-

---

10 Avraham Biran, "The Dancer from Dan, the Empty Tomb, and the Altar Room", *Israel Exploration Journal*, 36/3-4 (1986), 168-71, Fig. 2.

11 IAA, No. 33.1567, 16.-13. cent. BC., s. W. Flinders Petrie, *Ancient Gaza: Tell el Ajjul* (London 1933), vol. III, p. 8, Pl. XV.

12 IAA M969, 12. cent BC, s. G. M. Fitzgerald, *Beth-Shean Excavations 1921-1923* (Philadelphia 1931), p. 33, Pl. XXVI:2.

picted on at least thirty artifacts). We may also recall that there is no mention of a lute-type instrument in the Old Testament (except, perhaps, for the lone use of the word *shalishim,* 1. Samuel 18:6, "the most disputed musical term of the Hebrew language").[13]

When the lute re-appears, after nearly one thousand years of absence, we find it in the 4.-2. cent. BC in Hellenistic Marisa (Mareshah, Judea) in the hands of both a partly clad Bacchus (?) and a naked female figure[14] – two images alien to Israeli culture. To these two finds from Hellenistic-Roman Palestine we must add the depiction of the lute from the wall painting of the Dura Europa synagogue (2.-3. cent CE)[15] which until now has not been noticed by musicologists. Although found outside the borders of Palestine, the painting **(Fig. IV-1)** is of outstanding significance for undesrstanding the meaning of the lute in Jewish culture: it shows the legendary Dagon Temple in Ashdod (1.Sam. 5:1-5) with the Philistine god mutilated, and his temple implements scattered over the entire hall. Among the implements of the Dagon cult we clearly see a lute. There can be no more vivid confirmation of the lute as a pagan, and here hostile to Judaism, musical instrument.

Following this period nearly a millenium must pass before we find iconographical evidence that allows us to make some conclusions about the status of the lute in Jewish culture. The famous 13th century *Cantigas de Santa Maria* depicts some eighty musical instruments in forty miniatures, indeed, presenting a kind of ethnic anthology of musical instruments – Morish, Christian, Moslem and Jewish – residing in Spain at that time. Among the illuminations are two, which with certainty show Jewish musicians, as is made clear by the figures' head coverings and the illuminated backgrounds (fol. 89v, Cant. 70, and fol 341r, Cant. 380).[16] At least eleven lute players of all kinds are depicted in the manuscript, but not one

---

13 Sachs, *The History...*, p. 123; compare MGG, 2nd ed., vol. 1, clmn. 1533.
14 Mareshah Excavation No. 1386/XV/1, s. Amos Kloner, "Mareshah-1989," (in Hebrew), *Chadashot archeiologiot* (Archaeological news), 96 (1991), p. 33, Ill. 40; The Museum of Eretz-Israel (Tel-Aviv), Inv. No. 18762 (provenance unknown, probably Hellenistic-Roman Palestine, not published).
15 Erwin R. Goodenough, *Jewish Symbolism in the Greco-Roman Period* (New York, 1965), vol. X, pp. 74-97, and vol. XI, Pl. XIII, and Fig 334.
16 See Higinio Anglés, *La musica de las Cantingas de Santa Maria del rey Alfonso el Sabio*, vol. I, *Fascímil del códice j.b.2 de el Escorial* (Barcelona 1964).

lute is placed in the hands of a Jewish musician. The later are depicted only with plucked string instruments: two playing harps (fol. 341r), and two playing trapezoid psalteries (fol. 89v). Notably, the harps and psalteries are played only by the Jewish musicians (as has already been noted by Zoltan Falvy[17]). This can only be explained by the artist's desire to show the instruments Biblical affiliation. The Jewish affiliation is clearly demonstrated by the composition of the miniature fol. 341r, which like some Haggadah illuminations has in the background the traditional view of Jerusalem with elements of the Temple; this background, contrasts with all the other illuminations which have ornamental or dark plain backgrounds. The artist's intention here is obvious: the two instruments, played by the Jewish musicians, are supposed to represent the the two most popular biblical musical instruments, indisputably defined as chordophones – the *kinor* and *nebel*.[18] We can not, however, be sure which particular instrument is depicted in each of the images.

Both the LXX and the Vulgata translate *kinor* and *nebel* inconsistently: the Septuaginta usually translates them, respectively, as *kithara/ kinira* and *nabla/psalterion*, and the Vulgata as *cithara* and *psalterium*.[19] Thus, the dominant terms for the two biblical instruments are *kithara/ cithara* for *kinor* and *psalterion/psalterium* for *nebel*. From the 10th century the word *cithara* began to change from its original Roman-time meaning as lyre. Following several incarnatons, including its references to the lute (10th century *Stuttgart Psalter* Cod. bibl. fol. 23, Württembergische Landesbibliothek) and the harp (12.-13. cent., *Hortus deliciarum, cythara anglica*, St. Blasius ms.), its rendition as neck-instrument (*gittern, chitarrone, cetra, cittern, cithole*, etc.) prevailed.[20] The meaning of the term *psalterion/psalterium* is more stable. After its early period, when ancient Greek, Christian, and Jewish sources identified it as the harp, the meaning of the word during the Carolingian period became for some time

---

17 *Mediterranean Culture and Troubadour Music* (Budapest 1986), p. 53.
18 On the present state of research of these Biblical musical instruments, see 2MGG, vol. 1, clmn. 1516-17, and 1520-21.
19 See Joachim Braun, *Biblische Musikinstrumente*, in: 2MGG, vol. 1, Sp1516-7, and 1520-21.
20 See Sibyl Marcuse, *A Survey of Musical Instruments* (New York-London, 1975), pp. 373-4, and 440-1; Emmanuel Winternitz, *Musical Instrumnts and their Symbolism in Western Art* (London, 1967), pp. 57-65.

fluid (*quadratum*, or *modum deltae* -zither/harp?). Since the 12.-13. cent. its rendering as box-zither (trapezoidal, semitrapezoidal, wing-shaped, 'delta'-, 'pig-snout'-, or any other form) has been accepted.[21] However, in his commentary to Psalm 150 the Dominican friar Petrus de Palude (les than a century after the *Cantigas*) confirmed in text and drawing his understanding of the Biblical *kinor* as a trapezoid 'pig-snout' zither and the Biblical *nebel* as a pillar-harp.[22] This interpretation is to be found in a number of 13th-15th century sources, including those by such authoritative writers as Jean de Gerson and Nicholas Trivet, and, as well, in a number of anonymous manuscripts.[23] In this context Christopher Pages' assertion that "in most of this enormous literature of commentary the literal sense of words like *cithara* and *psalterium* was allowed to shrivel and die..., their meaning having withered and gone to be replaced by an echo of eternal truth,"[24] seems to be excessively pessimistic. The sense of the two instruments, probably, did not "shrivel and die", but rather, were subject to changes according to time and place. We must rediscover the meaning of the words in every case (see **Table IV-2**).

Meanwhile, we may claim that according to iconographical sources, for some two thousand years the string instruments of the Jewish people were the lyre, harp, and psalterium, while the lute player during this period was *persona non grata* in Jewish musical culture.

Beginnig with the 13th cent. the Jewish sources show a sudden change. One of the earliest most valuable and most beautiful, illuminated, Hebrew manuscripts in existance,[25] the Psalm manuscript Parma 1870 (Cod. De Rossi 510, Bibliotheca Regia Parmensis), which includes commentary of the great, Jewish scholar Abraham ibn Ezra (1089, Tudela, Spain – 1164, London) presents a new picture of the Jewish musical instrumentarium. Probably, written and illuminated in the central part of Italy, the manuscript may be dated between the late 13th and early 14th

---

21 James McKinnon, "Psalterium", 1NGD, 15:383-5; Marcuse, *A Survey...*, pp. 209-15.
22 Douai, Bibliothéque Municipale, MS 45, vol. 9, f. 262v; see the reproduction of Petrus texts and drawings in Christopher Page, *Voices and Instruments of the Middle Ages* (Berkeley-Los Angeles, 1986), Fig. 6, pp. 55-7, and 240.
23 idem., "Early 15th-century instruments in Jean de Gerson's *Tractatus de Canticis*", *Early Music* , 6 (1978), 340-2.
24 idem., *Voices and Instruments*, p. 55.
25 Now in the process of a fascimilie publication by Fascimilie Editions Ltd. (London).

century, probably, specifically about 1280-1300, and is the work of Jewish copyists.[26] Its 453 pages contain some 150 illuminations and miniatures, which are at the beginning of nearly every Psalm. Of these twelve are concerned with musical performance and musical instruments and are always relevant to the text – an extraordinary phenomenon for Jewish manuscripts of this time, and there is good reason to believe that the artist of the codex is of Jewish identity.[27]

The twelve musical illuminations depict a variety of scenes and instruments:

twice – a group of four-five men and a conductor with a music book (ff. 107v/Ps. 78, and 213v/ Ps. 150);

twice – a conductor (f. 139r/Ps. 98, and f. 160r/Ps. 109);

twice – a trumpet player (f. 87v/ps. 66, and f. 136r/Ps. 95, this latter with a person blowing a shofar);

once a pipe and tabor player (f. 116r/Ps. 81);

and five(!) times – either lute-type instruments alone or with other string instruments, some in animal images (f. 6v./Ps.6, f. 41v/Ps.33, f. 89r/Ps. 67, f.105r/Ps. 76, and f. 198r/Ps. 137; for the last three see **Fig. IV-2b, 2a** and **c**).

The explanation for the presence of the lute-instruments is provided by the Psalms' texts. Twice the illuminations illustrate the word *kinnor* (Ps.33 and 137; in the latter the two lute instruments are hung upon a tree, as prescribed by the text, **Fig. IV-2c**). In three Psalms (Ps. 6, 67, and 76) no particular musical instrument is mentioned, but the word *bineginot*, in its several variations, is found in the Psalms' headings; in the first case a lute is depicted by itself, in the second – the lute together with a psaltery (**Fig. IV-2b**), and in the third with a *fidel*, two gitterns, a lute, and a psaltery (**Fig. IV-2a**). There is an extensive critical discussion on

---

26 My sincer thanks are due to Prof. Dr. Malachi Beit-Arie (Jesselson Professor of Codicology and Palaeography at The Hebrew University of Jerusalem) who shared with me the information of his not yet published commentaries to the facsimilie edition in process.

27 See Thérèse Metzger, *Les illustrations d'un psautier hébreu italien de la fin du XIIIe siècle, le Ms. Parm 1870-De Rossi 510 de la Biblioteca Palatina de Parma*, in: *Cahiers archèologiques*, xxvi (1977), pp. 145-62. I thank Dr. Metzger for her kind letter from the 29th November, 1995, where she confirms her oppinion on the Jewish identity of the Parm. 1870 artist.

the meaning of the word *bineginot*, which appears seven times in the Psalms' headings, and everso can not be understood unequivocally (the root *ngn* stands for musician, musical instrument performer, song, melody, tune; s. 2MGG, vol. 1:1532). The Septuaginta translates it as *hymnoi*, the Vulgata – *in carminibus*, and the Greek Aquila-translation – *in psalmi*. Modern translations tend to the string-instrument interpretation: the American Version – "on string instruments", the Authorised Version, and Harkavy – "*neginot* and song", and the latest *Neue Jerusalemer Bibel* – "Mit Saitenspiel." There is no doubt about the interpretation of *bineginot* as "string instruments" in the Ms. Parma 1870, even more, as *kinnor* (lute) and *nebel* (psaltery).

I will not enter into the organology of all the different types of instruments, since this is not of decisive importance for our discussion. Let me note, however only, that Ps. 6 is illuminated by a short-necked lute-type instrument with six pegs, probably, an *'ud*; Ps.33 – by the Medieval gittern,[28] a plucked rebec-type instrument with a sickle-shaped peg-box terminating in a carved animal-head, and, probably, having eight pegs; Ps. 67 – by another *'ud* with incrustation along the resonance-body, played by a human being with an animal head and holding a plectrum in his right hand, and a semitrapezoid zither (**Fig. IV-2b**, a combination represnting, probably, *kinnor* and *nebel*, as was indicated by the *Cantigas de Santa Maria* manuscript); Ps. 137 – as illustrated on **Fig. IV-2c** shows two overlaping *'ud*-instruments. The richest illumination of the entire manuscript belongs to Ps. 76 and depicts five musical instruments (**Fig. IV-2a**). The miniature is dominated by a human being with a bird's head playing an oval-shaped *fidel* with an extremely long bow; the other four instruments are a semitrapezoid zither (in the center), an lute-type instrument with, probably, ten pegs (to the left), and two gitterns – the upper, seemingly, with frets and the lower without. Our gittern is shown both from the side and from the front and has all the features of this instrument type: a rounded back and sickle-shaped pegbox, the body and neck being of one piece, a rose visible on the upper side, the strings ter-

---

[28] s. Laurence Wright, *The Medieval Gittern and Citole: A Case of Mistaken Identity*, Galpin Society Journal, May 1977, pp. 8-42. This study certainly may be considered as the latest word on the gittern-discussion (see also Page, *Voices and Instruments*, p. 147).

minating at the bridge, and the instrument is being smaller than a lute. Tinctoris' tuning 4th-3rd-4th fits our gittern with four courses (eight pegs), which is considered the "traditional number"[29] of strings. The instruments of this type, *guitarra latina*, mentioned around 1330 by Juan Ruiz (*Libro de Buen Amor*, Stanza 1228), "had strong affinities with the lute and seem to have been imported from the Arabs via Spain."[30] It is of special interest for us, that the Greek/Hebrew word *kithara/kinnor* was used by the Arabs to designate different string instruments – the lyre in ancient times, and the lute even today[31]. Thus, *bineginot* undoubtably is "string instruments", and it is highly likely that in the context of the Parma 1870 manuscript the word *kinnor* is represented by lute-instruments.

This interpretation of the biblical term *kinnor*, as neck-instrument, is confirmed by a contemporary, written, Hebrew text, which is of especial importance for our discussion. This text, a 13th century commentary on Ps. 150 (Lambeth Palace, Ms 435, f. 131v),[32] includes both the Latin and French glosses of *vielle* for *nebel* and *gige* for *kinnor* (in this text both biblical string instruments are even interpreted as lute-instruments). It is this 13th century understanding of the biblical term, which served as a basis for the later transformation of the meaning of the word *kinnor* and turned it, in modern Hebrew, into the meaning "violin:" *kinnor* = violin.

The previous discussion allows for several suggestions:[33]

a. The artistic style of the Parma 1870 manuscript, its spiritual atmosphere (as indicated by the choice of the commentary by ibn Ezra), and the musical culture depicted by the illuminations are deeply rooted in the Jewish-Arab-Spanish milieu of the 13th-14th centuries.

---

29 idem., p. 18.
30 idem., p. 23.
31 idem.; Hans Hickmann, *Aegypten*: MGB II/1 (Leipzig, 1961), p. 136.
32 Page, *Musical Instruemnts...*, p. 54, Fig. 5.
33 Apart from our conclusions regarding the status of lute instruments in Jewish musical culture, it is of interest to note, that the Hebrew manuscripts (Parma 1870, and Lisbon, Biblioteca Nacional Ms Il. 72, fol. 440v) seem to present in the late 13th and early 14th century one of the earliest, if not *the* earliest, depictions of the gittern and bowed rebec in Europe. Wright, *Medieval Gittern* (p. 17, Pl. I.), mentions as the first certain iconographical evidence for the gittern a manuscript from 1330.

b. In the late 13th-early 14th centuries learned, Jewish men, probably, including the Rabbis, the wealthy, educated circles, and persons of status, who could order an illuminated manuscript of such richness as Parma 1870, accepted the lute-type instruments, particularly the gitterns – formerly tavern-, nightlife-, serenade-, even thieves'-instruments – as being the Temple-instruments of the past – the *kinnor* or *nevel.*

c. The illuminations are so "real", and so "contemporary", that a suggestion even is tempting to suppose the acceptance of neck-instruments and some other musical instruments of that time at certain communities for the accompaniment of Psalm-singing, as the *kinnor* and *nevel* were in ancient Israel.

The Ms. Parma 1870 is not the only example of the change in the lute's symbolic meaning from a pagan, secular, non-Jewish musical instrument to a sound tool completely accepted in Jewish culture. In the 14th century, Spanish *Farhi-Bible*[34] we see on fol. 186v the Jerusalem Temple, with its implements, among others two trumpets, two psalteries, two horns (shofars), one ornamented neck-instrument with segetal pegs and carved animal-head (gittern), and a portative organ (**Tab. IV-1:3; Fig. IV-3**). This illumination, in an even more convincing way, confirms the acceptance of the lute-instrument as part of the Temple service. It is this presence of the lute-instruments in Biblical manuscripts that most probably paved the way for it to take its place in other, non-religious, sectors of Jewish life.

The lute, widely popular in Spain at least from the 10th century penetrated the Iberian peninsula from the southern Islamic areas in the form of an *'ud*-type instrument and became part of the Mosarabic culture. In the process of musical acculturation of the Arab-Jewish population in Spain, the lute became a symbol of biblical music for some of the Jewish communities. This is, probably, also due to the terminological and semantic chain of *kinnor-cithara* (see **Tab. IV-2**).

The change of meaning in the Hebrew illuminated manuscripts actuated and stimulated the adoption of the lute into the Spanish, French and Italian Jewish communities, and turned this instrument into a para-

---

[34] See Bezalel Narkiss, *Jewish Illustrated Manuscripts* (Jerusalem, 1969), Pl. 16, and Therese and Mendel Metzger, *Jewish Life in the Middle Ages* (New York, 1982), Pl. 395.

liturgical, or secular *klezmer*-instrument to be used at weddings, at *brit-mila* (circumcisions), and on Jewish holidays. This process manifests itself in the illustrated Hebrew manuscripts of the late 14th-17th centuries.

Not only did this development occur diachronically, but as well as geographical migration from Sephardic manuscripts (Spain, and partly Italy) to Ashkenazi manuscripts (partly Italy, and Germany) took place (see **Tab. IV-1**). In the early Sephardic manuscripts the lute still acts as a biblical instrument (see **Tab. IV-1:1** and **3**), and it is probably not until the middle of the 14th century that the use of the lute as a para-liturgical and secular instrument becomes evident in Spanish Jewish illuminations (see **Tab. IV-1:4-5**). Only from the 15th century does the lute enter the Ashkenzi art of manuscript illuminations (probably via Italy into Germany). In these illuminations the lute usually plays the role of a secular instrument **(Tab. IV-1:6-10)**.

The two Biblical manuscripts (Parma 1870, and the Farhi Bible) mentioned above, stem either from Spain, or have a strong Sephardic affiliation. Both also belong to the tradition of th earliest 13th-14th century, Hebrew, illuminated manuscripts with musical instruments, and the function of the lute as a Temple instrument representing the *kinnor* is clear in both of them. Later manuscripts confirm the above mentioned changes.

An illustration in the Golden Hagaddah **(Tab. IV-1:2; Fig. IV-4)**, shows, as far as I know, for the first time in the history of Jewish illuminated manuscripts the episode from Ex. 15:20 ("And Miriam the prophetess, the sister of Aaron, took the timbrel in her hand...."). On the upper righthand compartment of the four-section panel on folio 15r we see seven maidens, two dancing, one playing a lute, one beating cymbals, one with a round frame drum, and one the rarely depicted concussion sticks; one maiden is holding a squere object (square drum?). An illustration from another Haggadah (Kaufman Collection, A422, see **Tab. IV-1:5**; see **Fig. V-4**) depicts the same episode (Ex.15:20): three maidens are playing, respectively a lute, a portative organ, and a square drum against a background of gothic architectural elements. In both illuminations Christian influences from some Parisian, or Italo-Byzantine prototypes can not be excluded. In a para-liturgical or even secular context, the lute is for the first time shown in the Barcelona-Haggadah **(Tab. IV-1:4)** where quite clearly the Catalonian ensemble *cobla,* known from the Middle Ages (pipe and tabor, rebec, lute, bag-pipe, nakers, **Fig. IV-5**), is depicted.[35] In the Vatican *Arba'ah Turim* (a codex of Halachik rulings, written in the first half of the 14th century in four parts, see **Tab. IV 1:6**), an illumination showing a court room has a wide ornamental frame **(Fig. IV-6)** on which musicians with musical instruments – the lute **(6a)** organ **(6b)**, drum, and tabor and fidel – are depicted in a purely secular manner. Another codex of the *Arba'ah Turim* (Tab. IV 1:7) has the depiction of a wedding feast where musicians with two lutes, a harp, and a frame drum are depicted. The Rotschild Miscellany, containing over fifty religious and secular books, was the work of several different scribes and at least three different artists.[36] Among the more than 300 illuminations three are connected to musical activities: one illustrats a wedding *piyut* (para-liturgical song) with social dancing and lute music **(Tab. IV-8a)**, the other illustrates a wedding meal with *Tafelmusik* performed by a harpist and a lutist. (s. **Tab. IV-1:8b; Fig. IV-7**). The third illumination depicts a Jewish legal scribe at work, with two lutes and a harp placed on the table in front of him: perhaps, the reference of the lute here is possibly the musical and intellectual background of the scribe (**Tab. IV-1:8c; Fig. IV-8**). These attributes are clearly indicative of the aesthetic and intellectual value of lute-instruments in the Jewish community, where lute music was supposed to be mainly functional. An illustration in the Oxford Siddur (prayer book, s. **Tab. IV-1:9; see Fig. IV:9**) shows nine musicians, some of them non-Jewish, with a great variety of instruments, including two lutes (one of the lutists is the only musician, depicted with his back to the viewer, and is, as is evidenced by his hair-cut, not Jewish), a harp, a fiddle, a bag-pipe, an S-shaped trumpet, a portative organ, a shawm (possibly, some type of the Moslem oboe *zamr)*, and a duct flute (or Arab vertical flute *nay* ?). The identification of the latter two instruments is questionable; one is tempted to suggest that this illumination from an Ashkenazi Siddur depicts an ethnically mixed ensemble, which, along with its Jewish members, includes Christian and Moslem musicians. It is impossible not to notice the close parallels between the Oxford Siddur and the 1411 French Bible (British Library, Royal 19.D.iii, fol. 458; **Fig. IV-**

---

35 Snir, "Musical Instruments...", p. 51.
36 Narkiss, *Jewish Illustrated...*, p. 152.

10).³⁷ However, as close as the relationship is (the entire composition, and the placing of each musician in an ornamental frame of leafs), the differences are striking: all direct Christian images (for example, Maria with child), and musicians with certain instruments are omitted (psaltery and nakers), while other figures (the musicians with portative organ, bagpipe, and the lute player with his back turned to the audience) are added or changed.

The last three drawings are from Ashkenazi Hagaddah Manuscripts (see. **Tab. 1:10** and **11a-b**), and depict the popular topoi of the marriage of Moses and Zipporah (Exodus 2:21; see **Fig. IV-11**, and Miriam's dance (Ex. 15:20). The *jongleur*-type musicians with lute and pipe, who accompany the Biblical episodes, show the degree to which the lute was part of Jewish community life at this time. The striking difference between the interpretations both artistic and musical of the episode from Ex.15:20 in the Haggadah Nürenberg 2 and the two Spanish manuscripts is symptomatic of the Sephardic and Ashkenazi traditions.

The penetration of the lute into Jewish life is extensivly documented by written sources, including those by authorities such as Moses ibn Ezra (11th-12th cent., a contemporary of the above mentioned Abraham ibn Ezra), and Al-Harizi (12th-13th cent). The latter wrote, in praise of a certain Isaiah, master of the the *'ud*: "he stirs up the Arabic lute strings to sing...like a child in mother's lap who smiles and emits exultant shouts, not weeping....His playing over a dead body would awaken it, and the spirit of life would dwell upon it again...."³⁸ These poetic words were written at the onset of the Jewish lute art in Sephardic musical culture. It is from this time that the early archive documents on Jewish lute players appears at the Catalonian court (1392).³⁹ In the second half of the 15th century lute playing among Jews is frequently documented in Germany (e.g. *Nansse lautensleher von forfort* in Frankfurt/Main, 1470, or Mosse from Fulda, *lawtenslager genannt* from the year 1519).⁴⁰ Lute playing among Jews was probably introduced to Germany via Italy, which had

---

37 see Jeremy Montagu, *The World of Medieval & Renaissance Musical Instruments* (London, 1976), pl. VI.
38 Hanoch Avenary, "Music", in *TheEcyclopedia Judaica* (Jerusalem, 1971), vol.12, p. 598.
39 Salmen, *Jüdische Musikanten...*, p.61.
40 idem., p. 62.

famous Jewish dance teachers, such as Guglielmo da Pesaro (Guglielmo Ebreo).

We have retraced the change of the function and symbolic meaning of the lute in Jewish ideology from that of a repugnant musical instrument to an accessory of the Temple service, as is attested to by the Biblical manuscripts. This change in artistic symbolism probably influenced Jewish musical life itself to such a degree that the lute was accepted as an indispensable part of musical culture. This process occured as result of both the change of the socio-ethnic environment and the change of the organological nomenclature. It even seems likely that in this case the primary stimulus for the change of the "Platz im Leben" of the musical instrument was not the general historical development in musical culture, but, rather the effect of the change in meaning provoked by written and visual sources on the musical instrument.

A parallel process may be observed in the change of the function and meaning of the organ, the discussion of which was one of the central controversies in Jewish thought and musical life.[41] Here I will limit myself suggesting that both the lute and the organ are musical instruments that have changed their functions and meanings in the Jewish musical world as a result of change in meanings and symbolism in the visual arts. This phenomenon of Jewish music culture – changes in musical reality resulting from changes in visual and later written sources – is probably unique for music history.

---

[41] The change in Jewish thought and musical life of the organ is discussed in the next Ch. V, pp. 143-155.

Nr.	Subject	Index	Folio	Provenance	Chronology	Topos
1a.	Psalms	Parma-1870	6v	Central Italy/ Spanish infl.	about 1300	Ps. 6; lute/'ud(?) in front of an animal image
1b.	Psalms	Parma-1870	41v	" "	" "	Ps. 33; gittern hold by two jongleurs(?)
1c.	Psalms	Parma-1870	89r	" "	" "	Ps. 67; lute/'ud and psaltery played by two animal images
1d.	Psalms	Parma-1870	105r	" "	" "	Ps. 76; Temple instruments – fidel (played), two gitterns, lute, psaltery
1e.	Psalms	Parma-1870	198r	" "	" "	Ps. 137; two lutes hanging on tree
2.	Haggadah, the Golden	BL-Add. 27210	15r	Spain, Barcelona	c.1320	Miriam with maidens dance, play a lute, beat cymbals, a drum, etc.
3.	Bible	Sassoon Coll., Ms. 1, 368 (6), Jerusalem	186r	Spain	1366-1382	Temple instruments: 2 trompets, 2 shofars, psaltery, gittern, fidel(?), organ
4.	Haggadah-Barcelona	BL-Add. 14761	61r	Spain	late 14. c.	Pessach orchestra: pipe and tabor, rebec, lute, bagpipe, neckers
5.	Haggadah	Kaufmann-A422 Budapest	3v	Spain	late 14. c.	Miriam with maidens dancing; musicians with drum, lute and organ
6	Arba'ah Turim	Vat. Libr. Cod. Rossiana-555	292/ 293	North Italy	1435	court scene; border show musicians, among others with lute and organ
7	Arba'ah Turim	Seminario Vescovile, Vercelli	13v	North Italy	15.c.	wedding feast; musicians with two lutes, harp, and frame drum
8a.	Miscellany	Israel Museum Rotschild-24	246r	Italy	1450-1470	Threni; three couples dancing to lute music
8b..	Miscellany	Rotschild-24	322v	Italy	" ".	wedding meal with harpist and lutist
8c.	Miscellany	Rotschild-24	446v	Italy	" "	scribe at table with two lutes
9.	Siddur	Bodleian Library Ms. Opp. 776	79v	Germany	15. c.	folk musicians, among others with lute and organ
10.	Haggadah Yahydda	IMJ-180/50	11r	Germany	15. c.	marriage of Moses and Zipporah; jongleurs with lute and pipe

| 11a | Hagaddah Nürenberg2 | Schocken Institute, Ms. 24087, vol. 1 | 12v | Germany | 15. c. | marriage of Moses and Zipporah; jongleur with lute |
| 11b | Haggadah Nürenberg2 | idem, vol. 2 | 22r | Germany | 15. c. | Miriam with maidens dancing; one lutist |

Table IV-1: Hebrew Manuscripts with Depictions of Lute-Instruments and Organ (13th-15th Cent.)

KINOR *kithara/kinira*; lyre	NEVEL *psalterion*; harp	CENTURY 2nd-3ed	SOURCE Septuaginta
cithara; lyre	*psalterium*; harp	4th-5th	Vulgata
cythara, lute-type	*psalterio*, harp	9th	Utrecht Psalter
cithara; lute-type	- -	10th	Stuttagart Psalter
cithara; harp	*psalterium di deca cor-dum*, triangular zither	12th	Hortus deliciarum
giga	viella	13th	Lambet Palace, Ms 435,f. 131v
cythara anglica, harp	*psalterium*; zither	12th-13th	Anonymus, in Gerbert "De cant.."
kinor; lute	*nevel*; zither	about 1300	Ms. Parma 1870
cithara, harp	psalterio, zither	early 14th	Nicholas Trivet, comm. on Ps. 150;
cithara; pillar-harp	*psalterio*, zither	13th/14th	Petrus de Palude

The term in the written source – *in italics*; the modern meaning of written term confirmed by iconographical image – underlined; the modern meaning of the written, or iconographical source cofirmed by context or research – in regular fonts.[42]

Table IV-2: Name and Meaning of the Biblical Kinor *and* Nevel *in the 13th-15th Cent.*

---

[42] for details on the sources of Table 2, see Hortense Panum, *The Stringed Instruments of the Middle Ages* (New York, De Capo 1971); ; Chrostopher Page , *Early 15th-century instruments in Jean de gerson's...*, in Early Music, 6 (1978), 339-49; Emanuel Winternitz, "The Survival of the Kithara...", in idem., *Musical Instruments and their Symbolism in Western Art* (London, 1967), pp. 57-65.

V. The Iconography of the Organ: Change in Jewish Though and Musical Life[*]

The organ and the lute – two musical instruments with negative associations in Jewish history of music, mainly due to their strong pagan, secular (the lute) and Christian (the organ) affiliations – exemplify the processes of change in Jewish musical thought and practice. Since I have discussed the case of the lute in detail at another place,[1] we will concentrate here on the organ, a musical instrument for many centuries much disputed in Jewish-Christian religious circles.[2] Let us take a short look at the transformation in the meaning and semantics of the instrument from its invention in the Hellenistic time (Egypt, middle of 3ed cent. B. C.) to the time of the Jewish Emancipation in Europe (18th cent.), and examine the part which iconography played in this process.

Some time ago the *Freiburger Rundbriefe* (1998:4) published an article on the organ in Jewish synagogues of the 19th century by the noted musicologist Walter Salmen. This latest informative contribution to the history of this instrument in Jewish musical life, reflects two stereotypes in the discussion of the subject: (a) the organ was probably used in the Jerusalem Temple, and (b) in European Jewish communities the history of the organ did not start before the eighteenh century. Both conclusions are misleading. The history of the organ in Jewish culture and Jewish thought, being a highly perplexed problem, appears to be a "musical" reflection of Jewish intercultural acculturation.

The term '*ugav*, which in contemporary Hebrew denotes the organ, appears four times in the Old Testament: in the mythological story of Gen. 4:21, as instrument of the godless (Job. 21:12), metaphorically as "voice of mourners" (Job. 30:31), and in the doxology of the Ps. 150:4.

---

[*] Published in: *Music in Art*, 27:55-69 (2004)
[1] J. Braun, "The Lute and Organ in Ancient Israel and Jewish Iconography," in: Ed. A. Beer et al., *Festschrift Christoph-Hellmut Mahling zum 65. Geburtstag*, vol. 1 (Tutzing, 1997), pp. 163-188.
[2] For a concise summary of the problem see Eric Werner, *A Voice Still Heard...* (University Park/London, 1976), pp. 116 and 195-8.

The root of the word '*ugav* points to the Hebrew-Arabic '*agava* (sensuality, lust, lasciviousness, comp. Ezekiel 23:5). In the apocryphal Ps. 151 (probably, 1st cent.) an image of an orpheic-Christian David appears as builder of musical instruments and here chronologically the interpretation of the '*ugav* (in the Hebrew version) as organ is a possibility.

The word '*ugav* is rendered inconsistently already in the Septuaginta: *kithara* (Gen. 4:21) and *psalmos* (Job 21:12, 30:31) may be interpreted as string instruments, and *organon* (Ps. 150:4) could be a wind instrument or just any instrument whatsoever. The Peshitta (Syriac translation of the Bible, 1st-2nd century) follows the translation of the Septuaginta; the Targum (Aramaic translation, 2nd–7th century), however, consequently translates '*ugav* as *abbuba* (the pipes of the Roman *ambubaiae*-girls, musician-harlots), and in the Vulgata it is *organum* consistently all four times. While in the Targum clearly is meant a mono- or double-pipe read-instrument, the interpretation of the Vulgata is uncertain: at the time when Jerome translated the Hebrew Bible (ca. 347-420), *organum* may have meant both a music instrument in general or an organ.[3] Jerome's contemporary St. Augustin (early 5th cent.) gives us the following comments on the understanding of the word *organum*: "*Organum* is the general term used of all musical instruments, although nowadays it is customary to apply the word *organum* to those which operate by bellows..."[4]

It is quite obvious that the translators of the Biblical text were not familiar with the real meaning of the word '*ugav*, which probably was lost long before. We also can not avoid the feeling of a camouflaged repugnance – probably because of its amorous affiliation – towards the mentioned instrument by both the writers of the original text and the translators. Contemporary musicology interprets the Biblical '*ugav* as a flute-

---

3   For the interpretation of the music instruments, see Joachim Braun, *Music in Ancient Israel/Palestine* (Gran Rapids, Mass./Cambridge, UK, 2002), pp. 12-32. The Gr. term "*organon*" is used in the Septuaginta for the translation of the Hebrew "*kinnor*" (Ps. 137:2), "*nebel*" (Amos 5:23 and 6:5) and the appelative "*kle shir*" (verbatim "instrument of singing" in 1Chr. 15:16; 16:5, and five times in 2Chr.); the Vulgata used "*organum*" for "*kinnor*" (Ps. 137:2), "*ugav*" (Gen. 4:21, Ps.150:4, Job 21:12 and 30:31), and seven times for "*klei shir*", similar to the Septuaginta.

4   James McKinnon, *Music in Early Christian Literature. Cabridge* Readings in the Literature of Music (Cambridge, Cambridge University Press, 1987), p. 160.

type instrument – the etymology and love-symbolism, similar to all ancient and contemporary Near Eastern flute instruments, suggests a *ma't* (Egypt), or *næy* (Israel/Palestine, Turkey) type instrument.[5]

Although sources are not unambiguous, we may suggest that the identification of the Biblical '*ugav* with the organ transpired at the time of the completion of the Talmud (4th-6th cent.). In the treatises TB Arakhin 10b and TJ Sukkah 55c we find the terms *ardablis, hardavlis, hardolism,* – all distorted forms of the Greek *hydraulus,* – water organ[6]. In the TJ (Sukkah 55c) it says unequivocally: "Rabbi Simeon ben Lakish said: '*ugav* – is an *ardablis*". And Rabbi Shimon ben Gamliel adds to the same passage that there was not such an instrument in the Temple, because its sound "disturbed the melody" (TB Arakhin 10b, TJ Sukkah 55c). There is also no Greek or other evidence of an organ in the Temple or on the territory of Israel/Palestine. We believe in this *argumentum ex silentio*: such an unusual instrument as the organ certainly would be noticed and broadly attested by the Greek-Roman writers, as was the organ somewhat north, in Syria (see below). Jewish sources of this period, however, never display an outspoken repugnance towards the organ, and we have to note, that the unsuitability of this instrument for the Temple service was thought to be of a purely aesthetic nature

In the Mischnah (2nd cent) and somewhat later in the Talmud is mentioned another sound tool – the *magrephah*. Rabbi bar Shila claimed that "there was a *magrephah* in the Temple" (TJ Arakhin 10b). The descriptions of this tool and its functions in the Talmud are quite confusing and contradictory, and later years brought about different interpretations[7]. Rashi (1040-1105), the great commentator of the Talmud, and some later authorities stressed three main functions of the *magrephah*: to sweep together the ashes from the altar after burning the offerings (Hebr. *garaph*, to scoop up); to produce a strong alarm sound for the priests by hurling

---

5 Curt Sachs, *History of Musical Instruments* (New York, 1940), p. 106.
6 At this time the commonly accepted word *hydraulicum* was frequently used also for the bellow organ (2MGG, 7:918).
7 Among the most popular Talmud passages which mention the *magrephah*, are the stories about its 100 holes with ten sounds from each, or ten holes with 100 sounds from each (TJ Sukkah 55c; TB Arakhin 10b-11a), and the story on the possibility to hear its sound in Jericho, which is some 30 km from the Jerusalem Temple (M Tamid 3,8). Some sources mention the shovel form of the *magrephah* (idem.).

the instrument, and to produce musical sounds similar to the *hydraulis*[8]. The well-known Renaissance scholar Abraham Portaleone (1542-1612, Mantua), was probably the first to claim that this instrument had pipes.[9] The discussions on the *magrephah* went on till the second half of the 20th century, without reaching any definitive opinion.[10] The musicologist and expert in Jewish studies Joseph Yasser claimed in the 1960s that the *magrephah* was not a musical instrument in the modern sense, and even less so an organ, but in older times (2nd-1st cent. B. C.) was a shovel to scoop away the ashes of the burned offerings, and later (1st century BC – 1st century CA) a shovel-shaped sound tool.[11] Yasser suggests, that, build possibly by some of the famous Alexandria craftsman, who used to be invited to Jerusalem for sound tool repairs (TB Arakhin 10b) its strong siren-like sound of uncontrolled pitch was activated by a stream of air and a number of pipes. This ritual sounding may have served as symbolic remainder of the impending judgment of God.

Be this as it may, we have good reasons to claim that during the pre-Christian and first Christian centuries the Jewish communities were acquainted with both – some kind of a Temple sound tool (*magrephah*) and the hydraulic or pneumatic organ. The last one is attested also by archaeological finds: on the territory of ancient Palestine a group of terracotta oil-lamps were discovered, which have on their front relief depictions of a framed row of seven organ pipes and two pairs of *crotala*. The artifacts are dated into the 3ed-4th century and attributed to the Samaritan culture (**Fig. V-1**).[12] Thus, a Roman Palestine community, in constant and close contact with the Jewish population (and sharing a related religion),

---

8   Alfred Sendrey, *Music in Ancient Israel* (New York, 1969), p. 397.
9   Israel Adler, ed., *Hebrew Writings Concerning Music* (=RISM BIX/2, Munich, 1975), pp. 259-60, Ms. 570, VI/6-42.
10 Even such distinguished scholars as Curt Sachs wrote that the *magrepha* is an organ, and was used in the Temple (Sachs, *History...*, p. 124).
11 Joseph Yasser, "The *Magrephah* of the Herodian Temple: A Five-Fold Hypothesis", in: *Journal of the American Musicological Society*, 13/1-3 (1960), 24-42; see also *Encyclopedia Judaica* (Jerusalem, 1971), vol. 12, p. 566.
12 Varda Susmann, "Samaritan Lamps of the Third-Fourth Century AD", in: *Israel Exploration Journal*, 28/4 (1978), 238-50. Unfortunately, the iconography of the oil-lamps was interpreted by archaeologist as depicting lyres, which for years confused the correct interpretation (see also Braun, *Music...*, pp. 238-9, ch. V/6).

was well acquainted with the organ, depicted this instrument as Temple implement, and, possibly, used it also for liturgical purpose. Another use of the organ in this Near Eastern area was documented in Hama (Syria), some 200 km north from Samaria, where a most remarkable mosaic from the 3ed century shows its use in everyday music-making. The mosaic depicts a group of female performers with musical instruments and among them an organ player (**Fig. V-2**).[13] Compared to the known third-century organ iconography, this instrument has remarkably developed features.[14]

Already from the time of the Mishnah (1st-2nd cent.) music in general and instrumental, particularly, was rejected by the Jewish clergy. Singing "ceased after the Sanhedrin," and the *erous* (wedding drum or bell) was forbidden (Sotah 9,11 and 14). Some two centuries later, in the Talmud, the language changed fiercely: "The ear which listens to song should be torn off" and "Rabba said: when there is song in the house there is destruction on its threshold" (TB Sotah 48a). Rabbi Johanan warns in the same passage with reference to Jesaja 5:11: *kinnor, nebel, toph, halil* and wine makes you forget God (TB Sotah 48a-b). Especially strong is the censure of women's singing: "Samuel said: the women's voice is unchaste, sexual incitement" (TB Berakhot 24a).

The prohibition of music and, in particular, of the organ by the Church Fathers was not less severe. In this case, from the beginning on this was not for aesthetic reasons, but rather because of the enticement of musical instruments. In this regard the depraving effect of the *organa* (the organ, or musical instruments in general) was stressed, especially for women: in his Epistle to Ps. CVII Jerome warns: "Let her be deaf to *organa*, let her not know why the *tibia*, lyre and *cithara* are made"[15].

Regardless of this, history went its own way. The situation is best described by Jean Perrot: "...we may never know the truth of the matter, since at present there is no known official text among the pontifical archives which authorizes the use of the instrument in church."[16] And there was good reason for it: although considering all instrumental music as

---

13 Abdul Rizaq Zaqzyq and Marcelle Duchesne-Gullemin, La mosaique de Mariamin, in: *Annales Arabes Syriennes*, XX/1 (1970), pp. 93-125, Pl. 1/2.
14 See Jean Perrot, *The Organ from its Invention in the Hellenistic Period to the End of the Thirteenth Century* (London, 1971), Pl. III/2, IV, VI, VIII, XIV etc.
15 McKinnon, *Music in Early...*, No. 324.
16 Perrot, *The Organ...*, pp. 218-219.

suspicios, the clergy turned a blind eye when the small portable organ was used at the service to accompany the singing of the faithful. In the 11th to 13th centuries a dual attitude to the organ was apparent. While the Sinode of Milano in 1287 declared organ music an important part of the service, the General Chapter of Ferrara (1290) ruled a strong *prohibitio* of the instrument.[17] Many clerics, however, "succumbed to the charm of the new instrument and were attracted by its sustained sound, which was to some extent religious in character... And so the organ, though never officially acknowledged in the pontifical decrees, and tolerated rather than accepted by the hierarchy, gradually established itself until, by the fourteenth century, it was the established servant of Christian worship".[18]

A similar process took place in Jewish thought. There is no known written text, or rabbinical *p'saq halaha* (rabbinical ruling), which did forbid or denounce the use of organ in a more severe way then any other musical instrument. A classical rabbinical sentence, the *Responsum* by Hayya ben Šerira (939-1038, Ga'on of Pumbedita, Babylonia), is one of the basic preserved documents on music of the post-Talmudic literature. Ben Šerira's answer to an inquiry from Tunisia whether music is allowed at weddings ("here, at the houses of the bridegroom and the bride it is the custom to play the drum and dance, and *goyim* (gentiles) are brought in with *nebel* and *kinnor* and *'ugav* to be merry"),[19] contains a permission for songs and laudations in honor of God and on occasions such as weddings, but strictly prohibits love songs, such as the Arab "songs of love". As regards instruments, only drums with dance are permitted and only at pure women's gatherings, while all instruments such as *"nebalim* and *kinnorot* and instruments which have strings and *'ugavim* and *halilim"* also here should be avoided, because "a prostitute is she who will use them"[20]. We can not be sure that in this context the word *'ugav* denotes the organ, although this should be quite probable considering the date of the document, the affiliation of the instruments with non-Jewish musicians and the clear reference to a wind instrument.

---

17 Grove 2001, 7:919.
18 Perrot, *The Organ*..., pp. 219.
19 Adler, *Hebrew Writings*..., p. 144.
20 idem, p. 145.

From now on Jewish habits changed rapidly. Quite a number of texts from the 12th to 14th century are preserved, which deal with the importance of music – both vocal and instrumental – in Judaism, while the attitude to the *'ugav* is ambivalent. Joseph b. Jehuda ibn 'Aqnin (Spain, ca. 1150-1220), for example, mentions in a positive way the "*'ugav* with cymbals"[21] (the typical ensemble of the late Middle Ages and Renaissance), while Moses ibn Ezra (Spain, ca. 1055-1135) reminds his readers of the relationship of the instrument to the "*šir 'ugavim*" (love songs, see Ezechiel 23:5 and 32), and he warns also from the *haṣoṣerah* (trumpet), *toph* (drum) and *halil* (pipe).[22] The greatest Jewish authority of this time Moses ben Maimonides (Cordova, 1135-Egypt, 1204) in his *Responsum* on music surprisingly does not mention the *'ugav* at all.

The very beginning of the process which may be designated as full legitimization of the organ can be traced back to iconography sources of the late 13th–early 14th century. A representation of the Talmudic *magrephah* appears for the first time in Hebrew sources as an illustration in the famous Second Kennicot Bible (Bodleian Library, Kenn. 2, **Fig. V-3**).[23] Painted and written by one of the most prominent Jewish scholars and manuscript authors Joshua ibn Ga'on (or his scribes) in 1306 in Soria (Spain), the manuscript presents on fol. 1v and 2r a detailed Temple plan, signed by Joshua himself. At the upper right corner of fol. 1v a fantasy drawing, accompanied by the inscription *magrephah* may be seen: a guitar-shaped body with a short, wide neck, ending in a double-faced eagle[24]. Three lines (strings?) are drawn across the body, ten round holes are placed on each side of the lines and the borders of the upper part are studded with dots.

Jewish writers, such as Ibn 'Aqnin (12th-13th century)[25], who mention the *magrephah*, refer to the above quoted Talmud passages on the number of pipes (TJ Sukkah 55c and TB Arakhin 10c/11a), and identify the instrument as some kind of musical instrument, possibly organ. In Arabic

---

21 idem, p. 157.
22 idem, p. 163.
23 Bezalel Narkiss, *Hebrew Illuminated Manuscripts in the British Isles* (New York, 1982), vol. I/1, pp. 24-30, and vol. I/2, Pl.III-IV (drawing).
24 See also, idem., p. 26.
25 *Hebrew Writings...*, pp. 158.

sources of the 11th-12th century[26], however, there are also interpretations of the *magrephah* as string instrument which could explain the presence of strings on the Kennicot instrument. Joshua ibn Ga'on seemed to strive in his drawing for all at his time existing interpretations of the *magrepha* – as a wind instrument (organ), a string instrument (*ma'azif* type), and an instrument in the form of a shovel (see footnote 7). Nevertheless, there is not the slightest organological or any other reason to see this drawing as anything but a fantasy, grown out of the Talmudic passages and oral traditions about the *magrepha*. It is for certain that Joshua ibn Ga'on did regard the *magrephah* as a musical instrument, but it is as well certain that he did not have the slightest idea what kind of musical instrument the *magrephah* was.

Starting with the 13th century several Christian manuscripts depict the image of King David as organ player (Belvoir Castle Psalter, Solomon Glossary) and he is even called *organista*.[27] This Christian David-iconography and the *Kennicot Bible*, produced by a great Jewish authority, probably stimulated a century or so later the penetration of the organ into Hebrew manuscript illuminations. The oldest and best example is the Farhi Bible (Spain, 1366-1382; see **Tab. V-1:1**; see **Fig. IV-3**): the illustration on fol. 186v under the heading *m'y klei šir b'mah š'haju mešorerim haleviim* (Hebr., some musical instruments which were played by the Levites) shows at the bottom the Jerusalem Temple and above it two trumpets with the inscription *haṣoṣerot*. In the center there is a large vessel (the "jar of manna"), surrounded by two shofars, two lutes, two psalteries and a portative organ. The last has eight pipes and some kind of pneumatic arrangement consisting of bellows and a tube.

This almost official acceptance of the organ as a Temple instrument, similar to the lute[28], made it possible for the organ to be reproduced in many other manuscripts. From the middle 14th-15th century the depictions of organs appear at least in three other manuscripts – first in a Sephardic, and after several decades in two Ashkenazi manuscripts (s. **Tab. V-1: 2, 3 and 4**). In the Spanish manuscripts the organ is depicted only as Temple

---

26 Amnon Shiloah, ed., *The Theology of Music in Arabic Writings* (RISM BX, Munich, 1979), p. 25. To my best knowledge no explanation for this interpretation was ever presented and in my opinion it is based on a misunderstanding.
27 Perrot, *The Organ...*, Pl. XXVII:2 and XXVIII: 2.
28 Braun, The Lute....

implement and in a Biblical context, while in the Ashkenazi paintings a secular approach to the instrument is evident.

An illustration in the Kaufmann *Haggadah* (Spain, late 14th cent., **Tab. V-1:2; Fig. V-4**) shows a group of women: three females with drum, lute and organ and eight maidens under them, depicted not in dance movement as the tradition of this topos requires, but rather as a choir. The organ, a portative one with seven or eight pipes, probably in two ranks, has a drone-pipe, nearly twice as long as the shortest pipe, which indicates a rather low sound of the drone (a similar instrument is depicted on the Belvoir Castle Psalter[29]). The organ player is shown at the performance, actually pressing the organ keys.

In the Vatican *Arba'ah Turim* (a codex of *halahik* rulings, first half of the 14th century, North Italy, **Table 1:3, Fig. IV-6b**), on the wide frame of an illuminated page an organ player is depicted at the lower left corner of the frame while at the other bends appear musicians with a fiddle, *shawm* and lute (see **Fig. IV-6**). All musicians are depicted in a pure secular manner. Another illustration in the Oxford *Siddur* (prayer book, early 15th century, Germany, **Table 1:4**, see **Fig. IV-9**) shows a musician with a portative organ among a group of musicians with a variety of instruments (lute, harp, fiddle, fiddle, bag-pipe, S-shape trumpet, shawm, vertical flute). The iconographical aspects of this illumination and its possible relationship to the drawing from the French Bible from 1411 (British Library, Royal 19.D.iii, fol. 458, see **Fig. IV-10**)[30] are discussed in relation to the lute.[31] It seems quite possible, that the basic elements of the illumination were applied from one manuscript to the other.

It is this presence of the organ in Biblical manuscripts, that paved the way for the instrument to be accepted into some synagogues, paraliturgical literature and extra-religious levels of Jewish social life.

The organ, similarly to the lute, migrated, from West to East Europe, from the Sephardic to the Ashkenazi communities, and, as in the case of the lute, first of all appears in the iconography of the Holy Scripture and religious literature, and only somewhat later, as result of the written af-

---

29 Perrot, *The Organ...*, p. 282.
30 see Jeremy Montagu, *The World of Medieval & Renaissance Musical Instruments* (London, 1976), pl. VI.
31 See Ch. IV, pp. 138-139.

firmation, "purified" and as Temple implement even "sanctified", the organ enters Jewish musical life.

Towards the second half of the 15th century intellectuals and partly the leadership of the European Jewish community accepted the organ as eligible musical instrument of high artistic esteem. Acknowledged as Temple instrument in Jewish art, and merged with the concept of the ancient Levite music's elite nature, Jewish Rabbis and scholars, such as Ibn Sahula (13th cent.), Anonymous Milan (15th cent.), Jacob Farissol (early 15th cent.), Judah ben Samuel Archivolti (1515-1611)[32] came to consider the organ as a suitable, in fact preferable musical instrument. The Jewish-Italian philosopher and biblical exegete Joahanan Allemanno (15th cent.) wrote in a most enraptured manner about the performance of a blind organist from Germany at the Mantua court (ca 1470), the famous Konrad Paumann[33]. A century later, also in Mantua, the prominent Rabbi, preacher and scholar Judah ben Joseph Moscato (1530-1590)[34] discusses the theological aspects of music in one of his sermons: men wer created according to musical proportions; the Biblical *kinnor*, interpreted by Moscato as organ, is compared to the human soul and affiliated to King David's "spiritual *kinnor*" (=organ). Just as the *kinnor* (=organ) player has to master his art to obtain perfect harmony, so the human soul has to act in accordance with the laws of harmony.[35]

This way of thinking was developed by the Venice Rabbi and scholar Leon Modena (1571-1648), who in the early 17th century introduced choral chant and musical instruments in the synagogue[36]. The Modena Rabbi Abraham Solomon Graziani (d. 1684) permitted in the middle of the 17th century the use of the organ in the synagogue.[37]

The reforms of the rabbis came to meet the requirements of the Italian Jewish communities, their musical taste and social behavior. In this context the testimony by Giulio Marosini (former Samuel Nahmias /1612-

---

32 *Hebrew Writings...*, No.No. 360, 120, 260, 180.
33 Hanoch Avenary, "Ein hebraeisches Zeugnis fuer den Aufenthalt Konrad Paumanns in Mantua (1470), in: *Die Musikforschung*, 16 (1963), pp. 156-7.
34 See Herzel Schmueli, *Betrachtung zum Leierspiel des Jehudah Moscato* (Ph. D. Univ. Zuerich) Tel-Aviv, 1953.
35 *Hebrew Writings...*, No. 530.
36 *Hebrew Writings...*, No.No. 520 and 530.
37 Sendrey, *The Music...*, p. 272.

1683/, a converted Jew) is quiet indicative; in his memoires he recalls his visit at a Venice synagogue in the year 1628: "Tra gl'instrumenti fù portatio in inagoga anche l'Organo, il qual però non fù permesso da I Rabbini, che si sonasse per essere instrumento che par ordinario si suona nelle nostre chiese. Ma che? Tutto qusto fù un fuoco di paglai, durò poco l'Accademia..."[38].

In the next century changes in the attitude to the organ occur as well in some other European Jewish communities. Johann Jacob Schudt in his *Jüdische Merckwürdigkeiten* (Frankfurt/Leipzig, 1714), for example, tells us about "Amsterdam...Jews (who) quite frequently visited churches to enjoy for hours organ music."[39]

The first evidence on the presence of the organ in a Prague synagogue is as early as from the year 1494, and it is again an iconographical source: the illustration from the Lobkovitz Prayer Book, 1494 (**Fig. V-5**)[40]. The drawing shows an organ in a Prague synagogue, which, surprisingly, is depicted here together with *neqqara* (small kettle drums) and a *Rauschpfeife* – a rare ensemble, indeed.

In the oldest synagogue of Prague – the Pinkas synagogue – build at the end of the 13th century, according to some sources, a portative organ was used already before the fire of 1689 and rebuilt after it.[41] In the *Altneue Synagoge* in Prague the organ was played at least from 1714, although only "for the Friday-Night Shabbat-welcoming prayer."[42] Organ music was part of Jewish festivities and ceremonies, as for example, in 1678 at a procession of the Jews of Prague in honor of the coronation of the Emperor Leopold I of Austria, or the *Freuden-Fest* on the occasion of the birth of the Crown-Prince in 1716 in Frankfurte, where the organs were carried by two boys in front of the Torah.[43]

Recalling the first depiction of the organ with *crotalum* on Samaritan clay oil lamps, it is not without surprise that we find the tradition of this ensemble not only in the late Renaissance, but also in 18th century Pra-

---

38 Quoted from Israel Adler, *La pratique musicale savante* (Paris, 1966), p. 65.
39 Johann Jacob Schudt, *Juedische Merckwuerdigkeiten* (Frankfurt/Leipzig, 1714), New edition by L. Lamm (Berlin 1922), Part II, Book VI, pp. 284-285.
40 Klementinium-Universitni Knihovna, Prague, Ms. XXIII F202.
41 Sendrey, *The Music...*, p. 340.
42 Schudt, *Juedische...*, Part I, Book IV, p. 218.
43 Schudt, *Juedische...*, Part IV, Continuation III (Farnkfurt am Main, 1717, p. 147).

gue. The information stems again from memoirs of a traveler – d'Abraham Levi (Ben Menahem Tall), who visited Prague between 1718 and 1724. In a synagogue, on a Sabbat day he listened to the performance of *Orgelpfeifen* with the accompaniment of *klappen-zymbels* or *klappcymbels*.[44] We can without hesitation claim that the first is an organ and the *klappencymbels* are just cymbals or *crotalum* (forked cymbals), rather than "tympanons" or "clavicymbals" as thought by some modern musicologists. The profession of a "klapzymbalist" was known in the early Prague Jewish community, as attested by epitaphs from 1636 at the old Prague cemetery [45]. We may suppose that this name was used for Jewish musicians/*klezmorim* in general and not only for cymbal players.

In the next centuries, with the Jewish Reform movement, the organ became a widely used instrument in the reformed synagogue. This, however, is a new chapter in the history of Jewish musical culture.

I will limit myself here to the suggestion that the organ, similar to the lute, is a musical instrument that has changed its function, meaning and symbolism in Jewish musical thought and musical reality as result of change or rather misinterpretation in Jewish visual arts. It seems tat the prohibition in Christian communities was dictated by theological-practical reasons and the permission accepted by esthetical considerations; in the Jewish world it was the theological aspect which ruled both prohibition and acceptance while the change was provoked by extra-musical factors. We witness here a unique phenomenon of musical culture – change in visual sources followed by change in theological writings and as result changes in musical life.

---

44 See Abraham Zvi Idelsohn, "Songs and Singers of the Eighteenth Century", in: *Hebrew Union College Annual*, Jubilee volume (1925), p. 403; see also Adler, *La pratique...*, p. 28; Werner, *A Voice...*, pp. 116 and 307
45 See Leopold and Moritz Popper, *Die Inschriften der alten Prager Judenfriedhöfe* (Braunschweig, 1893).

N	*MS.*	INDEX	FOL.	PLACE	*DATE*	TOPOS
1	Farhi Bible	Sassoon Coll., Ms. 1, 368 (6), Jerusalem	186r	Spain	1366-1382	Temple Instruments: 2 trumpets, 2 shofars, psaltery, gittern, fidel (?), **organ**
2	Haggadah	Kaufmann Coll., A422, Budapest	3v	Spain	Late 14th cent.	**Miriam with maidens:** drum, lute, **organ**
3	Arba'ah Turim	Vat. Lib., Cod. Rossiana-555	292/293	N. Italy	1435	Court scene: amomg others lute and **organ**
4	Siddur	Bodleian Lib., Opp. 776	79v	Germany	Early 15th cent.	Folk musicians (?): among others lute and **organ**

IAA – Israel Antiquity Authority
All FIGURES are published by courtesy of the indicated owners of the manuscripts and archaeological item.

Table V-1: *Sources of Organ Iconography in Hewbrew Manuscripts*

The Diaspora:
East Europe – Russia – Soviet Union

VI. The Unpublished Volumes of Moshe Beregovski's Jewish Musical Folklor*

The life and work of Moshe Beregovski, a unique personality in twentieth-century ethnomusicology, has not yet been studied sufficiently. A great part of his research was never published, while the published work was until recently hardly known even in professional circles. Because of this, Beregovski's contribution to the study of Jewish music was not evaluated in full. It is the purpose of this article to discuss the unpublished volumes of Beregovski's *Jewish Musical Folklore,* and point to some research perspectives of this material.

Born in 1892 near Kiev, Beregovski was brought up in a Jewish atmosphere. His father was a *melamed,* and according to Beregovski's own words, he was "singing at different synagogue choirs, where I acquired the basics of music theory and solfeggio."[1] He studied with the finest teachers of his time at the Kiev and Petrodgrad conservatories. These included Boleslav Yavorsky (1877-1942), one of Russia's great musicologists, who contributed largely to a more profound understanding of the modern concept of modality, but who was ignored in the Soviet Union after the 1920s. Beregovski's special interest in the ethos of Jewish modes, probably echos his experience with Yavorsky.[2] Beregovski taught at Jewish institutions of learning established during the first years of Soviet rule, and from 1927 worked at Jewish folklore institutions affiliated

---

* Published in: *Israel Studies in Musicology* IV, 1987:125-143., first presented at the Ninth World Congress of Jewish Studies, Jerusalem 1985.
1 Joachim Braun, "The Autobiography of Moshe Bereovski," *Tatzlil,* 19/10 (1979), p. 159.
2 Beregovski's interest in the hermeneutics of modes is apparent in most of his writings; see especially "Izmenennyi doriiskii lad v evreiskom muzikal'nom fol'klore: k voprosu o semanticheskikh svoistvakh lada" (in Russian, The altered dorian mode in Jewish folklore: on the question of the semantic features of the modes), I. I. Zemtcvkii, ed., *Problemy muzikal'novo fol'klora narodov SSSR* (The problems of music flklre of the people of the USSR), Moscow, 1973, pp. 367-382. English translation in Mark Slobin, ed. *Old Jewish Folk Music: The Collections of Writings of Moshe Beregovski* (Philadelphia, 1982), pp. 549-567.

with the Academy of Sciences of the Ukranian USSR. Here he came into close contact with another neglected scholar, the ethnomusicologist Klement Kvitka (1880-1953), whose influence on Beregovski was recently pointed out by Mark Slobin.[3] Until the last days of his life Beregovski seemingly believed in the dream of a Jewish culture in a socialistic multinational state. In 1948-51, however, Beregovski witnessed the total destruction of Jewish culture in the USSR and the ruin of his own work. (His unique collection of Jewish musical folklore at the Academy vanished, and has never been recovered). From 1951 until 1955 he was imprisoned for anti-Soviet activities. It seems that after these events, Beregovski took steps to preserve his work and sent some of his manuscripts outside Moscow and Kiev. Until his death in 1961 he continued to make corrections and additions to his unpublished works.

Beregovski's main opus, the work of his lifetime was his five-volume *Evreiskii muzykal'nyi fol'klor (Jewish Musical Folklore,* further *JMF),* an anthology of Jewish folk-songs and instrumental tunes selected from the huge Sound Archives at the Cabinet for the Studies of Jewish Literature, Language and Folklore of the Academy of Sciences of the Ukranian USSR (closed in 1948). Each volume was accompanied by an extensive analytical study and broad critical apparatus. Besides this monumental work, Beregovski wrote some thirty articles on a wide range of musical subjects covering questions of autonomous Jewish musical education and Jewish ethnomusicology, as well as problems of cultural interchange and musical semantics.

During Beregovski's life only a small part of his work was published. The main body of his research remained in manuscript. In 1934, the first volume of the *JMF*[4] appeared – 140 folksongs (more than half of them "revolutionary songs", the rest *bytovie pesni,* Russ. – "everyday songs"), an "Introduction", and information on the recorded items. This volume contained the most blunt political attacks on other musicologists written by Beregovski and it may be that because of this the musicological world was reluctant to accept his later work.

---

3   Slobin, *Old Jewish Folk Music.* pp. 5-8.
4   Moysei (Moshe) Beregovski, *Evreiskii muzykal'nyi fol'klor* (in Russian, Jewish musical folklore), Vol. 1, Moscow, 1934 (Engl. tr. Slobin, *Old Jewish Folk Music,* pp. 19-284).

After this volume, however, political polemics became less frequent. His later publications, in particular those dealing with questions of interchange between Jewish and non-Jewish folk music,[5] or studies on *klezmer* music[6] are most significant without any concessions to the peculiar conditions of Beregovski's life.

Two Beregovski studies were published posthumously: a major book containing 150 folk songs and instrumental tunes,[7] and a most valuable article on the ethos of the altered Dorian mode in Jewish music.[8] These works may be considered cornerstones of studies in East European Jewish music culture. The Bcregovski volume recently published in the United States incorporates the English translation of his two books and three articles,[9] and is a clear acknowledgement of Beregovski's achievements. The editor of this volume, Mark Slobin, refers to the author as a "significant but neglected ethnomusicologist of his day."[10]

A great part of Beregovski's work, however, remains unpublished. I refer here to Volumes II, III, IV and V of his *JMF*. These, in addition to the first published one, include more than 800 folk music items, four major analytical introductions (totaling some 350 typewritten pages), and a highly detailed ethnomusicological apparatus, the significance of which reaches well beyond pure musicological studies. These volumes show the real merit of Beregovski's field-work, which was actually the first of its kind – in scope and scholarship – in East European Jewish music. Most important is Beregovski's increasing interest in Jewish liturgical music, which he earlier ignored, probably for political reasons. These accom-

---

5 "Gegenzaytike virkungen tsvishen dem ukrainishen un yidishen muzik-folklor" (in Yiddish, The interaction of Ukrainian and Jewish music-folklore), in: *Visenshaft un revolutsie* (Science and revolution), 6 (1935), pp. 79-101 (Engl. tr. Slobin. *Old Jewish Folk music*, pp.5134-529).
6 *Yidishe insrumentale folk muzik* (in Yiddisch, Jewish instrumental folk music), Kiev, 1937 (Engl. tr. Slobin, *Old Jewish Folk Music,* pp. 530-548); "Yidishe klezmer, zeyer shafn un shtayger," (in Yiddish, Jewish klezmers, their creation and musical style), *Sovetish,* 12 (1941), pp. 412-450.
7 Evreiskie narodnye pesni (Moscow, 1962; Engl. tr. Slobin, *Old Jewish Folk Music*, pp. 285-510).
8 Beregovski, *"The Altered Dorian...."*
9 See footnotes 4, 5, 6 *and* 7.
10 Slobin, *Old Jewish Folk Music,* p. 8.

plishments make Beregovski comparable to such figures in Jewish folk music research as Abraham Zvi Idelsohn.

Volume II of *JMF* in the form of galley proofs, with corrections by the author, was discovered in 1981 at the *YIVO* Institute for Jewish Research in New York and considered by Mark Slobin in re-evaluating Beregovski's work in the 1982 Volume.[11] Somewhat later, on the basis of Volume II pointing out Beregovski's affiliation with the Russian formalist school (Y. Tynianov, R. Jacobson etc.), Slobin refers to Beregovski as a figure with a "vision of Jewish folkloristics which was unique in his day and a view of ethnomusicology which was somewhat ahead of its time."[12] Volume II was ready for print in 1938[13] or even 1934.[14]

In 1972 I was successful in taking out of the Soviet Union and bringing to Israel microfilms of Beregovski's typewritten manuscript of Volume III, *Jewish Instrumental Folkmusic,* Volume IV, *Jewish Folk Tunes Without Words,* and Volume V, *Introduction to the Purimshpil* (see Appendix). The manuscript copy is preserved at the Vilis Lacis Latvian U.S.S.R. State Library in Riga. The contents of these volumes were referred to for the first time in 1978.[15] At present one copy of the microfilms is in the Tel Aviv University Central Library [MF 1174 and 1175] and one is in my possession.

The Beregovski manuscript gives us exact information concerning the amount of Jewish folk music collected in Russia from 1912 until 1948 and preserved in the Soviet Union at the Sound Archives of the Cabinet for the Studies of Jewish Literature, Language and Folklore. This includes some three thousand items of folk music[16] recorded on 1265 sound cylinders: a) 435 cylinders recorded in 1912-1914 by the Jewish Historic Ethnographic Museum in St. Petersburg, which includes phonograms of the Jewish Folk Music Society; b) 30 cylinders recorded in 1912 by Joel

---

11 *Idem,* p. 3.
12 Slobin, "A Fresh Look at Beregovski's Folk Music Research," *Ethnomusicology,* 30/2 (1986), p. 259.
13 Slobin, *Old Jewish Folk Music,* p. 3.
14 Joachim Braun, *Jews and Jewish Elements in Soviet Music* (Tel-Aviv, 1978), p. 105.
15 *Idib.*
16 This is equal to the amount mentioned in Beregovski's posthumous volume (Slobin, *Old Jewish Folk Music,* p. 290). The number 7000 mentioned in my *Jews and Jewish Elements,* p. 104 is erroneous.

Engel in the Volynsk District; and c) 800 cylinders recorded mostly by Beregovski himself from 1928 to 1948 (IV, 158; further references to the unpublished volumes are in Roman numerals for volume(s) and Arabic numbers for pages). Among the written materials were the most valuable transcriptions from the archives of the Jewish Folk Music Society, including items dating back to 1885 (III, 317).

The fate of this collection is unknown. Beregovski himself vaguely indicated several times that the material was not available to him in 1949-50 and that he was not able to use the material collected after 1938 (III, 8). In 1960 he mentions in a somewhat obscure way that he has no access to the recordings (IV, 13-14). He never says what actually happened. If this material had been destroyed during the war, Beregovski would certainly have mentioned this in the most direct way. It is not known if part of the material is in the Beregovski archive at the Institute of Theatre, Music and Cinema in Leningrad (F 45).

The manuscripts in our possession are not dated. It is possible, however, to deduce from the text that Volume III was basically concluded in 1938 (III, 8 and 90); corrections and minor changes were made until 1960. At various times Beregovski hoped to publish the volume: on page 6 of Volume III, for example, the text reads: "more than forty years have passed since that time..."; the word "forty" was crossed out and "60" was written above. Volume IV was concluded in 1946 (IV, 139) with corrections added until 1960; the "Introduction" is signed "Kiev 1960". According to some sources Volume V was ready for publication in 1942.[17] From our manuscript copy, 1949 may be deduced as *terminus a quo* (V, 16). Our manuscript copy of this volume is incomplete: the music is lacking, the tables, most of the footnotes and "Addenda" are absent, and most of the chapters are not titled. Many question marks and some comments are seen in the margins. They are, however, not in Beregovski's handwriting.

Volumes III and IV, and probably V, have similar structures: a fairly extensive "Introduction", in fact a theoretical discussion of the subject (Vol. III – 91 pages; Vol. IV – 14 pages: Vol. V – 172 pages) is followed by transcriptions of the music (Vol. III – 254 items; Vol. IV, – 215 items). The last part of each volume provides a scientific apparatus for

---

[17] "Yidisher musikfolklor," *Sovetish Heimland,* 8 (1968), p. 146.

the transcriptions: several tables with extensive data on the informants, place, time and circumstances of the field recordings; indexes of musicians and persons helpful in collecting the material; lists of the first two bars of the tunes organized according to modes and first interval.

Parts of these manuscripts were previously published in the Soviet Union: in 1941 the "Introduction" to Vol. III appeared in Yiddish, somewhat changed and without illustrations as a separate article.[18] In the 1962 posthumous volume more than half of the textless and instrumental tunes are from Volumes III and IV (54 out of 80) and the "Introduction" of this publication draws heavily on material from the unpublished volumes.

The geography of the unpublished volumes is remarkable: Volume IV includes areas reaching far beyond the Ukraine, such as Leningrad, Moscow, Crakow, Vitebsk (IV, 189-192), and Volume V includes West Ukraine and Poland (V, 2). Many items were recorded at the Jewish agricultural colonies of Romanovka, Kalindorf (Seicemenucha) and Novozlatopol (III, 322).

Although most of the transcriptions belong to the late 1920s and 30s, some go back to the late 19th century, each case carefully documented by Beregovski. Volume III includes, for example, transcriptions notated by *klezmers* and music amateurs from about 1890 (III, 295-317). The material for Volume V was collected in the year 1937-40 (V, 24). Beregovski points out that the performers have restored for him music at least 20-30 years old (V, 214).

The social status of Beregovski's informants encompasses nearly all classes of society, from workers and members of kolkhozes, teachers and clerks, to distinguished scholars, artists, and members of noted hassidic families. Well known authorities in Jewish music and folklore, such as the composer Lev Pulver (1883-1970), the poet Samuel Galkin (1897-1960), the folklorist Yekhezkel Dobrushin (1883-1953) and the literary critic M. Vilner were also among his informants (III, 318; IV, 181-188).

Volume III, which deals with *klezmer* music, includes 254 tunes (without variants) from some 1500 preserved in 1948 at the Cabinet. The tunes of the volume are divided according to function: a) music for listening associated with the different stages of the wedding ceremony, like

---

18 M. Beregovski "Yidishe klezmer ..."

music while meeting the guests *(Mazltov, Dobriden*)*, seating the bride *(Kale-bazecn)*, at the meal *(Cumtiš Tiš-nign)*, and seeing off the guests *(Dobrinoč, Zajgezunt)*, and b) music for dancing *(Frejlexs, Sherf, Skočne, Pleskun, Baroygez-tanc, Xosid,* etc.). A similar functional division is maintained in Vol. IV which includes 215 textless tunes from some 800 owned by the Cabinet. The tunes are divided into a) table tunes *(tishnign)* and b) *frejlexs*, i.e. tunes for dancing.

As *Addenda* to the 254 tunes of Volume III, Beregovski has included four large forms by the two most famous *klezmers* of the second half of the 19th century. Partly recorded from informants and partly copied from hand-written *klezmer* notebooks – the authors themselves have never notated their compositions – every piece of this music exists in many variants, most of them probably unknown. The Beregovski volume includes a *"Luli – Viglid"* (Lullaby), *"Fantazie"* (Fantasy), and *"Cum-Tish"* (To the Table, For the Meal) by Avraham Moishe Kholodenko (Pedocer, 1828-1902), and the *"Jidisher koncert"* (Jewish concerto) by Alter from Chudnov (Goizman, 1846-1912).

Beregovski reached his highest level of musical-cultural analysis in the last volume (V), where the *Purimshpil* is discussed in detail. The analysis is based on historical published material, but mainly on variants of the *Akhashveyresh-shpil* and other *Purimshpils* recorded by Beregovski himself and his informants. Beregovski's field work includes six variants of the *Akhashveyresh-shpil*, three variants of the *Yaakov shpil*, three of "Selling of Yoseph", two Goliat plays, one "Wisdom of Solomon" and one "Benediction of Yaakov" (V, 16, 127 and 168). The material here is also divided into two functional parts: a) *Purimshpil* for home performance, and b) *Purimshpil* for public performance.

Beregovski's work is the first study on the music of the *Purimshpil* ever written and of special value because of the involvement of extensive fieldwork. In his discussion, Beregovski defines the *Akhashveyresh-shpil* as a "pure musical work" (V, 114) and closely explores the liturgical sources of the music, which is quite unusual in comparison with his earlier studies. He speaks about the "degradation" of the form in Russia and the USSR during the last fifty to seventy years and points out that in

---

*   The transliteration of Yiddish for the dance titles is kept as used by Beregovski, otherwise the generally accepted *YIVO* system of romanization is applied.

other countries (Poland) the genre is still alive (V, 2). Beregovski traces the *Akhashveyreslz-shpil* back to the musical Festnacht-Spiel parodies and mysteries. He considers the impact of Ukrainian and Polish music to be insignificant (V, 143). His most interesting conclusions are found when analyzing the recitative of the *Akhashveyresh-slzpil*, which is constructed as a chain of subsequent motifs (we may say, stringing of pearls) similar to the principle of Jewish liturgical cantillation. Beregovski also observes that the recitative is used only for non-Jewish persons of the play, and arrives at the conclusion that the recitative – the most ancient and Jewish core of the *Akhashveyreslz-shpil* – could not be derived directly from synagogue singing, but was adopted by the *Purimshpilers* as an element of Jewish culture through the mysteries, and then re-"Judaized" (V, 157).

To Beregovski's remarkable observations on the *Purimshpil*, we should also add his emphasis on instrumental elements in the music of the *Purimshpil*. Even more so, on the basis of the weight of the instrumental references in the entire musical output of all the transcribed sixteen *Purimshpils* (some 30%), he hypothesizes that the early *Purimshpil* was indeed a full-blooded, vocal-instrumental musical stage work (V, 168-169).

The corpus of Beregovski's musical transcriptions from Vol. III and IV (and, certainly also Vol. V, which are not in our disposal) – in all some 470 tunes without variants – is a real mine of information on the musical culture of East European Jewry. This is especially true if we take into account the rich critical apparatus which accompanies those tunes. At present it is even not possible to foresee all the directions in which research based on this material may develop. Let us point out here some of the research potential of this material.

As a first example I would mention a problem of classification posed by Beregovski's functional division of tunes for listening, and tunes for dance.

Beregovski's division according to the titles of the tunes, and the titles themselves presented by the informants, certainly, may be questioned. Why, for example, do the table tunes in Vol. IV include dances as well *(Sher, Frejlexs, Skochne, Rejdl*, etc.)? What, on the one hand, are the differences between the *freylekhs* and *skochne*, and, on the other, the differences between *freylekhs* and *skochne* for dancing, as compared to those for listening? Or what are the differences between the *freylekhs* and the *sher?* On this dubious problem of the tune classification both according to title and musical structure, Beregovski remarks that actually "the *klezmers* never performed the same piece for a *frejlexs* and a *sher* (although for the dance itself it would not be an obstacle). Every group had several certain melodies, which it always played for the *Sher.* Collecting the material from the *klezmers* in different areas we frequently received variants of the same piece, which in one place was considered a *sher,* and in the other one a *frejlexs,* and *vice versa"* (III, 24). This passage of Beregovski may lead us to the conclusion, that at present, while modern musical analysis is not yet able to build up a plausible classification of *klezmer* tunes, only a study of local sub-traditions (perhaps, even of an extra-musical nature), will be able to indicate the divisional frame for those genres.

Among the most notable transcriptions of the unpublished *JMF* volumes, which may well point to the research potential of this material, are the large instrumental forms (up to fifteen minutes in length) from Vol. III. Some are anonymous while others are attributed to certain *klezmers.* Let us consider, for example, No. 20, entitled *Taksim* (see **Mus. ex. VI-1**) which was transcribed by Beregovski himself in Kiev, 1935 from the performance by the sixty year-old clarinetist B. Dulitcki (III, 298). The *taksim* is an improvisational instrumental form of rhapsodic character based on the *maqam* principles and stemming from the Arab-Persian-Turkish musical milieu. Beregovski notes that he never saw a transcribed *taksim,* or even heard a performance of this eastern genre (III, 33). We may only guess now, what the path of this form was from the Middle East to the Ukraine. To follow up this musical emigration is by itself a challenge. The music of Beregovski's *Taksim* shows, that the intrinsic features of the Arab *taksim,* as described by Edith Gerson-Kiwi,[19] are preserved in Beregovski's Jewish-Ukraine *klezmer-taksim:* a) a common central sound and some identical degrees for various *maqams* in the Arab *taksim* and for various *shtaygers* in the Jewish *taksim;* b) the identical degrees of different *maqams/shtaygers* serve as a point of departure for mutual excursions; c) ornament patterns associated with specific sections of the piece;

---

[19] Edith Gerson-Kiwi, "On the Technique of Arab Taqsim Compositions," in: *Musik als Gestalt und Erlebnis,* Ed. E. Schenk, Vienna, 1970, pp. 66-73.

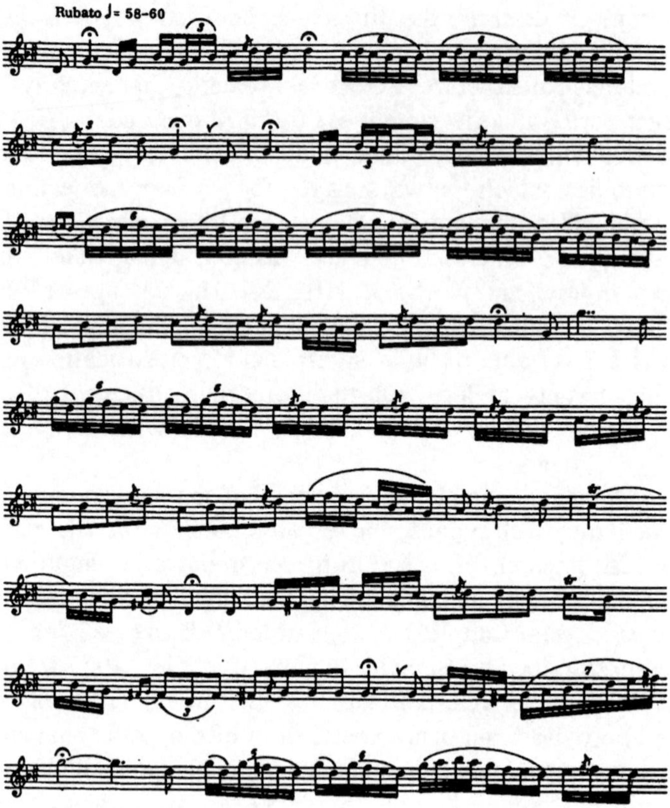
Rubato ♩ = 58-60

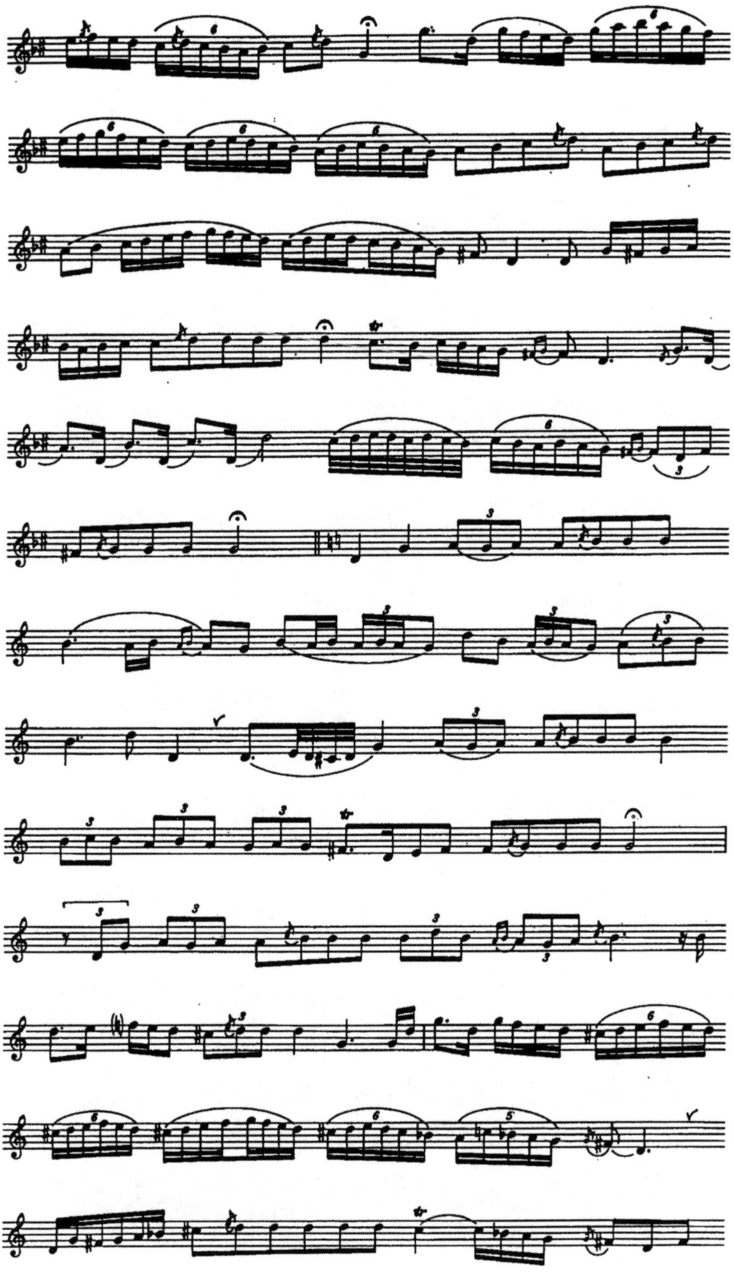

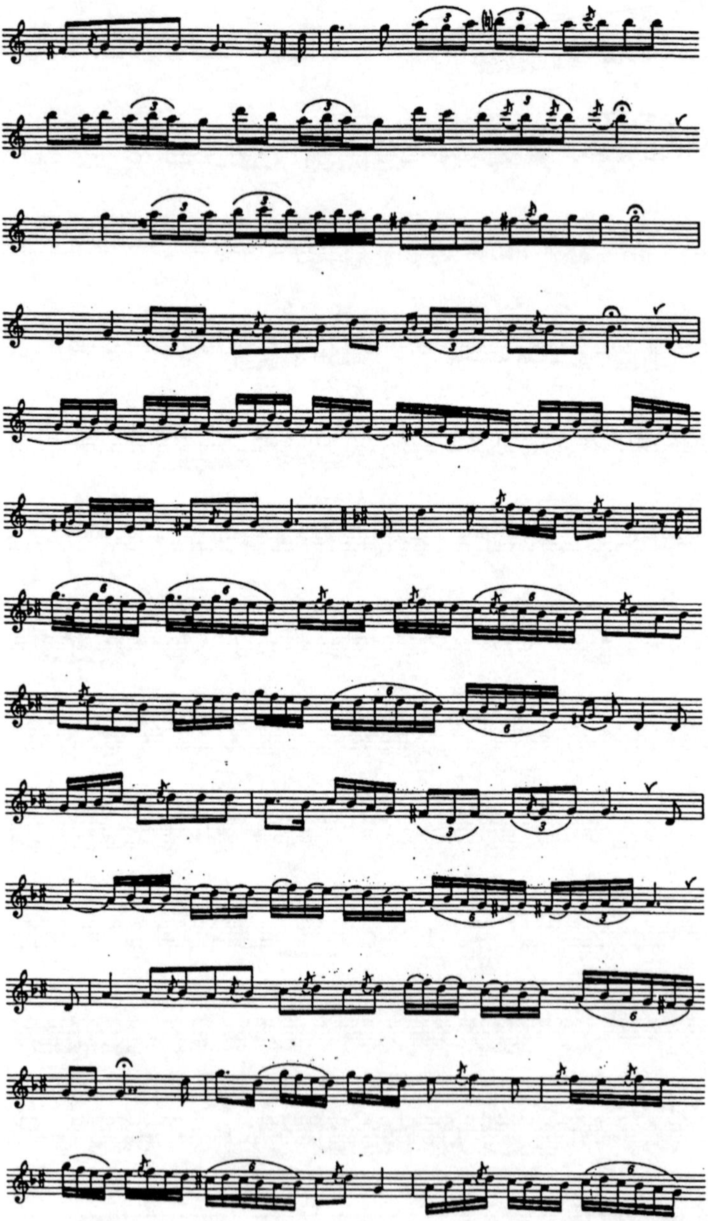

Mus. ex. VI-1: Beregovski Ms., no.20, Taksim

and d) an undulating sense of changing tension between related *maqams/ shtayger*. We join Gerson-Kiwi in claiming (substituting the word *maqam* with *shtayger*) that "nothing can equal the aesthetic pleasure of the listener in the detection of smooth soldering junctions between the related *maqam* sections."[20]

It is only natural that different manifestations of the intrinsic features of the *taksim* have changed in the Jewish-Ukrainian environment. The Jewish *taksim* consists of an ABA' improvisation in free rhythm, with A and A' in the altered dorian, and the middle part, B, in major. The improvisational part is followed by a 2 dance section C *(freylekhs-type)* – itself an aba structure – which concludes the work. The entire ABA'C form, although based on a common central sound, fluctuates between a g-d tension, with the d frequently predominating; at some moments the a emerges as the central sound (in section A'). A most refreshing turn is the G major at the end of the middle section of C. Hence, we have the "aesthetic pleasure ... in detection of smooth junctions between related *shtayger* sections", which oscillate between altered dorian (on g), harmonic and natural minor (on d), major (on g), and altered phrygian *(freygisch,* on a). The *klezmer-taksim* was performed at meals as a kind of *tish-nign* (III: 32), played on the clarinet or violin, and not on a plucked chordophone *(qanun* or *ud'),* the sound-row has changed from a *maqam*-stock of pitches to a *shtayger*-stock, the sectional division is more profound, and melodic elements dominate over *toccata* patterns. In short, the style of the work has changed to the extent that we may now talk about the *taksim* as a Jewish form, or, to use Beregovski's term, a "Judaization" (V, 138) of the form has occurred.

A different example of research possibilities which are opened up by Beregovski's collection is the comparison of different variants of a certain tune transcribed in Russia more than fifty years ago with variants transcribed in other parts of the world, let us say in Israel. In some cases a pattern of constant preservation seems to emerge. The *"Nign tsu zmires",* for example – transcribed by Beregovski as he recalled it from his father's home in Makarovo at the turn of the century (IV, 40) – appears in Israel in a publication of the hassidic music collector, Meir

---

20 Idem., p. 72

Shimon Geshuri.[21] The textless tune has changed to a song with text *(Rakhem b'khasdekha)* and is believed to originate from R. Yaakov Telkhaner. Here and there a change of ornament or passing note occurs, but otherwise the two abcb form transcriptions are identical, including the place and type of two inserted assymetrical transitional bars before and in the center of c.

Considering the possibilities of variant comparison Beregovski tends to stress the uniqueness of every transcription of a piece: "the variants coincide very rarely, in fact we have as many variants as transcriptions" (III, 16). For Beregovski this is valid not only in the case of small forms by anonymous authors, but also for larger works where the authorship is known to the transcriber, as in the case of the klezmer Padotser. As an example the "Lullaby" by this famous klezmer may be mentioned. Beregovski's version of this piece as compared to the variant published by J. Stutschewsky,[22] differs in the sense that it tends towards a one-movement fantasy, while Stutschewsky's variant is a clear-cut theme with variations. To a certain extent, we may detect in Beregovski's version the *taksim* pattern discussed earlier.

Another research aspect, significant for the understanding of the genesis of Jewish art music, should be the study of the music by the two mentioned klezmers Padotser and Goizman. The two pieces, besides the "Lullaby" – attributed to Pedotser – are elaborated improvisations which include the entire arsenal of romantic virtuoso violin music (from long sections *sul* G to left-hand *pizzicato* with *arco* accompaniment and harmonics). Goizman's "Jewish Concerto" is in fact a double variation in B major preceded by a broad improvisational introduction (B minor). Pedocer's and Goizman's music seems to have absorbed both the tradition of Russian 18th-century violin music (stress on variation form of the Khadoshkin type[23]), and the art of Moladavian lauters (folk violinists)[24] –

---

21 Meir Shimon Geshuri, *Ha-nigun v'ha-rikud b'hasidut* (Song and Dance in Hassidism), Vol. 2, Tel-Aviv, 1955, p. 189.

22 Joachim Stutschewsky, *Ha-klezmerim: toldotehem, orakh-hayehem v'yezirotehem* (The klezmers, their history, way of life and compositions), (Jerusalem, 1959), "Addenda", No. 1.

23 Israel Yampol'ski, *Russkoe skripichnoe iskusstvo* (Russian violin art), (Moscow-Leningrad, 1951), pp. 76-121; Anne Mischakoff, *Khandoshkin and the Beginning of*

contemporary with the *klezmers* – with their preference for improvisational elements and modal interplay. The main feature of this klezmer music, however, is the transformation of the formal musical elements into a Jewish idiom by the *klezmer*-performance itself, the process of "Judaization" of this music in the course of its audiosocial implementation. The compositions of Pedocer and Goizman are those rare recorded examples of Jewish music which appeared on the border of folk and art music, created by half-folk and half-professional musicians at the dawn of European Jewish art music. Consequently, we witness here a most characteristic process of incubation of professional art music from folk music, a process which Walter Salmen sees as a central feature for most European nations that were engaged in creating their art music during the second half of the 19th century.[25]

Beregovski's central goal for *JMF* was the presentation of a particular corpus of Jewish folk music, and in this sense his unpublished folk music transcriptions are of great scholarly interest. Not less significant, however, are Beregovski's theoretical and methodological concepts. Although not presented in a systematical way, they, nevertheless, penetrate his entire work like leitmotifs. We may sum up Beregovski's main concepts in three interrelated groups. The first two, in different ways, are reflected in his published studies:

1) The "inadequacy of notation concept": "notation does not provide the possibility to mark the manner of singing which, as is known, is quite different for singers of different nations. Even in Jewish and Ukrainian folklore, works which when notated look very similar, and sometimes even identical, sound in reality very different when performed by particular folk singers" (III, 19);

2) The "assimilation concept": "even with all of its originality, national art is devoid of any national insularity. The people always readily

---

Russian String Music (Russian Music Studies, No. 9, ed. M. H. Brown, Ann Arbor, 1983), Ch. 4, "Khandoshkin and the Independent Variation Sets", pp. 45-73.

24 Boris Kotljarov, *O skripichnoi kul'ture v Moldavii* (On the violin culture in Moldovia), (Kishenev, 1956).

25 Walter Salmen, *The Social Status of the Professional Musician from the Middle Ages to the 19th Century* (New York, 1983), pp. 14-15. See also Joachim Braun, "Aspects of Early Latvian Professional Musicianship," *Journal of Baltic Studies*, XVI/2 (1985), pp. 95-96.

accept new spiritually-related musical works, even if they do not have the typical features of that particular people. Often exactly because they bring with them new means of expression, typical of a different people, certain pieces become popular. The assimilation of foreign melodies is certainly typical not only of Jewish folklore" (III, 18 and 23).

3) The third concept never appeared in Beregovski's publications, and has not been formulated by Beregovski in the first volumes of his *JMF.* Only at a later stage while working on Vol. V, and probably, sharing ideas with the well-known Jewish composer Mikhail Gnesin (1883-1957)[26], Beregovski arrives at the "Judaization concept." A corrolary of the first two concepts, the "Judaization concept" refers to the interpretation of non-Jewish music by Jewish folk musicians, actually a process of acculturation. Changes in pitch, structure, tempo, addition of ornaments, changes of performance technique (articulation, embouchure, tone production, vibration, etc.) are introduced. This changes the music to such an extent that it takes on a new ethnic identity or ethnic meaning, or as Beregovski puts it, "a .Judaization of non-Jewish music occurs" (V, 138 and 157).

Considering these facts, the question arises: why was Beregovski's work not appreciated for some forty, nearly fifty years both in the Soviet Union and the West?

As regards the USSR, we are witnessing a typical case – more or less a routine matter – of general anti-Jewish policy which was especially strong in those areas of culture related to national self-identification. Even Beregovski's obituary speaks mainly of his general work in folklore and refers only in passing to his "studies in Jewish, Ukrainian and Bashkir(?!) folklore."[27] Beregovski's research on Jewish music was belittled in the Soviet Union because of its subject matter, and as a result appeared in publications in Ukrainian and Yiddish that were obscure and difficult to obtain, or in a ridiculously small number of copies. (The posthumous volume from 1962, for example, appeared in 1555 copies). Now a publi-

---

[26] Mikhail Gnesin, "O yumore v muzike" (in Russian, On humor in music), in M.F. Gnesin, *Stat'i, vospominaniia, materiali* (Articles, reminiscences, materials), ed. R.V. Glezer, Moscow, 1961, pp. 200-202.
[27] *Sovetskaya Muzika*, 11 (1961), p. 160.

cation of Volume III seems to be in process, and perhaps a revival of his work in the USSR can be anticipated.

In the West, the situation is more complex. Soviet politics achieved their goal and Beregovski's work has indeed not been a subject of scholarly exchange and attention until recently. A good example is his article on *klezmer* music which was published in a little-known Yiddish literature almanac in 2000 copies. So it happened that this valuable study was quoted at length in Israel without a citation of the source,[28] and was never mentioned in any discussion on East European Jewish music. It seems that Beregovski's biased ideology and the restrictions forced on him have shaped his image in the West. There is no entry on Beregovski in the *New Grove Dictionary of Music and Musicians* (London, 1980), and articles on Jewish music in this reference work do not include his most important studies. The *Encyclopedia Judaica* (Jerusalem, 1971) in its article "Music" does not mention Beregovski at all.

It seems that, along with the remoteness and isolation of Beregovski's activities, there was another reason for the disinterest of the Western world, in particular the Israeli scholarly community. Ethnomusicology, including Jewish, was involved mainly with non-European, exotic, oriental cultures; folk music of European, especially East European Jews, from whom most of the Israeli scholarly community itself stems – as does the entire Yiddish culture – was not considered a challenging, worthwhile research subject. In fact, it was not considered as ethnic culture at all.[29] This corresponds to the "minus one" definition of ethnicity, which does not consider as ethnic the culture of the dominant group in the particular society.[30] This conception also had an impact on me. When I brought the Beregovski microfilms to Israel in 1972, his name was

---

28 Stutchevski, *Haklezmerim*, pp. 91, 127, 189, etc.
29 See the bibliography for the articles "Israel" and "Jewish Music" in *The New Grove Dictionary of Music and Musicians*, vol. 9, ed. S. Sadie (London, 1980), pp. 360-361, 633-634, and 643-645. The first article does not mention studies on Yiddish folk music at all, and the second lists two items pertinent to our subject from some 15 studies on folk music by Israeli musicologists.
30 Michael Banton, *Racial and Ethnic Competition*, Cambridge, 1983, p. 65. See also Joachim Braun, "Aspekte der Musiksoziologie in Israel," *Studien zur systematischen Musikwissenschaft: Vladimir Karbusicky zum 60. Geburtstag*, Ed. C. Floros et alii, Hamburg, 1986, pp. 85-104 (see in this volume pp. 343-367).

hardly known in the West. Although I mentioned the unpublished volumes in my previous publications, the microfilms unfortunately remained unnoticed until recently. With the publication of the Beregovski volume in the U.S.A., which seems to mark the discovery of Beregovski in the West, new studies have begun at the musicology departments of Bar-Ilan and Tel Aviv Universities.

In the evaluation of Beregovski's work we have behind us a period of deliberate disregard and neglect as well as a period of underestimation and resistance towards his approach. We now acknowledge Beregovski as a most important forerunner of modern anthropology of music in the field of Jewish musical culture, as a unique, highly sophisticated collector of folk music, and – until today – as the one and only researcher in several areas of Jewish music.

Appendix

Contents of Moshe Beregovski's typewritten manuscript *JEWISH MUSICAL FOLKLORE:* Volumes III, IV and V*

JEWISH MUSICAL FOLKLORE
Vol. III
Jewish Instrumental Folk Music

I.	Introduction	6
	Ch. 1: Instrumental (klezmer) music – a constituent part of Jewish Folklore	13
	Ch. 2: Characteristics of klezmer music	25
	Ch. 3: Modes	39
	Ch. 4: Typical traits of klezmer interpretation	46
	Ch. 5: The klezmers of the 19th century	49
	Ch. 6: How the klezmers learned to play	67
	Ch. 7: The klezmer-type of the last quarter of the 19th century	73
	Ch. 8: Amateur musicians in Jewish everyday life	82
	Some remarks on the transcriptions of music	87

*) *The text in square brackets is by the author of this paper.*

II.	Transcriptions of Music		
	Part I: Musical works which were performed at weddings: greetings and seeing-off the guests; at the procession escorting the couple to and from the *khupa;* at the table, etc. [No. 1 – 84]		93
	Part II: Dances - a) Freylekhs [No. 85-176]		166
	b) Sher [No. 206-254]		225
	c) Other dances [No. 206-254]		241
Addenda:	Works for violin by the klezmers A.M. Kholodenko (Pedotser) and E. Goizman (Alter from Tchudnov)		267
III.	Information on the performers, place and time of transcriptions, and on the original tonality of the transcriptions and recordings		295
Table I:	Name index of performers		318
Table 11:	Name index of persons whose transcriptions are included in this book		319
	The numbers of the phonograms		321
Table III:	Places where the instrumental works included in this book have been in use or originated		321
	Short list of instrumental works included in this book (with Presentation of first bars) [20 illustrations]		324

JEWISH MUSICAL FOLKLORE
Vol. IV
Jewish Folk-Tunes Without Words

1.	Introduction		4
2.	Texts of Music: Part I [No. 1-158a]		15
	Part 2 [No. 159-215]		122
3.	Information on the performers, time and place of the transcriptions		158
4.	Table I: Name index of persons from whom the tunes were transcribed by ear, or were recorded, with numbers of those tunes		181
5.	Table II: Name index of persons whose transcriptions are included in this volume		187
6.	Table III: Places and dates of the transcriptions		189
7.	Classification of the tunes according to modality		
	a) Minor		193
	b) Altered Phrygian		199
	c) Major		201
	d) Altered Dorian		203

JEWISH MUSICAL FOLKLORE
Vol. V
Introduction to the Purimshpil

Introduction [Questions of bibliography]		1
Ch. 1:	[Historical and social aspects]	25
Ch. 3:	[The libretto of the "Akhashveyresh-shpil"]	58
Ch. 4:	[Aspects of genesis]	81
Ch. 5:	[Aspects of genre]	95
Ch. 6:	The Music of the "Akhashveyresh-shpil"	114
Ch. 7:	Common Traits in the Melodic Structure of the "Akhashveyresh-shpil"	126
Ch. 8:	The Sources of the Musical Language of the "Akhashveyresh-shpil	134
Ch. 9:	[On the recitative of the "Akhashveyresh-shpil"]	152
Ch. 10:	The place of the Instrumental Ensemble in the Purimshpil [six musical examples]	161

VII. The Large Forms of Klezmer Music: The "Missing Link"*

Until recently, musicological studies subdivided the written transcriptions of klezmer[1] music into either "tunes for listening" (e.g. *mazltov, dobriden, kale-bezecn*, etc.) or "tunes for dancing" (e.g. *freilekhs, šer, skochne, pleskun, bulgariš*, etc.). While this division corresponds to 19th-century klezmer vocabulary and musical life, many modern musicologists regard it as problematic for several reasons. First, it is not consistent with practical musicianship, as certain dances, such as *freilekhs* and *skochne*, appear as tunes for both listening and dancing. Second, musical analysis does not identify specific stylistic characteristics that distinguish between the two groups.

A rather limited corpus of discussions and examples of klezmer music appeared in anthologies (Idelsohn 1932, Beregovski/Fefer 1938, Beregovski 1962, Beregovski/Goldin 1987, Beregovski/Slobin/ 1982 and 2001[2]), monographs (Stutschewsky 1959, Salmen 1991, Ottens/Rubin 1999, Slobin 2000 and 2002, Strom 2002), and articles (Beregovski 1973,

---

* Based on a paper presented at the 3ed Congress on Jewish Music, London University, 2000.
1 *klezmorim* (pl. of *klezmer*, from *kley zemer*, Hebr. musical instruments) – accepted for the designation of European, esp. East European Jewish traditional semi-professional, semi-dilettante musicians, performers of instrumental music, whose repertoire was handed down for centuries by oral tradition. The earliest documented mention of the term appears in a 16th-century manuscript (Trinity College, Cambridge F. 12.45; see W. Salmen, *Judishe Musikaten und Taenzer vom 13. bis 20. Jahrhundert* [Innsbruck, 1991, 15), although the phenomenon itself, probably under a different name, was known at least from the 2nd century BCE (see J. Braun, *Die Musikkultur Altisraels/Palästinas*, Freburg/Göttingen, 1999, pp. 30 and 168). The modern use of the term "klezmer" for music performed by klezmorim (klezmer music), and the designation of the style as "klezmer" or klezmer-studies as "klezmerology" is a rather misleading vulgarism. The tradition of the negative symbolism of a "klezmer-performance" is still very strong, and not all musicologists who study klezmer music are in this sense necessarily "klezmerologists."
2 For full titles see RELEVANT BIBLIOGRAPHY at the end of the paper.

181

Slobin 1984, Braun 1987, Feldman 1994, Rubin 1997). While both Idelsohn's and Beregovski's publications offer two equally outstanding achievements, they were both created before World War II and not always meet modern reaserch requirement. More recent interest in the research of klezmer music started only in the 1980s with Marc Slobin's translation of Beregovski's published writings, and the first scholarly discussion on klezmer musical culture took place at an international musicological meeting in Schladming (Austria) at the ICTM 30th World Conference, July 1989 (sessions chaired by Walter Salmen and the author of this paper).[3] During this meeting, the subject of an unnoticed till then genre of klezmer music – the *Large Klezmer Forms* (LKF) – was discussed for the first time.

The transcriptions of the LKF pieces offer a unique document of recorded traditional music; an indispensable part of Beregovski's manuscript, they are a remarkable phenomenon of Jewish instrumental music. Beregovski's *Evreiskaya narodnaya instrumenral'naya muzika* (Jewish Instrumental Folk Music), the third volume of his monumental *Evreiskii muzykal'nii fol'klor* (Jewish Musical Folklore) was prepared for publication and basically completed by Beregovski in 1938. This volume includes five items that are the core of this discussion.[4]

At this point, a brief episode concerning the history of musicological research in Israel is worthy of our attention. In 1972 I brought to Israel a microfilm of the above mentioned third volume (*Beregovski Ms.*), as well as of volumes Four (*Jewish Folk Tunes Without Words*) and Five (*Purimshpil*). For several years the microfilm was kept at the Jerusalem National Library without registration; consequently I donated it to the Tel Aviv University Library (MF 1174). At that time no interest was shown in this manuscript, either by the Israeli musicological community, nor by any other musicologists.[5] Max Goldin, composer, ethnomusicologist, and

---

3 Not at Wesleyan University in 1996, as mentioned in *Judaism*, 47/1, 1998:3.
4 At the time of the presentation of this paper in 2000 (see footnote 1), the complete Beregovski volume with Jewish instrumental music was not yet published (see J. Braun, *Israel Studies in Musicology* iv, 1987:125-44, which includes the first publication and discussion of one of the LKF, the *Taksim*).
5 An anecdote from those years may illustrate the situation: in 1974 the late Prof. Eric Werner, one of the great experts on Jewish music, visited the Tel-Aviv University. Interested in the recent newcomer (the author of this article), he asked some ques-

expert in Jewish music, published Beregovski's *Jewish Instrumental Folk Music* in the Moscow publishing house "Soviet Composer" (1987). However, he did not include the five LKF found in this manuscript. Goldin insisted that these pieces, as well as some others, such as an interesting variant of the *Khatsot* (No. 19a in *Beregovski Ms.*), are not genuine klezmer music.[6] However, according to Beregovski himself, these are indeed examples of pure folk art (Moscow edition, p. 10). The complete volume *Jewish Instrumental Folk Music* was translated to English and published in 2001 by Marc Slobin 2001, however without necessary annotations. The St. Petersburg and Riga manuscripts are not quite identical; there are some minor bowing differences, possibly, as result of incorrect copying.

The informants or Beregovski himself entitled these five pieces in Yiddish and Russian as follows:

Taksim (Russ. *Taksim*)
Viglid (Russ. *Kolibel'naya*, Lullaby)
Fantasie (Russ. *Fantasia*, Fantasia)
Tcum Tiš (Russ. *Zastol'naya*, Table-music)
Yiddišer Kontsert (Russ. *Evreyskii Kontcert*, Jewish Concerto).

I venture to suggest that this small corpus of music is of the utmost historical interest and provides the **"missing link"** in the evolution of Jewish instrumental music. The corpus represents an intermediate stage, linking traditional music with the emerging Jewish European art music.

I have designated the five pieces discussed the generic term *Large Klezmer Forms* (*LKF*) for the following reasons:

1. <u>Size</u>. A standard klezmer piece without repetition, both for listening and dance, does not last more than about 3-4 minutes; an LKF can last up to 15 minutes.

2. <u>Form</u>. All the LKF pieces are clearly divided into several parts and consist of: (a) an impressive *Introduction* in an improvised rhapsodic virtuoso style; (b) a theme or even two themes (as for example in the *Jewish Concerto*) with a set of more or less standard variations; and (c) a

---

tions. "But on Jewish music there is nothing done in Russia?" I told him about the fate of the Institute of Jewish Culture at the Academy of Sciences in Kiev, and the work of Beregovski. "Not possible!" was his reaction, and he forgot about it.
6   Personal communication with Max Goldin (Riga, 1992).

coda, or, when the variation section is absent, a *freilekhs,* which concludes the piece. The sections, among other peculiarities, are linked by their modal structure: a common central sound for different modes (*shtaygers*). These compositions are incipient cyclical forms, which clearly differ from the regular klezmer miniature in their binary and ternary form.

3. Instrumental idiom. (a) Four of the five LKF are preserved in violin transcriptions; (b) the instrumental style is based on late 18th–early 19th-century virtuoso violin technique, and the music requires a highly skilled virtuoso performance.

4. Concert performance. The style and character of the pieces, as well as several preserved descriptions of performances, show that this music was intended as pure concert music, while the ordinary klezmer repertoire is always functional and performed at traditional events (e.g. weddings).

5. Authorship. Four of the five pieces are ascribed to two well-known klezmer-authors, as opposed to the usually anonymous klezmer music.

Little information survives about these LKF pieces. What we do know is summarized below:

Taksim (*Beregovski Ms.*, pp. 113-117, No. 20); transcribed by Beregovski from the clarinetist B. Dulitcky in Kiev, 1935; published by J. Braun (see footnote 4) and frequently performed by the Israeli klezmer, Mussa Berlin; a fragment of the piece has been recorded by the Joel Rubin Ensemble (SM 1614-2 CD, Well Musik, 1997) without indication of the source, but with a number of cuts and additions that entirely change the original *taksim* structure.

Viglid (*Beregovski Ms., Addendum* No. 1, pp. 269-275; published by M. Slobin in 2001; attributed by Beregovski (p. 269) to Aharon-Moshe Kholodenko (alias Pedhatsur, Berditchev, 1828-1902), one of the great klezmer virtuosi of the 19th century; copied by Beregovski (probably in the 1930s) from a handwritten music book of an unknown klezmer; the only comment in the *Beregovski Ms.* notes that the fingering and bowing are preserved as they appeared in the music book from which they were copied (p. 269). A shorter and somewhat different version was published by J. Stutschewsky in his *Haklezmorim* (1958, No. 1, pp. *bet-dalet*) and transcribed by him from Meir Frenkel (1894, Tchudnov, Ukraine – 1974, Jerusalem), the pupil of another well-known klezmer, Ehiel Goizman (Alter from Tchudnov, 1846-1912, see below), who allegedly had received this piece directly from Pedhatsur (*idem*, p. 112). Frenkel, who was originally educated by Goizman as a klezmer, later became a highly professional violinist. After World War II he joined the Jerusalem Radio Broadcasting Symphonic Orchestra, where he remained until the last days of his life. He memorized a rich repertoire of klezmer music, and frequently performed at family gatherings. The *Viglid* was among the pieces he loved best, and he often played it for his family.[7]

Fantasie (*Beregovski Ms., Addendum* No. 2, pp. 276-281; published by M. Slobin in 2001; the only information we have about this composition is that the *Beregovski Ms.* attributes it to Pedhatsur (p. 276).

Tsum Tiš (*Beregovski Ms., Addendum* No. 3, pp. 282-286; published by M. Slobin in 2001; Beregovski attributes this piece to Pedhatsur (p. 282).

Yiddišer Koncert (*Beregovski Ms., Addendum* No. 4, pp. 286-294; published by M. Slobin in 2001; the only composition Beregovski has ascribed to Goizman, a klezmer as popular as Pedhatsur, listed in the *Beregovski Ms.* as No. 258 (p. 323) and assigned to an anonymous handwritten klezmer music book from Tchudnov.

Beregovski admits that, despite his many efforts, he never had the opportunity to see any of this music in Pedhatsur's own handwriting, nor did he see two similar copies of any one piece.[8] All transcriptions of the music attributed to Pedhatsur and Goizman were made in the 1880s and '90s, or in the first decade of the 20th century. According to Beregovski, this music was copied from handwritten klezmer books that belonged to Pedhatsur's pupils and the sons of Goizman[9]. The sources of the information about Pedhatsur's manuscripts and his "Jewish Concerts" that appear in modern klezmer literature are not clear.[10]

For a better understanding of the LKF we should begin by comparing the two extant variants of the *Viglid*.

---

[7] From a telephone interview with Meir Frenkel's son Benjamin (Jerusalem, 14 July 2002). For the contact with the Frenkel family and other valuable advice, I am obliged to an anonymous reader of the manuscript of this paper.
[8] Beregovski/Goldin 1987, p. 10.
[9] Idem.
[10] For example, in Ottens/Rubin 1999, pp. 30 and 170.

STUTSCHEWSKY (1958)	BEREGOVSKI Ms (1930s)
Introduction, in *Freigish* on A	Introduction, in *Freigish* on A
Theme, in *Freigish* on A	1st Theme, in *Freigish* on A
Variations 1-5, in *Freigish* on A	Variations 1-7, in *Freigish* on A
	2nd Theme, in A-major
	Variation 1-3, in Altered Dorian (AD) on A
	Variation 4, from AD to a-minor natural
	Extended "herald-tone" (37 bars!) on e and g pedal
	Coda, A-major

Table 1

Noting Stutschewsky's shortened version of this piece, we do not know whether the author of the publication cut the original or whether the informant's memory was short. According to Stutschewsky (p. 112), the informant had claimed that the piece was produced "with perfect precision." It is clear that the Beregovski version is much closer to the typical late 19th-century LKF than Stutschewsky's variant. Beregovski's *Viglid,* as opposed to Stutschewsky's, shows most of the LKF characteristics – considerable length, developed form features, concert-level virtuosity, and, most important, the use of characteristic modes in different sections of the piece that mostly center on one central tone. The use of modality, which serves as a point of departure for "mutual musical excursions" (to borrow Gerson-Kiwi's expression),[11] can be observed in the undulating change of tension between related *shtayger/maqam* sections of both the Jewish-Ukrainian LKF and Arab *taksim*-form.

All of the LKF share a similar gross form and virtuosity, as mentioned before, as well as musical style. While this conclusion is based on a limited number of musical pieces whose authors were personally acquainted, it may indicate characteristics of a specific genre. The introductory improvisations in all of the pieces are written in a similar musical and – for the violin – idiomatic style, even when composed by different authors. Compare, for example, the beginning of the introductions in both the *Viglid* by Pedhatsur and Y*iddišer Koncert* by Alter Tchudnover:

---

11 Edith Gerson-Kiwi, "On the technique of the Arab Taqsim Compositios", in: *Musik als Gestalt und Erlebnis,* ed. E. Schenk (Vienna, 1970), p.72.

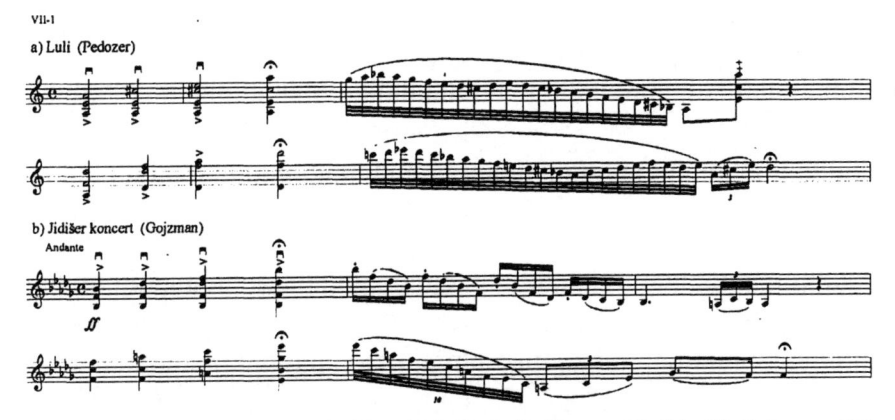

Mus. Ex. VII-1: (a) Beregovski Ms., Add. No.1, Pedhatsur, Viglid; (b) Goizman, Yiddišer Koncert.

The attached passages are "openings," intended to draw the attention of the listeners to what is to follow. In addition to the *virtuoso* texture, all of the introductions of the pieces share similar structures. The variations follow similar sequences: theme, figural variation, timbre figural variation (sul G), variation in flageolet tones, figural variation, leaps/bariolage/ left hand pizz. variation, coda (tremolo). The Beregovski *Viglid* and the *Koncert* – the two most developed compositions – have some peculiarities. The first has an unusually developed (37 bars) pre-coda, a "heraldtone" section, which focuses attention on the next part of the composition. Mostly composed in odd numbers of bars (3 or 5) in regular klezmer tunes, on a repeated tonic, sub-dominant, or dominant tone in different rhythmical and ornamental combinations, this motif appears as the introduction for a dance piece, or in between different parts of the piece.[12] The size of this section in the *Viglid*, its function on the dominant and position before the coda, seem to recall the organ pedal in classical forms. In the *Koncert*, the second half of the theme repeats after every variation (so-

---

12 See for example in Beregovski/Goldin 1987, Nos. 117, 131, 160; and Stutschewsky 1959, No. 27d.

metimes with a change of register), which creates a quasi-rondo or – typical for folk songs – refrain impression.

	Viglid-Stutschewsky	Viglid-Beregovski	Fantasie	*Tcum Tish*	*Yiddisher Koncert*
	Introduction	Introduction	Introduction	Introduction	Introduction
	Theme	Theme	Theme	Theme	Theme+rondo section
Var. 1	figural	figural	figural	figural	figural*
Var. 2	figural	figural	2 oct. leaps	figural	double ricochet in 8th.
Var. 3	Sul G	sul G	figural	sul G	l. h. pizz
Var. 4	flageolet	flageolet	oct. leaps	sul G	sul G
Var. 5	bariolage	figural	pizz./flag.	sul G	leaps
Var. 6		figural	sul G	flageolet	flageolet
Var. 7		bariolage	combined	bariolage	2nd theme sul G
		2nd theme+4 var.			+4 variations
		"herald-tone" etc., see Table 1			*after each var. follows a 8-bar rondo section
		Coda in A major			

Table 2

The most typical feature of this music, as we can clearly see, is the central role of the independent variation form.[13] A main feature of 18th- to first half of 19th-century Russian music, the generative period in which national Russian art music was emerging, the independent variation form was particularly characteristic for the compositions of the Ukrainian-born composer and violinist Ivan Khandoshkin (1747-1804). The forerunner of Russian violin music, Khandoshkin developed this music concept into the most significant form in his synthesis of Russian traditional and East European art music. While most 18th-century Western European music features the variation form as part of a multi-movement cycle (from Corelli, Leclaire, and Tartini to Stamitz, Haydn, and Mozart),

---

[13] I call "independent variation form" the compositions which are solely "theme and variations" without being part of a cyclical composition.

22 out of Khandoshkin's 28 extant works are independent *Themes and Variations*.[14] The number of variations is usually larger than five, which also differs from the Western European tradition. Most important, however, is the use of traditional melodies, in particular folk songs, as theme in all of his works. A similar method of composition occurs in the LKF – all of which are independent variations. These variations differ from the Russian compositions mainly in their more developed structure, which includes a free improvisational introduction and a final section in a dance character. The violin idiom reflects early 19th-century techniques (Spohr, Beriot, and even Paganini, Ernst and Wieniavsky) including long legato and staccato passages, broad sections *sul G*, flageolets, left hand *pizzicato* with parallel *arco* performance. The thematic material has concomitantly shifted from pure folk songs to themes of a traditional modal and structural type that include elements of folk songs.

The second source of the LKF is the Moldavian *lauter* music.[15] Musicians such as Barbu Lauter from Yassi (first half of 19th century), Yanku Perzha (Kishenev, 1830s-80s), Kostaki Marii (1830s-1911), and Kostaki Parno (1856-1912) were closely related to Jewish klezmers, both in their musical activities and social standing. Each had his own *taraph* (orchestra), and was a highly skilled violin virtuoso and inspired improviser. The musical parallels of the *lauter* and klezmer music are striking, as exemplified by the *doina* by Kostaki Marii and the *doina* transcibed by Beregovski[16] (see **Mus. ex. VII-2**).

In the second half of the 20th century Moldavian art music began to develop. Similar to many other Eastern European schools of national art music, traditional music served as an ethnic basis for the national musical culture. In Moldavian instrumental art music, the independent theme and variation form became the decisive form of the new nationalart music, similar to our observations regarding Jewish music.

---

14 A. Mischakoff, *Khandoshkin and the Beginning of Russian String Music* (Ann Arbor, Mich., 1978), Appendix A.
15 B. Kotliarov, *O skripichnoi kul'ture Moldavii* (On the Violin Culture of Moldavia, in Russian), Kishinev, 1955.
16 Idem., , mus. ex. No. 4, and Beregovski/Goldin, No. 21.

Mus. ex. VII-2: (a) Beregovski, Ms. No. 21, Doina; (b) Kotlyarov No. 4, Doina.

The LKF borders on both traditional and art music. Part traditional, part professional musicians created it at the dawn of East European Jewish art music in the middle and second half of the 19th century. We witness the emergence of professional art music from traditional music, a process that constituted a central feature for most European nations engaged in creating their own national art music during the second half of the 19th century.[17] In the specific conditions of 19th-century Eastern Europe, especially in Russia, Jewish art music developed from several sources, including such socio-musical factors as the development of national schools of music in Eastern Europe, and the particularly favorable conditions of Russian musical culture for Jewish art music. The primary musical factors that contributed to the formation of Jewish art music were the use of oriental and Jewish elements in Russian music, Jewish traditional

---

17 Comp. W. Salmen, *The Social Standing of the Professional Musician from the Middle Ages to the 19th Century* (New York, 1983), pp. 14-15; J. Braun, "Aspects of Early Latvian Professional Musicianship", in: *Studies: Music in Latvia* (Riga, 2002), pp. 159-160.

liturgical music, and Jewish traditional vocal and instrumental (klezmer) music.[18]

The LKF, defined by its variation form, and use of thematic, idiomatic klezmer music, was the decisive genre that generated East European Jewish instrumental art music. This genre later influenced American Jewish instrumental art music, and, after World War II, early Israeli instrumental art music. It is my conjecture that the LKF constitutes one of the decisive missing ethnic musical links, links that have not been recognized in the discourse on the birth of Jewish art music. In this regard, the role of the variation concept, in general, and the independent theme-and-variation-form in early Jewish and Israeli art music, in particular, are of utmost importance.

Analysis and evaluation of early Jewish and Israeli art music from this point of view requires a study of its own. Here I shall present merely a few brief preliminary examples that may indicate how the LKF tradition contributed to Jewish and Israeli art music.

Joel Engel (1868, Berdiansk – 1927, Tel Aviv), one of the founders of the St. Petersburg School of Jewish Music, was the first to direct public attention to Jewish musical folklore. His creative output is not large, but its deep interlacing with Jewish culture and the Jewish music tradition has great significance for Jewish art history. In addition to the fact that the variation serves as an "important fundament of his composition technique,"[19] the independent theme-and-variation-form provides the formal frame for some of the music written in his attempt to create a new Jewish/Israeli music. In 1926, shortly after settling in Palestine, Engel wrote music for a theater performance based on seven stories by the Yiddish writer Yitzhak Leib Peretz (1851-1915). Intended for the opening of the new Tel Aviv theater, "The Tent" (*HaOhel*), the preparation and actual performance of *Neshfey Peretz* (Peretz Festival) was a central event for those striving to create a national art form. The music for two highly important scenes in *Neshfey Peretz* was written in the form of theme and variations: Part II, *Shma Israel,* was based on a *khazanut* melody, and

---

18 J. Braun, "The Jewish National School in Russia," in: J. Cohen, ed., *Proceedings of the World Congress on Jewish Music Jerusalem 1978* (Tel Aviv, 1982), pp. 198-203.
19 R. Flomenboim, *The National School of Jewish Art Music: Joel Engel (1868-1927) and Michail Gnessin (1883-1957)*, Ph.D. Thesis, Bar-Ilan University (Ramat-Gan, 1996), p. 115.

Part IV, *From the Moon Stories/The Children*, featured variations on two contrasting melodies of an East European Jewish style.

Mikhail Gnesin (1883, Rostov-on-Don – 1957, Moscow) was one of the most significant figures in the new movement of Jewish national music in the first half of the 20th century. In 1925 he composed one of his first Jewish works – *Variations on a Jewish Theme*, op. 24 for String Quartet. In another work – *Theme and Variations*, op. 67 for Cello and Piano (1953), one of his last compositions,[20] the theme is based on the typical klezmer interplay of different *štayger* (mode) sections based on one central tone (see Braun 1987, pp. 132-133). In his most popular work, *The Jewish Orchestra at the Ball of the Town Bailiff*, op. 41 (1926) – composed for Gogol's comedy, *The Inspector General*, Gnesin used klezmer music motifs and variation form as a central means of ethnic expression.[21]

Paul Ben Haim (1897, Munich – 1984, Jerusalem), one of the founders of Israeli art music, composed his op. 42 for piano, *Melody and Variations*, in 1949. Although the composer regarded this piece as merely a little piano piece for children,[22] it greatly influenced future Israeli art music. He wrote this composition during a crucial period for the new Jewish music. Following the recent establishment of the State of Israel, the intellectual and musical community was involved in a heated discussion on what should be the essence of "Israeli music," "Israeli art," etc., especially in relation to European art music. In *Melody with Variation* the heterophonic texture dominates the fabric of the music, representing "an intrinsic feature of oriental music... – which appears in the work as a statement of opposition to organized harmonic writing."[23] It is remarkable that when Ben Haim ventured to introduce a new Mediterranean Israeli music style, he cast his music in the form of theme and variations, thus incorporating one of the immanent forms of Jewish traditional instrumental music – the LKF.

In conclusion, I would like to mention a recent CD – *Musique Juives Russe* (Le chant du monde/Harmonia mundi RUS 288166/HM 90) –

---

20 Written nearly 30 years later, during the period of Stalin's anti-Semitic campaign, the Jewish flavor of the theme had to be disguised.
21 Floenboim, op. cit., pp. 221-223.
22 J. Hirshberg, *Paul Ben-Haim: Life and Works* (Jerusalem, 1990), p. 241.
23 Idem., p. 246.

which presents three outstanding masterpieces of Jewish art music created under the influence, directly or indirectly, of the LKF: Sergey Prokofiev, *Overture on Hebrew Themes*, op. 34 (1919); Dmitri Shostakovitch, from *Jewish Folk Poetry*, op. 79a (1949), and Sergey Slonimsky, *Jewish Rhapsody, Concerto for Piano, Strings and Percussion* (1997). Each of these works symbolizes a different epoch: Prokofiev – the early 20th century, Shostakovich – the middle of the century amidst the turbulent 1950s of Soviet Russia, and Slonimsky – the end of the 20th century. While the musical style evolves from classical stylization, through the "new folklore wave," to post-modernism, all three compositions maintain the use of klezmer motifs and the variation form as a dominant structural concept.

Slonimsky's (b. 1932, St. Petersburg) *Jewish Rhapsody* is of particular interest, both because it is a relatively new and hardly known composition and also, as far as I know, the most recent work to draw upon elements of traditional klezmer music. I will not go into the details of Slonimsky's involvement with Jewish musical elements, but will only point out a few of them in the above mentioned *Rhapsody*. The title of the work itself indicates the free improvisational form; the three movements are performed *attaca*, thus creating the impression of a one-movement extemporary composition. The first movement, with its large harp-like *cadenza* of the solo instrument, is actually a kind of introduction; the second, a slow expressive variation on quasi-Eastern musical material, dominates the entire work, and explodes into an exciting dialogue between a klezmer *freilekh*-type tune and the popular Russian dance tune *Kamarinskaya*, actually the coda.[24] This latest work of Jewish art music still adheres to much of the structure of instrumental traditional music. Thus, at the end of the 20th century, it contributes to confirming the link between Jewish European art music and its rudimentary art form – the Large Klezmer Form.

---

24 Joachim Braun, *Musiques Juives Russes: Prokofiev, Chostakovitch, Slonimsky*. CD Le chant du monde/harmonia mundi (Paris, 2000), RUS 288 166/HM 90.

Relevant Bibliography

Beregovski, Moisei, 1962. *Evreiskie narodnie pesni* (in Russian, Jewish Folk Songs), Moscow. See Beregovski/Slobin, 1982, pp. 19-284.

Beregovski, Moisei and I. Fefer, 1938. *Evreiskie narodnie pesni* (Jewish Folk Songs), Kiev.

Beregovski, Moisei/Mark Slobin, 1982. *Old Jewish Folk Music: The Collections and Writings of Moshe Beregovski*, Philadelphia.

–, 1973. Izmenjonnyi doriiski lad ..., see Beregovski/Slobin 1982, pp. 549-567.

Beregovski, Moisei/Max Goldin, 1987, ed. and Introduction by M. Goldin. *Evreiskaya narodnaya instrumental'naya muzika* (in Russian, Jewish Instrumental Folk Music), Moscow.

Beregovski/Slobin, 2001, ed. and tr. by M. Slobin. *Jewish Instrumental Folk Music: The Collections and Writings of Moshe Beregovski*, Syracuse.

Feldman, W. Zwi, 1994. Bulgareasca/Bulgarish: the Transformation of a Klezmer Dance Genre, in *Ethnomusicology*, 38/1: 1-35.

Idelsohn, Abraham Zwi, 1932. *Hebraeisch-orientalischer Melodienschatz...*, vol. VIII, IX and X, Leipzig.

Ottens, Rita and J. Rubin, 1999. *Klezmer-Musik*, Kassel.

Rubin, Joel, 1997. 'alts nemt zikh fun der doyne': The Romanian-Jewish Doina – a Closer Stylistic Examination, in S. Stanton and A. Knapp, eds., *Proceedings of the First International Conference on Jewish Music*, London, pp. 133-164.

Salmen, Walter, 1991. *Judishe Musikaten und Taenzer vom 13. bis 20. Jahrhundert*, Innsbruck.

Slobin, Mark, 1984. Klezmer Music: An American Ethnic Genre, in *Yearbook for Traditional Music*, 9: 2-41.

–, 2000. *The Fiddler on the Move*, Oxford.

–, 2002. *American Klezmer: Its Roots and Offshoots*, Berkeley.

Strom, Yale, 2002. *The Book of Klezmer: The History, the Music, the Folklore from the 14th Century to the 21st*, Chicago.

Stutschewsky, Joachin, 1958. *Haklezmorim: History, Folkways and Composition*, Jerusalem.

VIII. The Jewish National School of Music in Russia[*]

In this paper I would like to refer to some aspects which may help, perhaps, to situate this chapter of Jewish music in a more balanced, historical and artistic perspective[1]. Some nuances might also be added to the over-all picture drawn by Albert Weisser, whose *Modern Renaissance of Jewish Music* (New York, 1954) is fundamental for any study in this field.

The founders of the Society for Jewish Folk Music, Engel and Kisselgof, nearly a century ago, thought that the only, or almost only possible and desirable method leading to the creation of a Jewish art music was the arrangement and use of East European Jewish folklore. The Jewish national musical school in Russia transcended these preliminary tasks and developed a much deeper and more comprehensive attitude towards the Jewish tradition. In modern literature, however, we may read about this school's "scanty and superficial"[2] concern with the mainstream of Jewish music – a statement which is not at all by way of exception.

The formal chronological borderlines of what is called the Jewish national school in Russia – a definition used, to the best of my knowledge, for the first time in 1924 by the Russian musicologist Leonid Sabaneev – extend from January 1909 to April 1926.

The earlier date is that of the first public concert of the "Society for Jewish Folk Music" in St. Petersburg. The original intention of the founders was not to establish a society for Jewish *folk* music, but rather a society for *Jewish music*. The reason for the change was the authoritatively

---

[*] Published in: *Proceedings of the World Congress on Jewish Music, Jerusalem 1978*, ed. J. Cohen, Tel-Aviv: The Institution of Translation of Hebrew Literature, 1982, pp. 198-204.

[1] I wish to express my sincere thanks to the YIVO Institute for Jewish Research and to the AMLI Tel-Aviv Central Music Library for kind permission to use archive materials.

[2] Eric Werner, "Prolegomenon", in *Contributions to a Historical Study of Jewish Music*, ed. Eric Werner (New York, 1976), p. 14.

pronounced conviction of a certain Tsarist police general, one Drachevsky, that Jewish art music does not and can not exist, an approach still common in some circles of our own time. The second date – April 1926 – is that of the last concert of the "Society for Jewish Music", established in 1923 and regarded as a continuation of the "Society for Jewish Folk Music", which was disbanded at the end of World War I.

I chose those two events not only because they mark the beginning and end of the socially organized activities of this school, but also because the 1909 concert presented for the first time in Russia – and perhaps in history – an entire program of Jewish art music, while the 1926 concert was the last event of this kind in the Soviet Union.

The programs of those two concerts[3] may symbolize the development of the Jewish school during these seventeen years. Let us illustrate this by comparing the two documents:

Number of works in programs	1909	1926
Folk song arrangements	5	0
Music on Jewish subjects written by non-Jewish composers	3	0
Large forms	0	2
Compositions using folk song material	3	3-4
Composition using traditional Jewish elements	1(?)	5-6
Jewish composers	2 (Schkliar, Kopet)	4 (Achron, Bloch, Gnessin, Milner)

We may define this development as a maturation process from folk song arrangements and borrowings to a genuine national art music.

However, an art trend or school cannot be confined within rigid chronological limits. The roots and sources of this school reach back to the musical tradition of nineteenth century Russia, strongly felt to this

---

[3] Program of the First Musical Evening of the Society for Jewish Folk Music, January 21, 1909, St. Petersburg (YIVO Institute for Jewish Research, Vilnius Archive: RG37, 2/118-120), and program of the Fourth Concert of Jewish Music of the Society for Jewish Music, April 29, 1926, Moscow (ibid., Box 9M, ½).

day. The nature and development of the Jewish national school in Russia were determined by five socio-musical factors – two of them non-Jewish, two Jewish and the fifth a result of Jewish-Russian interaction.

1. The development of national schools in Eastern Europe

Schools of national music – Russian, Polish, Czech, Hungarian, Norwegian, Finnish, Latvian, etc. – emerged during the second half of the nineteenth century. They all expressed a combination of national, artistic, and socio-political aims, and they all turned to folklore as a main source of inspiration. They all began by collecting folk songs and tunes, then went on to arrangements of these melodies, and later used them as thematic material for art forms. Only in the next and final stage did composers use the musical idiom of folklore as their own individual artistic medium. In the areas of Southern and Western Russia with a Jewish population, Jewish professional musicians followed a similar path during the period of emancipation.

2. The special conditions of Russian musical culture

The entire intellectual atmosphere of Russia in the late nineteenth and early twentieth centuries, was favourable to the development of Jewish national music. Especially strong was the impact of the spiritual leaders of Russian music – Nikolay Rimsky-Korsakov and Vladimir Stassov. In a letter to Yoel Engel, Stassov wrote:

> "I am continually gladdened by your project on Jewish folk songs a fundamental work. I always felt that it has long been overdue to introduce the *Jewish* contribution into the history and repository of the new European music. About a half and perhaps more all Gregorian, Ambrosian and other Christian melodies are based on Jewish roots... I think that a solid study of Jewish national melodies may become one of the first fundamental stones in the studies of contemporary European music..."[4]

---

4 Letter by Vladimir Stassov dated February 11, 1904, St. Petersburg (Yoel Engel, *Glazami Sovremennika* (in Russian, "In the eyes of a contemporary"), ed. I. Kunina [Moscow, 1971], p. 475.

This was written on February 11, 1904. The aphoristic pronouncements of Rimsky-Korsakov – why should you Jewish students imitate European and Russian composers? – are well known. Let us note also, that the first study of the Jewish national school was written by the non-Jewish musicologist Leonid Sabaneev, whom we have already mentioned. The climate of the non-Jewish environment was thus more than propitious.

3. Jewish folk music

Today we may adopt whatever attitude we choose towards the body of East European Jewish folk music, this alloy of multinational and multifunctional strains. However, the fact that for some 400 years East European Jewry has regarded this music as its own should remain our basic criterion. Musicians such as Engel, Kisselgof, Schkliar, Zhitomirsky, Lvov, etc., were chiefly active in collecting and arranging folk music. Achron, Saminsky, Zeitlin, Milner and others used folk tunes as quotations. Gnessin, Krein, Veprik, etc. used folk melodies in their art forms – operas, symphonies and chamber music – to nourish their creative work. Gnessin wrote in this context:[5]

> "Elements of Jewish music captured my musical feelings and imagination to-such an extent that, even when I did not intend to look for a Jewish style, those elements appeared in my works."

It should be noted that not only East European folk music appeared in the work of those composers. Visiting Palestine in 1914 and 1922, Gnessin became acquainted with Jewish musical material of Yemenite and Middle Eastern origins, which he used in his compositions.

---

[5] Mikhail Gnessin, *Statyi -Vospominaniya-Materyali* (in Russian, Articles – Recollections – Resources), ed. Raisa Glezer (Moscow, 1961), p. 202.

4. The Jewish liturgical musical tradition

Representatives of the school were seriously interested in Jewish traditional sacred chant. Research in this field was conducted by Saminsky, Maggid, Rozovsky, Beregovsky and many large scale forms were based on this tradition. Numerous compositions – operas, symphonic-and chamber works – by Klein, Milner, Saminsky, Gnessin and Veprik absorbed the melodies of the sacred chant. Nearly every member of the group wrote a "Kaddish" or some other semi-liturgical work. In connection with the work on his "Kaddish" Alexander Krein wrote about using – and here I quote from a letter I found recently[6] – "as much as possible material from *ancient* (Krein's italics – J.B.) books of the synagogue". By separating the Jewish national school from the genuine sources of Jewish traditional music and reducing if to a trend" of folk' '.song arrangements, we find ourselves trapped by General Drachevsky's pronouncement, echoed by official Soviet theories, proclaiming the non-continuity of Jewish spiritual life and culture.

5. The Oriental, or Jewish, elements in Russian music

The influx of Jewish elements into Russia may be traced back to the tenth century. From then onward Jewish strains are present in both Russian liturgical and vernacular music. The preoccupation of classical Russian music, from Glinka and Balakirev to Ippolitov-Ivanov and Prokofiev, with the Oriental or Jewish idiom (the two were frequently interchangeable) is not without a certain flavour of piquancy. However, "to view this merely as some strange whim or caprice on the part of Russian composers... is ridiculous and short-sighted."[7]

If one group of Russian composers – the "Five" – were closer to a musical and folkloristic approach to the Oriental element, another – Serov, Rubinstein – rather tended to interpret the Jewish idiom from a

---

6 Letter by Alexander Krein, probably written in 1923, Moscow (AMLI Tel-Aviv Central Music Library, Archive: R1/8/2/1509).
7 Vladimir Stassov, "Dvadtzat' pyat' let russkovo iskusstva: Nasha muzika" (in Russian, Twenty-five years of Russian art: Our music," in: *Vestnik Evropi* (Europian Herald, October, 1883).

199

philosophical and ethical angle. Although there was some confusion between an abstract Oriental style and the Jewish idiom, at the end of the century the Russian composers themselves were making an attempt to stress the genuineness of Jewish elements. Discussing a composition by one of his students, Rimsky Korsakov remarked:[8]

"Why did you call those pieces "Eastern Melodies"? Those are typical Jewish melodies! You cannot confuse them with the others."

The Eastern-Jewish trend of Russian music is deeply rooted in Russian history and culture, and this fact had a decisive influence on the development of the Jewish national school out of Russian music.

These then are the five sources, which, I believe, determined the genesis and growth of the Jewish national school in Russia.

The creative work or composers such as, Gnessin, Krein, Saminsky, Milner, Veprik and of writers on music, such as Beregovsky, Saminsky, Maggid, Rozovsky, together constitute the Russian Jewish national school. Some four hundred musical compositions, nearly a hundred books and articles, and numerous concerts over nearly a quarter century represent its output.

I would like to conclude by speaking of the tragic fate of this trend, which, to the best of my knowledge, has no precedent in history. With our information on the deliberate destruction of Jewish culture in the Soviet Union it is perhaps sufficient to quote from an unpublished letter of Gnessin, written in connection with the last activities of the Jewish Music Society:

> "As a person I am now not even a zero, I am a negative quantity... It is agonizing for me to speak to the Soviet officials... If you despise me – do so. I don't know if in the future I will be forgiven for all this, and I try not to think about it."[9]

The Jewish national school in Russia certainly does not represent the only possible path that Jewish art music in Europe in the late nineteenth and early twentieth centuries could have adopted. But it is the first and

---

8 Mikhail Gnessin, *Misli I vospomonaniya o Rimskom-Korsakove* (in Russian, Thoughts and recollections on Rimsky-Korsakov), Moscow, 1956, p. 208.
9 Letter by Mikhail Gnessin, January 8, 1924, Moscow (AMLI Tel-Aviv Central Music Library, Archive: R1/8/2/1518).

only school of European Jewish art music and in this sense its historical significance is unique.

The school was certainly not a "superficial" tangential tendency in the history of Jewish music. It is an organic, inseparable part of Jewish music at the very pivot of its mainstream. Its artistic-values are deeply rooted in Jewish tradition and social psychology, and in this sense its artistic significance is also unique.

IX. Jews in Soviet Music*

The topic we are concerned with is a complex one, as are most problems in the history of Jewish spiritual life in the Diaspora. It involves numerous issues outside the realm of music and overlaps many adjacent fields. As well as the general, well-known difficulties faced by students of Jews in the Soviet Union, especially with regard to the arts, the researcher of the Jewish idiom in Soviet music is confronted with certain other problems arising from the specific nature of music, for example, the still obscure question of national, in particular Jewish, expression of European musical performance; the significance of the use of Jewish musical intonations in the works of non-Jewish composers; the diffusion of different national musical styles etc. At the same time certain trends in the history of Soviet Jewry are seen more vividly and are more clearly expressed in music precisely because of that specific nature. The abstract nature of music made it possible for an aspiration towards Jewish self-expression to appear first in the field of music, even while Jewish culture was being suppressed – I refer to the Jewish folksong concerts given by Nekhama Lifshits and other singers in the early 1950s when Jewish spiritual life had been silenced by the Soviet authorities.

Until now scholars have been concerned with two topics: Jews in the Soviet Union, with hardly any reference to music; and music in the Soviet Union, with no mention of the Jewish aspect. The few articles in Western books or journals on the subject are usually limited to the 1920s[1] or consider particular problems within the subject.[2] The only article concerned with the subject as a whole is unfortunately of dubious value,

---

* Based on *Jews in Soviet Music*, Research Paper No. 22, The Hebrew University: Soviet and East European Research Center (Jerusalem, 1977), and *Jews in Soviet Culture*, ed. Jack Miller (London, 1984), pp. 65-106.
1 Irene Heskes and Arthur Wolfson, *The Historical Contribution of Russian Jewry to Jewish Music* (National Jewish Music Council, 1967).
2 E.G. Mlotek, 'Jewish Soviet life as reflected in the Jewish folk song', *The Workman's Circle Call*, January 1963, 13-16.

abounding in errors.[3] Soviet literature on music simply avoids the existence of Jewish musical values in Soviet music. The five volume *History of the Music of the People of the USSR*[4] which gives information on Chuvash, Yakut, Mari, Udmurt, Kabardin and Ossetian music, that is the music of people who number less than 500,000, makes no mention of the musical life of nearly three million Soviet Jews. Only one piece of research on Jewish music has been published during the fifty-seven years of Soviet rule.[5] During the years of Soviet rule 12 articles and books on Jewish music were published, while on Armenian or Azerbeidzhan music some 400 items appeared. There was a sharp decline in scholarly publications on Jewish music during the years 1917 and 1972. The following table illustrates the point:

	1917-22	1923-27	1928-32	1933-37	1938-42	1943-47	1948-52	1953-57
Music	8	9	17	16	8	2	0	2
Books	0	1	1	3	0	0	0	0

	1958-62	1963-67	1967-72
Music	3	0	8
Books	0	0	

Table 1: Music and Books on Music with a Jewish Subject Published in the USSR, 1917-72[6]

This table is even more eloquent if we bear in mind that, according to the third edition of the 'Great Soviet Encyclopaedia', vol. 10. pp. 60-62, in the entry 'Publishing' on p. 662, the number of publications in the USSR just in the period 1940-71 increased by an average of some 400

---

3   Gershon Svet, 'Evrei v russkoy muzykalnoy kulture v sovetskom periode' (in Russian, Jews in Russian musical culture in the Soviet period), in *Kniga o russkom evreystve: 1917-67* (Book on Russian Jewry) (New York 1968), 248-65.
4   *Istoriya muzyki narodov SSSR* (in Russian, History of the Music of the People of the USSR), vols. 1-5 (Moscow 1970-74).
5   See below on M. Beregovsky.
6   This table is based on both Soviet and Western sources and the personal archive of the author. In my opinion some items unavailable to the author do not alter the general picture.

percent, while the increase from 1917 can be estimated at about 600 percent.

It is possible to find reviews of Jewish folk song collections or other publications in Soviet periodicals, as well as some short articles on Jewish folk music. But in these cases the main purpose is always to prove that the 'idea of a distinct Jewish people is scientifically untenable, from a political point of view, reactionay'.[7] Reference books are the only sources for Jewish music in the Soviet Union. The *Bol'shaya Sovetskaya Entciklopedia* (in Russian, Large Soviet Encyclopedia), whose different editions were written according to the official policies prevailing at the time, shows an interesting development in treatment of our subject. The first edition of 1932 devotes three of the eighty-two pages of a general article on Jewish matters to Jewish music.[8] The one-page entry on Jews in the 1952 edition makes no reference to music at all. Information on music is also lacking in the 1972 edition, although a special entry is devoted to Jewish literature. The entry on Jewish music in the first edition of the only music reference book, *Encyclopaedic Dictionary of Music* (1959) merely gives some bibliography (M. Beregovsky, D. Magid, A. Idelson), without any text. The 1966 edition has three entries on Jewish music – 'Ancient Hebrew music', 'Jewish Music' and 'Israeli Music' – while other national musical styles come under one entry. This is evidently to demonstrate the thesis of the main Soviet reference book that 'Jews have no common culture'.[9]

It is not without interest that the entry 'Jewish Music' in the Soviet encyclopaedia of music, the reference literature directs the reader to E. Müller von Azov's article 'Das Judentum in der Musik', published in the classic antisemitic book of Th. Fritsch, *Handbuch der Judenfrage* (Leipzig, 1932).[10] Let us mention that Soviet reference books, as rule, present only officially approved bibliography. It is in this context that we shall quote the following passage from the mentioned opus:

---

7   *Sovetskaya muzyka*, 8:104 (1970).
8   The anonymous entry seems to be written by M. Gnesin..
9   "Jews," in: *Bolshaya*...(Moscow 1952).
10 *Entsiklopedichesky muzykalny slovar* (in Russian, Encyclopedic Dictionary of Music, Moscow 1966), p. 172.

'In music...more and more forces emerge which destroy harmony and melody and exclud all content from music. We now have music without logic, but which demands high virtuosity from the performers. This begins with the Jew Mahler; Schoenberg is their apostle...Among the young composers are Kšenek, Berg, Hindemith, Stravinsky.... Their aim is the destruction of the Western tone system... through dissonance,'

Not less indicative is the comparison of this passage with such well known Soviet sources as the *Resolution of the Central Committee of the CPSU* of 10 February 1948, and paper by Boris Asafjev at the *First Congress of Soviet Composers, Stenographic Report*.[11]

'The characteristic of this music is the negation of classical music, the propagation of atonality, dissonance.... negation of melody and logic, passion for chaos. This music... ruins the art of music.' 'What was started in the school of Arnold Schoenberg and in the expressionism of Alban Berg and Anton Webern, was developed by Ksenek and Hindemith and finished by Messiaen, Menotti and Britten...'

We can already see from these few examples that the history of Soviet Jewish music is the history of the contradiction between the suppression of Jewish musical life and the officially proclaimed right of every people in the Soviet Union to national development. On the one hand the existence of a common Jewish culture is denied and the very idea of a Jewish people is claimed to be reactionary, while on the other hand that culture exists, and a people sings and plays and has the right to express itself just like every other people.

What then are the general lines of development in the history of Soviet Jewish music and who are the central figures in this development?

The decades preceding the 1917 Revolution created a most favorable situation for the development of Jewish music. The establishment of national musical styles in Eastern Europe in the second half of the nineteenth century and the influential school of Russian national music, the emancipation of Jewish artists in Europe, activity in the field of folklore collecting and early examples of Jewish secular music, and last but not least the benevolent attitude of the Russian musical elite (see Ch. VIII) – all this led logically to the idea of a Jewish national style of music. It would be also wrong in this context to ignore the history of Russian-

---

11 Moscow, 1948, p.16.

Jewish musical interrelationship which reaches back to the 11th century (see ADDENDUM, pp.xxx). The idea of Jewish cultural revival crystallized especially in pre-Revolutionary Russia where famous figures such as N. Rimsky-Korsakov and V. Stasov were active and where there was a strong Jewish community. Jewish folk music first drew a large audience in the performance given by Y. Engel in November 1900 in the Moscow Polytechnic Museum. Rimsky-Korsakov expressed the general atmosphere when listening to 'A Romance on a Jewish Tune' by his student Ephraim Shklyar: 'Why should you Jewish students imitate European and Russian composers? The Jews possess tremendous folk treasuries . . . Jewish music awaits its Glinka.'[12]

A group of Jewish musicians, many of whom were students of Rimsky- Korsakov, applied for permission to set up a Jewish Music Society. The Tsarist Government, represented by General Drachevsky, refused permission, but on 30 November 1908 did allow the Petersburg Society for Jewish Folk Music to be established.[13] It is interesting that the Tsarist Russian authorities were more or less willing to accept Jewish folk music activities but not art music, likewise as it will be years later in Soviet Russia.

We can see how promising the situation was from the activities of this Society. It had about 389 active members throughout Russia, held some 150 concerts and lectures a year and published a large amount of music (eighty-five items between 1909 and 1917;[14] seventy-three items between 1917 and 1972); and was active in collecting folk music. Some of its most famous and talented composers at that time were: I. Akhron, S. Feynberg., M. Gnesin, A. Krein, M. Milner, S. Rozovsky, L. Saminsky, E. Shklyar; Y. Engel was one of its writers on music, and concerts were given by I. Press, E. Tsimbalist, Y. Heifez, F. Shalyapin, N. Milstein and others. We may add that famous schools of performance headed by Jewish musicians developed in pre-Revolutionary Russia, such as the L. Auer school of violin at the Petersburg Conservatory, the P. Stolyarsky school of violin in Odessa, and the K. Davidov school of cello in Petersburg. All

---

12 A. Soltes, "The Hebrew Folk Song Society of Petersburg," in: Heskes/Wolfson, *Historical Contribution*, p. 20.
13 A. Weisser. *The Modern Renaissance of Jewish Music* (New York 1954), p. 45
14 For a complete list of publications, see Weisser, *Modern*, pp. 67-9.

these activities brought about a situation which in the history of music is always characteristic of a speedy development of a 'classical' period in the particular national style. The famous non-Jewish musicologist of the period, L. Sabanejev, expressed this very well in the conclusions drawn from his research on the school of Jewish national music:

> All preconditions for a further development of this spirit exist: musical talent, a number of Jewish musicians, the artistic temperament of the nation, suitability to musical activity, an interest in national art, the example of past musicians of genius – all this justifies the assumption that the Jewish people will enrich world music literature with a stream of fresh and original works . . . At the present moment, when an intellectual stratum is emerging from the masses, it [the Jewish people] can and must attain world significance. The historical perspective has not yet been revealed. But we can justifiably assume that the blossoming of the Jewish people's culture has announced itself.[15]

This natural development was violently disrupted by the October Revolution of 1917. Among the first practical results of the change in situation was the dissolution of the Petersburg Jewish Folk Song Society, which was declared to be 'incompatible with the spirit of the time'.[16] The overall situation in musical life changed completely. Lenin's statement at a session of the Petrograd Society on 25 October 1917 was certainly equally true of music: "From today began a new period in the history of Russia...we must now devote ourselves to building the proletarian socialist state."[17] For music this meant, according to Lenin, that although "every artist takes it as his right to create freely, according to his ideal whether it is good or not", nevertheless, "we are Communists. We must not... allow the chaos to ferment as it chooses. We must... guide this development and mold and determine the results." The entire development of Soviet music moves from the first thesis to the second, from free creation to strict determination of the results of creation. For the Jews, as already suggested, this meant the contradiction between the complete ne-

---

15 L. Sabanejev, *Die nationale jüdische Schule in der Musik* (Vienna 1927), p. 24-5.
16 J. Yasser. "The Hebrew Folk Song Society," in: Heskes/Wolfson, *Historical Contribution...*, p. 41. This is the only statement so far by an eye-witness of the events. No records from Soviet sources are available. Probably, a certain element of self-dissolution was also present.
17 V.I. Lenin, *Polnoe sobranie sochineniy* (Complete Works), vol. 35, p. 2; and Klara Zetkin quoted in Louis Eisher. *The Life of Lenin* (New York 1967), p. 490.

gation of a Jewish people and the limited acceptance of spiritual life and art, 'national in form and socialist in content', for every people.

The Revolution divided the Russian musical world, including Jewish musicians, into many parts according to attitude to the events. Many welcomed the Revolution with hope for the future. The main figure in the new national Jewish school, M. Gnesin (see below) wrote, "I waited and yearned for the Revolution. I thirsted for activity, I wanted to see how the artistic life of the people would change."[18] The famous Jewish pianist, Samuel Feynberg (1890-1962), greeted the Revolution with enthusiasm and spoke proudly of the opportunity to play for Lenin in Sokolniki, January 1919.[19] It is interesting that the other pianist Lenin heard, Isay Dobroven (1894-1953), was also Jewish (these are the only two recorded instances of Lenin's listening to music after the Revolution). According to Maksim Gorky, Isay Dobroven played the *Appassionata* at E. Peshkova's Moscow home in the presence of Lenin.[20]

Other musicians were more reserved in their reaction. The well-known Jewish ballet conductor, Yuri Fayer (b. 1890-1971), who in those years was a violinist in the orchestra of the Moscow Bolshoy Theater, writes: "November found us in inertia and obscurity. No performance... To whom the theatre belonged was incomprehensible, and it was not as if the authorities would be interested in opera or ballet. The new revolution was met with even more embarrassment than the one in February."[21] Many figures in the world of music decided immediately or in the next few years to leave the socialist state forever. Let us mention only the names of the greatest both among Jews and in world music: the pianists Horovitz and Dobroven, the violinists Auer, Heifetz, Akhron, Tsimbalist, Milstein, the cellist Pyatigorsky, the musicologists Yasser and Slonimsky. Many of the active members of the Jewish Folk Song Society, the composers Saminsky, Rozovsky, Shklyar, the music critic Engel and many others, left Russia and so saved themselves for Jewish music.

---

18 M.F. Gnesin, *Stati, vospominaniya, materialy* (Articles, Reminiscences, Materials, Moscow 1961), 7.
19 S.E. Feynberg, *Pianism kak iskusstvo* (Piano-playing as Art) (Moscow 1969), 5-6.20.
20 A.V. Lunacharsky, *V mire muzyki* (In the World of Music, Moscow 1958), p. 552.
21 Yuri Fayer, *O sebe, o musyke, o balete* (About Myself, Music and Ballet, Moscow 1970), p. 96.

The fate of the Jewish composers who stayed in the Soviet Union was quite different. Mikhail Gnesin (1883-1957) was one of the most respected Soviet composers. Most of his works, and the best of them, are purely Jewish. Gnesin himself wrote: "Elements of Jewish music captured my musical feelings and imagination to such an extent that even when I did not have the mission to look for a Jewish style, those elements appeared in my works."[22] In 1966 this composer was described in Soviet reference sources as "Russian and Jewish composer"[23] but the new *Encyclopedia of Music* (Moscow 1973) refers to him simply as "Soviet composer" and in the 65-line article only one sentence mentions his place in Jewish music: "Was a well-known master of Jewish music" (vol. I:1025).

Until the end of the 1920s Gnesin wrote music deeply rooted in Jewish tradition and over forty-five of his sixty or so works were written before 1930. That is before he was fifty years old. His most significant works were composed in the late 1920s: the operas *The Youth of Abraham* (1921-23) and The *Maccabees* (1921), symphonic works, *Songs from the Old Country'* (1919), *The Jewish Orchestra at the Ball of the Town Bailiff* (1926), the song cycle *Red Headed Motele'* (1926-29), the *Quartet* (1929), *Ten Jewish Songs* (1927), *The Song of Songs* (1922), *Songs of the Knight-Errant* (1927) etc. Although Gnesin had been connected with Jewish music from 1912-14, his work of the 1920s was the result of hope for the revival of Jewish culture in a socialist state. But to understand the direction his mind took, it is also important to remember that he twice visited Palestine, in 1914 and 1922, where he collected folk melodies, some of which he used in his later works (e.g. *Variations on a Palestinian Melody, Galilean Songs)*. During his second trip he worked at, and was closely connected with, the Tel-Aviv Conservatory, 'Shulamit', which was an important period both for the composer and the local Conservatory.[24] He lived at Bab-el-Wad, and was considering to stay in Palestine and "live in a place with typical Palestinian nature."[25] This time he left Palestine with heavy feelings. Back in Moscow in 1923 he started work at the Jewish Habima Theater in Moscow – "a Jewish thea-

---

22 Gnesin, *Statyi*... p. 202.
23 *EMS*, 120.
24 I.Akhron's archive Mus12,j13, Jewish National and University Library, Ms. Department, Jerusalem.
25 Postcard written by Gnesin on 15. 2. 1922 (idem., A. Schwardon Fond).

ter can exist and flourish here."[26] But already a year later the tone of his letters changes. On March the 8th, 1924, he wrote the most tragic letter of this time drawing a horrifying picture of the impending spiritual disaster and capitulation of human dignity:[27]

> "It is now more difficult for me to write to you than to anyone else, and anyway, you will not understand me (underlined by Gnesin, JB). Everybody who has some connection with me has to know that I, as an active person, am even not a zero, but a negative quantity. You cannot count on me for anything. Even though I have the best intentions, I give up at the first difficulty... It is agonizing for me to speak to the 'authority officials' to achieve something... Outside music and teaching, I don't exist. If you despise me – do it. The non-existent is not ashamed and is not grieved...I do not know if I shall be justified for all this, and I try not to think about it, and I cannot do anything about it"

In the 1930s the Jewish idiom does not appear so constantly in Gnesis's music, while in the 1940s there is usually no reference to this idiom in the titles of the music (*Elegy*, 1940; *Trio*, 1943; *Sonata-Fantasia'* 1945, etc.). In the 1930s he started transcribing Azerbaydzhani, Armenian, Adygey, Mari, Circassian, Chuvash and other folk music. "The immersion in Jewish folk music helped me to understand folk art in general", he wrote in a letter of 13 March 1945 to the American musicologist Rene B. Fiher.[28] One has to see this document and read between the lines to sense the wound in the composer's heart. The letter is a confession, not a mere reply to a colleague. From 1917 to 1945 there was not a word on Jewish music in his many published writings, including the "Reminiscences", yet suddenly he answers a letter he had received over a year previously and then lost (?) in the VOKS (USSR Society for Cultural Relations with Foreign Countries – a secret department governed by the KGB, like every institution of this kind in the USSR). "Of course you no longer need my reply, nevertheless I should like to answer you."[29] After a few autobiographical sentences, which also indicate the personal nature of the document, there follows an eight-page effusion on Jewish music in general and on the Jewishness of his own creative work.

---

26 Idem., letter from March 19, 1923.
27 Idem., letter from March 8, 1924.
28 Gnesin, *Statyi*, p. 202
29 Idem., p. 196.

Gnesin was also one of the most famous teachers of composition in the USSR. Among his pupils are A. Khachaturian, T. Khrennikov, B. Kluzner, G. Mushel, A. Leman, N. Namizamidze, A. Eshpay, Z. Khabibulin and many others. One of his most famous pupils, the Armenian Aram Khachaturian wrote:[30]

> The strongest features of Gnesin the composer are the strikingly- expressed national character of his works, which are connected mainly with Jewish subjects. Gnesin reflected real Jewish folk intonations and characteristic psychological features with tremendous force and stylistic chastity. The feeling for folk intonations was so organic in Gnesin that he could create poetic songs in the style of folk improvisations such as 'On Her Tender Face', 'Songs of the Knight-Errant' and others, without using real melodies. M. F. [Mikhail Fabianovich Gnesin, JB] was one of the first to assert that the national character is one of the basic principles of musical creation...It is no accident that composers who subsequently occupied a significant place in the musical life of the national republics came precisely from M. F.'s class.

The Gnesin Music Institute in Moscow founded by the Gnesins in 1895 – Mikhail and his sisters, the piano teachers Elena (1883-1957), Evgeniya (1870-1940) and Mariya (1971-1918) – is regarded as one of the leading music schools in the country till our days; since 1944 called the Gnesin Music Pedagogical Institute.)

Gnesin's work is deeply Jewish, as the composer himself states and as is evident from his work. He took the advice of his teacher Rimsky Korsakov ('Why should you Jewish students imitate European and Russian composers?'), and this was one of the reasons for his success. If Soviet musicology today tries to erase this from human memory, it can change nothing.[31] The active and highly successful period of his creativity coincided with the time when he was connected with the Jewish idiom, that is, until the early 1930s. Afterwards his work declined in both quantity and quality.

---

30 A. Khachaturian, 'Slovo o moem pervon uchitele' (A word about my first teacher), ibid., 231-2.
31 The prestigious journal *Sovetskaya muzyka* (3:138, 1973) commemorates the 90th anniversary of the composer's birth in this way: "Gnesin successfully used in his works Russian, Ukrainian, Azerbaydzhan, Armenian, Chuvash, Jewish, Latvian, Mari, Mordovian, Kazakh and Adygey melodies"

The fate of the Krein family reveals the same picture of simultaneous decline of Jewishness and creative spirit. Old Abraham Krein (1838-1921), a *klezmer* (Jewish folk musician), violinist and folk-tune collector, had seven sons, five of whom became musicians. His son Aleksandr (1883-1951) was one of the most talented Jewish composers. Like Gnesin he was already mature at the time of the Revolution. From 1918-20 he was Secretary for Modern Music in the Commission for Folklore and from 1922 a member of the editorial board of the State Publishing House. In 1934 he was awarded the title of Honored Artist. Before the Revolution he had written numerous chamber works and songs in which synagogue laments and modern Jewish folk tunes were combined. After 1917 Krein turned to theater music. He wrote more than ten incidental works for the Habimah Theater, the Moscow, Belorussian and Ukrainian Jewish State Theaters. The Jewish idiom appears in his later works too: he wrote a symphonic cantata *Kaddish* (1922), *Ornaments for Voice and Piano* (1924-27) and *Ten Jewish Folksongs* (1937). His only opera *Zagbuk* (1950) is based on a drama by A. Glebov concerning a revolutionary plot in ancient Babylon. This was a veiled expression of his yearning for the Jewish idiom. He wrote: "As the plot takes place in ancient Babylon, in any case in the East, it demands some oriental coloring in the style of the opera as well as a specially chosen treatment of the orchestra and its colors. The music to *Zagbuk* must be the birth of a new musical orientalism."[32] A. Lunacharsky connected A. Krein's work on this libretto with his excellent knowledge of the skill in the field of Jewish music. But A. Krein had to turn to other subjects as well in order to please the authorities. We therefore find works with most curious titles, for example, a symphonic dithyramb called *The USSR – The Shock Brigade of the World Proletariat* (1932). He also wrote a *Funeral Ode for Lenin'* (1926), a *Tone Poem for Orchestra 'Birobidzhan'* (1935) and *Songs of the Stalinist Falcon* for violin and piano. In the 1930s and 1940s he wrote a number of works, including a popular ballet, *Laurentsia* (1937) in which he avoided Jewish intonations. Not one of his almost thirty Jewish works (out of a total of fifty-five works) is mentioned in the 1973 music encyclopedia. Articles on the occasion of his seventieth and eightieth

---

32 A. Krein, "O muzyke k Zagbuku" (On the music to Zagbuk), in A. Glebov, *Zagbuk*, p. 17.

birthdays do not mention at all that he has any connection with Jewish music.[33]

Aleksandr's brother, Grigory (1879-1955), was also a talented composer but he wrote only a few works with Jewish intonations and never found his own style of expression. Another brother, David (1869-1926), a violinist and, from 1918-26, professor at the Moscow Conservatory, according to eye-witness testimony was driven to suicide by anti-Semitism.[34] Grigory's son Yulian (1913-1996), a child prodigy who studied under Paul Dukas from 1926-32, never touched the Jewish idiom. He and his wife, Nana Ivanovna Rogozhina, wrote a book about their famous uncle (*Aleksandr Krein,* Moscow 1964), mainly to prove their family's loyalty to the regime and to dissociate the Kreins from anything Jewish. Leonid Sabaneyev again sees the historical situation exactly:

> The three Kreins felt like national Jewish musicians, pioneers of national music. If they did not succeed it was not their fault but because ideological considerations of an extra-musical nature saw their national trend as superfluous, harmful and as one that shakes the system's foundations.[35]

Perhaps the most Jewish of all these composers was Moses (Mikhail) Milner (1882-1955) who matured as a musician in the Jewish Folk Song Society. His fate was also the most tragic. He did not forsake Jewish music until the last days of his life. His music was not published, hardly performed, and today he has been expunged from Soviet historiography even though he was highly admired as a composer in the early 1920s and wrote the first opera in Yiddish to be performed in Russia – *The Heavens Aflame,* premiered on May, the 6th, 1923 at the Leningrad State Opera. After the second performance the opera was "forbidden even in concert form, by order... because of its mystical quality."[36] Later he wrote more than ten pieces of incidental theater music for Jewish theaters, voice and piano music, some orchestral works and two more operas – *The New Way*

---

33 *Sovetskaya muzyka* 12:87-8 (1943); *Muzykalnaya zhizn,* 17:19 (1963).
34 Interview with the Israeli cellist and composer Yoakhim Stuchevsky (Tel-Aviv, 1974).
35 *Novoe russkoe slovo* (in Russian, New Russian word) quoted in *Kniga o russkom evreystve* (Book on Russian Jewry), ed. F. Frumkin et al., (New York, 1968), p. 262.
36 Weisser, *Modern Renaissance...,* p. 95.

(1932) and *Josephus Flavius* (1935), all imbued with Jewish feeling and intonations. He was severely attcked for a second time after the performance of *Josephus Flavius,* which was declared 'reactionary'. A similar fate befell other Jewish composers: the choice between rejecting the Jewish idiom or sinking into oblivion. Most opted for the first, such as A. Veprik (1889-1958), from 1930 Professor and Head of the Department of Instrumentation at the Moscow Conservatory, or S. Feynberg (1890-1962), one of the most famous Soviet pianists and teachers and from 1922 was Professor and Head of the Piano Department of the same institution. In the 1920s Veprik still wrote some Jewish dances for orchestra. It is curious to see how in the 1930s Soviet musicology was trying to purge him of his Jewishness. After the performance of his *Five Dances for Orchestra,* opus 17, a review in the important *Sovetskaya muzyka* (3:100-1, 1936) stated: "The composer never speaks of the dances as Jewish. And although the foreign press calls Veprik a 'Soviet Jewish composer,' justice demands that this definition be strictly limited... The composer himself is willing to speak of the Jewish Ukrainian nature of his music."

Although Jewish music, *per se* declined during the late 1920s and 1930s and then vanished altogether, there was a large increase in the number of Jewish musicians in Soviet music at this time and in the following decades. The new status of the Jewish population after the Revolution made possible an influx of Jews into various fields of science, literature, and the arts. This was especially the case in such fields of music and performance, as teaching and musicology, in which the national idiom is not really evident. It was here that the concept 'Jewish brains and talent − yes, Jewish art and self-expression − no!' could be practiced most successfully. In the 1920s-40s the Soviet regime unreservedly accepted the creative spirit of Jewish musicians so long as they did not display their Jewishness, at least on the surface of their art.

During the first years after the Revolution musical life in Soviet Russia was headed by the young, modern-minded Jewish talented composer Arthur Lourie (1892-1966), now considered one of the first dodecaphonists. Lunacharsky, the first Commissar of Education and the main Party spokesman on culture, chose Lourie as his chief assistant in the field of music. In this capacity Lourie was responsible for most of the administrative work in music in those first years of Soviet rule and for working out the new policy of proletarian music, as the nationalization of theaters and conservatories, the closure of the Russian Music Society and apparently, of the Jewish Folk Song Society, reforms in music education, organization of the Association of Contemporary Music (ASM), etc. But in 1923 Lourie left the Soviet State. Perhaps none of the musicians involved in building up the new system of Soviet music from the first years after the Revolution to the present day is referred to in Soviet musicology with such hostility: "An aesthetic-decadent, a composer void of individuality, eclectic, with pretensions to innovation. Lourie used his official position to advertise himself and to support musical adventurists like himself."[37]

Jewish composers who were more or less Jewish in their art were among the most active and talented creative artists in the young Soviet State. Boris Asafjev, the highest authority in Soviet music, names three composers as the leading musicians in the field of song, among them A. Krein and S. Feynberg (1890-1962).[38] The new generation of composers was headed by Lev Knipper (1898-1974), Zinovy Kompanejets (1902-1987), Genrikh Litinsky (1901-1985) and Zara Levin (1906-76). The rise of the popular composers of 'mass songs', Isaak Dunaevsky and the brothers Daniil, Dmitry, and Samuil Pokrass, also occurred at this time (see below). None of these composers used the Jewish idiom as their main means of expression, and its appearance is somewhat fortuitous. Of course, future research into their life and work, and that of many other Jewish musicians, may reveal that their Jewishness had a deeper, indirect impact on their art or may suggest some deeper, hidden evidence of the Jewishness of their art.

Kompanejets was perhaps the only one who had an unexpressed urge for Jewish music throughout his life. In 1939 he wrote a 'Rhapsody on Jewish Themes' for symphony orchestra; he published a collection of folk songs in the 1940s and five original songs in 1960, and in 1970 he edited a collection of songs in Yiddish. This last collection included some of his own works, mostly based on the poetry of the officially approved Soviet Yiddish writer A. Vergelis. It is worth noting that the urge of

---

[37] *Istoriya muzyki narodov SSSR* (The history of music of the USSR people), vol. 1, 57.(Moscow, 1970).
[38] I. Glebov (=Boris Asafjev), "Perspektivy russkoy muzyki" (Perspectives of Russian music), in: *Zhizn iskusstva*, no. 1 (1926).

Jewish composers to express themselves through their own native idiom is invariably interpreted by Soviet musicology as the interest of a Russian composer in a general Eastern or Oriental idiom.[39] Kompaneets wrote a number of instrumental works as well as popular 'mass songs' (*The Song of Bygone Marches, The Lace-Maker and the Blacksmith*). He and especially Knipper wrote numerous works based on the folk tunes of Eastern peoples. Thus, Knipper wrote suites on Tadzhik, Turkmen, Buryat, Iranian, Kazakh etc. themes, and even *The Master Buddha's Stories*. He was very productive, writing works and some well-known mass songs. In the 1930s he was regarded as one of the pioneers of modernism. He was attacked both by the authorities and by great artists: the first condemned him as a fruitless experimenter and his music as 'unemotional', diminishing the pathos of the Revolution;[40] while Shostakovich claimed that he could see in Knipper's music "neither purity not simplicity."[41] Neither his *Far Eastern Red Army Symphony*, nor the *Poem of the Fighting Komsomol* (the popular song *Polyushko* is from this work), nor his ten suites based on various folk tunes (non-Jewish), and not even the article he wrote in 1951 under the eloquent title "Against cosmopolitanism, for a Russian national style,"[42] helped him to gain official recognition (although he was twice awarded a Stalin Prize and the title of Honored Artist by two republics; the highest title for composers, the title of People's Artist; and a chair at a conservatory he did not deserve). Of greater concern is the fact that the work of a talented composer never reached its potential level and that today it is quite forgotten. Rimsky-Korsakov's question is still relevant: "Why should you Jewish students..."?

Zara Levin (1906-1976) gained recognition mainly in the field of chamber song, especially children's songs. She wrote some music, for example, *Poem for Violin and Piano* (1930), and some songs, in which a Jewish idiom appears. Her childhood in Simferopol where her father, an amateur violinist, or *klezmer*, played Jewish folk tunes at home, naturally left some trace on her art. But today she recalls only one episode from this period, according to her Jewish biographer Noemi Mikhaylovskaya:

---

39 *Istoriya...*, vol. 1, 207.
40 Ibid., vol. 2, 163-4.
41 *Sovetskaya muzika*, no. 5 (1936).
42 Ibid., no. 2, 1951.

in 1914 the eight-year-old Zara wrote a waltz 'Salute to the Russian Warriors' for the recruits of the Tsar.[43] Her Jewishness finds no place in the entire book.

Even G. Litinsky, who was one of the talented modernists in the 1930s, attacked for his own conformity and lack of repentance,[44] and who was one of the few to remain consistent in those times, turned some years later to the national styles of music in the Russian peripheries and to musical theory.

Lev Pulver (1883-1970), a composer of an earlier generation but whose work is connected with the 1920s and 1930s, is also of interest. Until 1923 he was a violinist in the opera orchestra of the Bolshoy Theater. He then took over as musical adviser to the Jewish Theater in Moscow. During the years when the theater was active he wrote music for more than forty plays (e.g. *200,000 Tevye – the Milkman, Freylekhs, King Lear, The Vagabond Stars*). In 1925 Pulver and L. Shteynberg wrote the music for the *Purimshpil* (traditional play for the festival of Purim) at the Kharkov Jewish Theater. From 1949, when Jewish culture in the USSR was completely destroyed and the theater was closed, Pulver was silent as a composer except for some song arrangements. His greatest productivity was in the 1930s when he worked with Mikhoels and other great Jewish actors and wrote most of his incidental theater music. At that period he was highly recognized as a conductor and composer of Jewish theater music, and in 1939 he was even awarded the title of People's Artist. It was mere chance that he did not share the tragic fate of most of that theater's artists.

It is enough to note that forty-five percent of the newly appointed teachers at the Leningrad and Moscow conservatories in the 1920s were Jewish to demonstrate how great was the influx of Jewish musicians into Soviet music and how great their influence on it. The most famous of these were E. Volf-Israel, I. Eydlin, M. Polyakin, F. Zelikhman, I. Braudo, S. Ginzburg, M. Yudin, V. Sher in Leningrad; and M. Gnesin, F. Blumenfeld, S. Feynberg, I. Tseytlin, A. Yampolsky, A. Mogilevsky in Moscow. At this time Jewish participation in instrumental performance was especially high. Many scholars speak of a Russian Jewish school of

---

43 N. Mikhaylovskaya, *Zara Levin* (Moscow 1969), p. 5.
44 *Sovetskaya muzyka*, no. 5, 1936

violin founded by Leopold Auer and then developed by the famous teachers L. Tseytlin, A. Yampolsky, D. Oistrakh, V. Sher, I. Eydlin, I. Yankelevich.[45]

We can see the immense contribution of Jewish musicians to this field from the example of chamber music, in particular quartet music. One of the most famous and long-standing quartets in the Soviet Union was the *Glazunov Quartet*, founded in 1919. Three of its members – I. Lukashevsky, A. Rivkin and D. Zissermann – were Jewish. The *Lenin Quartet* was founded in the same year and included L. Tseytlin and G. Pyatigorsky. A. Mogilevsky played in the *Stradivarius Quartet*, founded in 1920, later included A. Knorre and B. Simsky, V. Pakelman and G. Gamburg, and after 1927 – P. Bondarenko. All the time at least three of its members were Jewish. This last Quartet was so named because of the Stradivarius instruments donated to the musicians by the government from the State Collection of Rare and Old Musical Instruments which had just been founded. Lunacharsky took a direct part in organizing the Quartet and its concerts in the early 1920s. He called it 'one of the creations of the Revolution',[46] and it very soon received high recognition. On 16 March 1923 *Pravda* wrote that it 'is already one of the best ensembles in the world'. The Quartet was active until the beginning of the 1930s.

The Glière Quartet (I. Targonsky, A. Targonsky, M. Lutsky, K. Blok) was completely Jewish. It shared first place with the Stradivarius Quartet at the Quartet competition in Moscow in 1927. Another all-Jewish Quartet was the excellent Vuillaume Quartet (M. Simkin, A. Staroselsky, G. Pekker, I. Vaks) which was active from the early 1920s to the 1950s. In the Ukraine there was the famous Leontovich Quartet (S. Bruzhenitsky,

---

45 *100 let Leningradskoy koservatorii* (100 Years of the Leningrad Conservatory) (Leningrad, 1962), pp. 219-85; *Moskovskaya konsrvatoriya: 1866-1966* (The Moscow Conservatory, 1866-1966) (Moscow, 1966), pp. 642-88. The overall number of Jewish teachers in the Leningrad Conservatory from 1917 to mid 1960s was some 160 (about 20 % of the entire teaching staff), and at the Moscow Conservatory 150 (about 15%). This and other figures on the nationality of the musicians are given somewhat approximately. As complete information, cannot be obtained from Soviet sources, this calculation is based on name studies, indirect evidence and the author's personal sources. The small degree of uncertainty hardly can change the general picture.

46 *Izvestiya*, 15,March 1925.

M. Levin, E. Shor, I. Gelfanbeyn). This list of fine quartets which existed in the Soviet Union at this time, not only in the main centers but also in the peripheries could be continued, and in each case the participation of Jewish musicians would be from fifty to hundred percent.[47]

Today it is impossible to reconstruct the position in orchestras, but the high number of Jewish musicians, especially in the string instrument section, is well known. New ideas in orchestral playing, the result of a 'revolt against the tyranny of the conductor', were also the product of the Jewish spirit. The *Persinfans* (Perviy simfonicheskii ansambl, First Symphony Ensemble), an orchestra without conductor, was founded in 1922 and spiritually guided by the violinist I. Tseytlin. It existed until 1932 and gained international fame from its first years: 'With such an orchestra the technique of execution reaches its maximum.'[48] The Persinfans had several followers in the Soviet Union, but this practice was not fully recognized, even for chamber orchestra most of which was conducted. Nevertheless, this idea had far-reaching consequences in increasing the consciousness and creativity of the orchestral musician.

Although Jewish music *per se* declined during the late 1920snd 1930s and then vanished altogether, there was a great increase in the number of Jewish musicians in Soviet music at that time as well as in the following years. The new status of the Jewish population after the revolution made it possible for an influx of Jews in different fields of science, literature and arts. In the 1920s-1940s the Soviet regime unreservedly accepted the creative spirit of Jewish musicians, so long as they did not display their Jewishness, at least on the surface of their art. This was especially the case in those fields of music, where the national idiom was not so evident, as for example, in performance and pedagogy, or in fields which could serve as substitute for national self-expression (among others, creation of other related national musical cultures). It was here that Jewish talent could be used, while at the same time rejecting Jewish art and self-consciousness.

---

47 See I. Raaben, *Mastera kamerno-instrumentalnogo ansamblya Gliera* (Masters of the Glière Chamber Instrumental Ensemble, Leningrad 1964).
48 Quoted from B. Schwarz, *Music and Musical Life in Soviet Russia, 1917-1970* (New York 1970), 47.

Historical and social conditions, still to be fully clarified, encouraged Jewish participation in the 1920s, 1930s and 1940s mainly in four fields: (1) popular music, (2) national music cultures, (3) instrumental performance, and (4) musicology. In general, the extent of the Jewish contribution to these four fields hardly changed in those decades. This is very different from the picture of creative activity in the field of Jewish music, which is indirectly depicted in Table 1. The powerful momentum of the activities of the Russian Jewish national school and the Jewish Folk Song Society could be maintained during the 1920s and 1930s despite the blow Jewish culture received in 1917. Although Jewish music lost a large number of creative minds in the 1920s and had to adjust itself to the new interpretation of Jewishness, at certain times it had an illusion of equality and hopes for an overall solution to the national problem in a communist state. An official Jewish folk song tells us that after the years of destruction and Civil War the Jewish mother could lift her head and sing:[49]

All my children have become
Teachers and engineers.

It is true that this demanded a complete rejection of all traditions, and more besides:

Who will lead you to the canopy, dear son?
– The whole Komsomol, mother dear!
Oh, who will bless you, dear son?
– Oh, Stalin and Kalinin, mother dear!

The idea of Birobidzhan and Jewish collective farms also appeared in the permitted folk song as one of the illusions which blinded the people. Only a few musicians had a real sense of the destruction which was taking place in traditional Jewish music, and even fewer could express it, and then, of course, only in personal documents as we can see from a letter written by the famous violinists Josiph Akhron's (1886-1943) grandfather who was cantor: 'Recently there has appeared Jewish litera-

---

[49] All folk songs are quoted in the translation by Ruth Rubin, *Voices of a People* (New York/London 1963), pp. 405 and 407.

ture which is not in the least Jewish, simply vile, you can't understand what's written there.'[50]

The Jews were permitted to have some Jewish music to nourish their national feelings at the given moment but they were not to develop their national idiom because, in any case, the future would dissolve the Jewish people into communist society. Thus Tsarist General Drachevsky's idea remained relevant: folk music – yes, serious music – no. Of the seventy-three items in Table 1 more than forty-five are connected with the transcriptions of folk music.

All this explains, too, the artistic, musical level of the composers active in the field of folk song transcription and publication this field. The names of R. Boyarskaya, I. Dobrushin, A. Yuditsky, I. Kogan. Sh. Kupershmid, who were active, in the field transcription and publication, or the names of I. Yampolsky, I. Shaynin, B. Riskind, M. Shalit, I. Bakst etc., who were active in the field of popular songs or brass music, are neither known nor really important. The most significant musical work on a Jewish theme in the 1930s is the *Overture on Jewish Themes for Sextet with Clarinet and Piano* written by Sergey Prokofiev in 1919 and transcribed for symphony orchestra in 1934, the time when some short-term hope for Jewish culture seemed to emerge.

Let us now turn to the main fields in which Jewish musicians were active.

The so-called mass song is a genre which arose in the Soviet Union and includes different groups of songs: patriotic and Revolutionary songs as well as work and love songs. The official requirement for these songs, however, remains ideological texts, in the Soviet sense, and simplified musical features. This genre originated from and absorbed various kinds of songs such as folk songs, prison and exile songs, urban folklore, and *blatnaya pesnya* – thieves songs. The last two were especially widespread in south Russia, in the Jewish centers of the Ukraine and Moldavia. Transformed and mixed with Jewish folklore, these songs developed into a genre of popular music which at an early stage revealed itself in the work of Avraham Goldfaden (1840, Starokonstantinov, Ukrain -1908, New York) and later formed a group of songs with catchy, declamatory

---

50 Letters from M. Morgalin to his grandson, Iosif Akhron, Leningrad, 3 May 1926 (The National and Hebrew University Library, Jerusalem, Mus 12 j 1).

intonations, elements of *Freylekhs*, and certain rhythmical patterns such as the march. These songs made up a large part of the Soviet mass song. It was Jewish professional and semi-professional composers, mainly from these areas of South Russia (M. Blanter was born near Mogilev, I. Dunaevsky – near Kharkov, the Pokrass brothers – in Kiev, O. Feltsman – in Odessa, A. Tsfasman – in Zaporozhe, F. Khayt – in Kiev, M. Fradkin – in Vitebsk etc.), who, sensitive to the signs of the times as Jews in the Diaspora are, and responding to the demands of the mass music market, created most of the popular music in the 1920s-1940s. Some 45% of the mass song composers mentioned by the *Encyclopaedic Dictionary of Music* (Moscow 1966) are Jewish. Out of the seventeen most popular mass songs in the Soviet Union named by that same *Encyclopaedia*, eight are written by Jewish composers (p. 297). Among the officially recognized and also most popular mass song composers are Matvey Blanter (1903-?), Isaak Dunaevsky (1900-55), Dmitry Pokrass (1899-1978), Daniil Pokrass (1903-54), Samuil Pokrass (1897-1939), Oskar Feltsman (1921-?), Aleksandr Tsfasman (1906-1971), Sigizmund Kats (1908-1984), Yuli (Ilya) Khayt (1897-1966), Lev Shvarts (1898-1962), Zinovy Kompaneets, Venyamin Basner (b. 1925), Mark Fradkin (1914-?), Yan Frenkel (1920-1989), David Pritsker (1900-1978), Eduard Kolmanovsky (1923-?).

Dunaevsky, Blanter and Dmitry Pokrass laid the foundations of the Soviet mass song. They developed the pattern of the melodious and march-like Soviet patriotic song. Intonations of Jewish urban folk music appears frequently in their songs and had a great impact on their whole work. This is so obvious that it was recognized even by Soviet musicology: 'Jewish folk music, song and dance melodies became one of the intonational components' of these songs.[51] The intonations of *Freylekhs* appear in the songs of Dunaevsky, Pokrass, Feltsman, Kompaneets, Pritsker and others. D. Pokrass's song *Those are Storm Clouds'* was so Jewish that the melody was popular in the Warsaw Ghetto resistance movement. We feel Jewish intonations in many of Dunaevsky's and Blanter's works including their stage works (operettas). This feature of the mass songs is not limited to the work of Jewish composers (Jewish intonations

---

51 *Sovetskaya muzyka*, no. 8, 1970, p. 105.

for example, are frequent in the songs of N. Boguslavsky). They appear then fused with other intonations from different national and social strata.

Songs by these composers which are most popular, and not only in the USSR, include the *Song of the Fatherland, Kakhovka, The Captain's Song, March of the Enthusiasts,* and *March of the Joyful Boys* by Dunaevsky, *On the Way* and *Katyusha* by Blanter, *If There Is War Tomorrow* and *Budenny's March* by the Pokrass brothers, *I Believe* by Feltsman, *The Song of Bygone Marches* by Kompaneets, *On the Nameless Height* and *What the Homeland Starts From* by Basner, *Aviamarch* by Khayt, and others. In the 1940s and 1950s lyrical intonations increasingly dominate in this genre and Jewish ones are more difficult to discover.

The operettas, musicals and cinema music by these composers were as popular throughout the Soviet Union as the Viennese operetta. Dunaevsky himself wrote twelve operettas including *The Free Wind* and music for the well-known films *Circus* and *Volga Volga*.

Jewish mass song composers wrote many of the apologetic songs of the time which became widespread due to their talent and the popularity of their style. It is enough to recall the popularity of the Stalin songs written by Dunaevsky, Blanter and others to see this genre in general and the work of those composers in proper perspective. Here the sentimental intonations of the Russian urban romance and features of the bellicose Revolutionary songs are combined.

Part of the Soviet nationality policy was to cultivate professional national styles of art which had no genuine art music background in the European sense. Those cultures were designed to serve the new system from the first day of their creation. About twenty such cultures appeared in the space of some ten to twenty years, and in the early stages Jewish participation in their creation was considerable. Jewish musicians who had received an excellent education in the 1910s-30s at the Moscow and Leningrad Conservatories turned to this field for several reasons: it was a vacuum in which recognition could be speedily gained; work was carried out in the peripheries, away from the central authorities and was therefore somewhat freer; it was a fascinating field for the questing Jewish mind. All this is true, but it seems to us that there is another, most significant reason: the frustrated urge for their own national idiom whose expression had been violently disrupted and was under constant repression, sought and found satisfaction in the creation of other national styles – a kind of national sublimation. Future research will perhaps demonstrate this in detail. Meanwhile, it can probably be substantiated by pointing to the large contribution of Jewish composers to the creation of Central Asia's musical cultures – Kazakh, Kirgiz, Uzbek, Turkmen – which are related to the Middle Eastern idiom. We could quote a number of transcriptions of the folk tunes of various small Central Asian peoples used by Jewish composers and which are very close to the Jewish idiom, for example a Changrian (Changri, in Turkey) song by A. Veprik.[52]

The older generation of Jewish composers – M. Gnesin, A. Krein, L. Kniper, M. Shteynberg, A. Veprik, etc. – had been interested in the folklore of the Russian periphery and had written a considerable number works in the style of certain national musical cultures. M. Gnesin wrote transcriptions of Tadzhik, Mari, Chuvash and other folk tunes, and in the 1930s he wrote a *String* Quartet on Azerbaydzhani Melodies and an *Adygey Sextet*, M. Shteynberg (1883-1946), a pupil of Rimsky-Korsakov and himself a prominent Soviet composer and teacher (D. Shostakovich was one of his pupils at the Leningrad Conservatory), wrote the *Turkish Symphony* with Kazakh themes, an opera, a symphony (no. 5) and some other works on Uzbek themes. He was the first to use the Uzbek and Kirgiz idiom in symphonic music. His only work written with Jewish intonations is his Third Symphony. Veprik wrote an opera *Tantagul* based on Kirgiz folklore, Kniper wrote some of the first Tadzhik symphonic works (*Vankh* and *Vakhio Bolo*). It is significant that it was Jewish composers who were most sympathetic to the needs of the national musical cultures. In 1928, for example, in response to a request from the Government of Turkmenistan, six Moscow composers wrote songs for Turkmen schoolchildren, four of them – Z. Levin, Z. Kompaneets, B. Shekhter, V. Bely – were Jewish.[53]

This trend was greatly developed. Many Jewish composers not only visited these parts of Russia for some time in order to write their works but even settled there for longer periods. According to official Soviet sources about thirty to thirty-five Jewish composers have been awarded

---

52 *Sovetskaya muzyka* (no. 10, 1936).
53 *Istoriya muzyki narodov SSSR*, vol. 1, p. 559.

the titles of Honored Artist and People's Artist by the national government of Soviet republics and autonomous republics.

Among significant Jewish composers in national styles are Evgeny Brusilovsky (1905-1981), who in the late 1930s wrote the first Kazakh opera (*Kiz Zhibek, Zhalbir, Er Targin*); Mikail Raukhverger (1901-1989), the composer of an early Kirgiz ballet and opera, written in 1942-43; Pavel Berlinsky (1900-?), composer of the first Buryat musical drama (*Zhargal*, 1941); Georgy Mushel (1909-1989), one of the creators of the Uzbek opera; Boris Shekhter (1900-1961), a highly talented musician who wrote the first Turkmen symphony works (*The Turkmenia Suite*, 1932) and the first opera (*Yusup und Akhmet*, 1941); Boris Tseydman (1908-?), composer of several Azerbaydzhani operas and symphonic works, taught well-known Azerbaydzhani and Uzbek composers in Baku and Tashkent; David Gershfeld (1911-?), author of the fist Moldavian opera (*Grozovan*, 1956); Genrikh Litinsky (1901-1985), one of the most prominent Soviet musicologists and composition teachers at the Gnesin Institute, wrote the fist Yakut operas and ballets (1947) etc.

The third field to which Jews contributed and in which they achieved the highest world renown is musical performance. This is not only true of Russian-born and Russian-educated Jews but is a general historical phenomenon. Soviet Jewish instrumental performance in the last half-century has maintained the highest standards, although different trends and periods can be discerned. The success of the Soviet school of performance may be attributed to a combination of factors: the talent of Jewish musicians, the totalitarian system of education in which no expense is spared to gain a victory at a competition, and the high tradition of musical performance in Russia.

Jews make up about 45% of Soviet musical performers.[54] Many of them come from south Russia, like the mass song composers. Pre-Revolutionary conditions – the Jewish Pale of Settlement (this restriction was occasionally lifted for those studying music), limitations in the choice of profession (music and medicine were permitted) – provided the

---

54 This and some following statements are based on an analysis of Soviet sources: *Sovetskaya muzyka, Muzykalnye konkursy v proshlom i nastoyashchem* (Music Competition in the Past and Present, Moscow 1966), newspapers, encyclopaedias, and books referred to above on the Moscow and Leningrad Conservatories.

social basis for the influx of Jews on to the concert platform. The musical basis was the art of the *klezmers*; nearly every one of the great Soviet Jewish instrumentalists has links with this tradition. The success was also based on the phenomenon of the Jewish child prodigy and the tradition of music education. Statistics show that for many nears (until the mid-1960s) about 50% of candidates for professional music schools in the large cities were Jewish. Nearly sixty percent of the prizes at Soviet and international competitions in the 1930s were awarded to Soviet Jewish musicians. Table 2 below, which gives the percentage of Jews in such competitions, indicates how the situation of Jews in the musical performing arts developed over the years. We must bear in mind that it is quite another question how far the Jewish heritage and their Jewish origin influenced the work of Jewish artists and how far we have the right to speak of Jewish features of musical performance. This question has not yet been thoroughly explored. We can, perhaps, point to such features of Soviet instrumental performance in the early period as a singing-declamatory sound quality, a distinctive melancholy tone, a strong subjective note in the interpretation as ones that could be traced to Jewish tradition. And perhaps the contemporary formal-virtuoso style of Soviet performance is related to the social and national alienation of the Jews from the regime.

The largest group of Jewish performers is concentrated in the field of bow instrument and pianoforte music where the percentage of Jewish musicians is as high as sixty-five to seventy percent. For example, at the six Chopin Competitions in Poland from 1927 to 1960, fourteen of the twenty-one Soviet prize winners were Jewish;[55] as well were Jewish seven of the eleven Soviet prize winners at the Wieniawski Competition in the same country from 1935 to 1962.[56] Thirteen of the twenty Soviet violinists who won prizes in the Eugene Izai and Queen Elizabeth Competitions in Brussels from 1937 to 1964, and five of the nine pianists,

---

55 In 1927 – G. Ginzburg; 1932 – A. Lufer, I. Segalov, T. Gutman, E. Grossman; 1937 – I. Zak, R. Tamarkina, T. Goldfarb; 1949 B. Davidovich, V. Merzhanov; 1955 – V. Ashkenazi, N. Shtarkman, D. Paperno; 1960 – I. Zaritskaya.
56 In 1935 – D. Oistrakh, B. Goldshteyn; 1952 – I. Oistrakh, I. Sitkovetsky; 1957 – R. Fayn, M. Komisarov; 1962 – M. Rusin.

were Jewish.[57] At the Marguerite Long and Jacques Thibaud Violin Competitions from 1953-63, ten of the sixteen Soviet prize-winners were Jewish;[58] at the two Tchaikovsky Competitions in Moscow (1958-62), fourteen out of twenty-five.[59] Between 1920 and 1940 fifteen of the twenty-three holders of the chair of piano in the Moscow Conservatory, and seventeen of the twenty-five heads of the violin classes from 1917 to 1966 were Jews.[60] The same source mentions that fourteen outstanding violinists graduated from the class of the famous violin teacher, Professor A. Yampolsky, eleven are Jewish. We can add to this list the young Jewish musicians who have gained high recognition in international competitions and on the concert platform in recent years: the violinists Feliks Hirshhorn, Gidon Kremer, Oleg Kagan, Vladimir Lantsman, Vladimir Spivakov; the cellists David Geringas, Mikhail Maysky; pianists Vladimir Lyubimov and B. Blokh.

Chamber ensembles and orchestras reveal a similar picture. We have already mentioned the quartets in the 1920s and 1930s. We can add the Jewish musicians from the *Soviet Composers' Union Quartet* (I. Targonsky, V. Vidrevich, I. Lipshits, and I. Firer); the *Bol'shoy Theater Quartet* (I. Zhuk, B. Veltman, M. Gurevich, S. Kneservitsky); the *Auer Quartet* (I. Lesman, A. Pergament, I. Shifman, and I. Livshits); and the *Tchaikovsky Quartet* (I. Liber, V. Pikayzen, V. Tsiporin). The best Soviet quartet at the present time, the Borodin Quartet, includes V. Berlinsky (first vio-

---

57 Violinists: in 1937 – D. Oistrakh, B. Goldshteyn, M. Fikhtengolts; 1951 – L. Kogan, M. Vayman; 1955 – I. Sitkovetsky, V. Pikayzen,I. Politkovsky; 1959 – A. Markov, R. Sobolevsky; 1963 – A. Mikhlin,S. Snitkovsy; pianists: in 1938 – E. Gilels, Flier; 1956 – V. Ashkenazi, L. Berman; 1964 E. Mogilevsky.
58 In 1938 – N. Shkolinikova, R. Sobolevsky; 1955 – E. Grach; 1957 – B. Gutnikov, V. Pikayzen, I. Politkovsky; 1961 – V. Zhuk; 1963 V. Lantsman, R. Nodel, N. Beylina.
59 In 1958 – violin: V. Pikayzen, N. Lubotsky, V. Liberman, V. Zhuk; piano: N. Shtarkman, E. Myansarov; 1962 – cello: V. Feygin, N. Gutman, M. Khomitser; violin: B. Gutnikov, N. Beylina, A. Markov, E. Grach; piano: V. Ashkenazi.
60 F. Blumenfeld, S. Feynberg,M. Nemenova Lunts, A. Shatskes, G. Ginzburg, E. Gilels, I. Flier, I. Zak, T. Gutman, E. Grossman, Y. Yokheles, L. Levinson, I. Milshteyn, B. Berlin, V. Natanson, M. Press, D. Krein. A. Mogilvsky, L. Tseytlin, B. Sibor,A. Yampolsky, B. Belensky, O. Oistrakh, I. Oistrakh, P. Bondarenko,I. Bezrodny, I. Yankelevich, L. Kogan, I. Rabinovich, M. Pitkus,M. Polyakin, N. Binder (*Moskovskaya konservatoriya* ..., pp. 412, and 446-62).

lin) and R. Dubinsky (cello).[61] Most of the string insturment orchestras are founded and led by Jewish musicians. We have already referred to the Persinfans; the *Moscow Chamber Orchestra* was founded and is led by Rudolf Barshay, the *Gnesin Institute Chamber Orchestra* by A. Gotlib, a second Moscow Chamber Orchestra by L. Markis, the *Latvian Philharmonic Chamber Orchestra* by T. Livshits, the *Bolshoy Theater Violin Ensemble* by I. Reentovich. About fifty percent of the musicians in these orchestras and the string sections of theater and symphony orchestras up to the 1960s were Jewish. We see, for example, from a 1964 description of the Bolshoy Theater orchestra that about fifty of the one hundred musicians playing bow instruments are Jewish.[62]

However, the decisive factor in music is, of course, not quantity but quality. All the musicians named above are excellent pianists, violinists, cellists etc. which is clear from their success at international competitions or membership of first-class ensembles and orchestras. Many of them are top masters whose fame is worldwide and whose art has been a historical contribution to their field. The pianists Emil Gilels (1916-1985) and Grigory Ginzburg (1904-61), the violinists David Oistrakh (1908-1974) and Leonid Kogan (1924-1982), the cellists Svyatoslav Knusevitsky (1907-63) and Daniel Shafran (1923-1997) are among the greatest musicians of our century. Among the younger generation (born in the 1930s and 1940s) we find top world names, such as Vladimir Ashkenazi, Gidon Kremer, Oleg Kagan, Igor Oistrakh, Natasha Gutman, Mikhail Maiski and many others. It is unnecessary to quote the world musical press to prove the range of these artists since their names speak for themselves. While speaking of instrumentalists we must mention the curious fact that the best Soviet organists are also Jewish even though this instrument has not historically been connected with Jewish tradition. For example, Isay Braudo (1896-1970), professor at the Leningrad Conservatory and author of studies on musical performance, Leonid Royzman (1915/16-1989), professor at the Moscow Conservatory, Maru Shakhin (b. 1917) and Gari Grodburg.

We must bear in mind that the highest level of artistry and world fame have not, in most cases, saved these people from being deprived of hu-

---

61 See L. Raabn, *Mastera . . .*
62 *Teatr*, no. 2, 1964, p. 187.

man and national dignity under the Soviet regime. We do not even speak of the performance by the Jewish musicians of Jewish music; their general repertoire was strictly confined within the framework of styles and composers accepted in the Soviet Union, and every move in their artistic and social life was controlled. The dying words of one of these great Soviet Jewish musicians are chilling: 'I have to die, it is impossible to live with this hatred in the heart.'[63]

These artists, for various reasons (mostly material), are taking the path of assimilation perhaps more so than the average Jew.[64] There has been no lack of anti-Israel declaration signed by D. Oistrakh, L. Kogan, E. Gilels and others, and some, such as I. Yankelevich, have written articles on the subject. However, the Jewish emigration movement in the Soviet Union affected these artists too, and many of them applied to go to Israel and left the Soviet Union (R. Barshay, G. Kremer, M. Maisky, F. Hirshhorn, B. Lantsman, I. Risin, B. Goldshteyn, etc.).

The second largest group of Jewish performers are the conductors. The leading figures in this field in the Soviet Union are Samuil Samosud (1884-1964), who for many years was the chief conductor of the Leningrad and the Moscow Bolshoy Theaters; Boris Haykin (1904-1978), professor and conductor at the same theaters; Karl Eliasberg (1907-1978), chief conductor of the Leningrad Great Radio Orchestra; Natan Rakhlin (1906-1979), chief conductor of the USSR State and Ukrainian State Symphony Orchestras; Yuri Fayer (1890-1971), chief ballet conductor of the Bolshoy Theater; Arye Pazovsky (1887-1953), chief conductor of the Bolshoy Theater; Mark Paverman (1907-?), chief conductor of the Sverdlovsk Philharmonic Orchestra; Leo Gingzburg (1907-1979), head of the department of conducting of the Moscow Radio Symphony Or-

---

[63] This was told to the author by the musician's widow, and for obvious reasons the name cannot be disclosed.

[64] The following anecdote is a clear example of both the assimilation and the self-determination trends. When fourteen year old Oleg Kagan applied in 1961 for a place in the violin class of the Moscow Conservatory, the late professor Isay Yankelevich wrote a letter to the boy's parents suggesting that since he was changing his native city of Riga for Moscow, it would be the right moment to change his nationality, too, from Jewish to Russian. In this case he would accept the new pupil. The boy's father, an army medicine general refused, and Oleg entered the class of Professor B. Kuznetsov. This is known to the author since he was then the violin teacher of the boy.

chestra. In all, Jewish conductors make up about thirty percent of the Soviet professionals in this field. Among the first four graduate conductors from the Moscow Conservatory were A. Braginsky, L. Ginzburg and B. Haykin.[65] The last two became long-standing professors of the same institution.

It is evident from the top Soviet Jewish conductors listed above that most Jewish conductors worked in the field of theater music rather than symphonic music. Perhaps they were attracted by the theatrical element of music, endeavoring to find a synthesis of music and drama (a legacy from the Purim plays, perhaps?). Important features in their style of conducting are improvisation (e.g. N. Rakhlin /1905-1979/, I. Aronovich) and a full-blooded temperament artistry (e.g. S. Samosud, Y. Fayer, M. Paverman).

Jews are less numerous in the fields of vocal music and wind instrument performance. There are several top vocalists, such as Debora Pantofel- Nechetskaya (1904-?), a *coloratura* soprano, and Mark Reyzen (b. 1895), a bass, both of whom are among the stars of the Bolshoy Theater. About nine percent of wind-instrument players are Jewish,[66] among whom are some excellent musicians.

The last group of musicians we have to consider is the musicologists. One-third of Soviet musicologists is Jewish: Jewish composers and musicologists, according to 1968 data, make up eighteen percent of the powerful Composers' Union of the USSR (cf. Jews are about one percent of the Soviet population). Out of a total 360 musicologists who are members of the Union, some 130 are Jews[67] These figures are even larger if we consider only musicologists from Moscow and Leningrad, that is, the

---

65 The reference book *Sovremennye dirizhery* (Contemporary Conductors), ed. L. Grigorev and I. Platek (Moscow 1969), names ninety-six Soviet conductors of whom twenty-eight are Jewish. As of 1st January 1969, nine out of twenty-nine theater orchestras and thirteen out of thirty-seven symphony orchestras were headed by Jewish conductors, (pp. 318-23).

66 S. Bolotin, *Biograficheskesky slovar muzykantov-ispoliteley na dukhovykh instrumentakh* (Biographical Dictionary of Musical Performers on Wind Instruments, Leningrad 1969).

67 *Soyuz kompozitorov SSSR: Spravochnik na 1968 god* (USSR Union of Composers: Handbook for 1968, Moscow 1968). A musicologist was accepted as a member of the union only if his publications are a contribution to Soviet musicology (from the statutes of the Union.).

leading members of the field: out of 187, eighty-five are Jewish. It is not only the number of Jews in Soviet musicology that is significant: they have produced important and fundamental works of Soviet early musicology relating music history to Marxism-Leninism. Among the first in the 1920s are the studies of Evgeny Braudo (1882-1939) and Boris Shteynpress (1908-1986).[68] The theory of so-called integral musical analysis was created by Lev Mazel (1907-?) and Viktor Tsukerman (1903-1988).[69] Later, in the 1960s, Mazel made the first attempt to justify more progressive styles in Soviet music. Viktor Berkov (1907-?) and G. Litinsky wrote basic works on musical theory. The first and only general history of music was written by Roman Gruber (1895-1962) and the first history of Soviet music by Semen Ginsburg (b. 1901). The first history of Russian music was published in the USSR by Mikhail Pekelis (b. 1899) and the first encyclopaedia of music, by Boris Shteynpress and Israel Yampolsky (1905-1976). Among the top Soviet musicologists are Arnold Alshvang, Lev Barenboym, Mikhail Druskin, Lev Ginzburg, Semyon Ginzburg, Yakov Milshteyn, Israel Nestev, Alexsandr Rabinovich, David Rabinovich, Semen Shlifshteyn, Grigory Shneerson, Daniel Zhitomirsky, and others.

Although Jewish music scholars were highly gifted and well educated, Jewish topics are absent from Soviet musicology. What is more, under the pressure of Soviet conditions prominent Jewish musicologists have tried to avoid any mention of Jewish aspects, even when directly relevant to the topic.[70] Only in the field of folk music, as mentioned above, several publications appeared.

The only musicologist active during these years in the field of Jewish folk music was Moisey Beregovsky (1892-1961). His whole life was de-

---

68 *Osnovy materialnoy kultury v muzyke* (The bases of material culture in music, Moscow 1924); *Voprosy materialnoy kultury v muzyke* (Problems of material culture in music, Moscow 1931).
69 *Fantaziya f-moll Shopena: Opyt analiza* (Chopin's Fantasy in f-minor: an attempt of analysis, Moscow 1973); *Stroenie muzykalnogo proizvedeniya* (The construction of a musical work, Moscow 1960); *Tselostny analiz muzykalnykh proizvedeniy i ego metodika* (Integral Analysis of Works of Music and its Methods), and *Intonazia i muzykalny obras* (Intonation and the Musical Image, Moscow 1969).
70 As example may be mentioned the article by I. Yampolsy (*Sovetskaya muzyka*, no. 10 1959, 134) on the great Jewish folk musician Yosif Guzikov.

voted to research and collection of Jewish music. Although controversial in some aspects (he wrote in Yiddish with Latin characters, he often was more concerned with the impact of Russian and Ukrainian folklore on Jewish folklore than with analyzing features of the Jewish heritage, etc.) – a direct consequence of working in Soviet conditions, he nevertheless remains one of the most important Jewish musicologist, and his work today may be considered congenial to Abraham Zwi Idelsohns contribution. He was educated at the Kiev and Leningrad Conservatories and from 1928 to 1936 was Head of the Musical Folklore Department of the Institute of Jewish Proletarian Culture at the Ukrainian Academy of Sciences in Kiev. He was later appointed to the Folklore Department of the Kiev Conservatory. From 1941-49 he was again at the Ukrainian Academy of Sciences, this time as Head of the Musical Folklore Section of the Institute of Literature's Department of Jewish Culture. In 1944 he received his doctor's degree in the subject *Jewish Instrumental Folk Music*.

Beregovsky published one major work, *Jidiser muzik-folklor* (Jewish Musical Folklore), vol. 1 (Moscow 1934), and *Yidishe Instrumentale Folksmuzik* (Kiev 1937). The other volumes of the first work, which was planned to appear in five volumes, have never been published in his lifetime. He also published a collection of folk songs *Yidishe Folks-lider* (Jewish folk-songs, Kiev 1938), together with Itsik Fefer, and a second collection was published posthumously (*Evreyskie narodnye pesni* – Jewish Folk Songs, Moscow 1962). About ten articles by him on Jewish folk music appeared in journals.

Beregovsky's devoted work at the Jewish Institute of the Ukrainian Academy of Sciences, the only institution in the Soviet Union at which research was carried out into Jewish culture, was very significant. This Institute was set up in the late 1920s and remained active until 1949. It had a group of literary specialists (I. Dobrushin, M. Viner, Z. Skuditsky, A. Yuditsky), and besides Beregovsky, M. Maydansky and R. Lerner worked there for some years in the field of music. In 1946 its archives contained about 7,000 records of musical folklore (in written music and tapes) most of which had been collected by Beregovsky. Only a small part of Beregovsky's work prepared at the Institute (the five-volume study of Jewish musical folklore, more than forty articles, etc.) has been published. He was very active during the war, as he himself described:

During the summer 1944 we received from our correspondents a number of ghetto songs, labor-camp songs and Jewish partisan songs.... We organized expeditions in 1944 in Chernovtsy..., and in August 1945 in the Vinnitsa area..., in 1946 we visited Vilnius and Kaunas where we collected material from the Vilnius and Kaunas Ghettos. We prepared for the publishing house the book *Jewish Folklore in the Period of the Great Patriotic War*[71].

After the destruction of Jewish culture in the USSR in 1949 Beregovsky had no opportunity to continue his work. Today he is not referred to in Soviet musical literature, and there is no mention of the Jewish musical folklore institutions in Kiev. Even the obituary to Beregovsky (*Sovetskaya muzyka*, no. 11, 1961, 160) speaks only of his general work on folklore, although it does mention that 'he wrote a number of articles and studies on Jewish, Ukrainian and Bashkir folklore.'[72] His life and work still awaits a complete and objective treatment.

Another example of musicological research on Jewish musical folklore is an article by A. Vinkovetsky, 'Jewish musical folklore in Russia'. This was written as preface to an *Anthology of Jewish Folk Song*, whose publication was discussed in the late 1960s in the Leningrad Music Publishing House. Dmitry Shostakovich wrote to him about this planned publication: 'I have made the acquaintance of your *Anthology of Jewish Folk Song* and I continue to do so every day. It is a very interesting work and I am very grateful to you for it'.[73] The preface gives a description and some analysis of the 244 songs in the *Anthology*. This letter has yet to be published, but the preface was recently published in an underground Jewish magazine in the Soviet Union, *Jews in the USSR*. We may draw from this the sad conclusion that the only Jewish musicology in the USSR today is underground.

When discussing the role Jews played in Soviet musicology, we must consider one more question. It is certainly true that there were six Jews

---

71 From the M. Beregovsky Archive at the Leningrad Institute for Theater, Music and Film; quoted from A. Vinkovetsky *Evreysky muzykalny folklor v Rossii* (Jewish musical folklore in Russia) in the Soviet underground publication *Jews in the USSR* (New York, September 1973, p. 91). The book Beregovsky refers to did not appear.
72 No Soviet reference source mentions any article by Beregovsky on Ukrainian or Bashkir music folklore.
73 Shostakovich's letter from November, 3ed, 1970, quoted in Vinkovetsky's *Evreysky...*, p. 79.

(more than 50%!) among the eleven musicologists who violently attacked modern music according to the Party line at the First Congress of the Soviet Composers' Union in 1948. It is also true that many Jewish names are among the most vocal and servile defenders of orthodox Soviet musicology.[74] None the less, the work of even more Jewish musicologists contains an important creative element, showing a quest for real, objective values. There are many different reasons for this relatively strong creative trend among Jewish musicologists (as well as among Jewish scholars in other fields of the humanities), and they naturally involve such factors as the democratic traditions of the East European Jewish intelligentsia, international contacts, knowledge of languages, and such like. The popularization and analysis of progressive musical trends which the Soviet authorities condemned in 1938 and 1948 were to a large extent linked with Jewish names.[75] This could not pass unnoticed by Soviet officialdom.

The attack on the most talented composers and musicologists in 1948-49 is well known. Professor Boris Schwarz has accurately defined the events of those days as 'musicologists on trial'. The destruction of Jewish culture and the wave of open antisemitism, which reached a peak at the same time, are equally well known. Although Schwarz points out, 'whether, in view of the anti-Jewish campaign which began in late 1948, any antisemitism played a part in the purge of musicologists is difficult to determine,'[76] to contemporaries of the events, the matter seems to be clear enough.

In the totalitarian Soviet system both the violent suppression of human freedom and the antisemitic state policy are manifestations of one and the same idea. Not so apparent in the 1920s and 1930s, it surfaced openly in the late 1940s. On page 206 and footnotes 9, 10 and 11, I quoted two similar statements on music from Nazi and Soviet sources. It is also no accident that we can present the following chronology of events from the 7th to the 13th January 1948:

---

[74] G. Shneerson, K. Rozenshild, A. Sokhor and I. Nest'ev distinguished themselves in this field.
[75] L. Mazel, I. Belza, I. Vaynkop, D. Zhitomirsky, G. Kogan, V. Berkov, S. Ginzburg, R. Gruber etc.
[76] B. Schwarz, *Music and Musical Life in Soviet Russia: 1917-1970*, New York, 1972, p. 251.

7th January:
Solomon Mikhoels, the great Jewish actor and head of the Soviet Jewish Anti-Fascist Committee, left Moscow for Minsk. At the railway station he told his relative, the composer Veynberg, with foreboding that Shostakovich, Prokofiev, Myasnovsky and some others had been summoned to the Party Central Committee.

10 January:
Stalin's confidant Zhdanov, who master-minded the ruin of modern music in the USSR, talked to the leading Soviet composers.

12 January:
Mikhoels was killed in Minsk. This was the prelude to the subsequent arrests and murders of most Jewish artists and writers and the closure of all Jewish institutions.

13 January:
At 13.00 the meeting of the Party Central Committee began at which the musicians were informed of the notorious resolution condemning 'Western modernism and homegrown formalism' in music. At 15.00 news of Mikhoel's death reached the musicians assembled in the Central Committee hall. In the evening Shostakovich said to some of his closest friends: 'This is a campaign which starts with the Jews and will end with the whole of the intelligentsia'.[77]

Thus the ideological struggle in music combined with the Jewish tragedy. Of the nineteen musicologists accused of 'anti-patriotic, harmful activity, aimed at undermining the ideological basis of Soviet music', denounced for 'cosmopolitan errors and groveling before Western music' and also for 'standing apart from current creative works,' fourteen were Jewish. Seventeen of the thirty musicologists blacklisted by the First Secretary of the Composers' Union Tikhon Khrennikov, were Jewish.[78]

All this is no accident, neither an average case of antisemitism nor the usual case of a struggle between the old and the new in art. It was a definite trend which started in the Soviet Union in the 1930s and continues to the present and which is motivated by deep social, political and aesthetic factors. It is a struggle by the authorities against aesthetic principles, which threaten the system or at least refuse to submit to its supervision. It is a struggle against a social and national community which does not fit

---

77 This time-table was related to the author from two participants of the events, whose names cannot yet be revealed.
78 *Sovetskaya musika*, no. 2, 1949, pp. 36 and 37.

into official policies. Not all the names in the Nazi and Soviet sources quoted above are Jewish: the social and national groups do not coincide exactly, but they do overlap by some seventy percent. The Soviet population supported the struggle against modern music because of the Jewish names the authorities constantly referred to. In Nazi Germany a number of non-Jewish musicians (Stravinsky, Hindemith, Stuckenschmidt) were attacked for their 'Jewish' art. In Soviet Russia the same people were attacked for 'anti-realistic, anti-social art'. The accent shifts from nationality to aesthetics and *vice versa*. The Jews are to be destroyed because of their corrupt musical aesthetics (according to Nazi theories) and hostile musical aesthetics can be attacked via the Jews (in the Soviet version). Antisemitism based on musical aesthetics and musical aesthetics molded by antisemitism are curious features of twentieth-century totalitarian regimes.

When this pattern emerged in the Soviet Union, Jews and the Jewish idiom began to be ousted from Soviet music. A *numerus clausus* was introduced first by an oral order at the end of the 1950s and then by a secret order of the USSR Minister of Culture, E. Furtseva, in 1969. The national cadres policy – the policy employing members of the native nationality in the various republics in preference to other nationalities – which was officially introduced to further the development of local cultures, in fact became a racial policy which officially recognized privileged nationalities, i.e. the local nationality of the republic and, of course, the Russian nationality.[79] There is no room for the Jews in this policy. Its results can be seen from Table 2.

1933	1938	1945	1947	1963	1969
54	60	25	23	12	9

(100% = number of Soviet prize winners)

Table 2: Soviet Jewish Prize-Winners at Music Competitions (in percentages)

---

[79] The author of this paper knows about the oral order from the Deputy Minister of Culture of the Latvian SSR, who confirmed it during an audience at his office (1967). The 1969 order I read in the office of the Director of the Riga Special Music School, the organist J. Sipolnieks.

This is one of the reasons for the decline over the past fifteen years in the number of significant Soviet musicians who have been awarded first prize at major international competitions. The case of Leonid Kogan is well known in Soviet music circles. In 1951 he was not accepted by the Soviet Ministry of Culture to compete in the Queen Elizabeth Competition in Brussels. But after Stalin had written on the list of candidates 'Get the first prize', the list was changed and Kogan included. Since then Jews have been included among the Soviet competitors at such events only when the authorities were especially interested in ensuring that the Soviet Union receives the main prizes. After the Jewish musician has performed this task he is often kept from the concert platform. This was the case with, for example, Gidon Kremer (first prize at the Tchaikovsky Competition), Natalya Gutman (second price at the same competition), Feliks Hirshhorn (first prize at the Queen Elizabeth Competition), Mikhail Veyman (second prize at the same competition), Vladimir Lantsman (first prize at the Montreal Competition), and others. We must, of course, bear in mind that the question of access to the concert platform in the Soviet Union is a sophisticated system of incentive and punishment.

The percentages of doctoral dissertations written by Jewish musicologists and accepted at the Moscow and Leningrad Conservatories has changed as follows.[80]

1934-41	1942-52	1955-62	1964-74
50	23	13	10

(100% = all dissertations accepted)

Table 3: Doctoral Dissertations by Jews at Moscow and Leningrad Conservatories

For Jewish musicologists the path to the doctor's degree is strewn with innumerable petty, artificial obstacles so that in some cases they find it impossible to get the degree and in others the whole process is very much protracted. Thus, for example, the musicologist and composer Maks Goldin (b. 1917) struggled to be granted the doctor's degree for more than seven years after he had completed his dissertation on Latvian

---

80 The figures for Table 2 and 3 are based on Soviet sources mentioned in footnote 45.

folk music. Goldin also devoted much time to research in the field of Jewish folklore, none of which has been published, and he wrote a number of instrumental pieces based on Jewish folk tunes. He was the author of the last publication of Jewish folk song transcriptions *Evreyskie narodnye pesni* (Jewish folk songs, Moscow 1972).

The new situation and trends which emerged in Jewish cultural life after 1948-50 had far-reaching, often indirect and complex consequences. The Soviet authorities do not always insist that Jews be completely ousted from musical life. In certain cases and situations they are willing to accept the Jewish idiom for propaganda purposes. This was the case with the Jewish folk singer Nehama Lifshits (b. 1927), who was sponsored by the authorities in the early stage of her career. She was sent to concerts in Paris in 1961. By the late 1960s she was not permitted to perform more than two or three Jewish songs at her concerts in the Soviet Union and many concert halls were completely closed to her. In 1971 she emigrated to Israel.

Some rare publications of Jewish folk songs are permitted for the same purpose of propaganda (see Table 1). The use of Jewish folk melodies in classical musical forms is much rarer and usually interpreted as an accidental deviation from the composer's main style (e.g. by Vaynberg, Basner). It is frequently condemned, as during the discussion of Vaynberg's Sinfonietta at the Composers' Union in 1948 when one of the leading musicologists was indignant that 'the music of *lapserdaks* and *peyses*' could be heard in Soviet music.[81] Yet a little later Tikhon Khrennikov, the General Secretary of the Composers' Union from 1948 onwards and Party spokesman for official music policy, decided to use this same Sinfonietta for propaganda and praised the composer as an example of 'reorientation' after the Resolutions of Music of 10 February 1948:

> We now have to check how our composers are liberating themselves from formalism, how they are fulfilling the Party's directive... how they are using the great treasures of folk art, how they are defending the national character of Soviet music against the reactionary idioms of bourgeois cosmpolitism.

---

[81] Related by a composer who attended the meeting.

During the antisemitic orgy of 1948-49, what could be better for world display than to give Vaynberg as an example. Khrennikov continues:

> As a composer he [Vaynberg] was strongly influenced by modernistic music which badly mangled his undoubted talent. By turning to the sources of Jewish folk music, Vaynberg has created a bright, optimistic work dedicated to the theme of the shining, free working life of the Jewish people in the land of socialism. In this work, Vaynberg has shown uncommon mastery and a wealth of creative imagination.[82]

After this dithyramb, extraordinary for the conditions of those times, the work was performed several times and then increasingly avoided. Today the Jewish idiom of the work is completely ignored and not even mentioned in articles about Vaynberg or in Soviet music history books.[83] Such are the complex, ambiguous destinies of a Jewish piece in Soviet music.

The authorities are more willing to accept Jewish musicians if they avoid their national idiom and contribute to Soviet music based on the idiom of the main nationalities of the USSR. Thus there emerged a new generation of talented Jewish composers who, unlike the older generation (Gnesin, Krein, etc.) turn to their Jewishness only occasionally and mainly work in the style of other national idioms or in a non-national, modern style which itself is not encouraged by Soviet ideology. This group includes musicians who are regarded as the most talented Soviet composers.

Yuri Levitin (b. 1912), pupil of Shostakovitch, a highly gifted composer, has written an opera, oratorios (Stalin Prize in 1952) and many works of symphonic and chamber music. He is active in the field of the Ukrainian and Russian mass song or writes in a modern, non-national style. However, he has often been accused of a 'dry and rational manner' or of 'a not sufficiently convincing interpretation of the heroic' in Soviet music, while if he attempts a more Jewish idiom the reaction becomes sharper. Thus, the music for his song cycle *Letters from Prison*, based on Nazim Hikmet's texts, was criticized as 'not individual, with some [quite

---

[82] T. Khrennikov in *Sovetskaya muzyka*, no. 1, 1949, p. 21.
[83] *Sovetskaya muzka*, no. 1, 1960, pp. 40-47; *Istoriya muzyki*..., IV, p. 294.

unexpected!] elements of Eastern song'.[84] By the mid-1960s Levitin was regarded as an established composer, conservative enough not to be dangerous and modern enough not to be entirely neglected by the younger generation. The authorities could rely on him as we see from the policy article he wrote on the situation in Soviet music in the Party newspaper *Pravda* (20 June 1965).

Moisey Vaynberg (b. 1919), whom we have already mentioned, came to the Soviet Union to study in 1939 and, when the Germans entered his native Warsaw, remained there. He is considered to be one of the top Soviet composers and one of the close followers of Shostkovich. He was married to Mikhoel's daughter and was therefore a victim of the anti-Jewish persecution. Arrested in January 1953 without charge, he was released some month later after Stalin's death. His work includes four operas, three ballets, eleven symphonies, twelve quartets, some instrumental concertos, numerous pieces of chamber music, about one hundred songs, film music, etc. It is mainly based on Moldavian, Russian, Byelorussian, Polish, Uzbek and Armenian folklore or else written with no connection with a particular national idiom. The Jewish idiom appears, as mentioned above, in the *Sinfonietta* and also in a *Trio* of 1943 and some songs of the 1940s based on poems by Y.L. Perets. Vaynberg is defined in the Soviet music encyclopaedia as 'one of the great Soviet symphonists',[85] but even so he has never received in the Soviet Union full official recognition or wide recognition in music-listening circles. His fate is characterized by the 'contradiction between the high and deserved recognition of Vaynberg's talent in professional musical circles and his relatively small popularity in wider circles of listeners, as a musicologist wrote in *Sovetskaya muzyka*, going on to complain that concert organizers made no attempt to have Vaynberg's works played, and some of these had yet to be performed:

> No musicological article has been written about a composer who has composed such a vast number of works, while special articles or even brochures are written about composers who have only just graduated from the conservatory!'[86]

---

84 *Istoriya muziki...*, IV, pp. 188, 264 and 294.
85 *Muzikal'naya encyclopedia*, I, p. 649.
86 *Sovetskaya muzyka*, no. 1, 1960, 46-7.

This was written in 1960. Since then there has been no other article on Vaynberg.

Venyamin Basner (b. 1925) is well known both in the field of symphonic chamber music, popular mass song, operetta and folk music. The love for music in the simple Jewish families of cobblers, the Basners, and on his mother's side, the Greditors, had a strong impact on the young composer. He has remembered some of the Jewish melodies he heard from his father and grandfather and used them in his works, for example, in the *Third Quartet*.[87] This was written in 1960 and is recognized as one of his best works, and the *Scherzo* of the quartet in which the Jewish element appears is the most significant movement of the work. Here the Jewish heart of the composer opened in impetuous joy and suppressed pain. Most of his works, however, have no connection with his Jewishness, nether in title nor in content.

The group of Soviet 'modernists', insofar as this term is applied to composers who use some dodecaphonic or aleatoric elements, include the Moscow Jewish composers Alfred Shnitke (b. 1934), who has written a number of vocal-instrumental and pure instrumental works, and Romuald Grinblat (b. 1930), until 1972 in Riga and now in Leningrad. The last has composed two ballets, five symphonies, chamber and film music. They are regarded in professional circles as highly talented composers. There are other composers of Jewish origin in this group, such as Yuri Falik and Lazar Feygin. All these composers have often been heavily criticized. Their works are not officially banned but are none the less ignored by philharmonic organizations.[88] R. Grinblat's music was prohibited in the Latvian SSR by the Director of the Philharmonic Society in Riga Filip Shveynik, himself a Jewish *Gulag* survivor. He became notorious throughout the Soviet Union for his hatred of any progressive movement in art as well as his hostility to Jewish musicians.[89] Shveynik was also the one who provoked the arrest of several young Jews when he called for

---

87 I. Beletsky, *Venyamin Basner* (Leningrad-Moscow 1972), p. 7.
88 For the Alfred-Shnitke-case see *Sovetskaya muzika*, no. 1, 1968, pp. 24-25 (Shnitke is now considered one of the great composers of the 20th century – JB).
89 When Director Shveynik was told that the singer Nehama Lifshits was leaving for Israel, he announced to a group of Philharmonic Society workers and musicians: 'I only hope that the first Arab bullet, which really is ours, will get her' (reported by L. Makhinson, and other witnesses to the author).

army units to come to the concert of Israeli singer Geula Gil in Riga in 1966.

We have no right to end an account of Soviet composers connected with the Jewish people or the Jewish idiom without mentioning the greatest and most famous Soviet musician, Dmitry Shostakovich. The tragic personality of this man is a subject to be discussed elsewhere. What concerns us here is his position on the Jewish question. Let us set aside his personal, unpublished pronouncements or sympathies,[90] and just say that he belongs to that part of the Soviet Russian intelligentsia whose views are often controversial, which sees in the Soviet Jewish situation a human tragedy and which, in its sympathy towards the Jews, expresses a kind of protest against the regime. The publication of collections of Jewish folk songs over the past ten years has usually been carried out under D. Shostakovich's supervision (e.g. the above-mentioned publication by Z. Kompaneets in 1970). But when we turn to his work a mere list of the compositions in which he uses Jewish melodies, intonations or subjects is sufficiently eloquent.

Trio, op. 67, 1944, written in memory of his close friend, the musicologist I. Sollertinsky, who was denounced by the Soviet authorities, at a time when the Russian intelligentsia became aware of the real dimensions of the Holocaust.
Concerto for Violin and Orchestra, Op. 77, and *Vocal Cycle 'From Jewish Folk Poetry', op. 79,* both written in 1948 during the Soviet Jewish tragedy. Both works were first performed only in 1955, after Stalin's death. The choice of texts for the vocal cycle is significant: eight of the eleven songs are tragic and some have clear connotations such as the songs *Warning, Lament on a Dead Infant,* and *The Abandoned Father.*
Quartet No. 4, op. 83, 1949, written in the year of the mass arrests of Jews and first performed only in 1953.
Quartet No. 8, op. 110, 1960, an autobiographical work with the use of the DSCH theme, a symbol of personal identification[91].
Symphony No. 13, Op. 113, 1962, inspired by Y Yevtushenko's poem *Baby Yar,* which had been attacked by Khrushchev. Shostakovich first wrote a symphonic poem *Baby Yar* and then turned it into the first movement of the Thirteenth Symphony, adding some other poems by Evtushenko.

---

90 We have mentioned some of them: the letter to A. Vinkovetsky, his words after the death of Mikhoels, his friendship with M. Vaynberg.
91 DSCH are the first letters of Dmitry Schostakovich's name (German transcription) which the composer used for a musical theme: $D = Re$, $S = Mi^b$, $C = Do$, $H = Si$.

In the 1950s and 1960s a new movement for Jewish national renaissance emerged in the Soviet Union as the result of various internal social and external political events: the suppression of Jewish spiritual life in the Soviet Union, the Soviet authorities' antisemitic actions, the establishment of the State of Israel and Soviet hostility to this State, the suppression of freedom in the Soviet Union and short periods of limited liberalization, certain cultural contacts between East and West, etc. Just as antisemitism was combined with political dictatorship and artistic conformity, so the Jewish renaissance of this period was linked with the Russian democratic (civil rights) movement and progressive tendencies in art. Both the act of self-expression in art by Jews and the act of solidarity by non-Jewish musicians became, in Soviet conditions, a symbol of humanism and resistance. National self-expression and self- determination were equal to human resistance. We have mentioned the creative work of D. Shostakovich. Another pregnant example is the Jewish popular song.

A new development in the field of Jewish song emerged in the late 1950s. Ruth Rubin is only partly right when she says that the

> Soviet-Yiddish folk songs of the Second World War were the close of Yiddish folk song in the USSR and that with the tragic destruction of Yiddish cultural institutions and of many prominent Jewish men of letters during the years 1948-53 this phase of Yiddish song may also have been brought to an abrupt end.[92]

It was only a certain phase which had come to an end. In the late 1950s the Yiddish song received fresh impetus, new life and new development. Jews started to hum and whistle the song *Yankele – You Have to Learn Khumesh*. In the early 1960s *The Song of Baby Yar*, and later *Next Year in Jerusalem* or *Pharaoh, Let My People Go*[93] were being sung by Jews in groups and private meetings, at home and at Holocaust memorial places (Baby Yar near Kiev, Rumbula near Riga, Paneri near Vilnius, Devyaty Fort near Kaunas), as well as outside the Moscow Synagogue.

The Jewish song is one of the most exciting developments in the history of Soviet Jewry: after the complete destruction of Jewish cultural life

---

92 Rubin (see footnote 48 above), p. 240.
93 The texts of the songs are published in Mlotek (see footnote 2), and the songs themselves recorded by Th. Bikel and J. Miron, *Silent No More* (Star Record Co., New York 1971).

in the Soviet Union, when there was a ban on Jewish language and art, there suddenly emerged in the mid-1950s a spiritual safety-valve, born by the creative instinct of the people. A number of amateur and semi-professional singers and reciters, not always sufficiently educated or artistically perfect, began to perform Jewish folk songs at concerts, first in various club-houses at amateur evenings and in amateur groups, then on more professional stages, and finally in philharmonic halls.

Amateur choirs were organized in Riga and Vilnius in club-hoses.[94] They were active intermittently until finally closed in the mid-1960s. The first Jewish folk song concert after more than ten years of silence took place on 1 August 1955 and was given by Saul Lyubimov who had returned home after exile under Stalin. The concert hall was packed and the success, despite a fairly modest artistic level was tremendous.[95] Lyubimov performed his programme of Jewish songs in many cities (Kiev, Kharkov, Chelyabinsk, Ufa, Omsk, etc.). A number of other folk singers appeared: Mariana Gordon, Rozalia Golubeva, Loyter Yakubovich, Emil Gorovets. The popular Soviet vaudeville actress and singer Anna Guzik (b. 1908), daughter of the well-known Jewish actor Yakov Guzik, included some Jewish folk songs in nearly every concert. She relates how frequently she would hear only one thing from a somewhat frightened Jewish member of the audience: 'Thank you'.[96]

The repertoire of all these singers was based on the Yiddish folk song of middle and south Russia of the nineteenth century and they dared not overstep this limit: the 'old Jewish songs', as we are told, 'some with a hint of sadness, some...with a sad smile, others humorous and lively' all have one function: 'to recreate scenes of the past',[97] and so to show that the Jewish song and Jewish culture in general are a matter of the sad past in Tsarist Russia. Nevertheless these concerts were enormously successful and understood correctly by the audience.

---

94 See David Garber, 'Choir and drama in Riga' in *Soviet Jewish Affairs*, vol. 4, no. 1, 1974, 39-44.
95 S. Schwartz, *Evrei v Sovetskom Soyuze* (Jews in the Soviet Union, New York 1966), p. 283.
96 From conversations the author had with A. Guzik, Tel Aviv, May 1974. A Guzik and many other Jewish song performers (N. Lifshits, M. Aleksandrovich, E. Gorovets) left for Israel in the 1970s.
97 From the record annotation *Recital by N. Lifshitsaite*, DO8341-42.

Some years later, at the end of the 1950s and the beginning of the 1960s, Jewish songs were being performed throughout the country, and in 1957 the number of people attending these concerts reached three million.[98]

The Jewish song received new impetus when artists of a high level appeared in this genre. Mkhail Aleksandrovich (b. 1914), a cantor in Latvia before the Second World War, an excellent singer of the Italian school, became famous in the Soviet Union during the war and was regarded as one of the top Soviet singers. He was awarded the title of Honored Artist in 1947 and received a Stalin Prize in 1948. His participation in concerts at the front during the war brought him this recognition. In an order issued by the Leningrad Philharmonic Society we read: 'Deserving of special mention is the courageous and patriotic attitude of Mikhail Aleksandrovich.... which was splendidly manifested during the Leningrad blockade when his concerts took place under sustained enemy fire'.[99] From the late 1950s he often included Jewish songs in his concert programmes. He would usually perform these songs as encores after the end of the programme. The Jewish audience knew of this habit and would wait impatiently for these songs to acclaim the artist not only as a singer but also as a Jew. And if for various reasons (frequently on the 'advice' of 'responsible workers of the Ministry of Culture') which were unknown to the audience, he did not sing Jewish songs, the audience would go home disappointed and distressed despite his excellent performance of arias and Neapolitan songs.[100]

In the early 1960s Aleksandrovich's insistence on performing Jewish songs increased along with the opposition of the authorities. The Ukrainian and Byelorussian SSR were closed to him because he performed some Jewish songs at a concert in Kiev after the Philharmonic authorities had removed them from his programme. In 1945, at the first Jewish New Year after the war, he had sung as cantor at the Moscow Synagogue at the invitation of the Moscow Party and city authorities. His singing of the *Kaddish* (Prayer for the Dead) was arranged as a big propaganda show to

---

98   Schwartz, *Yevrei...* p. 406.
99   N. Mikhaylovskaya (ed.), *Mikhail Aleksandrovich* (Moscow 1964), p. 2.
100 This and some other facts on Aleksandrovich's activities are known to the author from conversations with him in Tel Aviv, February 1974, and from personal reminiscences.

which diplomats, television, radio and the press were invited. But now, in the early 1960s, he was told that he could not be entrusted with the education of a Soviet audience as he was a cantor. However, after two years' battle he was eventually permitted not only to include some Jewish songs in his programme but also to devote an entire part of the concert to them. None the less he never managed to obtain permission for a whole concert of Jewish songs. Aleksandrovich included in his repertoire not only arrangements by Milner, Kogan, Likhtenshteyn and Yampolsky, and folk songs, but also the *Kaddish* by Ravel, the Joseph aria from Méhul's opera *Joseph in Egypt* and other classical works on Jewish themes. But the artist received the greatest satisfaction when he managed to perform, under a folk song title, a song such as *Dos Yidishe Lid* by Sinkop and could feel that the significance of the song for the present day was understood by the audience (*Men ruft im ben melakh/A yakhsn, a gvir/Un yedes land farmakht far im di tir* – He is called King's Son/A man of note of wealth/And every country shuts the door to him).

At the beginning of 1970 Mikhail Aleksandrovich applied to emigrate to Israel, and after a struggle of nearly two years (hunger strikes, petitions, demonstrations) without work or income, he received the permission to emigrate. Since then his name has been removed from Soviet reference books,[101] his records have been withdrawn from use on the radio, from music shops and libraries.

At the All Union Competitions of Variety Performers in 1958 the Vilna-born singer Nehama Lifshits (b.1927) was awarded the first prize. From an early age she had listened to Jewish songs and sung them by herself. When her teacher at the Vilna Conservatory, N. Karnaviciane, first heard her sing a Jewish song she said: 'This is your mission'. Her success at a concert in December 1956 when she performed a Jewish song for the first time in public, was decisive for her future. Some years later her performance was praised as high art:

> The great skill of the singer (Lifshits) is a veritable aesthetic synthesis of music and word. She brings to the listeners not only every intonation of the melody but also every detail of the text. Each song of the artist is a story in music, a complete genre scene or romantic novella, a three-minute story of human fate, or a humorous episode. Lifshits

---

101 The 1966 edition of the *Encyclopaedia of Music* has an entry on him; the 1973 *Encyclopaedicheski Slovar,* which is five times larger, has none.

performs with so much sympathy and heart that we can no longer call it singing; she lives the feelings of her heroes...We cannot find another explanation for this except the shortest and very likely, the only one: talent!

Thus writes the Soviet journal *Sovetskaya muzyka*, not overly generous with compliments.[102]

We have already mentioned the propagandist function her concerts were meant to perform in the Soviet Union and even more so abroad (Paris, Brussels, Vienna). Nevertheless her art spread throughout the country and hundreds of thousands listened to her Jewish songs. In nearly every Soviet city Jewish composers, both amateur (M. Gebirtik, E. Berdichever, B. Broder) and professional (I. Rozenfeld, D. Pokrass, G. Bruk, I. Kogan and the non-Jewish A. Barkauskas, etc) started working in the field of Jewish song and wrote specially for her. From 1961 she often sang at her concerts the song by D. Pokrass *Hot Lands* ('Hot lands, how am I to find the road to you, how am I not to mistake the road?'). This song is from a play with a Soviet Revolutionary theme and therefore acceptable to the censor, but the sensitive Jewish audiences would interpret the words in their own way. People listened, hummed the songs with her and dreamed about the hot Land. The effect of the Jewish song concerts became increasingly ambiguous, the audience's reaction was no longer one of pure musical enjoyment: 'Tears flowed down the joyous faces of the men and women in the audience, young and old people... they cried openly and unashamedly', relates one witness.[103] I myself remember some of Lifshits's concerts in Riga: a strange excitement imbued the halls of the Latvian Philharmonic Society. Simply attending a concert at which some ninety-five percent of the audience was Jewish was exciting: there was no place where Jews could meet except at the Jewish song concerts. And then the songs. Even if the performance was not always on the highest artistic level, every sound, every word was seized upon, overflowed with emotion and associations, was interpreted in every heart and mind in a hundred ways. This was the rebirth of national feelings and aspirations, of national consciousness and pride. The storm of applause which thundered through the hall and the pride contained in this applause expressed the pride of a people.

---

102 No.12, 1963, pp. 88-90.
103 From the diary of M. Kolb, quoted in Mlotek, footnote 14.

In the mid- and especially the late 1960s the situation became more difficult. Several concert halls were closed to Lifshits and to Jewish songs in general. These concerts had to take place in clubs or suburban halls. By the end of the 1960s she could perform only in her native republic of Lithuania where she was still employed as soloist of the Philharmonic Society. The pressure on Jewish songs and culture grew every day along with the anti-Israel and anti-Jewish campaign in the Soviet media and the systematic expulsion of Jews from Soviet musical life. With this development the Jewish song changed its social status from being the Jewish folk song officially accepted and used for propaganda to being the persecuted Jewish resistance and underground song.

These songs were composed or emerged spontaneously in collective creative spirit, as is the case with folk music. They were born in the Nazi ghettoes, changed their function and turned into resistance songs, were composed by Jewish partisans in the Second World War, and now were sung in new conditions. They were composed in secret in forests and Soviet labor camps, transmitted orally and preserved in the people's memory. They are sung in the family or at private gatherings, at memorial places outside the towns, at cemeteries or outside synagogues. They are sung during the arrest of Jewish emigration activists. These songs often have weak texts and melodies borrowed from other songs, or weak melodies and somewhat altered, borrowed texts. They are sung in Russian, Yiddish and occasionally Hebrew or with all these languages combined in one song, like the spoken language of Soviet Jews. They are lyrical, fiery, heroic or full of gentle humor. One feature alone unites them and secured their popularity: self-determination. Some of the songs have been brought to the West secretly and edited by folk music specialists in the USA. An excellent example is the record by Theodore Bikel and Issachar Miron, *Silent No More* (Star Record Co.), which includes the best Soviet Jewish underground songs. The song *Pharaoh – Let My People Go*, based on Soviet marching song intonations, appeals to historical analogies and so seemed to be less dangerous although its subject is perhaps the sharpest. It was frequently sung during the arrests of groups of Jews protesting at the Party Central Committee or Supreme Soviet in Moscow:

Oh, Pharaoh, Pharaoh, I tell you – Let my people go!
Let the Jewish people go to their proper homeland,
I shall never tire of repeating: Let my people go!
At your peril, at your peril do not keep my people.
To the Lord's own country let my people go.

A gypsy melody and changed text is used in the song *O my Clumsy Heart*:

So often in my dreams a wondrous land appears;
A land of blue skies and a red sea.[104]

We hear Jewish intonations in the song *Our People Lives*:

Our beautiful bright star will
Wondrously light our way,
Let them know, let them hear
Our song which says, We are alive!

Military motifs appear in a song similar to a Soviet mass song:

We are marching into dawn patrol;
The third wind blows out of the Sinai Desert.

Full of humor mixed with patriotic feelings is a song based on the old Russian song *Once Again*, half in Yiddish and half in Russian:

Outside there is a frost,
A real Russian snowstorm.
May our enemies perish –
I can hardly believe it could happen.

General Moshe Dayan –
He the angry one
Will not let the Jews
Be thrown out of Israel

---

[104] The English translations are from the record *Silent No more*. Some time the translations have been changed to keep close to the original.

Though they deliver more new MIGs
And new Katiusha rockets,
Yet the Fascist still will perish.
We will rock him fast asleep.

Frequently, as already mentioned, well-known Soviet mass songs were sung with a certain concealed meaning, a new interpretation of the words. This is the case with the song by I. Frenkel with the text of K. Vanshenkin:

It happened so that I am now far away
From our city,
Between us is an endless way
Which only in dreams is short.
The taiga is whimpering above the snow-covered valley . . .

This song was sung in memory of the Prisoners of Zion in Soviet labor camps.

The Soviet Jewish underground song is a new historical phenomenon, not older than the early 1970s, but it is a most important subject of musical folklore which deserves careful analysis in the future. These songs are a new contribution of Soviet-Jewry to Jewish and Soviet music.

In conclusion, we may formulate the situation of the Jews and the Jewish idiom in Soviet music at the present time as follows: a narrow margin of official Jewish musical culture is permitted for the purpose of propaganda; a somewhat broader participation of Jews in different fields of music is possible if they neglect their Jewish heritage. The policy of the authorities is moving toward the complete assimilation of Jews and Jewish music. As a result, a movement of Jewish national renaissance was born and Jewish underground music and musicology are now developing, historically linked to the Soviet liberal dissident movement.

The chapter of Jewish music in the Soviet Union and of the Jews in Soviet music is not yet closed, for a people's spirit – the Jewish people's spirit – cannot be destroyed by decrees.

Addendum

The Heritage of Jewish-Russian Musical Relations

Excerpts from *Jews and Jewish Elements in Soviet Music*
Tel Aviv, 1978, pp. 17-22.

The continuity of the Jewish musical tradition on the territory of the USSR and its relation to Slavonic alias Russian music goes back at least to the middle of the first millennium. Till recently the East-European channel of musical communication, Palestine-Byzantium-Slavonic areas (Russian-Central Europe) has not been sufficiently treated by historians. The existence of a strong East-European flow of the ancient Jewish musical culture was established in the late 1940s by the musicologists Egon Wellesz, Eric Werner[105] and Joseph Yasser.[106] The article of the last was an especially strong departure to serve studies in the field of Jewish-Russian musical relations.

It was proved by Yasser that the "tunes from Jerusalem", the "Hebrew verse", and "string from Jerusalem" so frequently mentioned in the Russian *bylinas* (medieval Russian heroic ballads) were not merely poetical metaphors, but indicate a certain body of ancient Jewish musical strains accumulated in medieval Russian musical culture. Furthermore, Yasser also observed the possibility of an occasional melodic borrowing from the oldest Jewish chant (*hazanut*) by the more recent Russian one (*demestvo*). Remarkably enough, Yasser's approach was ignored for a long time by Soviet musicology. But recently in one of the most important works ever written on the ancient Russian chant, Nicolay Uspensky joined Yasser and, to some degree, elaborated on this thesis. There existed a "broad influence into Kievskaya Russ" of a multiformed literature which originated in the Near East (Palestine, Syria and in the Mediterranean countries)... The path of its influx was first mediated by translated Bulgarian literature, but at the time of Jaroslav (i.e., the early 11th cen-

---

105 E. Wellesz, *Eastern Elements in Western Chant*, Oxford, 1947; E. Werner, "Hebrew and Oriental-Christian Metrical Hymns", in: *Hebrew Union College Annual*, Jubilee vol. ii, 1950.
106 J. Yasser, "Reference to Hebrew Music in Russian Medieval Ballads" in: *Jewish Social Studies*, xxi/1:21-49 (1949).

tury) it came straight from Byzantinium."[107] Uspensky shows that the "overseas music", the frequently mentioned "*tonets* from Jerusalem", was a reference to a certain musical idiom, perhaps connected with the tuning of the ancient Russian psalter-type instrumen *guslya*.

The Russian Jewish musical relations must have been so strong at the early stages that they could preserve elements of Jewish tradition even later. This can be traced in the terminology of the *znamennij raspev* (the entire body of Russian early liturgical chant). So among the so-called *fitniki* (a kind of embellished jubilation) from the 14th-17th centuries, are some with the names of *judeyiskaya*.[108]

It should be mentioned also that organological considerations contribute to the understanding of the East-European migration route. This was noticed in passing already by Curt Sachs,[109] and received further proof. Some forms of psalter and lute-type instruments have apparently come to Central Europe via this route and brought with them not only ergological features, but also certain forms of tuning. A still more explicit example is the ancient Russian wind instrument *surna* traced at least to the 15th century.[110] The name, construction and performance techniques of the *surna* stems from the Middle East. The Slavonic folk-musician himself (*skomoroch*, folk artist, jongleur) is a phenomenon of Eastern origin. This is reflected even in the name of the travelling folk, which according to different interpretations is of Semitic origin.[111] Still in the 14th-15th century the *skomorochi* were somehow connected and identified with the heretics *strigol'niki* and j*udaizers,* who came into prominence in the North of Russia.[112]

We may assume that this early period of Jewish-Russian communication has strongly contributed to the influx of the Jewish, or Eastern ele-

---

107 N. Uspensky, *Drevne Russkie pevcheskoe iskusstvo* (in Russian, Russian art of singing), Moscow, 1971, pp. 32-36.
108 M. Brazhnikov, *Drevnerusskaya teorija muziki* (in Russian, The music theory of ancient Russina music), Moscow 1972, p. 156.
109 *Reallexikon der Musikstrumente*, Berlin1913, p.307.
110 K. Vertkov et alii., *Atlas muzikal'nikh instrumentov narodov SSSR* (in Russian, Atlas of musical instruments of the people of the USSR), Moscow 1975, p. 27.
111 A. Famincin, *Skomorochi na Rossi* (Skomorokhi in Russia), St. Petersburg, 1889.
112 Russell Zguta, *Russian minstrels: A history of the skomorokhi*, University of Pensilvania Press, 1978, p. 29.

ments, into Russian, and especially Ukrainian, folk music. The "eastern" modes (Dorian with the increased IV degree, and the Phrygian with increased III degree) of the Ukrainian *duma* (recitative epic musical-poetic form of folklore) could have originated in the 11th-12th century in Kievskaya Russ, where, according to Russian musicologists, this folk form has emerged. The relationship of Ukrainian and Jewish musical folklore is apparent from the 17th century Ukrainian *vertep*, a folk-music puppet-show, where elements of Jewish music may be traced.[113] The Ukrainan-Jewish interrelationship, which seems to have surfaced in musical life in the 17th-19th centuries and is usually designated as local influence on Jewish culture, apparently goes back to the medieval period of Russian-Jewish history and should rather be considered as a phenomenon of acculturation.

Of interest is the great amount of Old Testament subjects found in Russian semi-liturgical music and even in folk music, a phenomenon quite rare for any other body of national music. Even a superficial glance at the so called "sacre verse", which was widely used in musical performances in Russia from the 12th century, shows the frequent use of passages on Adam, Cain, the Ark, Joseph, Moses, Samson, the City of David, and other biblical subjects and themes.[114] The earliest Russian liturgical dramas (*deistvo*) can be traced to the 16th century. The first such play mentioned in literature is the *Pechjnoje deistov* ("The Oven Play") based on the book of Daniel.

What Yasser called one of the "strangest and most difficult to explain paradoxes in Russian music,"[115] is the inverse correlation of Russian folk and art music in their usage of Old Testament subjects. Although there is a certain confusion of Russian semi-liturgical and folk music in Yasser's writings, the fact, nevertheless, remains that from the late 18th century on, when Russian art music made its first steps, biblical subjects are almost absent from the mainstream of Russian Music. Moreover, the use of Biblical subjects, as utilized by Alexander Serov, or Anton Rubinstein, in a broad humanistic context, was met by the National Russian School with

---

113 *Muzikal'naya...*, I, p. 758.
114 Brazhnikov, op. cit., p. 233.
115 J. Yasser, "Russkaya muzika na bibleiskie temi" (in Russian, Russian music on biblical themes), in: *Novoe Russkoe Slovo*, 1960, 1st May, p. 2.

open hostility in complete disregard of the incomparable success of those works (such as the operas *Judith* and *The Macabees*).

An explanation of this phenomenon may perhaps not only be found in the confrontation of the Russian people and its intelligentsia (as Yasser thought) but also in the strong trend of Russian Music to identify itself with the late 18th-19th century democratic movements in Europe, and the idea of the use of domestic folklore only as the main source of any art music. "Music is created by the people and we, the artists, only arrange it" – those well-known words by Michael Glinka constitute the quintessence of this approach.

X. Die Bekämpfung der Moderne und der Antisemitismus*

Der Kampf gegen die Moderne ist scheinbar so alt wie die Musik selber. Platon im Buch IV seines *Staates* sagt schon, man müsse „darüber wachen, dass keine ordnungswidrigen Neuerungen vorkommen in der Musik, denn es wird nicht an den Weisen gerüttelt, ohne dass die wichtigen Gesetze des Staates mit erschüttert werden." Ähnliche Aussagen finden wir im Konfuzianischen China. Schon damals war klar: Je strenger die Regeln in der Musik, desto stabiler die Stützen des Regimes. Nach mehr als 2000 Jahren schrieb d'Alamber in seiner *De la Liberte de la Musique*: „Die Freiheit in der Musik vermutet Freiheit der Gefühle; die Freiheit der Gefühle hat zur Folge die Freiheit der Gedanken; der Freiheit des Denkens folgt die Freiheit der Handlung; und diese ist der Ruin des Staates." Es ist also kein Wunder, dass die Avantgarde, deren *raison d'etre* die Änderung und Freiheit sind, nicht in totalitären Systemen geduldet werden kann.

Auch der Antisemitismus ist seit etwa 2000 Jahren dokumentiert. Er erscheint in den Schriften von Diodorus, Tacitus und in wachsendem Masse bei den Kirchenvätern. Einen Zusammenhang von Musik und jüdischem Charakter können wir (nach meinem besten Wissen) zum ersten Mal bei Johannes Chrysostom (4. Jh., *In psalmum*) finden, obschon seine Passagen keine ausgesprochen antisemitische Färbung zu haben scheinen. Ich kenne aber keine vollendete Theorie des Antisemitismus, die direkt mit der Musik verbunden ist, vor Richard Wagner. Hier wurde der Angriff gegen die Abfälligkeit der unerwünschten Musik zum ersten Mal mit dem Judentum und seiner totalen Vernichtung verbunden: „Aber bedenkt, dass nur Eines eure Erlösung von dem auf Euch lastenden Fluche sein kann, die Erlösung Ahasveros – der Untergang."[1] Dieses Phänomen

---

* Published in: *Die Musik des osteuropäischen Judentums: totalitäre Systeme – Nachklänge*, ed. F. Geisler, Leipzig/Dresden 1997, pp. 21-26.
1 Richard Wagner, „Das Judentum in der Musik," in: *Neue Zeitschrift für Musik*, No. 19, 3. September, 1850, p. 57. Ahasver (Gr. 'Assoueros), biblischer Name des persi-

– ich meine hier die ausdrückliche Verkoppelung von Ideen-Kampf in der Musik, und Rassenhass – erscheint erst wieder in den totalitären Systemen des 20. Jahrhunderts, jetzt aber im Rahmen einer Staatspolitik und im Kampf gegen die Avantgarde.

Wie schon erwähnt, ist die Avantgarde ihrem Wesen nach unzulässig im totalitären Staat. Hier würde es vielleicht interessant sein, daran zu erinnern, dass sowohl in Russland der ersten zwei Dekaden unseres Jahrhunderts, wie auch in Deutschland des zweiten und dritten Jahrzehntes die Moderne in allen Bereichen der Kunst, und auch in der Musik im Aufschwung war. In beiden totalitären Staaten war die Avantgarde in den Prä-Revolutionsjahren und kurz nachher die der Revolution würdige Neuerung, das Ethos der Neuen Musik, die Hoffnung und das Zeichen des Fortschrittes. Ein Teil der Elite, der Vorkämpfer der Moderne, war mit den revolutionären Parteien und deren Jugendorganisationen verbunden.[2] Wir wissen aber, dass es bald zu unvermeidlichem Konflikt zwischen dieser Lage in den Künsten und der Natur des totalitären Staates kam.

Im NS-Deutschland war der Antisemitismus vom Anfang an in die Ästhetik einprogrammiert; in der SU dagegen wurde der Antisemitismus für den Kampf gegen die Avantgarde hauptsächlich in den Nachkriegsjahren mobilisiert. Um nun aber die Essenz der anti-jüdischen und anti-modernen Allianz in der Staatsideologie und Kulturpolitik der totalitären Systeme zu demonstrieren, werde ich hier drei Quellen zitieren, die man als Modellbeispiele der beiden Systeme betrachten kann:

1. „Und in der ernsten Kunst... haben sich immer mehr Kräfte breit gemacht die Harmonie und Klang geopfert haben, und die alles Seelische ausschalten wollen. So haben wir jetzt eine Kunstmusik, die nur Töne gibt, die keinen Zusammenhang mehr haben... Schon bei dem Juden Gustav Mahler setzt diese Entwicklung deutlich ein. Arnold Schönberg wird ihr erster Prophet, und heute ist Igor Strawinsky ihr Fahnenträger. Die junge Generation der Hindemith, Korngold, Křenek, Weill usw. folgen ihren Spuren... Dazu gesellen sich Versuche, das ganze abendländische

---

schen Königs Xerxes I (5. Jh. for Chr.), der vorschrieb „man solle vertilgen, töten und umbringen alle Juden, jung und alt..." (Ester, 3:12-14).

2 F. K. Prieberg, *Musik im NS-Staat* (Frankfurt am Main, 1992), S. 125. In der SU: Lourie, Roslavez etc.

Tonsystem zu zerstören..., um so auch an ihrem Teil mit beizutragen zum seelischen Ruin des Abendlandes."

2. „Henry Prullieres..., the High Pontiff of the brand-new international Jewish musical church... told... to destroy romanticism, lyricism, feeling..., and to inoculate with cerebralism, materialism, and cynicism... Alfredo Casella and his friends are not innovators at all, they are, rather, simple and modest imitators of such Jewish musicians as Stravinsky, Honnegger, Milhaud etc. The music of Italy's so-called modernists and innovators derives... from these foreign Jewish musicians. It is music without a country! We do not want to be inoculated with the Jewish intellectual seed, and we do not want to become bastards, even if only in a spiritual sense."

3. „Das Typische dieser Musik ist die Negation der klassischen Musik die Propagandierung der Atonalität, Dissonanzen..., Negation der Melodie und Logik... Diese Musik ist die Zerstörung der Kunst der Musik... Die Tätigkeit der west-europäischen und amerikanischen Modernisten kam zum Abschluss mit dem Zerfall der tonalen Logik... Von der Schule Arnold Schönbergs angefangen, vom Expressionismus Alban Bergs und Anton Weberns weiterentwickelt, von Ernst Krenek und Paul Hindemith fortgesetzt kam sie zum endgültigen Ende in unseren Tagen bei den französischen *Vier*, geleitet von Olivier Messiaen, im Werk von Joan-Carlo Menotti, dem Engländer Benjamin Britten, und vielen anderen."

Das erste Zitat stammt von Erich Hermann Müller von Asows Beitrag „Das Judentum in der Musik," im *Handbuch der Judenfrage* des wohlbekannten Theodor Fritsch.[3] Interessanterweise ist dieser Beitrag von Dr. v. Asow im sowjetischen *Enciklopeditscheski Musikalni Slowar* (Russisch, Enzyklopadiches Musikwörterbuch, 1966, Moskau) im Verzeichnis der Nachweisliteratur zum Beitrag „Jüdische Musik" genannt.

Das zweite Zitat stammt aus Francesco Santoliquidos Schrift *Die jüdischen Musik-Blutsauger* (*La piovra musicale ebraico*).[4]

Das dritte Zitat ist zwei Quellen entnommen: dem Beschluss des Zentral Komitee der Kommunistischen Partei der Sowjetunion vom 10. Februar 1948 zur Oper von Vano Muradelli, und dem Vortrag des bekann-

---

3 Leipzig, 1932, S. 324-334.
4 *Il Tavera*, 1937, XV:40; Zitiert von H. Sachs, *Music in Facist Italy* (London, 1987), pp. 181-2.

ten Komponisten und Musikwissenschaftlers Boris Asafjew beim Ersten Kongress des Allsowjetischen Komponistenverbandes.[5]

Alle drei Zitate könnte man einer semiotischen Analyse unterziehen, aber auf den ersten Blick schon fällt die terminologische, stilistische und semantische Ähnlichkeit auf, auch die Komponistennamen sind sehr ähnlich. Besondere Aufmerksamkeit ruft jedoch das Folgende hervor:

a. Alle erwähnten Texte wurden von renommierten Musikern/Musikwissenschaftlern geschrieben, und nicht von Parteifunktionären oder Journalisten.

b. Das Jüdische wird direkt nur in den NS-Quellen hervorgehoben; in den sowjetischen Quellen ist die Anspielung auf das Jüdische, das Fremde dadurch gemacht, dass man den „Engländer" Britten erwähnt. Der semantische Sinn dieses Hinweises ist der, dass die Aufmerksamkeit des Lesers/Hörers auf das Nationale gelenkt wird, und dass er in anderen Namenslisten sich weiterhin selber zu orientieren wissen wird.

c. In allen Quellen ist nur ein kleiner Teil der Namen jüdisch, obwohl sie direkt als jüdisch gekennzeichnet sind. In den NS-Quellen sind die Komponisten, Musikwissenschaftler, und Interpreten entweder als Juden bezeichnet, oder als „Internationalisten", die sich unter dem jüdischen Einfluss befinden (in nazistischen Quellen),[6] oder als „Kosmopoliten", „vaterlandslose Kosmopoliten" (in der sowjet-sozialistischen Literatur).[7] Die sowjetischen Quellen, die laut Grundkonzept des Systems antisemitische Äusserungen nur in einer Camouflage-Form gebrauchten, entwickelten hier ein raffiniertes System von Verfahren und verschleierten Ausdruck: Enthüllung von Pseudonymen, wenn es sich um jüdische Namen handelte, Bezeichnungen, wie „Passlose Vagabunden," „Heimatlose Kosmopoliten" etc. Die „jüdische Gefahr in der Kunst" wurde hier dem Publikum mit Umsicht untergeschoben, der Gebote der „Brüderlichkeit und des proletarischen Internationalismus gedenkend". Die Verschmelzung des Antijüdischen mit der Diffamierung der Avantgarde kam in den verschiedensten Formen zu Tage: von der Ausstellung *Entartete Musik* bis zu den Ereignissen des 7.-13. Januar 1948, als zur selben Zeit die be-

---

5   B. Asafjew, „30 Jahre der sowjetischen Musik und die Aufgaben der sowjetischen Komponisten," in: *Der erste All-Unionkongress der sowjetischen Komponisten: Stenographisher Report* (Moskau, 1948), S. 7-23.
6   M. Meyer, *The Politics of Music in the Third Reich* (New York/Paris 1991), p. 273.
7   B. Pinkus/J. Fränkel, *The Soviet government and the Jews*, Cambridge, 1984, S. 147.

rüchtigte Komponistenversammlung im Kreml und der Mord am populärem jüdischem Schauspieler Samuel Michoels stattfanden. Der Mord diente als Signal zur Liquidierung jüdischer Kulturinstitutionen.[8] Sehr oft glitt man in der politischen Praxis vom Jüdischen zum Nichtjüdischen und ideologisch Unbequemen; in der Anti-Moderne wurde mit Leichtigkeit das Jüdische durch das Vorderasiatische und Barbarische ersetzt. Sehr ähnlich ist die Reihenfolge der Begriffe, derer man sich in beiden Systemen bediente. Im faschstischem Schrifttum: Atonalität – Juden – Mehrstimmigkeit der nicht-nordischen Rassen – vorderasiatische Menschen – Barbarei – Zerstörung der harmonischen Mehrstimmigkeit; oder in der sowjetischen Tagespresse: bürgerlicher Nationalismus – Kosmopolitismus – altjüdische religiöse Gesänge – Ritual Altpalästinas – antipatriotische Musik (welche dem Antistaatlichem gleichgestellt war); oder nach Chrennikow: aserbaidshanische Musik – mittelalterliche arabische Musik – anti-russische – bürgerlicher Kosmopolitismus – Anti-Parteilichkeit.[9]

Was wir also vor uns haben ist einerseits ein ideologischer Kampf gegen eine Ästhetik, gegen gesellschaftliche Konzepte, die die Existenz des Systems bedrohen; anderseits die Einbeziehung traditioneller Vorurteile gegen nationale Gemeinschaften, gegen Fremde. Die Bevölkerung unterstützte den Kampf gegen „schädliche" und „bolschewistische", „entartete" Musik im Nationalsozialismus, weil die Namen der Künstler jüdisch waren, oder ihre Kunst jüdische Elemente enthielt. Im Nationalsozialismus wurden Strawinsky, Hindemith und Stuckenschmidt für ihre „jüdische Musik" angegriffen, und dieselben Künstler wurden im sowjetischen Sozialismus für „anti-sozialistische", „antirealistische" Kunst verurteilt. Die Akzente verschoben sich vom Nationalen zum Ästhetischen und *vice versa*. Die Juden mussten vernichtet werden wegen ihrer entarten Musikästhetik, die „der totalen Zerstörung der natürlichen Tonordnung" zustrebt laut nationalsozialistischen Theorien[10] und die feindliche imperialistische, anti-sowjetische Ästhetik sollte bekämpft werden via ihrer kosmopolitischen, jüdischen Apologeten in der Sowjetunion (14 von

---

8 J. Braun, *Jews in Soviet Music*, in: J. Miller, ed., *Jews in Soviet Culture* (London, 1984), S. 88.
9 Vgl. bei R. Eichenauer, *Musik und Rasse* (München, 1937), S. 302; „Prawda Ukraini" vom 19.3.1949; *Sowjetskaja Musika*, 2:12 (1949).
10 Karl Blessinger, in: Meyer, op. cit. p. 269.

den 19 Musikwissenschaftlern, die des Kosmopolitismus, Formalismus, Avantgardismus und Antipatriotismus beschuldigt wurden, waren Juden). Antisemitismus auf anti-avantgardistischer Ästhetik gegründet, und die Anti-Moderne durch Anti-Semitismus bekräftigt und kanalisiert – das sind die Charakterzüge der europäischen totalitären Systeme des 20. Jahrhunderts.

Ich möchte versuchen, einige Zeichen dieser ästhetisch-national verflochtenen Kämpfe herauszuheben.

Was stand denn auf dem Banner der Musikästhetik der zwei „sozialistischen" Staaten hinsichtlich national-ästhetischer Aspekte geschrieben?

1. Im Dritten Reich war es das Schönheits-Ideal des „heroischen Realismus";[11] in der Sowjetunion der, laut den Statuten des Komponistenverbandes, der „sozialistische Realismus, die fundamentale Methode der sowjetischen Kunst", deren Hauptaufgabe es ist das „Progressive der Realität, das Heroische, Helle und Schöne" wiederzugeben, und „kompromisslos gegen antivölkische modernistische Richtungen zu kämpfen."[12] Das „Kämpferische" auch Heldenmut, das „Faustische", unter anderem in die „Herrschaft" gehören zum Wertekatalog des Rosenberg-Mythos.[13] Unter anderem, schon 1923, lange vor Alfred Rosenberg war in Moskau eine Malergruppe „Heroischer Realismus" tätig.[14] Der heroische Held war immer Russe oder Deutscher. In beiden Systemen war Kunstpolitik als Realpolitik gefasst.

2. Zum heroischem und sozialistischem Realismus fügt sich im NS-Staat das „Völkische," „Nordische," das als eine biologische Notwendigkeit vorgestellt wird.[15] Das Jüdische war also naturgetreu ausgeschaltet, wenn es nicht als ein negatives Element als Träger der Kunst selber erschien. In der Sowjetunion war es komplizierter, daher auch voll von Widerspruch. Das *primus inter pares* der russischen Kunst war ein beständiges Leitmotiv, und das „Völkische", die „völkischen Quellen", das

---

11 H.W. Heister u. H.G. Klein, Hrsg., *Musik im NS-Staat* (Frnkfurt am Mein, 1984), S. 49.
12 *Enziklopedisches Musikwörterbuch,* op. cit. S. 486.
13 S. Fussnote 11.
14 F. K, Prieberg, *Musik in der Swjetunion* (Koln, 1965), S. 113.
15 Eichenauer, op. cit., S. 316; Meyer, op.cit., S. 316.

Vorbild und die Hilfe der „fortschrittlichen russischen Musik"[16] ein Diktum der Realpolitik. Jede andere „narodnost" (Völkerschaft) wurde als „bürgerlicher Nationalismus" charakterisiert, und damit als anti-staatlich/ sowjetisch gebrandmarkt. Von hier aus können wir einige Folgerungen über die Behandlung des Jüdischen in den totalitären Systemen ziehen. Es wäre aber absurd, die prinzipiellen Differenzen in diesem Punkt nicht zu sehen. Wir können in dieser Hinsicht die Zentraltendenzen so charakterisieren:

a. Im NS-Staat war der konsequent ansteigende Antisemitismus, der von Isolation und ziviler Ausschaltung der jüdischen Bevölkerung und Kunst bis zur totalen Vernichtung führte, von konsequentem Antimodernismus begleitet. Die Entwicklung könnte man mit einer steigenden Geraden darstellen.

b. Im Sowjet-Staat ist eine zwischen Toleranz, Camouflage und beinahe offener Judenphobie schwankende Linie, mit „diminuendo"- und „crescendo"-Abschnitten zu sehen. Auf dem Lenin-Diktum: „die Idee eines selbständigen jüdischen Volkes ist wisschenschaftlich unhaltbar, und vom politischen Standpunkt aus reaktionär"[17] gegründet, entstand eine Situation, in der die jüdische Kultur und Musik auf der Grenze des Erlaubten und Unerwünschten, des Verbotenen, aber nicht Gesetzwidrigen existierte. Die Attitüde zur Moderne kann man ähnlich als schwankend beschreiben: von revolutionärem Aufschwung bis zur Verfolgung, als sie beinahe mit Antisowjetischem gleichgestellt wurde, und mit längeren Stagnationsperioden darin. Beides – der Antisemitismus und die Antimoderne, – entwickelten sich in mehr oder weniger parallel auf- und absteigenden Kurven, von der gegenwärtgen politischen Situation diktiert.

Auffallenderweise zeigt diese Lage neue Parallelen. In beiden Systemen funktionierten beide Erscheinungen – das Jüdische und die Moderne – und besonders die erste, als Musik-Idiom, einer Geheimsprache gleich, als eigenartige Aesopus-Sprache, als Sprache der Resistance. Wegen dem unterschiedlichem Charakter der Verhältnisse in jedem System, funktionierte diese Geheimsprache auch verschiedenartig. Schostakowitsch und Hartmann – um nur die zwei repräsentativsten Beispiele zu nennen – ge-

---

16 *Istoria muziki sovetskikh narodov* (Russ., Die Musikgeschchte der sowjetischen Völker, Moscow 1970) I, p. 23.
17 *Sovetskaia muzika,* 8:104 (1970).

brauchten beide eine Legierung von Jüdischem und Avantgardistischem, jeder seiner sozial-politischen Umgebung gemäss: Hartmann, der für die Öffentlichkeit in totalem Schweigen verblieb, komponierte die „Flaschenpost", Schostakowitsch schrieb entweder mit oberflächlicher, leicht zu durchschauender Camouflage, oder aus verborgenem musikalischem Untergrund kommunizierend (s. Kap. XI).

Es wäre eine höchst anregende Aufgabe für die Wissenschaft, die zwei Parallel-Fälle zu verfolgen, und ich hoffe, die Referate zu diesem Thema von unseren Kollegen werden dazu beitragen. Ich erlaube mir, in diesem Zusammenhang zwei Aussagen zu zitieren. Die eine ist aus Heisters Hartmann-Studie: der Komponist schrieb seine Musik „im Namen des Neuen, des Fortschritts", die beide „den Nazis keinen Ton und keine Technik überlassen, und im Namen einer Identifikation mit den Erniedrigten und Beleidigten."[18]

Das zweite Zitat ist aus meiner Schostakowtisch-Studie: „The social meaning of his work is deeply hidden in the labyrinths of polyphonic technique...very advanced for Soviet music of the early 1950s", where he used „the most elevated forms of the Jewish musical tradition, the *hazanut* melodies" (religiöser Gesang).[19]

Dieser Vortrag kann keineswegs eine vollendete Studie zum Thema „Musik in totalitären Systemen." Vielmehr wollte ich nur das Problem der Verbindung der zwei Phänomene stellen, und das Interesse an diesem Problem wecken.

---

18 Heister/Klein 1984, op.cit., S. 279.
19 See Ch. XIA, pp. 275-276.

XI. On the Double Meaning of Jewish Elements in Dmitri Shostakovich's Music*

A. The Double Meaning of Jewish Elements in Dmitri Shostakovich's Music

The definition of iconology suggested by the art-historian, Erwin Panofsky, may also be applied to musicology. Panofsky wrote: *The discovery and interpretation of "symbolic" values (which are often unknown to the artist himself and may even emphatically differ from what he consciously intended to express) is the object of what we may call "iconology"*.[1]

The concern of musicology is musical style. Insofar as musical style can be understood and interpreted only in the context of the particular culture or cultures where this style emerges, acts, and is perceived, and insofar as it is *"living matter"*, music, like belles lettres, *"demands a sense, not so much of what is really there, as of what is necessary to carry a particular situation off.*[2]

Assuming these postulates, the following questions may be asked: What is the meaning of Shostakovich's so-called Jewish works? When, where, why, and how are the Jewish subjects and idiom involved? How did this style function in Soviet music in general, and in Shostakovich's work in particular?

---

* (A) Based on the papers "The Double-Meaning of Jewish Elements in Shostakovich's Music" (2nd World Congress for Soviet and East European Studies, Garmish-Partenkirchen, 1980; and 13th International Congress of IMS, 1982, Strasbourg); published in: *The Musical Quarterly*, LXXI/1, 1985: 68-80; (B) excerpts from "Shostakovich's Song Cycle *From Jewish Folk Poetry*: Aspects of Style and Meaning," in: *Russian and Soviet Music: Essays for Boris Schwarz*, ed. M. H. Brown, Ann Arbor, Mich., 1984, pp. 259-286; and (C) based on the paper "The Shostakovich Discourse," presented at the International Shostakovich Symposium, Glasgow University (November 2000).

1 *Meaning in the Visual Arts* (Garden City, 1955), 31.
2 *Seven Types of Ambiguity*, 3rd ed. (Hammondsworth, 1961), p. 245.

But first we must define what is meant by Jewish elements or Jewish style in Shostakovich's music. Jewish elements may be considered as: (a) subjects defined as Jewish by the composer, or the author of the text used by the composer (e.g., Op. 113, or Op. 91; see Table I); (b) Jewish folk poetry (e.g., Op. 79); (c) a melos based on the transformation of well-known Jewish secular or liturgical melodies (e.g., Op. 79 and Op. 87): and (d) a musical idiom which shows modal, metro-rhythmical, and structural affiliation to East European Jewish folk music and is commonly accepted as Jewish by the Soviet listener, both professional and nonprofessional (e.g., Opp. 67, 77, 83, and 107).

To understand the meaning of Jewish elements in Shostakovich's music, it is essential to recall the controversial position of Jewish culture in the Soviet Union. Although the form and substance varied according to the period, the dominant ideological view attributed to Lenin that "the idea of a distinct Jewish people is scientifically untenable, and from a political point of view-reactionary"[3] is still prevalent. As a result, Jewish culture, including musical culture, existed and exists on the borderline of the permitted, and the undesirable even "anti-Soviet." This paradox of the permitted but undesired, and the forbidden but not unlawful, has created a highly ambiguous situation in Soviet culture regarding the employment of Jewish themes and motifs in art.

Shostakovich's interest in Jewish subjects both musical and nonmusical, although rooted in the tradition of Russian music, is without precedent in Russian music and, certainly, in Soviet music. In nineteenth-century Russian music, the use of a Jewish-melos-(or rather pseudo-melos) was, according to Vladimir Stasov, the expression of the Russian interest in everything Eastern,[4] and never went beyond a restrained Oriental "spicing" for coloration. Shostakovich's approach does not fit into this mainstream of "Russian interest" employed by Mussorgsky and Rimsky-Korsakov in their folkloristic style, nor does it fit into the philosophical-ethical category of Rubinstein and Serov in their use of Jewish

---

3 Quoted from *Sovetskaya muzyka*, VIII (1970), 104.
4 Selected *Essays* on *Music*, trans. Florence Jonas (London, 1968), p. 72.

subjects. Shostakovich's Jewish strains are of a basically different nature, both in quantity and in quality.[5]

Table I lists twelve Shostakovlch compositions which include Jewish elements: a symphony, a trio, two concertos, two string quartets, two vocal cycles for voice and piano, an instrumental cycle, and an orchestration of one vocal cycle. In two other works Shostakovich's contribution is limited to editing other composers' music.

Shostakovich used Jewish elements in three periods. The first, the years 1943-44, includes an orchestration of the opera, *Rothschild's Violin*, by his favorite pupil, Venyamin Fleishman (1913-1941), and the Piano Trio, Opus 67. His relationship with Fleishman during 1937-41, and his contribution to *Rothschild's Violin*, was Shostakovich's first encounter with the Jewish idiom.

In Fleishman's opera can be found in embryo most of the devices which set Shostakovich's Jewish style: the Jewish modes (Phrygian with a raised third, known in Yiddish as *freigish*; Dorian with a raised fourth, related to the so-called Ukrainian mode); the descending, "iambic prime" (Alexander Dolzhansky's term for a series of primes with the first sound of each prime on the weak beat); the klezmer "um-pa" accompaniment over a pedal harmony, which often creates a bitonal effect (a device that can be traced at least as far back as Hans Neusiedler's *Juden Tanz* of 1544).

Immediately after Shostakovich's work on the opera, he began the Trio with its tragic and macabre Finale, in which the Jewish idiom is exploited. During this time, the first information about the Holocaust was reaching the Soviet Union.

The second period, 1948 to 1952, includes most of the relevant works: the Violin Concerto, the Fourth Quartet, the vocal cycle *From Jewish Folk Poetry* (Op. 79), the Twenty-Four Preludes and Fugues, and the *Four Monologues*. Those are the very years of the consistent attempt to destroy Soviet Jewish culture and its institutions and the decimation of the Jewish intellectual elite. Over 400 writers, artists, musicians, and

---

5   See my *Jews and Jewish Elements in Soviet Music* (Tel-Aviv, 1978), pp. 145-66; and Ch. XIB.

other creative people were arrested in early 1949 and shot in August, 1952.[6]

The third period dates from 1959 to 1963 when Shostakovich wrote the Cello Concerto, the Eighth Quartet, the Thirteenth Symphony, and the orchestral version of Opus 79. This was the time when all hope for a permanent "thaw" (to use Ilya Ehrenburg's expression) had vanished. It was when a new wave of anti-Semitism forcefully struck Soviet society.

Shostakovich's last contact with Jewishness can be described as a gesture of protection-in-a mood of sentimental-reminiscence: in 1970 he appeared as editor-in-chief of a very mediocre Jewish song collection.

The large number of compositions containing Jewish elements and the chronology of these works are proof of a special meaning in Shostakovich's "Jewish" works. In fact, it is the fate of Soviet Jewry that is symbolized in this corpus of music.

The manner in which this symbolism was expressed in a particular composition can be illustrated by the transformation of the leitmotif of the vocal cycle, *From Jewish Folk Poetry* (see Ch. XI-B, pp. 277-309).

A considerable part, perhaps the finest part, of Soviet art and literature, contains social connotations of a dissident character.[7] To confirm this in the case of Shostakovich, we will quote two scholars who approach this matter from extremely opposite positions. The first is the judgment of Soviet party-line musicologist and critic of Shostakovich, Yuri Kremlev:

His [Shostakovich's] works are often penetrated by enigmatic associations, incomprehensible for the uninitiated listener.[8]

The second quotation comes from an essay on Shostakovich by the well-known mathematician and dissident, Igor Shefarevitch:

---

6   Joel Cang, *The Silent Millions: A History of the Jews in the Soviet Union* (New York, 1970), pp. 93-116.
7   Andrei Senyavsky, "Literaturniy prozess v Rossii," *Kontinent*, I (1974), 143-90; W. Kasack, "Formi inoskazaniya v sovremennoy ruskoy literature," in *Une ou deux Littératures russes? Colloque international* (Lausanne, 1981), pp. 123-35; my "Zur Hermeneutik der sowjetbaltischen Musik," *Zeitschrift für Ostforschung*, XXXI (1982), 76-93.
8   Yuli Kremlev, "O desyatoy simfonii D. Shostakovicha," *Sovetskaya muzyka*, IV (1957), 83.

	Composition	Composed	Published	First Performance	Jewish Subject
1	Edition and orchestration of V. Fleishman's opera *Rothschild's Violin*	1943	1965 Muzika M	20.7.60; M Soloists of the Moscow State Philharmonic Society	entire work
2	*Trio* for Violin, Cello and Piano, Op. 67	1944	1944 Muzgiz M	14.11.44; L Author (pf), D. Tciganov (vl), S. Shirinsky (vc)	4th movement Allegretto
3	*Concerto* for Violin and Orchestra, Op. 77	1947 1948	1956 Muzgiz M	19.10.55; L D. Oistrakh, and the Leningrad Philharmonic Orchestra under Y. Mravinsky	2nd movement Scherzo
4	*From Jewish Fold Poetry*, Vocal Cycle for Soprano, Contralto, Tenor and Piano, Op. 79	1948	1955 Muzikal'ny Fond M	15.1.55; L Author (pf), N. Dorliak (s), Z. Dolukhanova (ca), A. Maslennikov (t)	entire work
5	*Quartet No. 4* for Two Violins, Viola, and Cello, Op. 83	1949	1954 Muzgiz M	5.12.53; M Beethoven-Quartet (D. Tciganov, V. Shirinsky, V. Borisovsky, S. Shirinsky)	4th movement Allegretto
6	*24 Preludes and Fugues* for Piano; Op. 87	1950 1951	1952 Muzgiz M	23 and 28.12.52; M T. Nikolayeva	Pr/F No. 8; Pr No. 14; F No. 16; Pr No. 17; F No. 19; F No.24
7	*Four Monologues* on texts by A. Pushkin for Voice and Piano, Op. 91	1952	1960 Sovetski Kompozitor M	?	No. 1: *The Fragment*
8	*Concerto* for Cello, and Orchestra No. 1, Op. 107	1959	1960 Muzgiz M	4.10.59; L M. Rostropovich, and the Leningrad Philharmonic Orchestra under Y. Mravinsky	3rd movement Allegro con moto
9	*Quartet No. 8* for Two Violins, Viola, and Cello, Op. 110	1960	1961 Sov. Kompozitor M	2.10.60; L Beethoven-Quartet (see Op. 83)	2nd mov.: Allegro molto

10	Symphony No. 13 for Bass Solo, Bass Choir, and Orchestra, texts by Y. Yevtushenko, Op. 113	1962	1970 Leeds Music Canada	18.12.62; M Moscow Philharmonic Orchestra under K. Kondrashin, V. Gromadsky (bass), and choir under A. Yurlov	1st movement *Babiy Yar*
11	*From Jewish Folk Poetry*, Version for Voice and Orchestra Op. 79a (see 4)	*1963	1982 Muzika M	19.2.64; Gorki Philh. Orch. under Rozhdestvensky	entire work
12	Editor-in-Chief of Song Collection *New Jewish Songs*, compiled by Z. Kompanejetz	?	1970 Sov. Kompozitor M	?	entire work

Abbreviations: M – Moscow; L – Leningrad; Pr – Prelude; F – Fugue

* *All bibliographic and biographical sources mention 1963 or 1964 as the date of composition of this work. Only Volume 31 of Shostakovich's Collected Works (Moscow, 1982), which became available to me only after this article was in final proof, refers to October 1, 1948. This date seems dubious and raises many questions which cannot yet be answered (see my "Shostakovich's Vocal Cycle").*

Table 1: *Schostakovich's Compositions with Jewish Subjects and Jewish Compositions with his Participation*

It is for us of special importance to understand the creative work of Shostakovich, as it most completely reflects the spiritual life of a long and dramatic epoch ... As corollary of its pluralistic interpretation, and the difficulty of subjecting [it] to official control, [his music] acquired the significance of the samizdat.[9]

The question is then not if such connotations are present, but *where*, *when*, and *how* they are artistically implemented.

From Jewish Folk Poetry was withheld by Shostakovich from publication and performance until Stalin's death in 1955. How should this be explained? The cycle was precisely the kind of music required at this time (1948) by soviet official aesthetics. It was written in a democratic

---

9 Igor Shefarevitch, "D. D. Shostakovich," *Le Messagar*, 125/II (1978), 233.

form, using simple traditional musical language based on folklore and was easy for the listener to understand. The text was folk art. But we are confronted with a paradox: a work in complete agreement with the musical and artistic requirements of the Party is concealed by the author. However, even in an artistic and musical form acceptable to officialdom, the Jewish subject matter was, by its mere existence, provocative. At a time when Jewish culture was under fire, the performance of such a work would have been dangerous.

The connotations of Opus 79 are comparatively direct. Other works, especially instrumental compositions, are of a more complex nature. For example, the Trio, Opus 67, where Jewish strains appear for the first time in Shostakovich's own music, is dedicated to Ivan Sollertinsky (1902-1944), one of the finest thinkers of prewar Soviet Russia. Condemned by Soviet official criticism, and blamed for Shostakovich's "formalism," he was the composer's closest friend and the one who introduced him to twentieth-century modern music, art, and literature. The Trio culminates in a tragic finale based on two Jewish subjects. This movement has been interpreted as a representation of evil, of malice, of death itself, perhaps the forces that caused Sollertinsky's death. In this work personal and social feelings intermingle, and they are expressed in a Jewish idiom.

In the Twenty-Four Preludes and Fugues for piano, the Jewish elements are first expounded in the Prelude and Fugue in F# minor (No. 8). They also occur in Nos. 14, 16, 17, and 19, and finally most decisively in the Fugue in D minor (No. 24), the synthesis or summation of the entire cycle.

Jewish elements also frequently appear in works that employ the self-identification motive of the composer, D-eS-C-H (D. Shostakovich in German usage). This motive already appears (in transposed form) in Fleishman's *Rothschild's Violin*. Shostakovich himself first used the D-eS-C-H formula (also transposed) in the Scherzo of the Violin Concerto. In this movement the Jewish subject is clearly given; it is also the movement that dominates the entire work. In Opus 110, the so-called autobiographical Quartet, No. 8, the Jewish subject (a quotation from the Trio) is again juxtaposed with the self-identification motive.

The Thirteenth Symphony is our final example. The Jewish subject is a central theme in this composition, perhaps Shostakovich's most open work of dissidence. The first movement *Babiy-Yar*, refers to the place in the Ukraine where thousands of Jews were killed by the Nazis; the Soviets did not allow a memorial to be built there, but it later became a place of unofficial pilgrimage for Soviet Jewry. This part of the symphony was originally intended by the composer as a symphonic poem; the other four movements were added later.[10] *Babiy-Yar* is based on the poem of Yevgeni Yevtushenko, at the time a highly controversial figure, almost a dissident. Shostakovich added four other poems by this writer: *Humor, Fears, At the Grocery,* and *Career,* all openly critical of the regime.

The Thirteenth Symphony may also illustrate another point. The "Jewishness" of Shostakovich's music increased with the heightening of the abstractness of the musical form and the deepening of its esoteric meaning. The more hidden the meaning, the stronger is the ethnic coloring of the music, and the more intense is the Jewish musical idiom. Conversely, the more open and direct the meaning o the text, the less Jewish is the music, and the more doubtful is its ethnic provenance. There .are three different types of this interdependence:

1. In the Thirteenth Symphony, the text speaks an open language of resistance and there can be no doubt about the central concept of the composer. The specifically Jewish musical element is absent here and is, in fact, superfluous; it does not add anything to the clear intention of the text. On the contrary, the idiom is Russian: Russian chimes, Russian modes, the Russian vocal bass singing.

2. *From Jewish Folk Poetry* was a kind of stylized East European Jewish folk idiom. This work refutes the claim of several Soviet musicologists (Vasina-Grosman, Polyakova, Sokhor)[11] that Shostakovich made no use whatever of actual Jewish melodies. Songs Nos. 2 and 5 are versions of well-known Jewish folk tunes.[12]

---

10 Lev Danilevich, *Nash sovremennik: tvorchestvo Shostakovicha* (Moscow, 1965), p. 94.
11 Vera Vasina-Grossman, "Noviy vokal'niy cikl D. Shostakovicha," *Sovetskaya muzyka,* VI (1955), 10; Arnold Sokhor, "Bol'shaya praya o 'malen'kom' tcheloveke," in *Dmitri Shostakovich,* ed. Lev Danilevich (Moscow, 1967), p. 255; Polyakova, p. 9.
12 Emil Skoletz, *Yiddishe folk-lider* (Tel-Aviv, 1970), p. 147; Moisei Beregovsky, *Yevreyskiye narodniye pesni* (Moscow, 1962), Nos. 111 and 113.

XIA-1a

Shostakovich, Op. 79/2

S'loyfn, s'yong (Skoletz)

XIA-1b

B62 = Moshe Beregovsky: *Yevreiske narodnye pesni* 1962
Gnessin = Mikhail Gnessin: *The Jewish Orchestra at the Ball of the Town Bailiff*, opus 41

FP No 5

Freilikhs (Beregovsky)

B 62 No 111

B 62 No 113

(transposed - JB)

Gnessin op. 41

Mus. ex. XIA-1a and 1b: (a) Shostakovich op. 79/2, Skoletz, S'loyfen, s'yogn; (b) Shostakovich op.79/5, Beregovski 1962, no. 111 and 113, Gnessin, op. 41/33.

However, the basic musical elements of this song cycle are not purely Jewish. Apart from certain individual Shostakovichian features (flatted notes, for example), the work draws on a vernacular idiom that is of a general East European nature. The structure, meter, and rhythm as well as the modality are typical for the folk music of several East European cultures. In this work the composer is still concerned with the social meaning of the text – the, restoration of the original folk poetry in its orchestral

273

version is proof of this. Here the more or less obvious dissidence of the text is supplemented by the more or less Jewishness of the musical idiom.

Oddly enough, the folk text of this work is permissible and has even been cited as raw material par excellence for Soviet aesthetics. The Jewishness of this material, on the other hand, is suspicious and undesirable. Thus, while the work as a whole has dissident connotations, it was not actually prohibited. As it happened, Shostakovich's Opus 79 started a new trend in Soviet music, the so-called "New Folklore Wave", notable for its anti-establishment and "national" or ethnic overtones.[13]

From Jewish Folk Poetry helped define the concept of Shostakovich's Jewish style. Soviet musicologists, instead of defining the Jewish elements in Shostakovich's music, often refer to the relationship of a particular composition to Opus 79.[14] The identification of the musical style of this work with the Jewish idiom intensified the reception and awareness of the Jewishness in other works. Even such a typical Shostakovichian mannerism as a lowered second degree was frequently perceived as related to the Jewish *freigish*. However, the dual ethnic nature of the music of such works as the Violin Concerto, Fourth Quartet, and Cello Concerto lends itself to ambiguous interpretations on several levels. This can be demonstrated in the Cello Concerto (see **Mus. ex. XIA-2**).

The eight-measure subject in the Locrian mode on C # with the typical lowered fourth and seventh with the C#'-G# pedal accompaniment can be interpreted in the tradition of East European folk music performance practice detaching melody and' pedal accompaniment.[15] As a result, we have a typical Jewish *freigish* on A, even including the characteristic suffix for this mode. The two-measure structure is typical in Jewish Hassidic dance tunes, and characteristic of the *klezmer* performance style (glissando, "um-pa" accompaniment). This music, however, can also be interpreted as ethnically neutral: the Locrian mode, the rhythmical and structural features, the C#-G# pedal accompaniment, and the performance style also allow a general East European (Polish, Czech, or Roma-

---

13 Ramita Lampsatis, "Dodekaphonische Werke von Balsys, Juzeliunas und der jüngeren Komponistengeneration Litauens" (Ph.D. diss., Technische Universität Berlin, 1977); my "Zur Hermeneutik...."

14 Danilevich, p. 85; Alexander Dolzhansky, *24 preludii i fugi* (Leningrad, 1970), p. 64.

15 Bálint Sárosi, *Die Volksinstrumente Ungarns* (Leipzig, 1967), pp. 107-8.

XIA-2

Shostakovich Op. 107

Mus. ex. XIA-2: Shostakovich, Op. 107.

nian) interpretation. Soviet musicologist Lev Ginzburg writes in only a very general way about the "folk character" of this music.[16] The Soviet reader knows that any specific character – Russian or otherwise – will be pointed out except the Jewish aspect, which remains concealed. Composer, musicologist, and reader in tacit agreement exploit this Soviet Aesopian language.

3. In the Twenty-Four Preludes and Fugues the social meaning of the work is deeply hidden in the labyrinths of polyphonic technique The structure of this music and its language, very advanced for Soviet music of the early 1950s, was then considered very complex. The prelude and fugue form, and the abstractness of the connotations, demanded an exploitation of sources other than the vernacular klezmer tunes. In the

---

16 Lev Ginzburg, *Issledovaniya, stat'i, ocherki* (Moscow, 1971), p. 165.

Fugue in F# minor, for example, Shostakovich used as his model the most elevated form of the Jewish tradition, the *hazanut* melodies.[17]

Mus. ex. XIA-3: a) Shostakovich, Op. 87/8; b) weekday morning service (Eisenstein); c) Lebele Alukster's chanting (Ephros).

The musical structure of prelude and fugue as well as the semantic abstractness of modern instrumental music demanded the most authentic Jewish idiom of all. For this purpose, Shostakovich drew on the sovereign power of Jewish liturgical music. To understand this music, the listener must activate the deepest layers of memory and association.

The use of Jewish elements in Shostakovich's music reaches far beyond their specific and "colorful" Jewishness. The intrinsic meaning of these elements is of a socio-symbolic nature and may be interpreted as concealed dissidence. It is in fact a hidden language of resistance communicated to the aware listener of its subtle meaning. Dissidence and opposition are here represented by the Jewish element which, because of its

---

17 Judith Kaplan Eisenstein, *Heritage of Music* (New York, 1972), Ex. 14; Gershon Ephros, *Cantorial Anthology*, IV (New York, 1953), 368.

special place in Soviet culture, served as a perfect vehicle and "screening device"[18] for the expression of "symbolic values" consciously and, in part, unconsciously employed by the artist.

B. The Song Cycle *From Jewish Folk Poetry*: Aspects of Style and Meaning

Dmitri Shostakovich's interest in Jewish matters – both musical and nonmusical is without precedent in the history of Russian or Soviet music. Elements of a Jewish musical idiom may be found in at least ten of his major works, beginning with the Trio, opus 67 (1944), and continuing up to the Symphony No. 13, opus 113 (1962). He also expressed his interest in ways other than by original composition: he completed Benjamin [Veniamin] Fleishman's opera *Rothschild's Violin* (1943) and served as well as editor-in-chief for the, miscellaneous collection *New Jewish Songs* (1970).

Apart from its scope and persistence, Shostakovich's involvement with Jewish music and culture also differs from that of all earlier Russian composers in its very nature. The utilization of a pseuao-Jewish melodic idiom by nineteenth-century Russian composers reflected little more than a characteristically Russian "interest in everything Eastern,"[19] i.e., an interest in exotic coloration. But Shostakovich's appropriation of a Jewish idiom cannot be related either to the "folkloristic" concerns of a Musorgsky or a Rimsky-Korsakov or to the "philosophical" biases of a Rubinstein or a Serov. The uniqueness of his approach stems from the fact that Jewish culture in the U.S.S.R. exists on the borderline between the "permitted" *(de jure)* and the "anti-Soviet" *(de facto)*. Any Soviet composer's exploration of a Jewish idiom is consequently fraught with risk and potentially explosive. Shostakovich's fusion of East European Jewish *melos* with his own individual musical style (in particular, his use of modality, ostinato patterns, and the expressive interpolation of flatted scale

---

18 Edward E. Lowinsky, *Secret Chromatic Art in the Netherlands* (New York, 1946), p. 169. Lowinsky's theory of "secret art" has greatly influenced my approach to the interpretation of Soviet music.
19 V. Stassov, *Selected Essays on Music*, tr. Florence Jonas (New York, 1968), p. 72.

degrees e.g., the second and fourth, sometimes the fifth, and even the octave) is such, that the works composed in this special style seem equivocal when subjected to theoretical analysis, depending on whether emphasizes the ethnically Jewish connections encountered in particular style features or leaves such connections unremarked. This equivocality was probably what Shostakovich sought in his employment of the Jewish idiom. It allowed him the flexibility of symbolizing both autobiographical and social concerns, while shielding himself, as composer, his performers, and his listeners from possible harassment from Soviet officialdom.

I have discussed the general problem of Shostakovich's "Jewish" compositions elsewhere.[20] In this essay I shall focus on the song cycle, *From Jewish Folk Poetry*, attempting to account for its genesis and, by analyzing its text and music, to approach an interpretation of its style and meaning. The cycle is one of Shostakovich's most beautiful and richly symbolic compositions, a masterpiece of the composer's "secret language" of dissent. From the very hour of its creation, it was embroiled in controversy.

From Jewish Folk Poetry, opus 79, belongs to the second "Jewish period" (1948-52) of Shostakovich's compositional career, together with the Violin Concerto No. 1 in A Major, opus 77, the String Quartet No. 4 in D Major, opus 83, the Twenty-Four Preludes and Fugues for Piano, opus 87, and the Four Monologues on Pushkin texts, opus 91.[21] The exact

---

20 J. Braun, *Jews and Jewish Elements in Soviet Music* (Tel'-Aviv, 1978), pp. 146-66; Idem., "The Double-Meaning of Jewish Elements in the Music of Shostakovich," a paper read at the XIII Congress of the International Musicological Society (Strasbourg; August 1982); see Ch. XIA.

21 The works of Shostakovich concerned with Jewish subjects or employing a Jewish idiom fall into three chronological periods. The first, 1943-44, saw the composition of the Trio, opus 67, and the completion of Fleishman's opera and occurred during a time when information on the real dimensions of the Nazi Holocaust first reached the Soviet people. The second occurred during the last years of Stalinism, when Soviet Jewish culture was conspicuously and virtually destroyed. All the "Jewish" compositions from this period, with the exception of the Twenty-Four Preludes and Fugues for Piano, opus 87, were first performed only after a delay of between five and seven years. The third, 1959-63, saw the composition of the Cello Concerto No. 1, opus 107, the Quartet No. 8, opus 110, and the Symphony No. 13, opus 113, and the orchestral version of opus 79. This period coincided with the advance of a new wave of anti-Semitism in the USSR.

chronology of its composition, however, is not yet entirely certain. Unfortunately, it has not been possible to examine the manuscript owned by Shostakovich's widow Irina, but most secondary sources point to the year 1948.[22] Shostakovich's first biographer, David Rabinovich, locates the cycle in the year 1949,[23] but this could hardly be possible. The Soviet musicologist Vera Vasina-Grossman states that the source of Shostakovich's inspiration was "a small... book of translations from Jewish folk poetry, which came into his hands by accident."[24] This book was the collection *Jewish Folk Songs (Evreiskie narodnye pesni)*, compiled by Y.M. Dobrushin and A.D. Yuditsky, and edited by Y.M. Sokolov. The colophon of the book shows that it was signed for publication on 19 March 1947.[25] It is known from the practices of Soviet book

---

Of the twenty-three vocal-instrumental chamber works in Shostakovich's *oeuvre*, three form a separate corpus together with the opus 79: *Eight English and American Folk Songs*, without opus (1944), *Spanish Songs*, opus 100 (1956), and an *a capella* work, *Two Russian Folk Song Arrangements*, opus 104 (1957). All four are set to authentic folk poetry; all represent a musical style which may be described as stylized folk music; all, as can be shown by textual and musical analysis, are loaded with significant national and ideological connotations; and all were composed in the period 1944-57. These compositions brought to life a new style in Soviet music that was to influence those Soviet Russian and, especially, Soviet minority composers who, in the 1960s and '70s, formed the New Folklore Wave – a movement notable for its overtones of anti-establishmentarianism and national self-determination. See the interview with Edison Denisov in *Musica*, no. 4 (1970), pp. 391-92, and the response to that interview in *Sovetskaia muzyka*, no. 10 (1970), pp. 44-46; also R. Lampsatis, "Dodekaphone Werke von Balsys, Juzelinnas, und der jüngeren Komponisten generation Litauens," Ph. D. thesis, Technische Universität, Berlin, 1977; M. Tarakanov, "Neue gestalten und neue Mittel in der Musik," *Beiträge zu der Musikwissenschaft*, issue 1-2 (1968), pp. 42-64; J. Braun, "Zur Hermeneutik der Sowjetbaltischen Musik," Zeitschrift für Ostforschung, no. 1 (1982), pp. 76-93.

22 D. Shostakovich: *Notograficheskii spravochhik* [Reference guidet to the music] (Moscow, 1961), p. 39; *Dmitri Shostakovich: A Complete Catalogue*, comp. M. MacDonald (London, 1977), p. 25; L. Danilevich, *Nash sovremennik* [Our contemporary] (Moscow, 1965), p. 323.

23 D. Rabinovich, *D. Shostakovich: Composer* (Moscow, 1959), p. 124.

24 *Istoriia muzyki narodov SSSR* [Music history of the peoples of the U.S.S.R.], ed. Yu. Keldysh and M. Sabinina (Moscow, 1973), v. 4, p. 276.

25 *Evreiskie narodnye pesni* [Jewish folk songs], comp. Y. Dobrushin and A. Yuditsky, ed. Y. Sokolov (Moscow, 1947), p. 2.

printing and distribution that the publication could not have reached private hands before the end of the year. This sets the *terminus a quo*.

Ludmila Poliakova[26] has argued convincingly that composition took place in the summer of 1948, while the testimony of Natalia Mikhoels, who was a close-friend of the composer and the daughter of the great Jewish actor Salomon Mikhoels, seems to advance the date to the spring of 1948. According to Natalia Mikhoels, it was May 1948 when Shostakovich raised questions in her presence about the pronunciation of certain Yiddish words and about the rhythmic flow of the original folk texts, which Shostakovich knew only in Russian translation. Natalia was also present for the first home performance of the opus 79 on Shostakovich's birthday, 25 September 1948. (It was his habit to have new music performed at his birthday parties.) On this occasion Shostakovich, rubbing his hands nervously, introduced the recently finished cycle with the words: "I have here, you might say, some new songs."[27] This sets the *terminus ad quem*.

From Jewish Folk Poetry was thus created during the dark age of the *Zhdanovshchina,* a time which witnessed in the U.S.S.R. not only the greatest assault ever upon Western and Soviet art, but also the virtual destruction of Soviet Jewish culture. The two occurrences were not unrelated, as Svetlana Alliluyeva, Stalin's daughter, has testified:

> It was in the dark days of the Party's campaign against the so-called "cosmopolitans" in art, when the party would pounce upon the slightest sign of Western influence. As had happened many times before, this was merely an excuse to settle accounts with undesirables. In this instance, however, the struggle bore an openly anti-Semitic character.[28]

The increase in official anti-Semitism in the months during and preceding the composition of opus 79 must be understood against the background of the establishment of the state of Israel by the United Nations, accomplished in the period between November 1947 and May 1948, and the consequent fear among the Soviet leadership of increasing self-

---

26 L. Poliakova, *Vokal'nyi tsikl D. Shostakovich* [D. Shostakovich's vocal cycle] (Moscow, 1957), p. 3.
27 N. Mikhoels, personal interview conducted by the author on 12 March 1981, Tel-Aviv.
28 S. Alliluyeva, *Only One Year* (London, 1968), p. 148.

consciousness on the part of Soviet Jews. The equation of "Jew" with "ideological undesirable" started to figure at this time in one political incident after another, which suggests what must have aroused Shostakovich's social consciousness and attracted him to the Jewish musical idiom.

One sequence of political events is particularly laden with significance. In mid-December 1947, Yevgenia and Anna Alliluyeva, relatives of Stalin's wife, were arrested and accused of espionage.[29] Several Jewish friends of the Alliluyevas, many of them scholars, were arrested on 27 December and accused also of espionage and of suspicious contacts with Salomon Mikhoels.[30] Then on 12 January 1948, Mikhoels was killed in Minsk on Stalin's orders.[31] Six months later, during June and July 1948, immediately after the proclamation of the state of Israel, the accusations against the Alliluyevas' friends were changed; now they were accused of Zionist sympathies and of the intention to leave the U.S.S.R. for Israel.[32]

On the day after the murder of Mikhoels, Shostakovlch and other top Soviet musicians were attending the first day of a meeting convened by Andrei Zhdanov, Stalin's spokesman. Zhdanov gave his opening speech at 1:00 p.m. At 3:00 p.m., news of Mikhoel's death reached the assembled musicians.[33] At 5:00 p.m. Shostakovich spoke for the first time to the assembly. He accepted some of the criticisms leveled at him and publicly supported certain general goals for Soviet music: "Our art should advance, should be even better than it is now."[34] At 8:00 p.m. that evening, he joined Mikhoel's relatives and friends as they gathered at Mikhoel's home. (Also present was Shostakovich's biographer, David Rabinovich, who was to be arrested twelve days later and accused, of suspicious contact with foreigners.) Shostakovich spoke at the gathering about how "this" had started with the Jews but would end with the entire intelligentsia; then he added, "I wish I were in his [Mikhoel's] place".[35]

---

29 Ibid., p. 56.
30 L. Tumerman, *Moi put' v Izrail'* [My path to Israel] (Jerusalem, 1977), p. 72.
31 Alliluyeva, *Only...*, p. 149.
32 Tumerman, *Moi...*, p. 72.
33 N. Mikhoels, personal interview.
34 A. Werth, *Musical Uproar in Moscow* (reprint; London, 1968), p. 26.
35 N. Mikhoels, personal interview.

On the day of the meeting of musicians called by the Central Committee, Shostakovich spoke for the second time; now he fully acknowledged the Party's criticisms: "I have made mistakes; I shall accept critical instructions...."[36]

Shostakovich had to endure an onslaught of denunciation in the months to follow. The Central Committee's Resolution of 10 February 1948 accused Shostakovich and other leading Soviet composers of "formalism" and "anti-people" tendencies in their music. Tikhon Khrennikoy, the powerful First Secretary of the Soviet Composers' Union, further condemned the leading Western and Soviet composers, including Shostakovich, during the First All-Union Congress of Soviet Composers (19-25 April 1948). Then, the Soviet-dominated International Congress of Composers and Musicologists convened in Prague, 20-29 May 1948, and announced its support for the Central Committee's resolution condemning "cosmopolitanism" in music,[37] and in June and July, *Sovetskaia muzyka*, nos. 2 and 3,[38] carried a two-part article by the composer Marian Koval pronouncing Shostakovich's music "worthless," "fallacious," and "anti-people." Soon afterwards, nineteen leading musicologists, fourteen of them Jewish, were accused of "anti-patriotic activities" and "cosmopolitanism"; the latter designation became at this time a virtual synonym for "Jewish."[39] With the arrests of many of his Jewish friends, the mounting attracks in the press against the newly established Jewish state, and the official denunciations of Jewish intellectuals for their "cosmopolitanism," is it any wonder that Shostakovich should have adopted a Jewish idiom as a language of dissent?

The opus 79 was not released by the author for public performance until two years after the death of Stalin. These first public performances

---

36 Werth, op. cit., p: 26.
37 *Sovetskaia muzyka*, no. 4 (1948), p. 97. The resolution of support was signed by H. Eisler, A. Bush, M. Flothuis, and A. Mendelssohn, among others.
38 The half-year delay in the February and March issues of *Sovetskaia muzyka* (nos. 2 and 3) was apparently the result of uncertainty about how to handle the new situation; or perhaps there was simply a lack of authors willing to deal with the subject.
39 See *Sovetskaia muzyka*, no. 2 (1949), p. 36. Increasing anti-Semitism moved hand in hand with increasing Zhdanovism in literature and the arts. Anti-Semitism based on musical esthetics and musical esthetics molded by anti-Semitism emerged as a particular characteristic of twentieth-century totalitarian systems.

took place on 15 January 1955 in Leningrad, and five days later in Moscow. The performers were Nina Dorliak (soprano), Zara Dolukhanova (mezzo), Alexei Maslennikov (tenor), with the composer at the piano. In June of the same year, the cycle was published by the Musical Fund of the U.S.S.R. (Moscow) in an edition of 3000 copies.[40] On 19 February 1964, under the baton of Gennady Rozhdestvensky, the composer presented an orchestral version of the cycle in Gorki on the occasion of the Second Festival of Contemporary Music.

The distinguished subject of our *festschrift* explains the delay of the first performance in the following way:

> For the next few years [1947-52], Shostakovich planned his creative output in such a manner as to avoid political controversy. He wrote works that were ideologically unassailable – scores for patriotic films..., the oratorio *Song of the Forests*..., and so on. On the other hand, he composed several important works in a more complex idiom and laid them aside...; he obviously decided to postpone the premieres until the artistic climate would be more relaxed... Among the latter works are the Violin Concerto,... the String Quartet No. 4,... and the vocal cycle "From Jewish Folk Peotry."[41]

This account of Shostakovich's strategy during these years is not entirely plausible with regard to the song cycle. The Violin Concerto and the Quartet may indeed be considered works of a "complex idiom." In fact, even after their first performances (in 1953 and 1955, respectively), they were still considered too involute by the conservative music critics.[42] *From Jewish Folk Poetry*, on the contrary; is an example of stylized urban folk art. The text is genuine folk poetry, and as such should have been regarded by Soviet aesthetic standards as raw material *par excellence* for musical setting. The music is written in complete accordance with the features of a popular genre: couplet form, a predominance of simple melody lines, and a folk-type accompaniment. This was the sort of

---

40 Stanley Krebs errs in his statement that the work is unpublished; see his *Soviet Composers and the Development of Soviet Music* (London, 1970), p. 198. All of the later publications of opus 79, including that in Shostakovich's *Collected Works*, v. 32 (Moscow, 1982), are reprinted from the first edition.

41 B. Schwarz, *Music and Musical Life in Soviet Russia: Enlarged Edition, 1917-1981* (Bloomington, 1983), p. A similar account is presented in K. Meyer, *Dmitri Shostakowitsch* (Leipzig, 1980), p. 152.

42 *Sovetskaia muzyka*, no. 7 (1956), pp. 6-7.

music required by the Resolution of February 1948 – "democratic," "melodious," and "understandable for the people" – as was pointed out by many Soviet musicologists, including one as mindful of political correctness as Israel Nestyev. Nestyev refers *to* the opus 79 – together with the oratorio *Song of the Forests,* the cantata *The Sun Shines Over Our Motherland,* and some songs for films – as music written in response to the February Resolution.[43]

Why would a work written in complete accordance with the artistic requirements of the Party Resolution be withheld by the composer until a time when he though the "artistic climate would be more relaxed"? There is, however, a possible explanation for this: At the time of the work's completion in summer-fall 1948, it had not been Shostakovich's intention to delay public performance. His having arranged a home performance in September was a risky move in itself, given the political climate during 1948. By way of contrast, he seems to have told no one about the existence of the Concerto or the Quartet, because he must have intended these works to be concealed from the beginning. By the autumn of 1948, the shock waves over the February arrests had subsided. Despite, or perhaps because of, the murder of Mikhoels and the imprisonment of other intellectuals, Shostakovich might now have thought of going ahead with a public performance. This interpretation would help to explain the choice of texts, the popular musical idiom, and the transparently propagandistic songs that end the cycle. Soviet Jewish culture, although endangered, had not yet been anathematized. For Shostakovich, an artist in despair and bowed-down under pressure from the state, the gloomy fate of Soviet Jews accorded with his own frame of mind and served as a vehicle for the expression of his feelings. But during November and December, only two months after the private home performance, the situation changed drastically: all things Jewish were now anathematized and equated with anti-Sovietism. The entire Jewish intellectual elite was either under suspicion or under arrest, including the compilers of *Jewish Folk Songs,* Dobrushin and Yuditsky.[44] There was now no chance for any

---

43 I. Nestyev, "Put' iskanii" [The Path of explorations], *Sovetskaia muzyka,* no. 11 (1956), pp. 12, 13.

44 Some four hundred Jewish scholars, writers, artists, and musicians were arrested in the period from November 1948 to February 1949; most of them were shot in August 1952. See J. Cang, *The Silent Millions* (New York, 1969), pp. 93-116.

public performances whatsoever of Jewish works, even those in a musical style completely in accordance with official requirements.[45]

Conceived and composed as an expression of human desperation, *From Jewish Folk Poetry* had been turned overnight into an ideological protest of potentally nation-wide political significance – a remarkable case of sudden change in value and meaning of an artistic work due to circumstances independent of its creator. Shostakovich apparently as in mind the cycle's unexpected enhanced political clout when he turned in 1963, during a time of renewed anti-Semitism in the U.S.S.R., to arranging an orchestral version, having just completed his Thirteenth Symphony with the famous "Baby Yar".[46]

Of the eleven songs Shostakovich selected from Dobrushin and Yuditsky's Russian edition of *Jewish Folk Songs*, all but one were translations from the original Yiddish edition published by the same compilers in 1940. The translations are literal for the most part, except for euphemistic "corrections" of Yiddish vulgarisms, the change of "engineers" to "doctors," and the substitution of "star" for "sun" as a symbol of happiness in the eleventh song (see table 3). The fifth song in the cycle was taken not from *Jewish Folk Songs,* but from a collection by Z. Skudinsky.[47] Shostakovich also adhered essentially to the order of the songs as they appeared in both the Russian and the Yiddish editions. This fact refutes the assertions of Soviet musicologists that Shostakovich designed the cycle to create a picture of human life from "birth" to "old age," and

---

[45] When this manuscript was in print a new source came to my attention: Shostakovich's letter written on the 22nd January 1949 to a friend, the well-known composer Kara Karayev. Shostakovich wrote: "Dear Karik! Thank you for your letter. I am not very well... I have not yet presented my Jewish songs, I will do this in some ten days. As their fate is of interest for you, I will write you more about this presentation...." (D. Schostakovitsch, *Erfahrungen,* ed. Christoph Hellmundt and Krysztof Meyer / Leipzig: Reclame, 1983 / pp. 215-216). Shostakovich is probably speaking about a presentation at the Composer Union. Did this take place or not? In any case the letter confirms that the composer thought about going ahead with the performance of op. 79. The revision of this decision indeed came only in late January or February 1949, at the height of the anti-Semitic wave, perhaps in connection with the attack on musicologists in February.

[46] The unpublished orchestral score of opus 79 was made available to me through the courtesy of Hans Sikorski Verlag in Hamburg, BRD, for which I express my sincere thanks.

[47] Z. Skudinsky, *Folklor-lider,* v. 2 (Moscow, 1936), p. 161.

from "poverty" to "happiness."[48] The order of songs was predetermined by Dobrushin's collection, and Shostakovich just followed an approved folk song publication.[49] He did invent titles of his own for the individual songs.[50] In the orchestral version of the cycle, he replaced these titles with the first lines of the original songs (see table 1). It is difficult from this vantage point to speculate about Shostakovich's reasons for assigning new titles in the first place – state censorship? Self-censorship?

In four cases Shostakovich altered the original folk song texts (see table 3): The change in the first song seems to be of purely artistic significance. Two of the changes, however, are of political nature. In the third song, Shostakovich added the line "The Tsar holds him in prison" following the line "Your father is in Siberia" in the original – surely an attempt to avoid any possible misinterpretation. In the sixth song, the words "has converted" were replaced by "left with the police officer," thus substituting a secular, social issue for a religious one. The change in gender in the tenth song does not seem to be motivated by a clear-cut reason.[51]

---

48 Poliakova, op; cit., p. 6; T: Kurisheva, "Kamernyi vokal'nyi tsikl v sovremennoi sovetskoi muzyke" [The vocal chamber, cycle in contemporary Soviet music], candidate's thesis, Tchaikovsky State Conservatory of Music, Moscow, 1968, pp. 29-30.
49 It seems possible that Shostakovich's selection of texts for songs No. 9, and No: 10 was influenced by the example set by M. Vainberg. On 13 May 1948, Vainberg's *Sinfonietta* was praised at a meeting to the Composers' Union. The work carries the epigraph: "Jewish songs also begin to sound on the kolkhoz fields – not the songs of the past, full of sadness and misery, but new happy songs of productivity and labor" [see *Sovetskaia muzyka*, no. 4 (1948), p. 97]. Vainberg was the husband of Natalia Mikhoels and a close friend of Shostakovich.
50 The reference to "aunt" in the title of the second song of opus 79 is a mistranslation. The Yiddish "tatyunya" (the diminutive of "tate" – daddy) is mistakenly translated as the Russian "tyotia" (aunt).
51 The reason for the change in the tenth song from a male noun to a female noun is rather puzzling. Why should the kolkhoz shepherd be a girl? The argument that this change was engendered for artistic reasons, because songs No. 9 and No. 10 are "male" songs, is not compelling. No. 9 is a much more appropriately "female" song than No. 10, and Shostakovich himself changed the order of these two, deviating from that in the Russian edition of *Jewish Folk Songs*. A shepherd's work was not usually performed on the Kolkhoz by a female. Could it be that the change was intended to point up the lack of reality in this depiction of "happiness?"

Of greater implicit significance are the changes initiated in the orchestral version of the cycle, all of which, in fact, amount to restorations of the original texts from the Russian edition of *Jewish Folk Songs*. Shostakovich dropped his invented song titles, returned to the unaltered folk text of the first song, and removed the cautious reference to the Tsar in the third song. They also indicate how strongly Shostakovich cared about the richly Aesopian language of the genuine folk texts, leaving little doubt in particular about his motivations in restoring the original text of the third song.[52]

Let us turn our attention to the division of the song cycle into tragic songs and songs that affirm happiness (nos. 1-8 and 9-11, respectively; see table 2). Soviet audiences are accustomed, indeed conditioned, to tolerate in works of Soviet art a certain degree of official propaganda and extraneous Marxist-Leninist rhetoric. While tacitly accepted by both artist and audience, this aspect of the work of art may be disregarded or detached from the "intentional content" (using Roman Ingarden's term) of the work itself. In accordance with the "rules of the game," this extraneous content must nevertheless be present and in proper proportion to the other elements in the work of art, as well as in proper setting and style.

"Tragic" songs and "happy" songs appear in the proportion 8:3 in Shostakovich's cycle, thus, directly contradicting the explicit dictate of Socialist Realism that "the victorious... heroic, bright, and beautiful" should be the focus of attention in a work of art.[53] The three "happy" songs, clumped together at the end of the cycle, obviously stand apart from the main body of the work. The subject matter changes abruptly from texts about poverty and misery to texts inflated with optimism, quite unlike the transition provided in *Jewish Fold Songs*, where texts about work, fighting, and war form a bridge between the "tragic" and the "happy" songs. Distinct topical and formal features also divide the two song groups. The first (nos. 1-8) presents genre scenes, the second (nos. 9-11) presents pronouncements and slogans; the text of the first is based on folkloric elements and uses folk lexemes, that of the second exploits

---

52 In consideration of this fact, an edition of the opus 79 with the original Yiddish text put to Shostakovich's music seems entirely justified (in preparation by J. Braun at the H. Sikorski-Verlag, Hamburg).

53 B. S. Shteinpress and I. M. Yampol'sky, authors-compilers, *Entsiklopedicheskii muzykal'nyi slovar:* 2nd ed., rev. and enl. (Moscow, 1966), p. 486.

features of art song and uses the vocabulary of Soviet mass songs; the first uses the dialogue form typical of Jewish folk songs, the second eschews this structure; the first approximates stylized Jewish folk music, with ample use of "speech intonations," while the second reflects a mixture of the conventional *melos* of the Soviet mass song and the Russian art song. All of these differences create the sense that these two groups of songs are independent of, indeed alien to, one another.

Nearly every song of the cycle exploits the elliptical and connotative language characteristic of Jewish folk poetry in order to suggest certain half-hidden meanings. Dobroshin, the editor of *Jewish Folk Songs* wrote in this connection:

> Here [in Jewish folk songs] maximal concreteness and exactness often turn into reticence. When two persons talk on things well know to them, they can speak in hints.... In Jewish folk poetry, phrases and verses of this kind, built on innuendo, are very often present.[54]

	Title in opus 79	Title in opus 79 (orchestral)	Page no. in Dobrushin original (Russian)	(Yiddish)
1.	Lament about a dead baby	Sun and rain	43	18
2.	The attentive mother and aunt	Hush-a-by	46	45
3.	Lullaby	My son is the most beautiful	50	388
4.	Before the parting	Oh, Abram!	71	84
5.	The warning	Listen, Khasya	110	99
6.	The abandoned father	Elye, the innkeeper	135	227
7.	A song of privation	The roof is sleeping on the garret	171	327
8.	Winter	My Shayndl is in bed	170	325
9.	The good life	Oh, spacious fields	231	433
10.	A girl's song	On the glade, near the forest	230	432
11.	Happiness	I took my husband by the arm	234	460

Tab. XI-1. From Jewish Folk Poetry. Titles and sources.

---

54 Dobrushin, *Evreiskie narodnyi pesni*, p. 9.

Summary

1. The song – a question and answer rhyme – tells of Moyshele, a baby who is born, rocked in a cradle, nurtured with bread and onion, and buried in a little grave.
2. A lullaby: Daddy will go to the village and bring us an apple (or chicken, nuts, etc.) to make the head (or tummy, hand, etc,) strong.
3. A cradle song about an exiled father: Sleep; your father is in Siberia, and my grief is great...Hush-a-by.
4. Parting with the beloved. The refrain "Oij, Abram, how can I stand being without you?!" alternates with reminiscences about the lovers' first dates.
5. "Listen, Khasya! You mustn't go... with anyone! Else, you will weep..."
6. Zirele, the daughter of an innkeeper has departed with a police officer *(pristav)*. The desperate father offers her dresses, jewelry, etc., but she repels him and asks the police officer to "drive out the old Jew."
7. A dance refrain, "Hop, hop, hop," alternates with the description of a baby in the cradle, hungry and "naked, without diapers."
8. A song about abject poverty: My Shayndl is in bed with her sick child, There is no fire, and the wind blows. "Oij, children, weep; the winter is here again!"
9. In the past I had only sad songs, and the fields did not blossom for me; now the kolkhoz is my home, and I am happy.
10. Shepherdess's song: I play my little flute, and admire my country. Little flute, don't cry, do you hear; I am happy, and you have to play more gaily.
11. The old shoemaker's wife goes to the theater with her husband. She recalls the blessings that surround her, and wishes to tell the whole country about her happiness: "The star shines above our heads... our sons have become doctors."

Tab. XI-2. From Jewish Folk Poetry. Summaries of songs.

No.	Dobrushin (Yiddish) DY	Dobrushin (Russian) DR	Op. 79 (piano)	Op. 79 (orchestral)
1	The sun and the rain, The bride and the baby, The groom arrived, The bride floated away.	Same as DY	The sun and the rain, The shine and the mist, The fog is low, The moon has darkened.	same as DR
2		Same as DY	Same as DR	same as DR
3	Sleep, my child, my beauty Sleep, my little son, Your father is a young Siberian, Sleep,....	My little son is the most beautiful in the world, I do not sleep, Your father is in chains in Siberia, Sleep, hush-a-by...	My little son is the most beautiful in the world, A light in the darkness, Your father is in chains in Siberia, The Tsar holds him in prison	same as DR
4	Oij, Rebecca, give me your pussy! ("Pussy" should be understood here in its bawdy sense, which accurately renders the Yiddish *piskenyu*.)	Oij, oij, Rebecca, give me your mouth, baby! (The Soviet editors' squeamishness in the face of the folk vulgarism is reflected in their substitution of the word "mouth.")	same as DR	same as DR
5		from Skudinsky		
6	Elye, the innkeeper Has put on his robe, So he was told, His daughter has converted.	Same as DY	Elye, the junkman Has put on his robe; It is said, His daughter has left with the police office.	same as opus 79
7		Same as DY	same as DR	same as DR
8		Same as DY	same as DR	same as DR
9		Same as DY	same as DR	same as DR
10	I am happy in the kolkhoz.	I [masc.] am happy in my kolkhoz.	I[fem.] am happy in my kolkhoz.	same as opus 79
11	My sons have become engineers - Only the sun shines above our heads.	My sons have become doctors The star shines above our heads.	same as DR	same as DR

Tab. XI-3. From Jewish Folk Poetry. Comperison of texts.

This innuendo possesses concrete meaning only for the initiated – in the case of Shostakovich's song cycle, for those acquainted with a particular social and artistic climate. Let me cite some examples. An implicit reference to the millions exiled to Siberia by the Soviet regime is obvious in the third song of the cycle, although the text itself refers to events during the 1905 Revolution.[55]

The third song also relates to the fourth song, with its recurrent, desperate outcry, "Oij, Abram, how shall I live without you? / I, without you – you, without me /How shall we live apart?" The dramatic situation enacted here is clearly a consequence of the Siberian banishment depicted in the third song. The theme of religious conversion in the sixth song was widely construed by the Jewish audience – and afterwards by the non-Jewish audience, especially those belonging to ethnic minorities – as a warning about the possible loss of ethnic identity and the danger of assimilation.

The three "happiness" songs may well have been forcibly included in the original collection. The idiomatic wording of the Russian translation in the tenth song certainly suggests the presence of coercion:

Tol'ko, dukochka, ne plakat'!	Only, little flute, no weeping!
………………..	……………………
Slishish, zhizn' moya polna!	Don't you hear? My life is full!
Veselee, veselee,	More gaily, more gaily,
Dudochka, ty pet' dolzhna!	Little flute, you have to sing!

The "only no weeping," "don't you hear" and the "more gaily," followed by the "have to" are more an *argumentum baculinum* than an overwhelming afflux of happiness. The concluding verse of the cycle, with its reference to "doctors" (implicitly Jewish ones at that!) and to a "star" on, the head of the shoemaker's wife, was perceived by Soviet audiences as pure mockery. With the "Doctor's Plot" of Stalin's last days and the "yellow stars" of Nazi Germany still firmly in mind, these lines

---

55 The symbiotic semantics of "Jewish" and "Siberia" is not a singular occurrence in Shostakovich's vocal works. In his *Four Monologues on Pushkin Texts,* Shostakovich juxtaposed "The Candle in the Jewish hut" [V evreiskoi khizhine lampada] and "In Deep Siberian mines" [V glubine sibirskikh rud], thereby drawing an unavoidable analogy between the two tragic events of Soviet history in 1952.

struck such a vein of accumulated grievance and fear that the effect could hardly be concealed. An eyewitness to the first performance relates: "a shivering, half-giggle, half-shudder swept through the audience."[56] Yet another detail of the first public performance confirms that already by 1955 wide circles were aware of the political implications of this work. The master of ceremonies who announced the program appended a significant word of explanation about the third song: "A mother sings a lullaby about her baby's father, who is in Siberia," he said. Then he added pointedly, "This takes place in Tsarist Russia." With these words, "the audience sat stunned," remembered the same eyewitness.

The Jewish musical idiom probably came to Shostakovich's direct attention in the late 1930s when the young Jewish composer Benjamin Fleishman (1913-41) studied with him at the Leningrad Conservatory. Fleishman had already begun work on *Rothschild's Violin,* a one-act opera based on Chekhov's novel of the same title, when, in September 1941, he was killed in, the war. Shostakovich completed the work, editing and orchestrating what Fleishman had left incomplete. "His memory is sacred to me," Shostakovich would write many years later.[57]

In Fleishman's opera some of Shostakovich's Jewish style is foreshadowed. Three episodes – the orchestral opening with the first chorus, the second orchestral *tutti* (rehearsal numbers 30-42),[58] and Rothschild's flute solo (42-46) – establish all the musical material of the work. Most of the music is strictly modal, with the use of flatted scale degrees and bitonal effects. The latter originate to a certain extent in genuine *klezmer*[59] performance, which often sounds out of tune, although in reality it is based on untempered scales. The modal tunes are set against a pedal accompaniment, which produces a primitive type of bitonality.[60] Minor

---

56 N. Mikhoels, from personal interview with the auhtor.
57 *Sovetskaia muzyka,* no. 3 (1980), p. 31.
58 V. Fleishman, *Skripka Rotshil'da* [Rothschild's Violin] (Moscow, 1965).
59 M. Gnessin, *Stat'i, Vospominaniia, Materialy* [Articles, Reminiscences, Materials] (Moscow, 1961), p. 205. *Klezmer* (Hebrew: kley + zemer = musical instrument) refers to Jewish folk musicians known from the late Middle Ages in Europe, but especially active and popular among both the Jewish and non-Jewish populations of the Ukraine and Byelorussia in the eighteenth and nineteenth centuries.
60 The classic example of this type of bitonality is found in Hans Neusiedler's *Juden Tanz* from 1544, probably the first piece of notated *klezmer* music.

modes, extensively used in East European Jewish folk music, are dominant. The use of an "um-pa" accompaniment and the highly characteristic "iambic prima"[61] suggest the sound of a folk orchestra. Traits of Shostakovich's individual style are also present, as in the case of the transposed D-eS-C-H motif (bars 1-4).[62] The opera makes characteristic use of "musicalized speech," a type of recitative imitating speech intonations, which originated from two quite different sources – the Dargomyzhsky-Musorgsky approach to text setting in art music and the ancient practice of cantillation in rendering Jewish liturgical texts.

Songs 1, 3, 4, 5, 6, and 8 of Shostakovich's opus 79 all employ the device of "musicalized speech." Although the Musorgskian strains in Shostakovich's music in general are well-known, his "Musorgsky-ism" [*musorgskianstvo*][63] is of special significance for his "Jewish style." Musorgsky wrote about his interest in "musical declamation" that he was "departing from the conviction that human speech is strictly controlled by musical laws," and that he considered "the mission of the art of music to be the reproduction in musical sounds of not only the nuances of the emotions but, even more important, the nuances of human speech.[64] Dobrushin, speaking about the East European Jewish folk song, wrote that what "vividly stands out [as] the one most characteristic folksong feature [is] the fundamental connection with spoken language, with the manner of speaking of the Jewish masses.[65] Thus, we witness in Shostakovich a case of overlap between principles cultivated in Russian art music and traditional features found in Jewish folk art. Shostakovich drew upon these two related approaches in order to create his own kind of "musicalized speech," which Soviet audiences perceived to be inspired

---

61 The (a) "iambic prima" and (b) the "trochaic prima" are terms introduced by Alexander Dolzhansky in his 24 *Preliudii i fugi* D. *Shostakovicha* [D. Shostakovich's 24 preludes and fugues] (Leningrad, 1963), pp. 42, 63, to describe two types of melodic-rhythmic figures with a unison repetition: see **Mus. ex. XIB-10**.

62 The D-eS-C-H (D-E*b*-C-B) is a musical transcription of the composers' name in German: D. SCHostakowitsch.

63 M. Sabinina, *Shostakovich-simfonist* [Shostakovich the symphonist] (Moscow, 1976), p. 283.

64 From *Musorgsky: In Memoriam 1881-1981*, ed. Malcolm Hamrick Brown (Ann Arbor, 1982), p. 3.

65 Dobrushin., *Evreiskie narodnye pesni*, p. 9.

by Jewish traditions, but which could also be interpreted as purely Russian in origin – a typical manifestation of Shostakovich's twofold-style.

The genre-scene character and subject matter *(zhanrovost'; siuzhetnost)* of *From Jewish Folk Poetry* also reflect Shostakovich's conjuncture of Russian classical tradition and Jewish folk tradition. Musorgsky's "folk-scenes" *(narodnye kartiniki)* characteristically dealt with the fate of the "little man" or the "humble man," a familiar figure in Russian literature and art from the time of Gogol. The comic and the tragic converged in the "little man's" everyday life, with the tragic perhaps predominating. The Soviet musicologist Arnold Sokhor claims that *From Jewish Folk Poetry* "is in fact the first composition which revived in our time the tradition of vocal scenes, pictures, and portrait sketches that comes from Dargomyzhsky and Musorgsky."[66] Similarly, the miniature genre scene is also found in Jewish folk song where it stems to a great extent from the Jewish folk theater *(Purimshpil:* Purim-games), and particularly from the art of the *badkhan*.[67] "The Jewish folk song is always inclined towards a story," wrote Dobrushin, and the Yiddish folk song "was born in the cellars of the poor man, in the cramped tailor-shop, in the shoemaker's closet, at the sewing-machine, and at the joiner's bench."[68] With a few changes in social setting, then, the hero of the Jewish folk-scenes, with his "laughter through tears," is very like the "little man" we encounter in Gogol's stories and Musorgsky's songs.

There is an important distinction, however, between these two cultural concepts of the "little man." The "little man" of Russian art song suffers from social inferiority and spiritual impoverishment. The Jewish "little man" is,' first and foremost, economically impoverished; but, though oppressed by a dark social power and by rigid officialdom, as with any folk hero, his reason and his spirit remain strong and dominant. This distinction was ignored by Soviet musicologists, who felt constrained to interpret the cycle only in terms of 19th Century Russian art music tradition; the intelligent Soviet listener, however, generally accepted the Jewish "little man" on his, own terms.

---

66 A. Sokhor, "Bol'shaia pravda o 'malen'kom' chelovke" [The big truth about the "little" man], in *Dmitri Shostakovich*, ed. L. Danilevich (Moscow, 1967), p. 257.
67 *Badkhan* is a Jewish folk comedian or jester; also, a musician *(klezmer)* or actor, akin to the medieval jongleur.
68 Dobrushin, *Evreislie narodnye pesni*, p. 9.

Stylistic interpretation of *From Jewish Folk Poetry* can be complete only by taking into account all three of the cycle's aspects: the Jewish, the Russian, and the Shostakovichian. The latter two have been widely discussed, but the Jewish element has hardly ever been mentioned, and occasionally even concealed. Aside from short periodical reviews,[69] four musicological studies on the cycle have been written. The first, by Vera Vasina-Grossman, a leading Soviet expert on vocal chamber music, appeared five months after the cycle's first performance. In her nine-page article, she devotes all of *nine lines* to the subject of our interest here:

> The new vocal cycle is written on texts from Jewish folk poetry. The composer used only the poetry of the folk songs, which he viewed only as a poetical creation. By setting his music to texts of folk songs, Dmitri Shostakovich, naturally, could not avoid the folk-song genres and the intonational and modal features of Jewish folklore.[70]

Eighteen years later, in *Istoriia muzyki narodov SSSR* (1973), Vasina-Grossman added not a single word to her reconsideration of the piece.[71]

The second study, after Vasina-Grossman's article, was by Ludmila Poliakova, who devoted twenty lines of her twenty-five-page booklet (1957) to the Jewish sources of opus 79; expanding on Vasina-Grossman's points, she declares that the music is "certainly Russian in its humanitarian content, is real Russian music about another people."[72]

An elaboration of this idea appears in two other studies from the late 1960s. Arnold Sokhor's article, "The Big Truth about the 'Little Man,'" typifies the best Soviet musicological writing, but even Sokhor denies the use of actual folk melodies and the pervasive connections with Jewish musical tradition.[73] The most significant point encountered in the article relates to Sokhor's brief reference – for the first time in Soviet musicology – to a Jewish "national character;" thereby touching upon a controversial Marxian concept which at that period was finding its way back

---

69 *Sovetskaia muzyka.* no. 3 (1955), pp. 103-4; no. 12 (1956), p. 109.
70 V. Vasina-Grossman, "Novyi vokal'nyi tsikl D. Shostakovicha" [D. Shostakovich's new vocal cycle], *Sovetskaia muzyka.* no. 6 (1955), p. 10.
71 *Istoriia muzyki narodov SSSR,* v. 4, pp. 276-79.
72 Poliakova, op. cit., p. 9.
73 Sokhor, op. cit., p. 255.

into Soviet aesthetics.⁷⁴ "Shostakovich achieved in his music deep psychological truthfulness, which was the main requirement for a faithful reproduction of the national character."⁷⁵

The most recent study, Tatiana Kurisheva's doctoral thesis of 1968, contains an eighty-one-page chapter devoted to opus 79 that is an example of how, Soviet formal analysis typically avoids considering the dangerous area of cultural context and meaning by hiding away in the purely structural aspects of the music. Although she is much more specific, Kurisheva basically concurs with Vasina-Grossman's interpretation of the Jewish element in opus 79 as exotic flavoring. While recognizing that this tiny song cycle "belongs to the most important works of the composer,"⁷⁶ Kurisheva never actually discloses the reasons for its importance.

In examining the musical message of *From Jewish Folk Poetry*, we must reject, first of all, the recurrent assertion that Shostakoyich made no use of Jewish folk tunes. The second song is Shostakovich's version of the folk song "Are rushing, are flowing..." (S'loyfn, s'yogn...), which appears in Emil Seculetz's collection, and, in fragmentary form, in a collection of Moshe Beregovsky and Itzik Fefer.⁷⁷ It is of interest that the original text of the melody in the Seculetz collection reads: "Black clouds rush, and flow / Your father sends greetings from Siberia... / He digs deeper, and deeper / Digs the grave for the lie... / He is not the first, and not the last / Who dies in the field" (see **Mus. ex. XIA-1a**). Can this text have been unknown to Shostakovich; can his choice of a melody associated with a Siberian subject have been purely accidental?

Generally considered to be "bright" and "humorous," Song No. 2 has tragic strains which probably derive from the original text, a typical *Hobelbanklied*. Shostakovich stresses the tragic by inserting into the tune's 2/4 flow, four 3/4 bars, and this always on the flat sixth. This $C_♭$ is interpreted by Kurisheva as the "Russian 'romance' sixth."⁷⁸ From our perspective, however, a "Jewish" interpretation seems more accurate: the $C_♭$

---

74 M. Kagan, *Lektsii po marksistsko-leninskoi estetike* [Lectures on Marxist-Leninist aesthetics] (Leningrad, 1971), pp. 641-46.
75 Sokhor, op. cit., p. 258.
76 Kurisheva, op. cit., p. 77.
77 E. Seculetz, *Yiddishe folks-lider* (Tel-Aviv, 1970), p. 147; *Yiddishe folks-lider*, comp. M. Beregovsky and I. Fefer (Kiev, 1938), p. 318.
78 Kurisheva, op. cit., p. 95.

is the sixth of the *freigish*, the altered Phrygian – a typical Jewish *shteiger* which, according to Beregovsky, bears equally with the "altered Dorian" the semantics of "lamentation, complaint, and grief."[79]

An interpretation of Song No. 2 as being in E Major is not the only one possible. The *g* natural may be considered the raised third of the *freigish* on $e_♭$, rather than the usual major third of E Major. The implied Phrygian $f_♭$ is just a bar away, and the accompaniment is careful not to overstep the "hollow" fifth ($e_♭$-$b_♭$). If a $d_♭$ appears, it is the $d_♭$ of the modal suffix (see explanation in Note 1); and when the accompaniment adds something, it is the altered Dorian, using another Jewish mode together with the characteristic device of switching from one mode to another. With the addition of the neighbor-note motion on *d*, we have a compound Jewish mode with the characteristic modal suffix. In this way, this "most Russian" song (as Kurisheva describes it) can be interpreted just as easily as a Jewish song.[80]

This is not the only case of a direct relationship between opus 79 and Jewish folk tunes. Song No. 5 is a version of a Jewish *freilekhs* (dance tune) transcribed in 1935 by Beregovsky from performers at the Moscow Jewish Theater.[81] A similar fragment appears in Mikhail Gnessin's symphonic piece, *The Jewish Orchestra at the Ball of the Town Bailiff* (1926), a classic of Soviet Jewish music, and widely known among musicians in Moscow (see **Mus. ex. XIA-1b**).

Yet another example is provided by the melody of the folk song "Oij Abram," which can be regarded as a primitive prototype of Shostakovich's Song No. 4.[82] The descending fourth *e'-b* (again, as in Song No. 5, at the same pitch) provides the skeleton of both melodies. The Hasidic tune from Idelsohn's *Melodienschatz* is also closely related to Shostakovich's song.[83]

---

[79] M. Beregovsky, "Izmennyi doriiskii lad v evreiskom muzykal'nom fol'klore" [The altered Dorian mode in Jewish musical folklore], in *Problemy muzykal'nogo fol'klora narodov SSSR* [Issues in the musical folklore of the U:S:S.R.] (Moscow, 1973), p. 388. **See Note 1.**
[80] Kurisheva, op. cit., p. 94.
[81] Beregovsky, *Evreiskie narodnye pesni*, songs no. 14 and 113, p. 23.
[82] Seculetz, op. cit., song no. 37.
[83] Idelsohn, *Hebräisch-orientalischer Melodienschatz*, v. 9, songs nos. 153 and 560.

Song No. 6 presents an interesting case of the "re-Westernization" of a Jewish tune. Written in 3/4 meter, the song approaches its dramatic high point – "Drive out the old Jew!" – through a section wherein Zirele announces her decision to marry the police officer. Here the rhythm aquires the character of a waltz, with rests on the downbeat. Sharp dissonance appear in the waltz accompaniment, along with stylized scale passages *á la* Weber, endowing the music with a bitterly sarcastic quality typical of Shostakovich's method of suggesting "evil" by means of parody. The waltz itself is alien, of course, to Jewish folklore, so that the very sound of such a characteristically Western genre underscores the unnatural character of Zirele's action. But there is more. Many tunes in the *klezmer* repertory, in particular the songs of the popular *badkhan* Elyokum Zunser (1840-1915), were "created" through modal and textural transformation of popular Western melodies. In the case of Song No. 6, Shostakovich started with a Zunser–derived melody (see **Mus. ex. XIB-4**), restored its purely Western major scale basis and texture, and thereby "re-Westernized" what had become a Jewish tune. What more effective way to stress for Jews the alien and tragic character of religious conversion![84]

XIB-4
(transposed and abbreviated - JB)

Mus. ex. XIB-4: (a) Shostakovich, op. 79/6; (b) Idelsohn, Thesaurus, vol. 9/581.

---

84 Ibid., song no. 581.

Song No. 11, which caps the group of so-called "happiness" songs, often elicits discomfort or vexation from Soviet audiences. It was not really an appropriate choice as the final song for the cycle. The entire section referring to the "blessings" that now surround the Jewish shoemaker's wife seems somehow ridiculous. Moreover, the "humor" in this "good-natured" song lacks "good humor," contrary to what has often been asserted.[85] Much has been written about Shostakovich's "malicious humor," achieved by transformations of popular urban folk melodies or genres (as in the use of the valse in Song No. 6). Sarcasm and scorn are certainly present in this particular "happy" song. Its melody is strongly related to, if not directly derived from, familiar Hasidic tunes. In Shostakovich's version, however, the melody has acquired a blunt, rhythmical monotony, with its dull repetition of every tone.

Mus. ex. XIB-5: (a) Shostakovich, op. 79/11; (b)Idelsohn, Thesaurus, vol. 10/52; (c) ib., 10/73.

---

85 Poliakova, op. cit., p. 23.

The c_b (lowered fifth) that appears at the climax of the song on the words "we got (c_b) two tickets for the parterre" clearly distorts the pure Hasidic melody. Then again, the "darkening" effect occurs on the words "the star (c_b) shines above our heads."

An obtuse "um-pa" accompaniment dominates the entire song (44 bars out of 58). In the second stanza every line is accompanied by a Phrygian motif "Oij!" which Shostakovich has added to the text: "And I want to tell the entire country, Oij! / About my happy and bright fate, Oij! / My sons became doctors, doctors, Oij! / The star shines above our heads, Oij!" In this context the "Oij!" – a typical feature of Jewish folk songs – sounds parodistic. To complete the sense of parody, a sudden modulation takes place in the last bars of the song from F minor to F Major, with octave leaps *á la* Soviet mass song. The chromatic line g-g_b-f-e adds a mocking laugh. The entire song, a parody of a folk tune, thus reveals itself as a parody of the idea of happiness.

The Jewish sources of opus 79 do not suggest themselves purely through musical parallels. Most of the songs are written in genres typical of Jewish folk music: lamentation (nos. 1 and 8), lullaby (nos. 2 and *3), freilekfhs*, (nos. 4 and 7), and genre scenes (nos. 5 and 6). The ethnically unmarked genres of lyrical song (nos. 9 and 10) and of parody (no. 11) appear in the last group of "happy" songs, thus underlining once again their alien nature.

Perhaps the most characteristic feature of East European Jewish folk music is its tendency to an "extrapolation of mood."[86] This peculiar trait is richly explored in opus 79: a single, gay dance-motif develops into ecstatic, self-obsessed automatism (nos. 4 and 7); a lyrical, melancholy subject turns into tragic music, bordering on a state of catharsis (nos. 1 and 8); a calm piece of everyday advice concludes in a deliriously whispered warning (no. 5). Only in the last three songs, where the mood is constant and unequivocal, do we miss this sort of development.

All the songs are basically composed in the two simplest song forms: the binary or couplet form (nos. 2, 4, 7, 8, 10, and 11) and the ternary form (nos. I, 3, 5, 6, and 9). Song No. 8, the last of the "tragic" songs, represents with its developmental couplet form (ab a'b' a") a kind of

---

[86] Gnessin, op. cit., p. 201.

culmination. This culmination, or sense of finality, is also evident in the distribution of the vocal parts:

No.		No.		No.	
1.	S + A	3.	A	9.	T
2.	S + A	4.	S + T	10.	S
		5.	S	11.	S + A + T
		6.	A + T		
		7.	T		
		8.	S + A + T		

(S – soprano; A – contralto; T – tenor)

Opening with an introduction (nos. 1 and 2) and moving through a progressive interchange between the singers (nos. 3-7), the cycle culminates in the vocal trio of no. 8. The last three songs of the cycle follow a more formal approach to the "appended" trio in no. 11. The accumulation of intensity that culminates in Song No. 8 is also supported by the expanded ambitus of both the solo parts and the piano score at the point: in no. 8, G#-b' for the singers and CCC-b' for the piano; while in no. 11, only F-g' for the singers and FFF-g' for the piano.

Throughout the cycle, rhythmic patterns and formulas of articulation characteristic of Jewish folk music are used extensively. Subdivisions of the strong beat, syncopations, and the "iambic prima" occur in all eleven songs. Oftentimes, identical rhythmic structures can be found for the melodies in opus 79 and for folk melodies (e.g., Song No. 7 and the folk song "Good evening, Brayne").[87] In eight songs Shostakovich has used the "um-pa" accompaniment (mostly on a pedal bass) typical of *klezmer* bands. It is absent only in songs no. 5, which is based on a folk melody, no. 6, where its absence may stress the alien quality of the situation (i.e., the religious conversion), and no. 9, the first of the "happy" songs. (In the latter song, the entrance into an artificial, marionette world is marked by an accompaniment *á la* Schubert.)

Shostakovich's use of modality is probably the most complex feature of his music. The various investigations of his melodic-harmonic system suggest a multitude of possible interpretations, from a relatively conventional major-minor approach by the traditionalist (L. Danilevich, A.

---

87 Beregovsky and Fefer, *Yiddishe folk-lider*, p. 284.

Dolzhansky, V. Bobrovsky) to those of more recent researchers who stress the Western and Eastern folk roots of his highly individual and modal style (E. Fedosova, S. Skrebkov, Y. Tyulin, V. Sereda). The very existence of such a wide spectrum of theoretical possibilities seems to substantiate the equivocality of Shostakovich's music. Skrebkov, for example, points out that the distinctive Shostakovichian lowered fourth degrees serves as a significant source of auditory deception, since it sounds as a major third.[88] From our perspective, the melodic-harmonic system on which opus 79 is based should not be construed as the major-minor system with instances of altered scale degrees, but as a distinctive modal system with a strong affinity for the Jewish *shteiger*. We have already mentioned this in connection with Song No. 2; it also has implications for the D-eS-C-H formula (see Note 1). Let us add some other examples.

Song No. 4 is referred to in all studies as being in A minor. The first twelve bars, over a pedal on a, consist of three modal nuclei. The first, with an oscillation between the lower and upper neighbor notes, d# and f focuses on e; the next, with a diminished fourth, a d_b, sounds above a F-minor chord; the last one encompasses the oscillating d# within a raised third, and through a Phrygian c resolves both unstable units into a *freigish* mode on b. This, as substantiated by the following main subject of the song *(meno mosso)*, turns out to be the upper tetrachord of a mode centered on e. A Hasidic dance tune establishes a *freigish* on the same e. The tonal feel of the song is not A minor, despite the A-minor ending. The A minor here is only a kind of "deception," while the actual modal center is e. The scale basis of the song corresponds to an artificial symmetrical mode that leans towards the *freigish* (see **Mus. ex. XI-6**).

Further instance of auditory deception in opus 79 are: major third = raised third from the *freigish* (Song No. 2); lowered second = Phrygian natural (nos. 3, 6, 10); lowered fourth = raised third from the *freigish* (nos. 3, 5); lowered fifth = raised fourth from the altered Dorian (no. 11).

---

[88] S. Skrebkov, "Kak traktovat' tonal'nost'" [How to interpret tonality], *Sovetskaia muzyka*, no. 2 (1965), p. 92.

XIB-6

Mus. ex. XIB-6: Freigish mode.

The middle part of Song No. 1, for example, is usually interpreted as Mixolydian on $e♭$ with lowered second.[89] Our ears tell us, however, that this section is Phrygian with the raised third of the *freigish*, along with the typical modal suffix of $d♭$ and c. Modal ambiguity is further secured by the instability of tonal focus throughout the song, where B minor, $B♭$ Major, and $E♭$ Major vacillate (see **Mus. ex. XIB-7**).

XIB-7

Mus. ex. XIB-7: Shostakovich, op. 79/1. Modal ambiguity.

The harmonic frame of Song No. 3 may be interpreted as C minor with a lowered second and a "split" fourth. Yet another interpretation might be to regard the entire song as in *freigish* on c. The e that occurs each time with an $e♭$ can be explained as a splitting of the third to imitate the untempered augmented second which occurs naturally in Jewish folk performance. (A similar device – simultaneous use of the minor and ma-

---

89 Kurisheva, op. cit., p. 36.

jor third – is found in the final bars of Gnessin's "Romance" from *The Jewish Orchestra* [see **Mus. ex. XIB-8**].

XIB-8

Mus. ex. XIB-8: Shostakovich, op. 79/3. Simultaneous use of minor/major third.

The frequent occurrence of the "split" fourth (nos. 3, 4, and 5) can be explained as an "interaction of the two modal tendencies"; that is to say, the raised fourth belongs to the Jewish altered Dorian, while the lowered fourth characterizes Shostakovich's personal style.[90] The "split" fourth may also involve the interaction of two Jewish modes: the raised third (lowered fourth) of the *freigish*, which becomes manifest because of the Phrygian second, and the above mentioned altered Dorian fourth. This sort of instability, which results from two modal collections on a single fundamental, is a typical feature of Jewish traditional music. Such an interpretation of the chromatic inflections in Shostakovich's music, i.e., their being derived from the *freigish* and the altered Dorian modes, opens up new possibilities for insight into *From Jewish Folk Poetry*, yet in no way limits more traditional analytical descriptions. Such a musical dualism, auditory and theoretical, symbolizes the delicate interplay between the established Soviet and the "semi-official" Jewish in Shostakovich's cycle.

A degree of tonal instability rare in the first eight songs may also be intended to underscore the ephemerality of the "happiness" represented in the last three songs. Song No. 9 concludes on a first-inversion F#-Major triad. No. 10 begins in *freigish* on *c* and ends in Mixolydianon on

---

90 Ibid., p.70.

a. And No. 11 concludes the entire cycle, or, perhaps, leaves it open in a tritone relationship with No. 1 (B:F).

One of the most striking structural devices utilized in opus 79 is the leitmotive. Its significance here is certainly not "pure[ly] musical," as maintained by Kurisheva,[91] if one takes into account its strong ethnic coloration. Although the basic structure of the motive remains constant enough, and it clearly dominates the entire cycle, it never appears twice in the same form and therefore may be defined as a leitmotive only with some reservation. Nonetheless, its integrity as a motive is secured by both modal and rhythmic-melodic features, namely, the augmented second, typical of the two Jewish modes *(freigish* and altered Dorian), and the descending, stepwise chain of "iambic primas"

"Iambic primas" are certainly not the exclusive property of Jewish folk music. Western musicians from the time of the Baroque have also exploited the device. Its distinctive structure, with the double accentuation of each scale degree, inevitably highlights the individual melodic traits of whatever mode constitutes the scale basis. This quality is of decisive semantic significance in the case at hand: in East European Jewish folk music, the *freigish* and the altered Dorian impart to the "iambic prima" its specific Jewish flavor. The device is widely used in Jewish folk songs. In Beregovsky's collection, for example 33 of the 150 tunes make use of the "iambic prima," and some 60% of these are in *freigish* or altered Dorian.[92] In *From Jewish Folk Poetry,* the "iambic prima" of the leitmotive is linked to an altered *freigish,* an alloy of the pure *freigish* and the altered Dorian (½ – 1 – 1½ – ½ – ½).

In its most complete form the leitmotive appears in No. 3 (see **Mus. ex. XIB-9:3**), the Siberian song, which seems to embody the idea of the cycle *a toute outrance*. Four times the entire motive appears, and the melodic subject of the song itself is a variation of the motive (or *vice versa)*. In Songs Nos. 2, 4, and 5, only fragments appear, while the motive is absent from Songs Nos. 1, 7, and 8. In Song No. 6, the motive appears for the last time in the first and principal part of the cycle (nos. 1-8). Here, at the height of tragedy, the moment of ideological collapse, the motive sounds on the words "Come back, Zirele, my daughter!" after the

---

91 Ibid., p. 78.
92 see Beregovsky, *Evreiskie narodnye pesni.*

XIB-10

Mus. ex. XIB-10 Iambic prime

converted daughter shouts, "Drive out the old Jew!" Although its basic structure is preserved, the motive is now expanded to a diminished octave extending downward from the flat sixth, moving through the tonic *c*, the ending on the natural sixth on the weak beat. In the process, it acquires a highly unstable character, emphasized by a *fortissimo* C-major *tirata* in the contra-octave, which concludes with a descending leap of a seventh to CCC just as the final two notes of the leitmotive (b_b-a) sound *pianissimo* in the vocal part on the whisper, "Zirele, my daughter." This radical transformation of the leitmotive and its dramatic confrontation with the alien-sounding tirata suggest the breakdown of a tradition, the confrontation with "evil" (in this case, religious conversion), and a final cry of despair at the loss of posterity.

Following the climax in Song No. 6, the leitmotive does not appear for two songs. No further spiritual devastation is possible; only physical well-being can deteriorate, and this indeed happens in Songs Nos. 7 and 8. With Song No. 9, the motive rapidly loses its, ethnic character as well. It has assumed a pure Phrygian coloration by the end of Song No. 9, and in No. 10, it even loses its augmented second, coming to conclusion with an authentic cadence, which is entirely alien to the Jewish modes. In Song No. 11, the characteristic descending motion of the "iambic prima" disappears as well, replaced by movement both upward and downward. 'The Picardy third in the final F-minor chord concludes the metamorphosis, obliterating any sense of ethnic intrinsicality. The transformation, indeed the destruction, of a spiritual world has been accomplished.

From Jewish Folk Poetry stands as striking evidence of the complexity and ambiguity characteristic of both the culture in which the composer lived and created, and his own life: It seems to me that the work's uniqueness, its special place in Soviet music, and perhaps in world music, is secured by its distinctive Aesopian language, its remarkable inter-

XIB-9

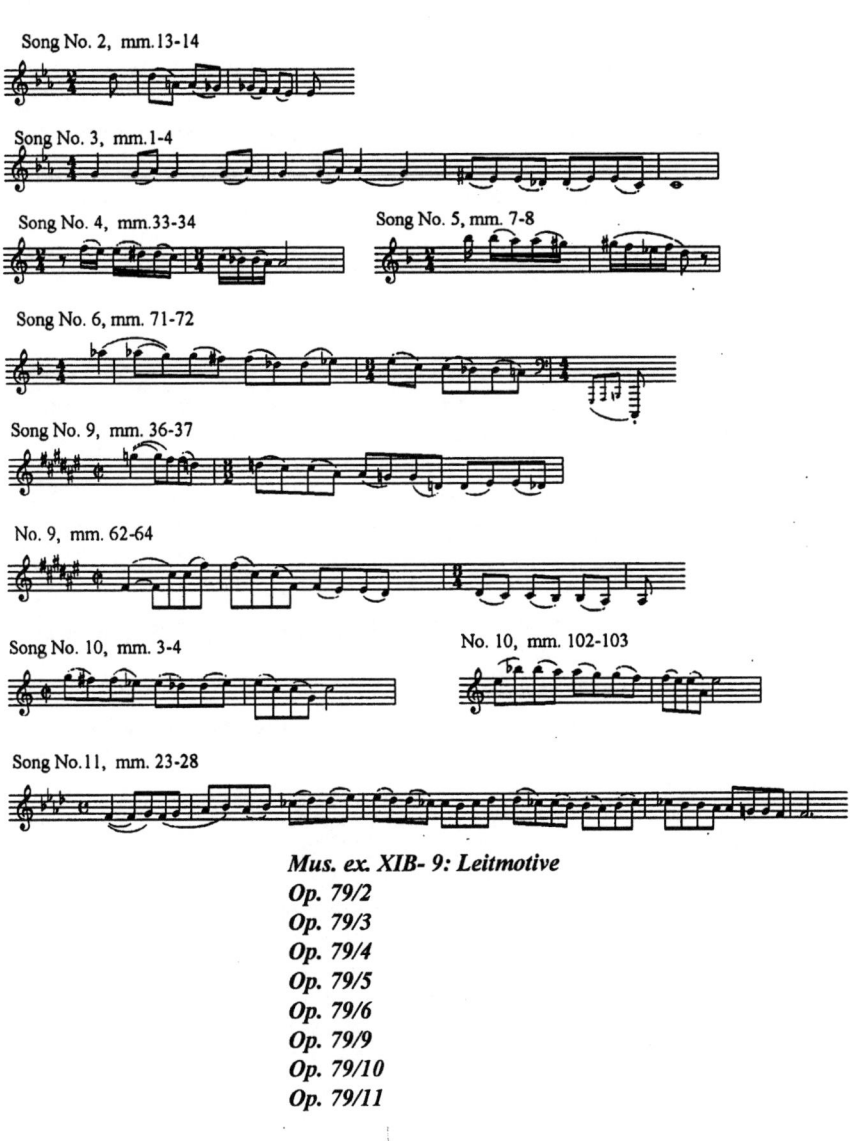

Song No. 2, mm. 13-14

Song No. 3, mm. 1-4

Song No. 4, mm. 33-34

Song No. 5, mm. 7-8

Song No. 6, mm. 71-72

Song No. 9, mm. 36-37

No. 9, mm. 62-64

Song No. 10, mm. 3-4

No. 10, mm. 102-103

Song No. 11, mm. 23-28

Mus. ex. XIB- 9: Leitmotive
Op. 79/2
Op. 79/3
Op. 79/4
Op. 79/5
Op. 79/6
Op. 79/9
Op. 79/10
Op. 79/11

mingling of the obvious and the latent, which constitutes its real meaning and its symbolism. The fate of Soviet peoples, the complications of Soviet life, and the ironies of an officially imposed doctrine of optimism and happiness have been expressed by Shostakovich through a Jewish musical idiom that, because of its special status in Soviet society, was able to serve at the time of its creation as an ideal vehicle, and simultaneously as a "screening device,"[93] for the composer's artistic and ethical self-expression.

Note 1

Besides the natural minor the two most characteristic East European Jewish folk music modes *(shteigers)* are the *freigish* (Phrygian with a raised third) and the "altered Dorian" (Dorian with a raised fourth). The latter is related to the "Ukrainian" mode, and the fusion of the two is close to the "Hungarian" mode. In different sources a somewhat different rendering of the *shteigers* is given, but the modal "suffix" is a constant feature:

XIB-11

Mus. ex. XIB- 11: *Altered Phrygian or freigish and altered Dorian.*

The augmented second in these modes goes back to the traditional Jewish *ahava-raba* mode; it allows for distinctive modulational possibilities to other modes, as well as for shifts of the same mode to other scale degress (see Idelsohn, *Jewish Music,* p. 190). The positioning of the diminished fourth – the "D. SCHostakowitsch" interval – in these modes also suggests the possibility of relating the formula D-eS-C-H to them, in addition to the regular modal implications involving a *finalis* on d or $b♭$, as pointed out in E. Fedosova, *Diatonicheskie lady v tvorchestve D. Shostakovicha* [The diatonic modes in the works of D. Shostakovich] (Moscow, 1980). A good example, from among several possibilities, is the "*study-shteiger*" from Idelsohn's *Jewish Music:*

---

[93] I am using Edward Lowinsky's term, from his *Secret Chromatic Art in the Netherlands Motet* (New York, 1946), p. 169, which has inspired to a great extent my approach to the interpretation of Soviet music.

XIB-12

Mus. ex. XIB-12: Study-shteiger, A. Idelsohn, Jewish Music, p. 189.

See: H. Avenary, "Music," *Encyclopedia Judaica,* ed. Cecil Roth and Geofrey Wigoder (Jerusalem, 1972), v. 12, p. 621; M. Beregovsky, *Evreiskie narodnye pesni* [Jewish folk songs] (Moscow, 1962), pp. 16-18; A.Z. Idelsohn, *Jewish Music in its Historical Development* (reprinted, New York, 1975), pp. 25-26, 137-43, 184-92; Idelsohn, *Hebräisch-orientalischer Melodienschatz,* v. 9, (Leipzig, 1932), pp. x-xv.

C. On the Present Shostkovich Discourse

Some years ago to my attention came the article by Laurel E. Fay in the *New York Times* (April 14th, 1996), which was actually the opening of a "post-revisionist" discussion on Shostakovich's personality. The title of Fay's article – "The Composer Was Courageous, But Not as Much as in Myth" – marks the central agenda: it was just "the rotten luck of the composer" when he picked up Jewish folklore for his op. 79. The subtexts and chilling ironies of which have "engraved themselves" in the score and the double meaning of the music should be authored rather to Stalin than to Shostakovich, suggests Fay. The focus of the discussion, aimed to the person, instead the music, is put very clearly – Shostakovich, the hero is a myth. In the Oxford UP volume[94] Fay's picturing of the political ambiance of the years preceding the op.79 (1947-1948) remained as superficial and misleading, as before. She ignores facts and evidence on the state of mind of the composer and the intellectuals of his environment, and music analysis is absent here as it was in the newspaper hit.

---

94 Fay, Laurel E., *Shostakovich: A Life,* New York 2000, pp. 167-170.

Let us recall the reality of those days: fear was the perpetual state of mind, and among others – the fear of being Jewish.[95] Stalin could be as creative as he wanted – if op. 79 from the hour of its creation would not possess some intrinsic anti-Soviet resistance-symbolism, no one could plant it there. Only the combined effect of music, text and the particular historical situation could produce the double meaning of op. 79, as it would have done in 1948, if the cycle would be performed, and indeed did produce in later years while collective memory was alive.

The question – was Shostakovish a dissident or was he not – is now in the center of the discussion, which became non-academic and unpleasantly overstrained. Ironically enough, this discussion is linked to Solomon Volkov's *Testimony* – this very doubtful and, to use Richard Taruskin's expression, "shameless"[96] piece of literature, and is reduced to *pro* and *contra Testimony*. This futile discussion on the authenticity of Volkov's book goes on till our days, as, for example, in Michael Koball's "Vom Machwerk zum Authentikum,"[97] in which, according to the

---

95 On p. 170 Fay explains that "by the summer 1948, Shostakovich, like the majority of his countrymen, could not yet have known about Stalin's plan" for the eradication of Soviet Jewry. The reader should believe that no signs of trouble were apparent, and if the composer postponed the first performance of op. 79 till 1955, this was an act of "belated panic" (from Fay's NY Times writings). Reality, however, was different: already in December 1947 a number of Jewish intellectuals were arrested and accused of contacts with Salomon Mikhoels. January 1948: Mikhoels was killed during the days of the Zhdanov's infamous meeting with musicians, and Shostakovich's's reaction to this event was – "this started with Mikhoels and will end with the entire intelligence" (see p. 281). From 19 musicologists branded by the 1948 February Resolution as "cosmopolitans" (a sign for persecution), 14 were Jewish. Shostakovich, perhaps, did not know about Stalin's plan for the eradication of Soviet Jewry, as claims Fay, but does this mean there was no foreboding of danger? There are enough testimonies to the contrary, among others the memories of Svetlana Alliluyeva, Stalin's daughter, not to mention the well known descriptions of those days by such eye witnesses as the first performer of op. 79, singer and friend Nina Dorliak, the musicologist Abraham Gozenpud and composer Edison Denisov (see in: El. Wilson, *Shostakovich: A Life Remembered* /London, 1994/, pp. 234-238).
96 Richard Taruskin, *Defining Russia Musically*, Princeton, NJ, 1997, pp. 472.
97 In: G. Wolter and E.Kuhn, ed., *Dmitri Schostakowitsch - Komponist und Zeitzeuge*, Berlin, 2000, pp. 1-18.

authors statement "Die Geschichte der Debatte um Schostakowitsch's Memoiren ... sollen hier entfaltet werden." A one-sided and incomplete overview of the history of the debate is followed by a section confronting "Die letzte Zweiflerin: Irina Antonowna Schostakowitsch" (why "die letzte"?) and quoting "berühmte Persönlichkeiten des Russischen Musiklebens"[98].

But we certainly do not have to prove or disprove the authenticity of the *Testimony*, in order to confirm Shostakovich's dissidence, which is manifested by his music. This is what I wrote to Ian MacDonald, when he approached me in 1997 with the request to react in his book *Shostakovich Reconsidered* on Dr. Fay's article.[99]

While in the Soviet Union open intellectual resistance was forcedly destroyed, a thin layer of latent dissent nevertheless has been glimmering. During all the years through the 30s, the 40s and into the early post-Stalin era, these early tremors remained nearly unnoticed by broader professional circles as well as the public opinion on both sides of the Iron Curtain and came to light only in the 1960s. In this connection Juri Jelagin's[100] very early writing is of utmost interest – it contains one of the first and most shattering documents of Shostakovich's camouflaged musical language of dissent. Jelagin, a young violinist at the Moscow Art Theater, attended in Leningrad on December 21, 1937 at the White Auditorium the premier of Shostakovich's *Fifth Symphony* performed under Yevgenij Mravinski by the Leningrad Symphony Orchestra. The main part of this document was quoted by Richard Taruskin, who nevertheless felt the necessity to minimize it's weight for the Shostakovich case by branding Jelagin memories as "somewhat tentative, from a defector," and "from his musician's perspective, construed narrowly."[101] If,

---

98 Indeed, many well-known musicians, when asked about the *Testimony*, confirmed, it was true; reacting otherwise, would mean to be equated with the official Soviet propaganda. To say "yes" to the *Testimony* was everyone's personal vendetta.
99 Allan B. Ho and D. Feofanov, *Shostakovich Reconsidered*, Toccata Press, 1998, pp. 228-229; see ADDENDUM 1.
100 Juri Jelagin, *Taming of the Arts*, tr. by N. Wreden, New York, 1951, pp. 164-169; *Ukroshchenie iskusstv*, New York, 1952, pp. 220-222.
101 Richard Taruskin, "Public lies and unspeakable truth interpreting Shostakovich's Fifth Symphony," in: D. Fanning, ed., *Shostakovich Studies*, Cambridge UP, 1995, p. 36.

however, Jelagin's memories are quoted from the German translation (signed in Huston, Texas, June 1959), including the *Nachwort*, we will see that the post-modernist nihilists are quite wrong by underestimating the spirit and genius of the Soviet intelligentsia. This is how Jelagin recalls the events and describes the perception of the *Fifth* by the audience at the premier:

> .... In seiner *Fünften Symphonie* (klangen) durch die technische Vollendung der reifen Meisterscheft, durch die ungeheuere kunstlerische Uberzeugunskraft völlig neue Töne an: es war die 'grosse Linie' der ständigen Niederdrückung des Schreckgefühls und der Verzweiflung, im ersten Teil; die plumpe Groteske und der schlechte Sarkasmus im Scherzo; im dritten Satz das betrübte, seltsam ruhige Thema, dass in einer unerwarteten Explosion sich aufbäumt zu einer wahnsinigen Anspannung; der stetige Schritt einer kalten, unmenschlichen Gewalt, die alles auf ihrem Weg zermalmt, im Finale. Die Fünfte Symphonie und viele der späteren Werke von Schostakowitsch sind in ihrer Haltung, in ihrer inneren Bewegung die antikommunistischste, antisowjetischste Musik, die irgendwann auf unserem Planeten geschrieben wurde.[102]

When Jelagin published the two first editions of his book in the early 1950s – the Soviet state after WW II at the peak of its power, and many circles in the West full of illusions and admiration for this system – it was premature to publish this text; only some years later, after Stalin's death, the author could expect understanding for his words even in the Western world.

For "a fuller contemporary reading" for the *Fifth* Taruskin turned to the critical review of Georgiy Khubov, a top servant of the Soviet establishment, among others advisor on arts at the Central Committee of the USSR Communist Party. But, in fact, even Khubov in his critical zeal pointed to some characteristics of Shostakovich's music which, if seen in the right light, could be interpreted as a negative depiction of Soviet reality. Taruskin resorts to Khubov for proof, that "public dissent or even principal criticism were simply unknown" in the Soviet Union of the late 30s, thus attempting to turn Soviet orthodox writing (by any Khubov-type musicologist) into a text with "a rich vein of rhetorical ambiguity inviting

---

102 *Kunst und Künstler im Sowjetstaat*, tr. by H. D. Mueller, Frankfurt/Main - Hamburg, 1961, pp. 205.

readerly irony, in short, of doublespeak as classically defined."[103] We are offered here by Taruskin a reading of the Soviet hyper-official musicology, which implicates "doublespeak," and a Shosotakovich who was a loyal Soviet citizen rather than dissident.

The first attempts to re-evaluate Soviet music were made in the second half of the 50s and the 60s,[104] by choosing mostly a soft middle-line, as did, for example, Boris Schwarz' in his classic work of that time *Music and Musical Life in Soviet Russia 1917-1970* by (New York, 1972): "Shostakovich belonged to all, and to none," he wrote. In a certain way it expresses the multifarious possibilities of interpreting Shostakovich – the man and his music, allowing the composer both to survive the system and to keep some fractions of freedom of expression, some elements of esoteric communication. When a quarter of a century later this is repeated by Richard Taruskin: "The fact is, no one owns the meaning of this music,"[105] this statement sounds somewhat naive.

With the second half of the 50s hidden musical dissent in the Soviet Union gained strength. It appeared in several ways: by using avant-garde music styles (in particular, dodecaphony), employing early, especially Baroque, music stylization and performance, or in the New Folklore Wave and use of esoteric poetry from exotic cultures.[106] Only in the 60's we find in Soviet musicology the foremost latent indications of the sense of these new artistic means, as, for example, Mikhael Tarakanov's articles, in particular on the use of ancient folklore layers.[107] The first studies

---

103 Taruskin, "Public lies...," p. 38.
104 Andrei Olkhovsky, *Music under the Soviets: the agony of an art*, New York and Routledge, London, 1955; Fred Prieberg, *Musik in der Sowjetunion*, Cologne, 1965; Detlef Gojowy, *Moderne Musik in der Sowjetunion bis 1930*, Ph. D. Goettingen, 1965.
105 Taruskin, *Defining Russia...*, p. 476; a overlapping passage by Taruskin in "Shostakovich and Us" (in: R. Bartlett, *Shostakovitch in Context*, Oxford,2000, p. 8) additionally accuses "many others" in dishonesty for attempting a revised interpretation of the "Soviet" Shostakovich.
106 J. Braun, "Zur Hermeneutik der sowjetbaltischen Musik," in: *Zeitschrift für Ostforschung*, 32/1 (1982), 76-93 (reprinted in: *Studies: Music in Latvia*, Riga, 2002, pp.204-226).
107 M. Tarakanov, "Neue Gestalten und neue Mittel in der Musik", in: *Beitraege zur Musikwissenschaft*, Berlin, 1968, 1/2, pp. 42-64.

on the double meaning or Aesopian language of Shostakovich's music appeared, to my best knowledge, in the 70's in the West.[108]

Dissidence – certainly a non-musical term – in the arts is probably much older than the word itself. The oldest documented musical example is that of the hidden language of the secret chromatic art in the Netherland madrigal;[109] a most powerful text on music and the Aesopian language of music is Heinrich Heine's description of the esoteric meaning of the *opera buffa* in Italy of the 1820's. The famous passage from his *Reise von München nach Genua* can convince anyone of the tremendous volcanic power of moral and political resistance which music can develop, and in certain circumstances communicate hidden meaning, if necessary, *"tödliche Befreiungsgedanken"*[110] from alien, hostile powers.

Hidden musical dissidence in Soviet music we find not only in Shostakovich's works; we have only to mention some composers of the Baltic Republics.[111] Even Nicolay Myaskovsky, the conformist, wrote some compositions with hidden religious allusions;[112] and there is a rich list of such compositions outside the Soviet Union by Polish and Czech composers, in particular Krzysztof Pendereczki.

Did somebody define dissidence in music? Has it to be open, noisy and public or can it be hidden, quite, just a hint? Should it be only the persecuted, arrested, preferably executed martyr-dissident, or could it be the prosperous, free and very much alive dissident? It can be shown that the best composers of the Soviet Baltic Republics, carrier of the high titles "Honored Art Workers" and "Peoples Artists" wrote dissident music,

---

108 J. Braun, *Jews in Soviet Music*, Research Paper No. 22, The Hebrew University, The Soviet and East European Research Center, Jerusalem, 1977, pp. 71-76; *Jews and Jewish Elements in Soviet Music*, Tel-Aviv, 1978, pp. 149-165, see ADDENDUM 2; Marc Honigger et al., *La Musique le rite sacre et profane: Actes du xiiie Congres de la SIM 1982*, Strasbourg 1986, p.749.
109 E. E. Lowinsky, *The Secret Chromatic Art in the Netherlands*, New York, 1946.
110 Heinrich Heine, *Reise von München nach Genua;* see the full quotation in Ch. XII, p. xxx.
111 See footnote 13
112 Prof. Dr. Vladimir Karbusicky (Hamburg University) was preparing a study on the Aesopian musical language of some Soviet composers, mostly Myaskovsky (from personal contact, 1984, Hamburg).

because they knew how to do it, and were talented enough to master the new hidden language of communication.[113] I don't think that because Sostakovich "never suffered a dissident's trial but ended his career a multiple 'Hero of Socialist Labor,"[114] his music could not be dissident. What is a "genuine dissident" and a non-genuine one? Is an artist, who has chosen "inner emigration" (Karl Hartmann, Mikhail Gnessin) less dissident than one who sets himself on fire publicly? But, above all, is it of real importance, if Shostakovich every moment of his life was a dissident or not? Starting with maturity, his music, his artistic message was communicating dissident symbolic values, which, using Erwin Panofsky's wording, "sometimes, possibly, were unknown to the artist himself and may even have emphatically differed from what he consciously intended to express."[115] And again, the question is not weather there is hidden dissident meaning in Shostakovich's music, but our task rather is to discover this meaning and to disclose its artistic implementation.

Shostakovich's musical dissent, which we musicologists not always have cared to notice, was not an exclusively 20th century phenomenon, his hidden musical language was not the first in history. Shostakovich did not stand alone as a lonely romantic hero, his dissentient activities where perhaps not always and not in any situation "heroic," and his dissentient music not always the best one, but they nevertheless were not a myth. His dissent was deeply rooted in the culture of the better part of Russian and the entire Soviet intelligencia, who in the periphery were fighting both a social and national war for independence. We may hardly accept the view, that "in the failing Soviet Union he (Shostakovich, JB) was cast as a 'dissident' of a sort that simply did not exist during the better (or rather, the worse) part of his lifetime." We should be careful to claim, that "there were no dissidents in Stalin's Russia." Especially, if some pages before the same author claims that "the social value (of Sostakovichs's music, JB)... was precisely the result of the play of subtexts – the uncontrollable

---

113 See footnote 106.
114 Taruskin, *Defining Russia*..., p. 536.
115 Erwin Panofsky, *Meaning in Visual Arts*, New York, 1955, p. 31.

play of subtexts, it is important to add."[116] What is this "play of subtexts" if not hidden camouflaged language of dissent?

And now, a few words on the Jewish elements in Shostakovitch's music.[117] The mentioned contribution in *New York Times* by Laurel Fay is in full devoted to the Jewish subject. This clearly shows that the author considers this aspect highly important both in Shostakovich's music and as acute subject of research, and by the publication in the *New York Times* has moved this aspect into the political center of the discourse. In her recent book, however, Laurel Fay does not seem to attach great importance to the Jewish topic in Shostakovich's music any more.[118] Worth noticing is the fact, that other publications of the post-revisionist strain equally avoid the discussion of the Jewish elements in Shostakovich's music. The more then 20-page long article by Dorothea Redepenning titled "Shostakovich's Song-cycles", published in David Fanning's *Shostakovich Studies* (1995), hardly mentions the op. 79 at all (somehow, this article reminded me of earlier Soviet publications).

Moreover, in his book on Shostakovich's Tenth Symphony David Fanning presents a very interesting detailed list of thematic allusions in the first movement of the *Tenth Symphony*, but unfortunately fails to mention a very obvious one to op. 79 of the C motive in the first thematic group – the so-called typical "iambic prima," a central feature of Jewish traditional music;[119] also, several central musical concepts, which Fanning convincingly and in detail discusses in connection with the *Tenth*, appear already in op. 79, for example the concept of thematic transformation, and the concept of modal (*ladovy*) interplay (related to the Jewish *stayger* nature).[120]

---

116 Taruskin, *Defining Russia...*, pp. 472, 496 and 535.
117 See also ADDENDUM 2
118 Laurel Fay, *Shostakovich: A Life*, New York, 2000.
119 David Fanning, *The Breath of the Symphonist: Shostakovich's Tenth*, London. 1988, pp. 13-14.
120 Idem., p. 60 etc. These last two were discussed years earlier in my publications on Shostakovich (see Ch. XI A and B) as carriers of musical double meaning. While considering their role in creating the sub-text of the *Tenth*, Fanning replaces the term "double-meaning" with "doublespeak" and "doublethink" (?) I believe the Talmud saying "to quote with due" (*amar davar b'shem omro*, in Hebrew) is still valid in our days.

Along with writings disregarding the Jewish features, the abundant literature on Shostakovitsh lately offers farfetched theories on the "Jewishness" of Shostakovitch's music, as, for example, Timothy L. Jackson's article with the eloquent title "Dmitry Shostakovitch: the Composer as Jew."[121] The identification with Yevtushenko's text in the 13th symphony ("I seem to be a Jew"), the autobiographical *Eighth Quartet* with the DSCH anagram merging with the Jewish theme from the Piano Trio leads the author to the rather forced thesis of "Shostakovitch as Jew." True, the Jewish element may be considered the Rosetta stone to intertextuality in Shostakovitch, as proposed by Jackson, but, regrettably, his conclusions are based on such wrong notions as the "Amen" cadence being "very prominent in the Jewish service." In fact, Jewish liturgy does not have a constant musical motif for the "Amen."[122] Even more problematic is Jackson's profuse talk about 'Shostakovitch-as-Jesus,' the 'selfrepresentation both as Jew and as Crucified Christ" or the obscure idea of "putting Shostakovitch-as-Jew back into Christ."[123]

I would like to conclude with a paragraph from Donald Grove's paper "Current Historiography and Music History," which written nearly forty years ago seems as live and true as pronounced today:

> while value judgements are to be admitted in historical studies, there are nonetheless certain rough but generally satisfactory criteria of objectivity (in a broader sense of the word)... criteria such as respect for truth, no blinking at awkward facts, no gratuitous moralizing, no ulterior interest (as in propaganda).[124]

---

121 In: *Shostakovitch reconsidered,* ed. Allan Ho et al., London 1998, p. 597.
122 No source on Jewish music indicates a constant formula for the Amen, nor does oral tradition confirms it (see for example, *Encyclopedia Judaica* [entries 'Amen" and 'Music'], and NGD2 [entry 'Amen']).
123 T. Jackson, in: *Dmitri Schostakowitsch und das jüdische musikalische Erbe,* ed. E. Kuhn et al., Berlin, 2001, p. 19.
124 In: *Studies in Music History: Essays for Oliver Strunk,* ed. H. Powers, Princeton 1968, p. 27.

Addendum 1

From: Allan B. Ho and Dmitry Feofanov, *Shostakovich Reconsidered* (pp. 228-229)

When contacted by the authors in September 1997, he [...Joachim Braun] provided the following statement for publication:
The conditions of Soviet artistic life were more complex than some Western musicologists may imagine (I say this both as a scholar of this culture and its witness). No greater harm can be done to and no greater danger exists for scholarship than vulgar simplification. Dr. Fay has used in her *New York Times* article journalistic style of quoting selectively out of context, without referring to sources and to the authors of the material used. My position on Shostakovitch's Op. 79 is clear enough from the title of the mentioned MQ (*Musical Quarterly*) article: "The Double meaning of Jewish Elements in Dmitri Shostakovich's Music."

In December '47 to January' 48 there was hardly anyone among the Soviet intellectuals who had illusions about anti-Semitic tendencies in Soviet politics. To claim that the case of Weinberg, who was complimented by Khrennikov, was a sign of tolerance is equivalent to proclaiming that the slogan over the gates of Theresienstadt 'Arbeit macht frei' ('In work there is freedom') was a true reflection of life in Nazi concentration camps (cf. my 'Jews in Soviet Music,' in J. Miller, ed. *Jews on Soviet Culture*, London, 1984, p. 91). The falsehood of public and personal life in the Soviet Union usually made straightforward, unequivocal behavior impossible, especially for intellectuals. As a great artist, Shostakovich – consciously or unconsciously – reflected dissidence in nearly every one of his works. To bring this meaning to the surface, certain conditions or perception were needed. I must quote another passage from my Boris-Schwarz-Fs. (Festschrift) article: 'Conceived and composed as an expression of human desperation, *From Jewish Folk Poetry* had been turned overnight into an ideological protest of potentially nation-wide political significance – a remarkable case of sudden change in value and meaning of an artistic work due to circumstances independent of the creator' (pp. 263-64). The meaning of Shostakovich's music is disclosed to the 'aware listener' (Braun). It is his 'rotten luck' (Fay) that among the unaware are also some musicologists.

Shostakovich's dissidence is manifested by his music and his music only. I have to add, in this regard, that this fact cannot be confirmed nor disproved by the authenticity or unauthenticity of the Volkov/Shostakovich *Testimony*, a collection of lobby gossip, in my opinion a clever (both in terms of legality and content) piece of falsification. It is regretful that the author who wrote a convincing review on this, to use an expression of Richard Taruslin, 'shameful' publication, falls in the trap of a style she condemned.

Addendum 2

From: Joachim Braun, *Jews and Jewish Elements in Soviet Music,* Israeli Music Publications Ltd., Tel Aviv, 1978, pp.162-166.

We may now summarize the impressions gained from the use of the Jewish idiom by Dmitri Shostakovich.

1. In all of Shostakovich's works in which the Jewish idiom appears along with other material, it is used to climax an entire work, or a movement, in juxtaposition of outmost stress, strain, and crisis.

2. The Jewish idiom in vocal-instrumental works indicates a hidden declaration of resistance. Where the idea of dissidence is evident in the text, as in the Thirteenth Symphony, there is no need for Jewish musical symbols.

3. In instrumental music, the Jewish idiom usually coincides with episodes of high harmonical tension and sharp dissonance. Of course in terms of the given historical and social context both the Jewish and the dissonant are under Soviet conditions regarded as alien to real art.

4. The fusion of the Jewish idiom and the DSCH self-identification subject shows the merging of the social and the personal in Shostakovich's art. It also underlines the general humanitarian meaning of the Jewish idiom in his works.

5. The Jewish idiom appears in Shostakovich's works in two different periods (excluding the 1944 Trio). The first "Jewish period" of Shostakovich is the period between 1947-1951, the time of the first combined anti-Jewish and anti-modernist attack by Soviet officialdom; the second period includes the years 1960-1962, the time of approaching reaction and of the second Soviet attack on Jewishness and progressive art.

6. The delay of the first performance and the publication of almost every "Jewish work" by Shostakovich and the rare performances of these works in later years show that Soviet officialdom was aware of their anti-establishment undertones. However, it was never quite clear where the confrontation occurred, whether on a musical or a social-national basis, it constantly switched from one to the other.

7. The interpretation of the Jewish material by Shostakovich was always in his characteristic mood of the sarcastic, hostile, dissident and resistant. In the 1940s and the early 1950s those elements were denounced as alien to Soviet reality. In the 1960s and 1970s there was made an attempt to interpret them as references to the past or to forces outside the realm of Soviet reality. However, the Soviet listener, used to broad implications and connotations in all fields of art and literature, developed his own semantic code, his "Aesopian language." According to this code both modern musical techniques and Jewish strains were interchangeable phenomenal, permutable forms of one humanistic symbol.

8. In those circumstances the Jewish idiom based on folkloristic officially adopted means emerged as flexible and vital. On the one hand, it was hardly possible for Soviet officials to prove the dissident, or "Western modernistic" character of a Jewish folk tune; on the other hand it was associated with the forbidden, socially dissident, musically dis-

sonant. At the same time it was difficult to discover a national musical strain hidden in contemporary instrumental dressing. Only the elite of the musical community could be fully aware of the interplay of meaning, associations and connotations.

The double meaning, the hidden ideology, or even political implications of a work of art, so characteristic in 20th century totalitarian systems, are by no means phenomena of our times.

"Great turning points in the history of the arts, aside from the inevitable controversy between old and new, are usually marked by an intensification of intellectual efforts, shown both in the concentration of the artist on technical and stylistic problems and in theoretical discussions of the aesthetic and technical issues involved. Such turning points often occur contemporaneously in more than one art: they are ordinarily the expression of deep, underlying social and cultural changes, strains and stresses. Chromaticism was frowned upon by the church: the composers of the secret chromatic art were inclined to Reform, if they were not outright heretics. The suppression of new ideas by the Inquisition was a pervasive strand of the fabric of contemporaneous intellectual life; the fear of detection on the part of reform-minded musicians living in the Netherlands under the Spanish yoke was a prime factor in the secrecy in which the new art was shrouded. The curious ambivalence in the secret chromatic art, which allowed a diatonic interpretation, but whose chromatic realization was infinitely more expressive, was a unifying bond in the intellectual make-up of the whole epoch".

This quote comes from Edward E. Lovinsky's[125] observations with regard to 16th century secret chromatic art; they read like a description of contemporary Soviet conditions if we make just a few minor adjustments.

Almost half a century ago Walter Benjamin wrote:

The logical result of Fascism is the introduction of aesthetics into political life. The violation of the masses, whom Fascism, with its "Führer"-cult forces to their knees, has its counterpart in the violation of an apparatus which is pressed into the production of ritual values.... This is the situation of politics which Fascism is rendering aesthetic. Communism responds by politicizing art.[126]

Both Fascism and Communism are inherently anti-semitic and anti-artistic; hence both are destructive to Jewish art. The fate of Jewish music in the Soviet Union seems to be foredoomed. Confronted with an antinomy – the negation of Jewish culture, its history and peculiarity, on the one hand, and of the existence of a Jewish people which, as every

---

125 Edward E. Lovinsky, "Secret Chromatic Art Re-examined," *Perspectives in Musicology*, ed. B. S. Brook, New York, 1972, p. 116.
126 Walter Benjamin, *Illuminations*, ed. H. Arendt, London, 1968, pp. 243-244.

people should according to the letter of Soviet ideology have the right to national spiritual life, on the other hand – the Soviet state permits a narrow margin of Jewish official culture for propaganda purposes. This residual phenomenon devoid of the nutritive roots of developing vital national art, must disappear sooner or later. The nationalistically inclined part of Soviet Jewry has either been destroyed or has succeeded in emigrating. The remaining Jewish population has assimilated or at least has neutralized its Jewishness. An attempt to restrict or to oppose this development seems almost hopeless.

Visible social phenomena and their development, however, are illusory in the Soviet Union. Life of people, of Jews in particular, is dualistic. This is especially true for *hommes de lettres* and artists. Their existence and position in a totalitarian society are contingent on the visible part of their art, and at the same time their art itself, its significance and power, is a function of their artistic integrity and candidness. This very condition of duplicity creates a situation loaded with unpredictable potential for change and explosion.

As Jews recall periods in their history when their national existence was protected by secretly-preserved identity, thus has intellectual leadership of other nations concealed its own creative essence in order to ensure the continuation of their spiritual life.

Our study attempted to draw a general picture of the Jewish contribution to Soviet music and the fate of Jewish music in the Soviet Union. Future research will probably reveal new facts and explain many still obscure problems in the history of Soviet Jewish music.

XII. Christian and Jewish Religious Elements in Music: A Hidden Language of Resistance in Soviet Riga[*]

I had two reasons to choose the mentioned subject for a paper at this conference:

a. In my article from 1982 "Zur Hermeneutik der sowjetbaltischen Musik"[1] I pointed out five groups of musical style which were used by Soviet Baltic composers to communicate a hidden meaning of dissidence: Baroque stylization, Latin headings, Far Eastern stylization, Composition methods of the "New Folklore Wave" and avant-garde composition techniques. For some reasons I did not include liturgical music or the use of liturgical elements in secular music as an independent group. Now I would like to correct this omission. And

b. Since this first attempt of an analytical approach to the intrinsic meaning of Soviet-Baltic music, this subject, to my best knowledge, was neglected, avoided or ignored by musicology. Just to mention a latest example – in an article on the problems and perspectives of Baltic music history writing in *Acta musicologica* LXXI/1 (1999)[2] this aspect of research and historiography is not mentioned at all and the author stops short before acknowledging the existence of such a phenomenon. As regards Jewish music the situation is even worse – an article (by the way, the only one) on Jewish musicians in Latvia published in independent Latvia of 1997[3], the part on the Soviet period can be classified only as a gross falsification. The ideas of *Geschichtsaufarbeitung* and *Vergangenheitsbewältigung* still seem to be quite foreign to Baltic musicology.

It is my conviction that one of the most important tasks of contemporary musical historiography, when discussing the music from our recent past, is the discovery of it's symbolic values, which, to quote the great art

---

[*] Published in: *Musikgeschichte zwischen Ost- und Westeuropa: Kirchenmusik – geistliche Musik – religiöse Musik.* Ed. H. Loos/Kl.-P. Koch, Sinzig, 2002, pp. 77-82.
[1] In: *Zeitschrift für Ostforschung*, 31/1 (1982), p.76ff.
[2] Urve Lippus, *Baltic Music History Writing: Problems and Perspectives*, p. 50ff.
[3] Lija Krasinska and Marina Mihailjeca, *Muuzika*, in: *Sava kraasa varaviiksnee* (Its own colour in the rainbow), Riga, 1997, p. 10ff.

historian Edwin Panofsky "*are often unknown to the artist himself and may even emphatically differ from what he consciously intended to express.*"[4] Let me remind you, in this connection, that Baltic music was by no means the only case of an Aesopian language of resistance. We know – to mention an example from history – the classical case of the "*secret chromatic art*" in the Netherlands madrigals, researched by Erwin Lowinsky[5]. And from modern times we may refer to the amphibology of Shostakovich's compositions with the Jewish idiom. To this last example I will come back later.

There can be no better start for our discussion than to read a passage on the *opera buffa* from 1828 and to imagine the conditions of the Soviet Balticum:

> Dem armen geknechteten Italien ist ja das Sprechen verboten, und es darf nur durch Musik die Gefühle seines Herzens kundgeben. All sein Groll gegen fremde Herrschaft, seine Begeisterung für die Freiheit, sein Wahnsinn über das Gefühl der Ohnmacht, seine Wehmut bei der Erinnerung an vergangene Herrlichkeit, dabei sein leises Hoffen, sein Lauschen, sein Lechzen nach Hülfe, alles dieses verkappt sich in jene Melodien, die von grotesker Lebenstrunkenheit zu elegischer Weichheit herabgleitet, und in jene Pantomimen, die von schmeichelnden Karessen zu drohendem Ingrimm überschanppen.
>
> Das ist der esoterische Sinn der Opera Buffa. Die exoterische Schildwache, in deren Gegenwart sie gesungen und dargestellt wird, ahnt nimmermehr die Bedeutung dieser heiteren Liebesgeschichten, Liebesnöte und Liebesneckereien, worunter der Italiener seine tödlsiche Befreiungsgedanken verbirgt.
>
> Heinrich Heine, *Reise von München nach Genua*.

The meaning of a musical style or a particular composition can be understood and interpreted only in the context of the relevant culture and social atmosphere where this style emerged, acts and is perceived. Insofar as music is a "living matter" (to use William Empson's wording), it, "*like belles-lettres, demands a sense, not so much of what is really there, as of what is necessary to carry a particular situation off*".[6]

Therefore approaching our first example of musical ambiguity in Soviet Latvia, we should keep in mind the socio-political atmosphere of the

---

4 *Meaning in Visual Arts*, New York, 1955, p. 51
5 *Secret ChromaticArt Re-examined*, in: Barry S. Brook et al., ed., *Perspectives in Musicology*, New York, 1972, p. 91ff.
6 William Empson, *Seven Types of Ambiguity*, Hammondsworth, 1961, p. 245.

late 40s – early 50s: the occupation, the repressions – a large number of citizens was at this time banished to Sibiria, the suppression of religion – churches were closed and often used as farming buildings, the crosses of the orthodox cathedral in the center of Riga were cut down and the church turned into a planetarium. At this time, in 1951, in the Riga Anna church the first performance of Alfred Kalnin'sh *Variations on a Theme by Jaazeps Viitols for organ* by his last student Estere Didrichsone took place.

Alfred Kalnin'sh (1879-1951), one of the great classics of Latvian music, was in 1945, after the re-establishment of the Soviet order in Latvia, immediately pronounced by the new rulers "Peoples Artist" and given the position of Rector of the State Conservatory (1944-48). He was presented as an example of harmonic collaboration of the old Latvian intelligentsia with the new system. The quite and mostly ironical composer accepted all this silently. But soon, Kalnin'sh could not suit any more the Soviet establishment. The great composer asked for and was assigned a new job at the Conservatory – teacher of obligatory piano for students of the orchestra and vocal departments.

On the day of his 70s birthday on August, 27, 1949, Alfred Kalnin'sh, as stated by his biographer, withdraw into his city apartment to be alone and write his swan song – the *Variations on a Theme by Jāzeps Vītols for Organ*.[7] The first performance had to wait for two years – the time it took to make this composition acceptable: Jāzeps Vītols (1863-1948), the patriarch of Latvian music, still in disgrace at this time, died in emigration. His death opened the way for his rehabilitation by the Soviet establishment – his surroundings was made responsible for the flight from the Soviet regime. His name as classic was cleaned and the performance of variations on his theme was in 1951 a reminiscence on the founder of Latvian classical music. Kalnin'sh Variationes were dedicated to Vītols and culminated on a funeral march.

There was, however, more to it. To my best knowledge, neither Soviet, nor Western musicology specializing on Kalnin'sh (Jēkabs Vītolin'sh, Nīls Grīnfelds, and others) ever mentioned that the source of the theme for the *Variations* was one of the most beatiful and – this is of special importance – most popular chorals by Jāzeps Vītols – *Jēsus, mana*

---

7   Arnolds Klotinsch, *Alfreeds Kalninsch*, Riga, 1979, p. 348.

saule (Jesus, my sun), published in 1939 in his *Melody Book for Evangelic Lutheran communities*.[8] Was this conscious or aimed taciturnity? Or was it, in some cases, just lack of knowledge?

To choose this choral for the theme of variations for organ, the church instrument *par excellence,* in the Stalinist Soviet Union of 1949 can hardly be interpreted otherwise as an act of dissidence. The public performance of this work was, probably, possible only by both – the tacit consent of the performers and the listeners and the ignorance of the Soviet musical administration. The well known text of the choral does not leave much doubts on the spiritual condition of Kalnin'sh at this time: *"Jesus, my sun[...], Pardon my sins[...] Give new strength[...] Only for You will I live, only Yours will I be, my God..."*

We have to admit that this early case of a latent message in Soviet Latvian music, when the religious character of dissidence was covered with the acknowledged name of a great Latvian composer, was a comparatively naive and straightforward attempt of hidden language. In later years, confronted with more sophisticated methods of suppression and censorship, the metaphorical systems of associative equivocal musical styles became also more sophisticated, ambiguous and obscure. The hidden message submerged into deeper layers of music and was using more enigmatic means of cover.

One of those methods used in the 60s and 70s was the employment of liturgical Latin titles, such as the *Credo* by Arvo Paert (b.1935, comp. 1968) and Raimo Kangro (b. 1949. comp. 1977), and the *Concertrequiem* by Pauls Dambis (b. 1936) on the text of Imants Lassmanis. Written for double-chorus, two boy voices, organ and chimes, the *concert-requiem* was composed in 1969 in memory of the fallen in World Wore II.

The Riga listener trained since 1962 by a local concert tradition of annual performances of Dmitry Kabalevski's *Requiem,* was used to a naive-primitive musical language of this and other compositions *in memoria* of war victims and developed certain musical reception patterns. Now, at the first performance of Dambis *Concertrequiem* in the Riga Dome, the public was shocked: the new means of expression – aleatory, clusters, shouts, glissandos and whispers in the chorus, the amalgamation of organ

---

8   J. Wihtols, *Meldiju graamata evang'eliskaam luteraan'u draudzeem,* Riga, 1939, p. 43, No. 110.

sounds, chimes and stylized elements of traditional folk music, and the use of Latin titles (two sections bear the names *Kyrie* and *Dies ire;* no elements of traditional liturgical music are, however, used) – all this did not belong to the accepted techniques of Soviet music of mourning for World War II victims, and provided a quite new sets of associations. This musical language was to such a degree strange and inadequate, that the entire semantic world of the listeners seemed to be shaken up. For years branded as foreign, formalist and hostile, this music obviously was carrying new, hidden meaning. The *Concertrequiem* was not perceived according to the announced title as memoria for the fallen some twenty years ago – but rather as expression of contemporary, present in Soviet reality, personal pain, longing and hatred.

I will restrict myself to these two examples, but I hope the *Dies ire* in Jaanis Ivanovs 4th Symphony, the *Lectionaries* of Imants Zemazaris, some compositions of Lucia Gaaruta, Romuald Jermak, Artur Griinups and some others will be considered from this point of view.

Now I will turn to liturgical musical elements in Jewish musical life of Riga. This problem seems much more complex and the amount of music is comparatively meager. Two preliminary points, however, have to be considered in this connection.

First of all, Jews and Jewish culture were and remained in the former Soviet Union, regardless of the announced and officially proclaimed politics of equality of all people, a controversial phenomenon, a foreign, undesired body. Although the form and substance varied according to the period, the prevalent view was (according to Lenin) that the idea of a distinct Jewish people is scientifically untenable and in practice reactionary. As result, Jewish culture, including musical culture, existed on the borderline of the permitted and undesired, the forbidden but not unlawful. This created a highly ambigious situation in Soviet culture regarding the employment of Jewish themes and motifs in art. Any exploration of a Jewish idiom or subject was fraught with risk and potentially explosive. Any performance of such music – even if written in the best traditions of "socialist realism", was unwanted, mostly censored. A striking example is the op. 79 of Dmitry Shostakovich *From Jewish Folk-Poetry*, written in 1948 and performed in Leningrad and Moscow for the first and only time after Stalin's death in 1955. The local administration of the Riga

Philharmony could not tolerate the performance of this work till the 70's.[9]

Secondly, there is the nature of Jewish music by itself. The borderline between the liturgical and secular musical style is often very blurry. There are a lot of para-liturgical forms, as, for example, the songs and dances of the Hassidim, a religious movement that became very popular in Eastern Europe from the early 18th century. A great part of this music, and certainly liturgical music, which is based on a certain skeleton, modal pattern, a so called *shtayger* in Ashkenazi (German/European) liturgy, is till our days mostly not notated, not canonized, and preserved only in oral tradition. Elements of improvisation belong to the nature of this music, and the performer, or cantor is in a sense partly also the creator of the music, the composer.

In this connection, the activity of the tenor and cantor Misha Aleksandrovich in Riga was significant. Born in Latvia, he studied at the Jewish Folk Conservatory in Riga, was in the 20 and 30 cantor in Riga, Kaunas, Manchester and London and became one of the most popular cantors in Europe. After studies in Italy he was also acknowledged as an excellent performer of chamber music. During the years of WW II he was one of the most popular artists on the battlefronts of the Red Army and was awarded the Stalin Prize. In 1945 he was asked to sing at the Moscow Great Synagogue the *kaddish* (prayer for the dead) on May, the 9th; Alexandrovich's performance as cantor was broadcast throughout the world. He performed once more this prayer at the Riga synagogue, at that time a small place in the old city. After these propaganda performances he was not permitted any more to repeat this prayer in public. He became a concert tenor, mainly with an Italian repertory. But very soon he started the tradition of performing at his concerts – as encores – Jewish folk songs, mixed with para-liturgical melodies, which was received enthusiastic by the audience. In fact, knowing this, people were arriving especially to the second half of the concert, and his performances turned clearly into declarations of national self-consciousness and dissidence, by means of a existing tacit code of the intrinsic meaning of Jewish liturgical and para-

---

[9] See J. Braun, *Jews in Soviet Music*, in: *Jews in Soviet Culture*, ed. J. Miller, London, 1984, p. 65ff; idem., *The Double Meaning of Jewish Elements in Dmitri Shostakovich's Music*, in: *The Musical Quaterly*, LXXI/1, 1985, p. 68ff.

liturgical music in the given circumstances. The Latvian State Philharmony administration reacted soon and he was asked to stop the performances of the encore songs, or not to visit Riga any more. Similarly, the Latvian ethnomusicologist and composer Professor Max Goldin (b. 1917) was not permitted to perform at concerts his arrangements of Jewish folktunes. In both cases we only have the interview with the two musicians to confirm our story. As Jewish liturgical music itself, much of its history is preserved in oral tradition only.

Finely, I would like to mention a composition by Dmitry Shostakovich, the several performances of which in Riga may be considered as part of Latvian musical life. In at least some ten compositions Shostakovich uses the Jewish idiom, mostly based on Jewish folk songs, to communicate some kind of dissidence. But in two of his *24 Preludes and Fugues for Piano* (op. 87) we encounter Jewish liturgical melodies.[10] Only in this type of composition, the most abstract musical form, written in an advanced for his time musical language, when there are no texts (as in op. 79, 91, or 113), no titles (as in op. 67) or no musical symbols (as the DeSCH-formula in op.110) to communicate a message – only here the composer drew on the sovereign power of Jewish liturgical music. To understand the meaning of this music, which is deeply hidden in the labyrinths of polyphonic techniques, the listener must activate the deepest layers of his memory and associations. This is the case in the *Fugue* fis-moll op. 87: the theme of this fugue is based on the tune of the *Weekday Morning Prayer*.

The present paper was in no way intended as a comprehensive survey of the material, especially because my access to the relevant literature is restricted. If the interest to this approach will be to some extent generated, I will consider my mission accomplished.

---

10 J. Braun, *The Double Meaning of Jewish Elements in Dmitri Shostakovich's Music*, in: *The Musical Quaterly*, LXXI/1, 1985, pp. 79-80.

XIII. Music – Survival – Resistance*

There are phenomena of World War II never witnessed in history before. So the music of the Holocaust, it's meaning and place in society. What makes the Nazi Holocaust unique is the method – the systematization, the order and the industrialization of the events, the proceedings. And as never before, music was part of it. As far as music history is known, music was never before used to ensure the order of organized mass murder and to assist in its execution. Music was frequently involved in supporting survival and sponsoring resistance; in killing, dehumanization and oppression under conditions of coercion and deceit – never. This is why the study of music and its function in the Holocaust is one of the most important challenges not only for musical scholarship, but also for the understanding of human behavior. The most diabolical use of music was made in such concentration camps as Auschwitz, Maydanek, Treblinka, Belzetc. This chapter of Holocaust history is described in Moshe Hoch's Ph. D. thesis, now published as book.[1] The Baltic area as far as we know, was spared from this aspect of musical activity.

The function and the character of music in the ghettos and concentration-camps was, on one hand, the product of the Nazi system; on the other – it was also based on the history, culture and tradition of the particular country, on the local musical culture in the areas under occupation. Therefore it is only natural that the micro-culture of every ghetto or camp had its own character and degree of musical activity, which was the

---

* This chapter is based on a paper at the Conference *Reichskommissariat Ostland* (Stockholm and Uppsala Universities, April 2002), and published in D. Gaunt, P.A. Levine & L. Palusuo, *Collaboration and Resistance During the Holocaust: Belorus, Estonia, Latvia, Lithuania* (Bern-Wien: Peter Lang, 2004), pp. 421-429.

1 Moshe Hoch, *Jewish Musical Culture in Poland under the Nazi Regime* (1939-1945). Ph. D. Thesis, Bar-Ilan Univrsity, 1992, Israel (advisors Prof. J. Braun and Dr. H. Yaoz). Published as *Kolot m'tokh hakhoshekh: hamusika b'gettaot v'bmakhanot b'polin* (in Hebrew, Voices From the Dark: Music in the Ghettos and Camps in Poland), Jerusalem: Yad Vashem, 2002.

function of Nazi-policy in this camp and the musical tradition of the majority of it's inhabitants. This activity, often performed with danger of death, was to bring hope for survival and for freedom to the performers and the ghetto population. However, it had often also to please the ghetto command and authorities. This contradiction, as we will see, accompanied music during the entire Holocaust period.

Although we have a multitudinous literature on the Holocaust, there is definitely a neglect of music in the general Holocaust research.[2] Most of the available literature consists from memoirs and song collections, which means, that we in fact deal here with an oral tradition. Only rarely we may refer to documented research, facts and events confirmed by documents, as in the case of the broadly discussed Theresienstadt KZ – rather a case-study for international fraud, than a research subject for the understanding of music in the Holocaust. We have to say that especially for the Baltics – the *Reichskommissariat Ostland* – the state of the art is far from being satisfactory. At this stage we can say nearly nothing about Estonia[3], and little about Latvia and Belorussia. From Lithuania, in contrary, a remarkable corpus of evidence on musical activities and songs is preserved. The, probably, best bibliography of music in the Holocaust is presented by *The New Grove Dictionary of Music and Musicians* (Macmillan 2000) in the article Jewish music (vol. 13:111). It lists 32 items, but even here 13 are on Teresienstadt. The other are mostly song collections, often without mentioning the authors of texts and music. It is for us not without interest that the five earliest song collections published from

---

[2] There is no mention of music in many fundamental reference works, among the latest are *The Holocaust Encyclopedia*, ed. W. Laquear (Yale University, 2001); *The Complete History of the Holocaust* (San Diego, 2001); G. Feldman, *Understanding of the Holocaust* (Detroit-London, 1998). In most reference sources the information on music is extremely meagre, as for example in *The Columbia Guide to the Holocaust* (New York: Columbia University Press, 2000), or the *Encyclopedia of the Holocaust*, 3:1022-26 (London: Macmillan, 1990) and the *Enzyclopedie des Holocaust*, 2:978-81 (Argon, 1997), which present identical articles (mainly song collections) and 15 item bibliographies.

[3] The only study on music in Estonian ghettos and camps is Mark Dworzecki's *Histoire des camps Nazis en Estonie* (Ph.D. Thesis, Sorbonne, Paris, 1967; published also in Hebrew and Yiddish, Jerusalem 1970). The musical material quoted by the author is mostly of Lithuanian provenance.

1946 to 1949[4], are mostly songs from Lithuania and Latvia. Among the mentioned collections with songs from the three occupied Baltic countries, was such a basic work, as Shmaria Kacherginsky's (1908-1953) collection (NY 1948) with one hundred items. But even this remarkable corpus, re-published several times (1947), was ever scholarly discussed.

Let me, in short, give an overview of two almost unknown and never analyzed sources, which may represent the character of the material which reached us. These two are of special importance because both belong to the Baltics, they were completed during the time of captivity and were the earliest to appear immediately after liberation.

In Vienna of early 1947 was published the song collection *Ghetto- und KZ -Lieder aus Lettland und Litauen* by Johanna Spector (b. in Liepaja, 1920). She has survived the Liepaja ghetto, the "Kaiserwald" and "Prechu" KZ's near Riga, and the KZ's "Stutthof", "Stolp" and "Burggraben". She was liberated by the English troops in Mai 1945, came in 1947 to the USA and received her Ph.D. in musicology at the Columbia University, served at this University as professor of musicology until the 1990's, and is now retired. During the years I had many opportunities to talk with Professor Spector both in New York and Israel. She never mentioned the Holocaust and in her broad ethnomusicological research never returned to this subject.

Spector's song collection, the only from Latvia, includes 15 songs and is provided with minimal commentary. In the short introduction she states (p. 4):

Die vorliegende Sammlung von Liedern soll ein historisches Dokument sein....Sie haben nicht den Anspruch, als Kunstwerk zu gelten....Diese Lieder drücken lediglich die Sangesfreude der jüdischen Volksmassen aus, die unter den härtesten Bedingungen nicht hat erstickt werden können...

As if she was anticipating one of the central questions in future research: the Holocaust song as document rather than work of art, and the

---

4 Zami Feder, *Zamlung fun katzet un geto lider* (Bergen Belsen, 1946, in Yiddish); Mordekhai Gebirtik, *S'brent: 1939-1942* (Krakov, 1946, in Yiddish); Shmeryahu Kacherginski, *Dos gezang fun Vilner geto* (Paris, 1947, in Yiddish); Johanna Spektor, *Ghetto- und KZ-Lieder aus Lettland und Litauen* (Wien, 1947); S. Kacherginski, *Lider fun getos un lagern* (New York, 1948; in Yiddissh).

333

song as means of survival. We should avoid to present, interpret and perform these songs as great art".[5] The presentation of ghetto songs out of the authentic social context is a difficult and often treacherous task; this subject certainly deserves a separate discussion.

Ten songs of the collection are documented from Latvia, the others are of unknown provenance; they all are written on German and Yiddish texts, the prevailing languages of Latvian Jewry. Spector herself is the author of text and music of seven songs, which she composed in the Liepaja ghetto (three songs, 1942) and KZ Prechu" (three songs, 1944), and one soon after liberation in 1945. The songs in the collection tell us about the horrible conditions of life and about death, but each of them towards the end turns into a song of hope and freedom. Three songs are written by a certain Yasha Rabinovich, one of which actually documents and describes in detail the transport of Liepajas ghetto-Jews to the "Prechu"-KZ: We are shattered and crushed, only few of us from Libau remained" (Song No. 5; Spector comments to this song: "815 Überlebende von ca. 9,000.") And another song by the same author, who wrote all his three songs in Yiddish: "I want to see the time when my brothers are freed,/The time is not far away... /But I will die in martyrdom (*kiddush hashem*)/, My vehement songs will be my testament..." (Song No. 11, tr. JB). According to Spector, Rabinovitch was shot in Neustadt (Schleswig-Holstein) on May, the 3ed, 1945, several hours before the English troops liberated the place (p. 16). The songs from Spector's collection are based on the tradition of the Latvian German-oriented Jewry, and present the popular musical romantic-lyrical style of the 30th, characteristic for the pre-WW-II ambience of this community. While there are no songs with elements of the Latvian musical tradition, at least six songs borrowed the music from the contemporary popular German, Russian, and Jewish repertoire (No. 1, 3, 5, 7, 10, etc.). The remaining songs also rest upon the musical style of pre-War East-European popular music. The songs composed by Spector differ from the others, as they have a broader ambitus and include elements of chromatics. Overall, they show a certain professional artistic touch.

---

5   This happened with the recently published CD *Jewish music in a changing world: Riga ghetto songs*, produced by V. Shulman, Riga: Riga Synagogue 2001.

The pre-war bound of Latvian Jews with the Jewish-German culture was to some extent, although under very different circumstances, prolonged in the Riga ghetto, which was divided into two parts: one for the local Latvian Jews, the other, "Reichsjuden-Ghetto," for Jews from German. A rare description of musical contacts between Latvian and German Jews is the testimony of Gertrude Schneider, a German-Jewish survivor from the Riga ghetto[6]. The musicians from the Latvian part of the ghetto "received passes to be able to cross into the German ghetto and back to their own ghetto again..., where no cultural event was ever held..., and the atmosphere was entirely different from that of its German counterpart"[7]. Together with their Austrian, German and Czech colleagues, who were brought to Riga to be exterminated here,[8] Latvian Jews participated in symphonical, chamber and popular music concerts. But, confirms Schneider, at the same time, there seems to have been a certain boycott of these events by the Latvian Jews, "who felt that the efforts of the German Jews to lead a relatively normal life in the ghetto were a mockery...."[9] This was an attitude similar to that of Lithuanian Jews, who, as we will see, at the early stages of ghetto-life were opposed to musical activities.

It seems, however, that the testimony of Shneider about the lack of musical activities in the Latvian part of the ghetto, is not quite correct. In anoher set of memories by Max Kaufmann[10], is preserved, probably, the only testimony about a number of well-know Riga musicians, who performed in the Latvian part of the ghetto. Among the musicians are mentioned the singer Yacob Yoffe, the cantor Serensen, indicated as author of the popular song "Bombes, bombes falt arop" (Yidd., Bombs, bombs,

---

6 Gertruda Schneider, Professor Emeritus of History at the City Uiversity New York, resides at present in Harrington Park, New Jersey U.S.A. At the US Holocaust Memorial Museum, are preserved recordings of four songs from the Riga ghetto performed by Schneider (I am thankful to the Music Specialist of the Museum Bret Werb for this as well as for some additional information).
7 G. Schneider, *Journay intoTerror* (New York, 1979), p. 81.
8 According to Schneider (idem) of the more than 5,000 Jews sent to Riga by a certain gestapo official Anton Brunner (convicted to death in Vienna after the war), only about 900 were still alive in summer 1942.
9 Schneider, *Journay...*, p. 84
10 M. Kaufmann, *Churban Lettland: Die Vernichtung der Juden Lettlands,* Hrsg. Erhard Roy Wiehn (Konstanz, 1999; 1st ed. M?nchen 1947).

335

fell down)[11], or the pianist Hermann Godess, a Latvain Conervatory absolevent, who made his artistic carrier in the U.S.A after the war. The most notable artistic personality of the ghetto was the Latvian Conservatory Professor Adolf Metz (1880-1943), a pupil of the famous violin teacher at the Petersburg Conservatory Leopold Auer, who was invited in 1922 by Jazeps Vitols to put the foundation of the modern Latvian violin school.[12] Metz was the teacher of an entire generation of Latvian violinists. In the ghetto he presented two remarkable concerts, one of which he devoted to the great Russian composer and founder of the Petersburg conservatory Anton Rubinstein. The large audience was asked by Metz to refrain from applaus. "Der Applaus zeigte sich nur in unseren Tränen," remarks Kaufmann.[13]

The situation in occupied Vilnius and Kaunas was quite different. In this part of Lithuania – two important East-European centers of Jewish culture – the ghettos turned into hotbeds of resistance – armed, spiritual and musical. Documents from Vilnius and Kaunas show a unbelievably active for those conditions music life – symphonical and chamber music performances, chorus concerts, musical reviews and theater, the going-on of a conservatory, musical criticism and music competitions.[14]

Some information about the nature of this musical life is preserved in the diary of Elena Kutorgiene, a Lithuanian doctor from Kaunas, who, although at risk to her life, maintained contact with the ghetto inhabitants and gave help to many Jewish people, among them musicians. She describes in her diary the cultural life of the Kunas ghetto, and among others, tells how musical instruments were smuggled into the ghetto through the sewerage system: "The music of the symphonical orchestra," she wrote, "was for the inhabitants of the ghetto as mountain air for the consumptive."[15] In both cities, however, there was a strong opposition to theater and music on the part of the religious establishment. There were long discussions regarding the pros and cons of musical activities. The

---

11 This is a good example of uncertainty of song authorship from this time – in other sources, e.g., Hoch, *Kolot...*, 2002, 241 this song's authorship is assumed tobe a different person.
12 See Joahims Brauns, *Vijolmplmakslas attisitiba Latvija* (Riga 1962), pp.179-184.
13 Kaufmann, op. Cit., p. 242.
14 See Hoch, *Jewish musical...*, 1992, 120-131.
15 Yad-Vaschem Archive, File M-35/10, fol. 10.

slogan "In the cemetery you don't dance" was spread in both the Vilnius and Kaunas ghettos and Yeshiva students wrote poetry against musical and theater performance. Despite this the famous Kaunas Slobodka yeshiva was soon turned into a concert and theater hall, where in 1942/43 seventy seven concerts for the Jewish population and three concerts for the local SS took place.[16] Leading musicians and theater people not only defended the artistic activities, but were convinced that the ghetto Jews have to fight the enemy with the weapon of arts and music as well. The Kaunas conductor Misha Hofmekler, furiously defended the establishment of the symphonical ochestra in the Kaunas ghetto, and is quoted by and anonymous witness to have proclaimed: "music is not just only an expression of joy".[17] The same witness testifies:

> The first concert took place in August 1942. Tears of painful, proud joy were shed by the listeners and the musicians when the first cords cut the silence of he hall....The consolation of 'the Jewish people live!' was transferred to the numerous flowing listeners all the time of the existence of the orchestra.[18]

The artistic activities in the ghetto indeed granted the ghetto inhabitants a short respite of freedom and went hand in hand with resistance activities; along with the active musical life, a strong underground resistance movement was developing in the Lithuanian ghettos. The musical activities, however, often attended by the German officials, helped the *Aelternrat* and the German officials to maintain order in the ghetto and keep the inhabitants quite. It was this contradiction that was at the root of the confrontation of the two approaches.

The spirit of Lithuanian Jewry is well reflected in the collection *Kazet un ghetto Lider* by Sami Ferer (in Yiddish), who during his KZ and ghetto years several times wrote down, destroyed, and re-wrote again most of the songs. The collection (31 songs, mostly from Lithuanian

---

16 Idem., file M-1/F 1230, fol. 4
17 Idem., fol. 2.
18 idem., fol. 2-3. The quotation from the anonymous manuscript written in Yiddish with Latin letters reads as follows: Der erste koncert hot statgefunen in August 1942. Trenen hoben sich gegosen baj di zuherer vi oich bay di musiker ven di ersteen Akorde hoben durchgeszniten di stilkajt fun sal...Der trejst dos geht fun am Jisrael Chai!- hot zich durch di gance cajt fun existenc fun orchester zich ibergeben ojf di massenvajz sztermende cuherer

ghettos) was first made public in January 1946, in Bergen-Belzen, less than a year after liberation. All song texts and the introduction are in Yiddish. Unfortunately, only seven of them are with music – five transcribed in Vilnius, one in Kaunas and one of unknown provenience. We have in this collection again two texts by Yasha Rabinovich from Latvia, which in the above mentioned Spector's collection appears with the music. Ferer choose Rabinovich's *Testament* as an epigraph to his collection, to indicate its character – not only hope for freedom, but songs of resistance, active fight for liberation. The collection starts with the popular pre-War prophetic song from 1936 by Mordekhai Gebirtig (1877, Krakov-1942, killed in the Belzhetz death camp) *Es brent, briderlekh, s' brent...*(Yidd., It burns, brothers, it burns". p.4). Two songs follow, with popular texts by the young talented Vilnus poet and ghetto partisan Hirsh (Hirshke) Glik (Vilnius, 1922 – late1944, north Estonia): the famous hymn of the Jewish partisans *Sog nisht keinmol, az du geist dem letzten weg...*(Yidd., Never say you walk your last path...", p.5), to the music of a mass-song by the popular Soviet composer Dmitry Pokras, and the *Partisan Song*, set to music by an unknown author (p.7). Unknown are the composers of music to other songs in the collection – all from Vilnius and all imbued with a strong resistance spirit. It is not by accident that Pokras' music was chosen by Glik for the partisan hymn: texts and elements of Soviet mass song were a part of the "collective memory" and the "collective hope" in the eraly Soviet Union and in ghettos and the KZ. These melodies, written mostly by Jewish composers and to some degree influenced by Russian-Jewish folklore, responded strongly to the cultural tradition and social fate of those people, and the anonymous authors of majority of Lithuanian ghetto songs used this melos of the Soviet mass-song. It was the irony of history, that melodies by the brothers Pokras, Isaac Dunajevsky, Yan Frenkel and others Soviet composers, the symbol of revolution and resistance, became a symbol of another totalitarian system of Jewish suppression, the Soviet Union.

On the other hand, a sound social strain is expressed in such songs as *The ghetto-elite*, which brands the ghetto Jewish establishment (p. 16). A number of these songs which we may define as songs of social protest, full of despise and hate against the ghetto *Aeltestenrat*, appear on the recently recorded CD of the US Holocaust Memorial Museum *Hidden History: Songs of the Kovno Ghetto* (edition and commentary by Bret

Werb, Washington, D.C., 1997). By the way, this CD contains the only Holocaust song I know of, with music belonging to the Lithuanian national tradition – it is, sarcastically enough, a song set to the music of the old Lithuanian anthem *Lietuva, tevyne musu* (Lithuania, our motherland) underlined as with a new Lithuanian text *Lietuva, kraujuota zeme* (Lith., "Lithuania, bloody land", No12).

Both song collections show the three main text-music patterns of Holocaust songs, which may be classified as follows:

a. old songs with pre-war texts and music, as Gebirtig's most popular *Es brent...*;

b. "new-old" songs, which had new texts, set to pre-war music, as the mentioned *Lietuva, kraujuota zeme*, or the hymn of the Jewish partisans *Zog nisht...* (Never say...); to this category belongs the majority of songs performed in the ghettos and death camps;

c. entirely new songs, with new texts and new music, as the songs by Johanna Spector, or Rabinowich's *Lullaby*; a relatively little number of preserved songs belong to this group, probably, not more than some 20 such songs have reached us; there are not known "old-new" songs with old texts and new music.

Research of music, especially of the oral tradition – the art in time which disappears with the performance itself – is a most difficult, often even impossible task, and this is certainly one of the reasons for the state of the art in Holocaust music research. But music is also a most important social, often political factor, which may disclose aspects and hidden phenomena, which no other field of social life is able to reveal. There are methods that may reveal to us the *Platz im Leben*, the conditions and the symbolism, the intrinsic meaning of music in the most inhuman conditions of the Holocaust. I would suggest that an intercultural project of the study of music in the *Reichskommissariat Ostland* should be initiated. The project may concentrate on the following desideratum:

a. research of archival material and collection of still available musical oral evidence;

b. comparison of the musical conditions in different locations at the time of the Holocaust and the pre-WW II period;

c. preparation of an educational program of music of the totalitarian systems of 20th century Europe, in particular of the Baltic states.

Israel Today

XIV. Aspekte der Musiksoziologie in Israel*

Schon 1957, kaum zehn Jahre nach der Gründung des Staates Israel, schrieb Alphons Silbermann in seinen bekannten *Prinzipien der Musiksoziologie:* „*Ein für den Musiksoziologen* [...] *besonders beachtenswertes Feld hat sich in dem Musikleben des jungen Staates Israel eröffnet. Dort berühren sich Publikumsgruppen, die aus 'Zentraleuropa abstammen* [...] *mit solchen, die aus arabischen Ländern gekommen sind* [...] *Sie, zusammen mit zahlreichen anderen Gruppen, funktionieren nun wie eine Art musikalischer Filter, so daß ihre Berührungsprozesse auf die Dauer zur Kristallisierung eines israelischen Musikstiles führen können.*"[1] Silbermann hatte hiermit nicht nur die Bedeutung der musiksoziologischen Forschung in Israel hervorgehoben und die musikkulturelle Dynamik skizziert, die dem sozialpolitischen Denken der Gründer Israels entsprach – von diversen ethnischen Gruppen und Musikkulturen zur Kristallisierung einer Nation und nationalen Musik –, sondern auch das Ethnische als Zentralfaktor der Musikkultur Israels bezeichnet.

In nicht minderem Maße als der „outsider" Silbermann sahen auch die heimischen Musikwissenschaftler die einzigartige Situation der Sozialstruktur Israels und ihre Perspektiven für die Musikforschung. Die damals noch ganz junge Johanna Spector beschrieb schon einige Jahre vor Silbermann die israelische Musikwissenschaft als ein Teilgebiet der Sozialwissenschaft. Nachdem sie auf die vielfältigen Kulturaspekte der etwa einhundert jüdischen Gemeinden (*edot*[2]) infolge des „*ingetherings of exils"* hingewiesen hatte (von den Verwandtschaftssystemen, ökonomischen Mikrostrukturen und Sprachproblemen bis zum Kunsthandwerk und zur Zeremonie- Sitten- und Glaubenssymbolik), meinte sie, dass „*all these various fields present themselves to the researcher as interconnec-*

---
* Published in: *Studien zur systematischen Musikwissenschaft =Hamburger Jahrbuch für Musikwissenshaft* 9, ed. P. Petersen, Hamburg, 1986, pp. 85-104.
1 Silbermann, A., *Wovon lebt die Musik? Die Prinzipien der Musiksoziologie* (Regensburg, 1957), S. 153.
2 Sie Anmerkung 1.

ted and related, because it is life itself he is studying. "Also folgert Spector: *„a musicologist becomes an anthropologist.* "[3]

Zur selben Zeit äußerte sich auch der 1938 nach Palästina gekommene große Vorkämpfer der modernen Musikpädagogik, Leo Kestenberg. Mit Blick auf die Zukunft der Musik in Israel schrieb Kestenberg, der ansonsten die soziale Komponente an musikalischen Prozessen unterstrich, 1955 ganz im Geist Rousseaus und der klassischen deutschen Philosophie: *„The real import of all musical education is, perhaps, particularly clear to us in Israel. We are particularly close to the divine source of the Judaic-Christian stream of European culture [. ..] At every level we must devote ourselves to exalting the soul to transcendental heights.* "[4]

Hanoch Avenary, einer der Gründer der israelischen Musikwissenschaft, übertrug diese humanistische Perspektive auf das Studium der Musikgeschichte *per se: „Music will no longer be treated as the concern of a certain social layer, nor as an arabesque on the margin of great political and cultural events: for the old Mediterranean civilizations have already acknowledged it as a power interwoven in all human affairs.* "[5] Auch zwanzig Jahre später sieht Eric Werner in einer musiksoziologischen Theorie und Methodologie das End- und Hauptziel der israelischen Musikwissenschaft. Als deren Ausfluß soll eine auf statistischer Analyse gegründete Typologie der jüdischen Musik entwickelt werden: *„social, religious, political, even communication conditions contribute in various degrees to an everfluctuating, fictitious, yet homogeneous image of an entire tradition, in short, to a typology.* "[6]

All dieses, oder sagen wir, das meiste davon verblieb aber im Bereich der Wunschideen. Die israelische Musikwissenschaft schlug stattdessen einen viel begrenzteren, nämlich rein ethnomusikologischen Weg ein. Die Musikwissenschaftler in Israel sahen in noch größerem Maße als Silbermann das Ethnische als Zentralproblem der Forschung. Eine solche

---

3   Spector, J., „Anthropologic Approach to Jewish Music", in: *Jewish Music Notes* (Okt. 1954), S. 4
4   Kestenberg, L., L., „*The* Present State of Music Education in the Occidental World," in: *Music in Education* (Paris: UNESCO, 1955), S. 55-56.
5   Avenary, H., „Towards an Israeli Design of Music History," in: idem, *Encounters of East and West in Music* (Tel-Aviv, 1979), S. 198.
6   Werner, E., *Contributions to a Historical Study of Jewish Music* (USA, 1976), S. 29.

Einstellung war damals wegen der diversen Bevölkerungsgruppen Israels durchaus berechtigt.

Zunächst muss an die einzigartige Bevölkerungsexplosion in Israel erinnert werden. Es gibt kaum ein anderes Beispiel einer so kurzfristigen und turbulenten Bevölkerungsdynamik. Es genügt, darauf hinzuweisen, daß die Totalbevölkerung Israels sich in den zwölf Jahren von 1948 bis 1960 mehr als verdoppelt hat (von etwa 850.000 auf 2 Millionen) und sich in den nächsten zwölf Jahren bis 1972 verdreifachte (auf fast 3 Millionen). Es ist ganz klar, daß so ein Wachstum nur teilweise auf Grund der natürlichen Geburtenrate geschah; mehr als 60 % des Zuwachses kamen von den verschiedenen Immigrationswellen, die in den Jahren 1948-50, 1955-56, 1962-64 und 1969-73 besonders hoch schlugen und die erwähnten mehr als 100 Kulturgruppen (von Äthiopien bis Schweden und von Mexiko bis China) ins Land brachten.[7] Dazu kommt die Veränderung der Infrastruktur der Bevölkerung in Richtung einer kraß steigenden Dominanz der asiatisch-afrikanischen Kulturgruppen: 1948 bestand die jüdische Bevölkerung aus etwa 35 % in Israel geborenen, 10 % aus Asien und Afrika gekommenen und 55 % von Europa und Amerika nach Israel eingewanderten Menschen. Bis 1970 veränderte sich das Verhältnis entsprechend auf 43 %, 30 % und 28 %. Diese dramatischen demographischen Veränderungen hatten einen tiefgreifenden Einfluß auf die Musikkultur Israels. Das Studium dieser Veränderungen, aber auch die Untersuchung der Musikkulturen neu eingewanderter Gruppen war vor allem ethnisch ausgerichtet. Folglich stand eine ethnisch orientierte Musikwissenschaft, die durch die demographischen Prozesse des Landes bedingt war, im Vordergrund.

Die Tendenz, sich den ethnischen Aspekten der Musikkultur zu widmen, wurde auch durch die Natur der jüdischen Musik, wie sie Curt Sachs 1957 bestimmte, gefördert. Dessen Definition wurde analog zur traditionellen jüdischen Musik selbst mündlich überliefert. In seiner Eröffnungsrede zum Ersten Internationalen Kongreß für jüdische Musik soll Sachs gesagt haben: „*Jewish music is that music which is made by Jews, for Jews, as Jews.*" Diese Definition lebt noch heute in verschiede-

---

7 *Society in Israel 1980* (Jerusalem: Central Bureau of Statistics, 1980), S. 5-7.

nen Varianten fort und wurde sogar (bewußt oder unbewußt?) von Kunsthistorikern übernommen.[8]

Die Fragwürdigkeit der Sachs-Definition wird indessen offensichtlich, sobald man die enorme Zahl der so nicht erfaßbaren Musik in Betracht zieht. Überdies ist der Wert einer Definition zu bezweifeln, wenn sie nicht auf andere Erscheinungen derselben Reihe angewendet werden kann, in diesem Fall auf andere Musikkulturen. Viel überzeugender ist in dieser Hinsicht eine andere Definition des Kunsthistorikers Bezalel Narkiss;[9] bezeichnenderweise sind die zwei Narkiss-Definitionen, von denen eine mit Sachs übereinstimmt, die andere von Sachs abweicht, nur in einem journalistischen Kontext erschienen. Auf die Musik angewendet würde sie bedeuten, daß alles in der Musik, womit Juden sich identifizieren können, als jüdische Musik bezeichnet werden könne. Dieser Standpunkt kommt dem von Mark Slobin nahe: *„ it is not the form, but the understood* meaning *of a particular item that puts it inside that* [ethnic, J. B.] *boundary.*"[10] Obwohl aus modern-semiotischer Sicht diese Definition überzeugend ist, verlieren wir mit ihr den Boden unter den Füßen, sobald wir es mit historischem Material zu tun haben, das ohne Sozialkontext betrachtet wird.

Allan Merriam versteht Musik im weitesten Sinn als *„ Verhalten des Menschen"* genauer *„geformtes Verhalten" („patterned behaviour")*[11]. Akzeptiert man dies, so könnten wir sagen, daß nationale bzw. ethnische Musik national bzw. ethnisch bedingtes Verhalten ist, und daß folglich jüdische Musik jüdisch bedingtes Verhalten oder mit anderen Worten solche Musik wäre, die in formaler, stilistischer oder semantischer Hinsicht Anzeichen eines jüdischen Verhaltens und einer jüdischen Kultur hat und übermittelt.

---

8 *Encyclopedia Judaica* (Jerusalem, 1971), 12:555; *Proceedings of the World Congress on Jewish Music: Jerusalem 1978,* Hrsg. v. J. Cohen (Tel-Aviv, 1982), S. 16; Narkiss, B., „Ma'hi amanut jehudit" (Was ist jüdische Kunst), in: *Ha'aretz* (16. Juni 1985).

9 Narkiss, B., *„Jewish Art Week,"* Interview, in: *Jerusalem Post Supplement,* 17. Mai 1985.

10 Slobin, M., „Klezmer Music: An American Ethnic Genre," in: *Yearbook for Traditional Music* 16 (1984), S. 38.

11 Merriam, A., „Purposes of Ethnomusicology: An Anthropological View," in: *Ethnomusicology* 3 (1963), S. 212.

Trotz ihrer Unhaltbarkeit aus heutiger Sicht hatte die Sachs-Definition zu ihrer Zeit die Zentralstellung der ethnischen Problematik in der jüdischen Musik treffend widergespiegelt. Ausprägung und Geist der jüdischen Musik sind durch die sozial-historischen Prozesse der Geschichte des jüdischen Volkes bestimmt. Die jüdische Musik – die liturgische und die weltliche Volks- und Kunstmusik – hat sich während der mehr als zweitausend Jahre der Diaspora entsprechend der jüdischen Kultur in Regionalstile der verschiedenen *edot* aufgespalten, die vorwiegend ethnisch bedingt waren. Und obwohl Preservation und Kontinuität ebenso wie Assimilation, Konformation, Integration, Akkulturation oder Autonomie sozial geschichtet sein konnten und sicherlich von Sozialfaktoren nicht weniger als von ethnischen beeinflußt waren, blieb die Musikwissenschaft vornehmlich ethnisch ausgerichtet; andere Ansätze, die vielleicht die bisherigen Konzepte und Einstellungen ins Schwanken hätten bringen können, blieben ihr verschlossen. Die Forschung konzentrierte sich ganz auf die ethnischen Charakteristiken der Musik der einzelnen *edot* Die Rechtfertigung einer solchen Einstellung war darin zu erblicken, daß das bisher auf alle Kontinente und in mehr als hundert Länder und in unzählige Gemeinschaften verstreute Musikrepertoire nun in Israel konzentriert war und hier notiert, aufgezeichnet, systematisiert und erforscht werden konnte. Das Gemeinsame und das Unterscheidende dieses Repertoires hervorzuheben, war von jeher der Traum der Vergleichenden Musikwissenschaft Der Rekonstruktion eines jüdischen „Ur-Melos" auf der Basis eines solchen Vergleichs galt das Lebenswerk des Avraham Zvi Idelsohn.[12] Von den Ideen Idelsohns und Robert Lachmanns (der sich im Unterschied zu Idelsohn auf einzelne musikethnologische Fallstudien konzentrierte), war es kein Wunder, daß die israelische Musikwissenschaft sich hauptsächlich der ethno-musikalischen Forschung widmete.

Alle vier von Allan Merriam so vortrefflich beschriebenen Konzepte der traditionellen Ethnomusikologie fanden in Israel einen fruchtbaren Boden.[13] Mit der Vielfalt eines kaum übersehbaren Materials konfrontiert, kam erstens das „*duty of preservation concept*" zum Zuge. Die Arbeit an dem 1935 von Robert Lachmann gegründeten Schallarchiv (heute

---

[12] Idelsohn, A. Z., *Hebräisch-Orientalischer Melodienschatz*, Bd. I–X (Leipzig 1914–1932); und *Jewish Music in its Historical Development* (New York 1929).
[13] Merriam, op. cit.

„Phonothek" genannt) der Hebräischen Universität in Jerusalem konnte ohne weiteres fortgesetzt werden. Etwa 30.000 Schallaufzeichnungen jüdischer Musik sind hier aufbewahrt. Das *„preservation concept"* hatte auch einen negativ-restaurativen Effekt: in ihrem Wunsch, die Tradition um jeden Preis zu bewahren und festzuhalten, kamen die Wissenschaftler bald von der reinen Sammeltätigkeit zu einer Art Mumifizierung der Tradition sowie zur gewollten Konservierung der Musikkulturen: *„despite the removal of almost the entire community to Israel* [in diesem Fall von Indien; J. B.], *it is to be hoped that this tradition will be preserved in its new locale.* "[14] Ähnliche Wunschvorstellungen, die selbsverständlich den Prozess der nationalen Amalgamierung aufhalten, wurden sogar noch beim Weltkongreß für jüdische Musik in Jerusalem 1978 geäußert.

Auch das *„commumcation concept"*, das Hand in Hand mit den zionistischen Ideen der nationalen jüdischen Renaissance ging und zur Verständigung der diversen Bevölkerungsgruppen beitragen sollte, fand eine sehr weite Verbreitung in Israel.[15] Das dritte von Merriam beschriebene Konzept, ist das *„shotgun concept."* Es äußert sich dadurch, daß die in Israel vorhandenen ethnischen Reichtümer von den verschiedenen Interessenten – Musikforschern, Psychologen, Anthropologen, Komponisten, etc. –, besonders aber von westlich orientierten Musikern ausgebeutet werden.[16]

Schließlich postuliert Merriam noch das *„white knight concept"*, das es dem westlichen Musikwissenschaftler[17] geradezu zur Pflicht macht, sich für die östliche Musik einzusetzen, die doch immer vernachlässigt und diskriminiert worden sei. In Israel, in dem die östliche Welt einen wichtigen Bestandteil des wieder zusammengekommenen Volkes bildete, war dieses Konzept besonders bedeutsam; es führte allerdings auch zu lokalen Komplikationen. In den östlichen jüdischen Musikkulturen erblickte man nicht nur das Exotische, das Orientalische und das Nicht-Europäische, sondern auch die „ältesten", „authentischsten" und „wert-

---

14 Ross, I. J., „Cross Cultural Dynamics in Musical Tradition," in: *Musica Judaica* 1:72 (1977); s. *Proceeding...,* S. 57.
15 Gerson-Kiwi, E., „Synthesis and Symbiosis of Styles in Jewish-Oriental Music," in: idem, *Migrations and Mutations* of the Music in East and Wes (Tel-Aviv, 1980), S. 7–14.
16 *Aspects...,* op.cit., S. 3–30.
17 Sie Anmerkung 2.

vollsten" Schichten der jüdischen Musiktradition. Das „*searching for roots*" – ein gewisser Drang zur Ur-Kultur amalgamiert mit dem „*white-knight*"-Syndrom – führte zu einer vorwiegend östlich orientierten Ethnomusikologie: nicht weniger als 80 % der einschlägigen Literatur beziehen sich bis heute auf die östlichen asiatisch-afrikanischen *edot*.[18] In dieser Einseitigkeit kommt übrigens auch eine gewisse „minus-Eins"-Position zum Tragen, die eine Tendenz der jeweils dominanten soziokulturellen Gruppe charakterisiert, stets nur andere als „*ethnics*" zu bezeichnen, sich selbst aber „*not as ethnics but as setting the standard by which others are to be judged.*"[19] In Israel, wo die aus westlichen Ländern gekommenen und westlich orientierten Gruppen das sozio-kulturelle Establishment bildeten, betrachtete man folglich hauptsächlich das östliche Judentum als eine ethnische Gruppe, die westliche Musikkultur wurde dagegen von der Ethnomusikologie nicht eigentlich als ihr Forschungsobjekt betrachtet, und so kam es zu einer Vernachlässigung der Erforschung des westlich orientierten Teils des Musiklebens. Dies führte auch zu einer Vernachlässigung der für die Musiksoziologie im besonderen kennzeichnenden Forschungsgebiete (Soziologie der Musikgattungen, Sozialdechiffrierung von Musikwerken, Musikrezeption, Musik und Ideologie, Massenkultur, die Musikkultur von Stadtgemeinden, etc.).

Auch die geistig-ideologische Atmosphäre des jungen Israel darf in diesem Kontext nicht vergessen werden – die zionistische Idee selbst, die als fördernder Faktor der Ethnomusikologie betrachtet werden kann. Eine der zentralen Ideen des gesellschaftlichen Denkens im Staate Israel war und ist in gewissem Maße noch heute die Idee der Verschmelzung der diversen jüdischen Kulturmodule in ein monolithisches Nationalsystem. So äußerte David Ben Gurion 1951: „*This is a people unique, hurled to all the ends of the earth, speaking with many tongues, apprenticed to alien culture, as under in different communities and tribes within the House of Israel. We must melt down this fantastically diversified assemblage and cast it afresh in the die of a renewed nationhood. We must break down the barriers of geography and culture, of society and speech, which keep the different sections apart, and endow them with a single language,*

---

18 „Jewish music", in: *The New Grove* 9:xx (1980); Shiloah, A. & Gerson-Kiwi, E., „Musicology in Israel: 1960–1980," in: *Acta Musicologica* 2: 200–216 (1981).
19 Banton, M., *Racial and Ethnic Competition*, (Cambridge UP, 1983), S. 65.

a single culture, a single citizenship, a single loyality, with new legislation and new laws. We must give them a new spirit, a culture and literature, science and art."[20] Ben Gurion akzentuiert vor allem ethnische und kulturelle Divergenzen; sozialpolitische, -ideologische und -ökonomische Aspekte erscheinen demgegenüber sekundär. Mit den Ideologen kamen die Künstler, Schriftsteller und auch Musiker, um nach künstlerischen und sozialen Kommunikationskanälen und Ausdrucksmöglichkeiten zu suchen, die diese neue Kultur fördern könnten. Das Gemeinsame konnte aber nicht künstlich aus dem Nichts geschaffen werden; das Gemeinsame mußte aus der Vielfalt herausgefunden und im Vergleich studiert werden (siehe z. B. typische Diskussions-Titel wie *Synthesis and Symbiosis of Styles..., The Legacy of Jewish Music thorugh the Ages, Diversity within Unity...*etc.), die Musikkulturen der verschiedenen *edot* mußten erst erforscht werden. Wir stoßen daher wieder auf die immanente Notwendigkeit, in erster Linie ethnomusikologische Studien zu betreiben.

So kam es in Israel zur jahrelangen Vorherrschaft einer ethnisch eingestellten Musikwissenschaft. Die Haupttendenzen der israelischen Ethnomusikologie wurden vor kurzem kritisch gesondert;[21] demnach lassen sich drei Tendenzen hervorheben (s. auch Kap. XV):

a) Die erste Tendenz, zu der der größte Teil aller Publikationen rechnet, ist hauptsächlich der Beschreibung und formalen Analyse des ethnischen Musikrepertoires gewidmet und hat in diesem Ansatz eine Menge ethnischer Musik ans Licht gebracht.[22] Das Material stammte von Einzelinformanten *(„culture beares", „key informants")*, wurde allerdings von deren sozialem und kulturellem Kontext isoliert betrachtet; und obwohl die Informanten hervorragende Kenner der Tradition waren, blieben die Belege oft vereinzelte und kulturell isolierte Beispiele. Die Musik wurde bloß als Endprodukt, statisch und von konstantem Wert gesehen; sie wurde insoweit als „Museum" betrachtet; die gesamte ethnische

---

20 Ben Gurion, D., „The Call of Spirit in Israel," in: idem, *Rebirth and Destiny of Israel* (New York, 1954), S.401.
21 Braun, J. u. Sharvit, U., *Anthropology of Music: The Israeli Aspect,* Paper at Annual Conference of Israel Musicological Society (April 1982).
22 Gerson-Kiwi, E., „The Music of the Persian Jews", in: *Dukkhan* 3, 1962, S. 60–62 (Hebräisch); Hoffmann. Sh., „Two Versions of a Yemenite Tune," in: *Tatzlil* 4/9, 1969, S. 150–151 (Hebräisch); Weich-Shahak, S. „The Wedding Songs of the Bulgarian-Sephardic Jewish Tradition," in: *Orbis Musicae* 7, 1979/80, S. 81–107.

Gruppe „*serves as an instance of rare stability and remoteness in all its folkways.*"[23] Die Idee einer „antiken" bzw. „authentischen" Musikkultur, die nicht nur in Schallarchiven, sondern auch in der Musikpraxis konserviert sein sollte,[24] beherrschte diesen Trend. In ihrem Grundkonzept widersprach diese Idee der Natur gesellschaftlicher Prozesse und zudem auch noch den Idealen des neuen Staates.

b) Die zweite Strömung in der Ethnomusikologie betrachtet die Volksmusik in gewisser Hinsicht als lebenden Organismus und setzt die Musik in einen sozialen Kontext. Die Kulturaspekte und -ereignisse werden aber nur als Hintergrund angesehen. Eine gesonderte Beschreibung, ja sogar getrennte Analyse von Zeremonie und Musik kann weder die Interdependenz von Musik und Wort noch die von Musik und sozialem Hintergrund erklären.[25] Die Studien dieser Gruppe bleiben der Methodik der ersten Gruppe verpflichtet, obwohl in Einzelfällen öfters auch statistische Analysemethoden einbezogen werden.[26] In dieser Hinsicht sind aber die Versuche, Verallgemeinerungen der Befunde auf ganze ethnische Gruppen oder komplexe soziale Kulturprozesse vorzunehmen, sehr riskant.

c) Der dritte Trend unter den Ethnomusikologen ist eine ziemlich neue Erscheinung in der Musikwissenschaft Israels (seit etwa 10–15 Jahren); er kommt der modernen Musik-Anthropologie und -Soziologie am nächsten. Diese Richtung betrachtet die Musik als „patterned behaviour", als Symbol. Im Zentrum dieser Studien steht die Funktionsanalyse des Musikrepertoires und auch teilweise die semantische Strukturanalyse. Die Musik wird als eine Teilmanifestation der Sozial- und Kulturereignisse analysiert (in Anlehnung an Studien von John Blacking und Allan Mer-

---

23 Gerson-Kiwi, E., „Women's Songs from Yemen: Their Tonal Structure and Form" (1965), in: Gerson-Kiwi, *Migration...*, 1980, S. 147–153.
24 Sieh Fussnote 14.
25 Avenary, H., The Experience of Nature and Scenary in the Israeli Song (1975), in: idem., *Encounters...*, S. 97–104. Gerson-Kiwi, E., „Halleluia and Jubilus in Hebrew-Oriental Chant" (1961), in: idem., *Migration...*, S. 54–60. Shiloah, A. „Group of Arabic Wedding Songs from the Village of Deyr al-Asad", in: *Studies in Marriage Customs* (Jerusalem, 1974), S. 167–196.
26 Katz, R., „The Singing of the *baqqashot* of the Aleppo Jews," in: *Acta Musicologica* 1968, S. 267–296; idem., „The Reliability of Oral Transmission: The case of Samaritan Music," in: *Yuval* 1974, S. 109-135.

riam). So sprechen z. B. Bruno Nettl und Amnon Schiloah in einer Studie zur Musikkultur der iranisch-jüdischen Gruppen in Israel über *„modernization of musical sound and musical behaviour that has resulted from the exposure of Iranians to the multi-faceted musical society in Israel."*[27] In einer Analyse der Kulturmodelle der jüdisch-jemenitischen Tradition wird die Strukturgemeinschaft des Musikverhaltens mit anderen Gesellschafts- und Kultur-Phänomenen aufgezeigt. Die ganze Methodologie ist aber auch hier auf die Erforschung des Ethnischen konzentriert; indem also die empirisch-soziologische Analyse unterbleibt, ist ein Problem wie das der Gruppennormen kaum diskutierbar.[28]

Alle drei Richtungen der israelischen Ethnomusikologie haben also einige konzeptionelle und methodische Züge gemeinsam:

a) Die Musikkultur und ihre Prozesse werden hauptsächlich ethnisch gesehen; alle anderen sozialen Parameter werden mehr oder minder im Schatten belassen.

b) Das Ethnische selbst wird wiederum hauptsächlich im orientalischen Element gesehen.

c) Dem folgt das weitgehende Ignorieren des Musiklebens westlicher Prägung und somit auch des Stadt-Milieus.

d) Die Forschungsmethodik stützt sich vorzüglich auf Einzelinformanten wodurch eine statistisch begründete Analyse nicht möglich ist. Validität und Reliabilität der Folgerungen erscheinen so nicht hinreichend gesichert.

Die Rückständigkeit der Forschung auf dem Gebiet der Musiksoziologie und die Vernachlässigung von deren Konzepten zeigen sich klar in den publizierten Mitteilungen über den Forschungsstand der Musikwissenschaft Israels. Der erste, schon 1958 erschienene Bericht erwähnt die Musiksoziologie überhaupt nicht;[29] auch unter Desiderata ist dieses Forschungsgebiet nicht genannt. Noch 1968 ist die Musiksoziologie als Dis-

---

27 Nettl, B. /Shiloah, A., „Persian classical music in Israel," in: *Israel Studies in Musicology* (IMS) 2, 1980, S. 33–49.
28 Hajdu, A., „Le Niggun Meron," in: *Yuval* 2 (1971), S. 73–113; Sharvit, U., „The Role of Music in the Jewish Yemenite Heder," in: IMS 2, 1980, S. 33–49; idem., „On Arts and Aristic Patterns in the Jewish Tradition," in: *Pe'amin* 10, 1981, S. 119–130.
29 Gerson-Kiwi, E., „Musicology in Israel," in: *Acta Musicologica* 30, 1958, S. 17–28.

ziplin abwesend obwohl die Sozialgeschichte der Musik als Forschungsthema erwähnt wird.[30]

Der letzte Forschungsbericht wurde 1981 von Schiloah und Gerson-Kiwi vorgelegt. Von den 22 hier genannten Musikwissenschaftlern die den aktiven Kern der israelischen Musikwissenschaft bilden und sich mit der jüdischen Musik befassen, arbeiten etwa fünf historisch und fünf systematisch; der größere Teil der Forscher ist heute in beiden Bereichen aktiv. Das spiegelt wiederum die Spezifik der jüdischen Musik wider, die sowohl historischen als auch systematischen Aspekten zugänglich und deren Erforschung nur durch eine Verschmelzung der beiden Bereiche möglich ist. Was die Musiksoziologie betrifft, so ist diese in diesem letzten Report wiederum nur einmal als potentielles Forschungsgebiet eines Musikwissenschaftlers genannt.[31]

Das Programm des Welt-Kongresses für jüdische Musik im Jahre 1978 vermittelt zumindest ein indirektes Bild der Forschungsschwerpunkte und Interessen der israelischen Musikwissenschaft, wobei die Geringschätzung der Musiksoziologie klar zutage tritt: Von 33 Kongreßvorträgen operierte kein einziger mit soziologischen Konzepten, obwohl sich alle in der einen oder anderen Form mit sozialen Problemen befaßten.[32] Dieses negative Bild bestätigte sich schließlich auch anhand der Musikartikel der israelischen enzyklopädischen Literatur, deren Information und Darlegung im Grunde soziologisch irrelevant ist.[33]

In den erwähnten Forschungsberichten, in der enzyklopädischen Literatur, in Kongreßvorträgen usw. tritt in gewissem Maße nicht nur die aktuelle Konzeption der Musikwissenschaft zu Tage, sondern oft auch die Einstellung der israelischen Musikwissenschaftler. Zwar werden die Musik und das Soziale nicht selten und sogar konsequent in guter Nachbarschaft diskutiert, die Kontaktstelle aber zwischen Musikwissenschaft und Sozialwissenschaft (von einer interdisziplinären Einstellung ganz zu

---

30 Harran, D., „Musical Research in Israel: Its History, Resources, and Institutions," in: *Current Musicology* 7, (1968), S. 120–127.
31 Shiloah, A. & Gerson-Kiwi, E., „Musicology in Israel 1960-1980," *Acta Musicologica*, 53/2:200-216 (1981).
32 *Proceedings...*, sieh Anm. 3.
33 Gradenwitz, P.E., „Eretz-Israel: Musika, in: *Ha'enzklopedia ha'ivrit* (Hebräische Enzyklopädie) 6 (1957), S. 1121–1129; Boehm, Y., „Music in Modern Israel", in: *Encyclopedia Judaica* (1971), 12:668–675.

schweigen) bleibt unreflektiert. Die ungenügende Verbindung von Musikwissenschaft und Sozialwissenschaft ist leider von beiden Seiten verschuldet. Aspekte der Musik oder des Musiklebens sind den Sozialwissenschaften (von seltenen Ausnahmen abgesehen) völlig fremd geblieben. Das kann am Beispiel der *Enzyklopädia l'madei ha'chevra* (Enzyklopädie der Sozialwissenschaften; Enziklopedia 1962–1970) am besten demonstriert werden: Dieses fünfbändige Werk hatte keinen Fachredakteur für die Künste (im Gegensatz zu den meisten anderen Gebieten), es enthält folglich nur einen insgesamt zwei Seiten langen (kurzen!) Artikel über die Künste, in dem die Musik nur ganz beiläufig erwähnt ist (man sollte dies mit dem Artikel „Music" von Merriam und Engel in der *International Encyclopedia of Social Sciences* vergleichen). Erst 1981 erscheint im Addenda-Band der *Enzyklopädia l'madei ha'chevra* ein etwa vier Seiten langer Artikel „Musik und Gesellschaft".

Bis vor kurzem hatte also die soziologische Forschung in Israel kaum ein Interesse für die Musik. Sogar solche klassischen Werke wie Schmuel N. Eisenstadts *Israel Society* bringen das Wort „Musik" nicht einmal im Sachregister,[34] und in einer Bibliographie zum Thema *„Kultur und Werte"* ist keine einzige Arbeit über die Künste erwähnt.[35] Stattdessen sind die veralteten Konzepte der „universellen Musik" noch wirksam: *„The most universal non-local artistic sphere was that of music, a sphere which is certainly not marginal. Here both consumption and production were generally geared to universal musical creativity, a fact which is fully borne out by the Israel Philharmonic Orchestra with its string of international conductors and its own international repertoire."* Was die Volksmusik anbetrifft, so heißt es knapp: *„Naturally folk music and dances etc. have also developped in this sphere."*[36] Es ist nur nicht klar, ob die Voksmusik zu den *„universal"* oder zu den *„non-local"* Eigenschaften der Musik gezählt werden soll.

Eine vereinzelte, aber höchst anregende Studie der Kulturverhältnisse in Israel haben Eliahu Katz und Michael Gurevitch unter dem Titel *The Secularization of Leisure: Cultur and Communication in Israel* vorgelegt.

---

34 Eisenstadt, Sh. N., *Israel Society*. London 1970.
35 *Integration and Development in Israel.* Hrsg. v. S. Eisenstadt. Jerusalem 1970, S. 691-703.
36 Eisenstadt, Sh. N., *Israel Society*, S. 377.

Daten über Konzertbesuch, Musikinstrumenten- und Schallplatten-Besitz, Radiohören, Vergnügungsaktivitäten etc. werden hier erstmalig präsentiert und analysiert und zwar größtenteils in dreidimensionaler Korrelation (Alter, Abstammung, Bildung). Die Studie wurde im Auftrag des Ministeriums für Bildung und Kultur durchgeführt und basiert auf Feldarbeiten aus dem Jahre 1970. Leider sind Terminologie und Präsentationsform der Daten nicht immer auf den Bereich der Musikkultur übertragbar. Auf welchen Typ von Musik bezieht sich z. B. die erwähnte *„concert attendance"*? Sind *„entertainment"*, *„light entertainment"* und *„popular music"* identisch?[37] Radiohören kann als Variable eigentlich nicht gebraucht werden, wenn der musikalische Teil der Sendungen nicht gesondert ausgewiesen wird. Aber gerade das Radiohören wäre wegen der stilistisch strikt geteilten Musiktypen der vier Programme des „Kol Israel" (Israels Radio „Die Stimme Israels") besonders günstig für die Erforschung der Musikrezeption.[38] Bestätigt wirklich ein hoher Prozentsatz von Leuten, die ein Musikinstrument besitzen (23 % der Bevölkerung), *„the high interest in musical expression"*? Inwiefern kann auch für Musik in Betracht gezogen werden, daß *„education supersedes ethnicity"*? Ist die These, daß *„all groups, regardless of ethnicity, generation or education, favour the continuity of ethnic pluralism in culture, that is in things having to do with customs, holidays, music and the like,"*[39] auch im Bereich der Musik haltbar, oder sind es nur ganz bestimmte Musikverhältnisse, die durch Religion und Sitte bestimmt sind? Solche und viele andere Fragen verlangen zusätzlich zu allgemein-soziologischen Erhebungen die Berücksichtigung spezifisch musikwissenschaftlicher Probleme.[40]

Wenn wir uns jetzt wieder der Musikwissenschaft *per se* zuwenden, können wir konstatieren, daß Elemente der Musiksoziologie in einem bestimmten Teil der Musikforschung immerhin zu erblicken sind. Obwohl die Präferenzen der Ethnomusikologie für exotische Kulturen, isoliert gelegene außerstädtische Gemeinden, ethnische Forschungsparameter und eine deskriptive Methodik (im Gegensatz zu den Präferenzen der

---

37 Katz, E. & Gurevitch, M. *The Secularization of Leisure: Culture and Communication in Israel* (Cambridge, 1976), S. 108, 125, 133.
38 Sieh Anm. 4.
39 Katz & Gurevitch, *The Secularization...*, S. (S. 115, 163 u. 191).
40 Sieh Anm. 5.

Musiksoziologie, die sich westlichen Kulturen und Stadtgemeinden in einer Vielfalt von Parametern auf der Basis einer quantitativ orientierten Methodik widmet) die israelische Forschung beherrscht, sollen einige Arbeiten, die der dritten Strömung der Ethnomusikologie entstammen, als soziologisch orientiert hervorgehoben werden. Es handelt sich um Arbeiten seit den siebziger Jahren, in denen die Musik *„against a wider background"* als *„a component of* [...] *culture"* betrachtet wird. In diesem Zusammenhang schrieb Professor Shiloah: *„I realised that the search for novelty, and the emphasis on preservation, in fact, narrowed my field of operation, and threatened to obscure the view of traditional music as an activity expressing man's outlook and forming part of his being and culture."*[41] Besonders nahe stehen der Musiksoziologie jene Studien, die dem Sozialstatus des Musikers gewidmet sind, einem Gebiet, das bis vor kurzem ganz außer Acht gelassen wurde.[42] Die charakteristische ethnozentrische Einstellung bleibt aber auch hier bestehen: Von Interesse ist hauptsächlich der Status der orientalischen Musiker, soweit diese *„fall into the clutches of foreign impressarios"* und ihre Kunst dem degenerierenden Einfluß des Radios ausgesetzt sei.[43] Die Methodik dieser Arbeiten verbleibt deskriptiv und stützt sich nur auf Einzelzeugnisse. Um ein Beispiel aus dem hier zitiertem ansonsten höchst anregenden Artikel von Gerson-Kiwi „The Musician in Society: East and West" zu nennen: Das östliche Bildungssystem wird hier mit 7 Musiker-Interviews exemplifiziert, das westliche nur abstrakt beschrieben; die Gegenüberstellung von West und Ost (ein thematischer Dauerbrenner), die an der Musikausbildung durchgeführt wird, ergibt daß die östliche Musikausbildung angeblich anti-institutionell, die westliche dagegen strikt institutionell gebunden sei, eine Entgegenstellung, die wie soviele Kontrastbildungen von Ost und West den historischen Tatsachen widerspricht (die westliche Musikausbildung der Stadtmusikanten des 16./17. Jahrhunderts war antiinstitutionell andererseits war die östliche des jemenitisch-jüdischen

---

41 Shiloah, A. , „Leaves from the Diary," in: *Ariel* 31 (1972), S. 18 u. 19.
42 Gerson-Kiwi, E. „Musiker des Orients – ihr Werden und Werdegang," in: *Studia Musicologica* 3 (1962), S. 127–132; „The Oriental Musician," in: *The World of Music* 43 (1968), S. 8–18; Shiloah, A.(a), „The Status of the Oriental Artist", in: *Ariel* 36 (1974), S. 79–83.
43 Gerson-Kiwi, E., „The Musician in Society: East and West" (1973), in: idem., *Migration...*, 1980, S. 190 u. 195.

Cheders höchst institutionell gebunden.[44] Den soziologischen Aspekten am nächsten kommt wohl Shiloah, der die Statuskonzepte der östlichen Musiker am Beispiel der Musiker des Orientalen-Ensembles des Israelischen Radios analysiert.[45]

Auch zwei andere Studien nähern sich der Musiksoziologie, und zwar sowohl von der stilanalytischen wie von der sozialpsychologischen Seite. Smoira-Rolls Analyse des israelischen Volksliedes (oder Massenliedes, die Grenze zwischen den beiden ist in der Musikkultur Israels nicht ganz klar) führt auf Sozialprozesse zurück und bezieht eine statistische Beweisführung in die Stilanalyse ein.[46] Diese vor etwa zwanzig Jahren erschienene Studie hätte einer der Bausteine der Musiksoziologie Israels werden können. Die Richtung fand aber keine weitere Entwicklung, vielleicht wegen einer konzeptionellen Unsicherheit, die Smoira-Roll selbst anspricht: Fünfzehn Jahre später schrieb sie: *„it is, perhaps, strange that I found it necessary to use national landmarks as if to indicate the change in artistic-musical developments."*[47]

Die andere Studie befaßt sich mit dem Thema „Das Israelische in der israelischen Musik.[48] Einer Gruppe von 95 Personen (Israelis/Emigranten – professionelle Musiker/nicht-professionelle Musiker) wurde ein *„klingender Fragebogen"* (10 israelische Kompositionen, 10 nicht-israelische) vorgelegt. Die Resultate waren deutlich negativ: Der Begriff des *„Israelischen in der Musik"* ist vage, obwohl erwartet wurde, daß die israelische Musik sich von nicht-israelischer unterscheidet. Das Konzept des *„Israelischen in der Musik"* scheint noch nicht ausgereift zu sein. Andererseits könnten auch methodologische Mängel zu diesem Untersuchungsergebnis geführt haben.

Zuletzt sollen einige Publikationen erwähnt werden, die im vollen Sinn des Wortes zur Musiksoziologie gezählt werden können. Es sind insgesamt vier, also eine Publikation pro neun Jahre Musikwissenschaft

---

44 Braun, J. *Vijolmakslas attistiba Latvija* (Die Entwicklung der Geigenkunst in Lettland), (Riga, 1962), S. 69; Sharvit, U., „The role of music in the Jewish Yemenite Heder", in: ISM 2 (1980), S.33-49.
45 Sieh Fussnote 42, Shiloah, „The Status..."
46 Smoira-Roll (Zmora), M. *Folk Song in Israel: An Analysis Attempted.* Tel-Aviv 1963.
47 *Proceedings...*, Hebreiher Teil, S. 16.
48 Hirshberg, J., The „Israeli" in Israel Music: The Audience Responds, in: ISM, 1:159-173 (1978).

in Israel, von denen drei zudem von Nicht-Israelis geschrieben wurden und die vierte von einem israelischen Komponisten. Dieser Umstand scheint mir die Einstellung der israelischen Musikwissenschaft, die hier schon mehrmals zur Sprache kam, sehr anschaulich zu beleuchten. Der bekannte Komponist Joseph Tal hat 1955 als Direktor des Jerusalemer Konservatoriums mit seinem Essay *Die musiksoziologische Einflußsphäre des israeli-schen Radios* den Anfang der israelischen Musiksoziologie markiert.[49] Im Rundfunk – dem heutigen Auftraggeber für Komponisten in Israel – sieht Tal eine Institution, die *„die kulturpolitische Aufgabe hat, die Kristallisierung eines israelischen Musikstils* [man achte auf die Wortidentität mit Silbermann! – J. B.] *zu fördern;"* (S. 419); diese Aufgabe würde vom Rundfunk sowohl qualitativ wie auch quantitativ erfüllt. Die Einstellung Tals liegt – wie schon erwähnt – ganz im Sinne des geistigen Klimas im Israel der fünfziger Jahre (hatte wohl Silbermann seine Bemerkungen von Tal übernommen?). Jedoch sind hier wie bei vielen anderen Behauptungen Tals Zweifel angebracht. Kann man wirklich sagen, daß für die Realisierung der Forderung der Gesellschaft nach einem *„israelischen Ausdruck in der Musik"* das Radio der ideale Protagonist ist (S. 422)? Ist der *„Kontakt zwischen Komponist und Publikum in diesem Land zweifellos ein engerer als in der Mehrzahl anderer Länder"* (S. 424)?

Nicht viel besser ist es um die Validität der Urteile im Essay von Elie Yarden bestellt, obwohl seine Beobachtungen von ganz entgegengesetztem Charakter sind.[50] Ist es wirklich so, daß *„some of the fiscal policies reflect the view of the political decision-makers that music is relatively devoid of significant cultural values,"* (S. 131)? Erinnern wir uns an die oben zitierten Worte Ben Gurions von 1951 oder denken wir an die neuerlichen Äußerungen von Premier Shimon Peres: *„Ich sehe die Musik nicht als Unterhaltungsmittel oder Belustigung; sie ist für mich ein Teil des schöpferischen Prozesses des Volkes; die Musik ist eine Ausdrucksform, die das ganze geistige Leben des Volkes bereichert [...]."*[51] Und

---

49 Tal, J., Die musiksoziologische Einflußsphäre des israelischen Radios, in: *Cahiers d'Etudes de Radio-Télévision:* Radio, Musique et Société, 3–4, Paris 1955, S. 419–424.
50 Yarden, E., „The Israeli Composer and his Milieu," in: *Perspectives of New Music* 2, 1966, S. 130–139.
51 Peres, Sh., *Rede aus Anlaß der Überreichung des Premierminister-Preises an den Komponisten Yitzhak Sadai* (Jerusalem, Van Leer Institut), 12. Juni 1985.

sind die Thesen wissenschaftlich haltbar, daß „*music in Israel [...] is subjected to the rules of the market even more than in the most advanced countries of the West*" (S. 131), oder daß „incipient Zhdanovism shows up in the conduct of the State Broadcasting Service" (ebd.), oder, daß „*the Radio was responsible for the destruction of the nascent Israeli folk music*" (S. 132)?

Die Aussichten, die Friedrich Klausmeier in seinem Aufsatz Musik als Mittel sozialer Integration in Israel ausbreitet, nähern sich wieder denen von Tal. Er meint, der Staat Israel hätte „*einen direkten Grund [...], Volksgesang zu fördern*", da das Lied „*das Gemeinschaftsleben zum Ausdruck bringt*", das in Israel von sozialistischen Ideen inspiriert sei.[52] In Israel gälten Lied und Tanz „*umgekehrt wie in Westeuropa [...] vor allem für obere, geistig aktivere Schichten*", und „*Volksmusiktradition wird durch Volksmusikpflege ersetzt*" (S. 22). Trotz der Fülle biblischer Texte in Liedersammlungen (etwa 20 %) sei die Musik nicht in der Restauration der eigenen Folklore erstarrt, sondern eher als „*Umdeutung in gegenwärtigen lebendigen Ausdruck*" (S. 23) zu begreifen. Daneben klassifiziert er eine Schlagerindustrie, die durch Radio und Schallplatten in die Hörerrezeption eindringt, eine revue-artige Musik des Militärs und eine symphonische Musik, „*die über eine Adaption von folkloristischen Einflüssen den Anschluß an die Dodekaphonie gefunden hat*" (S. 23). Klausmeier scheint auch der erste gewesen zu sein, der für Israel einen „*musikalischen Pluralismus*" konstatierte, indem er schrieb: „*Wie in Europa wird sich auch in Israel ein einheitlicher Musikstil nicht mehr durchsetzen; sondern die verschiedenen Stile und Musikformen befriedigen in fruchtbarer Anpassung das Ausdrucksbedürfnis der heutigen Mittelstandsgesellschaft*" (S. 24). So wurde auch bezüglich der Musik eine neue Realität akzeptiert und sogar als wünschenswerte Entwicklungstendenz gekennzeichnet, die schon einige Jahre früher in der Soziologie zu Tage trat: „*There is [...] a kind of synthesis between authentic cultural elements of some of the Oriental communities and dominant cultural elements in Israel society. Together with these changes in the bases of conformity of the new immigrants [...] there has been a complete recess, on the part of the political and cultural élite, from the conformity model*

---

52 Klausmeier, Fr., „Musik als Mittel sozialer Integration in Israel", in: *Musik und Bildung* 4, 1972, S. 20-25.

which compelled the immigrants to accept unselectively the cultural patterns of the old timers [...] There has been a de facto recognition of cultural pluralism. "[53]

Bereits 1962 entstand die Dissertation von Marvin Greenberg über *Music Education in Israel*.[54] Er legte einen ab 1960 erhobenen Bestandsreport des israelischen Musikbildungswesens vor. Diese einzigartige Studie – eigentlich eine Soziographie des Musiklebens in Israel – wurde leider nicht fortgesetzt. Einige Folgerungen Greenbergs sind bis heute aktuell (z. B. die noch von Kestenberg stammende Idee einer universalen Musikausbildung), und der Informationswert seiner Arbeit ist unbestreitbar. Obwohl die Studie auf viel soliderem Boden steht als die ersten drei, sind Greenbergs Schlußfolgerungen oft voreilig. So kann man fragen, auf welche empirischen Daten er sich stützt, wenn er sagt, daß *„there is lack of understanding of the values of music for the Israeli citizen,"* eine These, die auch bei Yarden Widerhall findet.[55]

Der wissenschaftliche Wert der zuletzt erwähnten vier Studien ist vor allem in der Fokussierung auf gesellschaftliche Tatbestände der Musik zu sehen. Andererseits sind sie typische Beispiele für die phänomenologisch orientierte Soziologie und basieren insoweit nicht auf empirischer Forschung. Der offensichtliche Mangel empirischer Forschung im Bereich der Musikkultur hat z. T. weitreichende und unerwünschte Konsequenzen. So lesen wir zum Beispiel in einem Heft der UNESCO – einer Publikation von internationalem Status und sogar wissenschaftlichem Anspruch, wie ihr Titel unterstreicht (*Studies and Documents on Culture Policies: Culture Policy in Israel*), das folgende: *„The concert-going public is conservative and adjust itself with difficulty to modern music in any form. This made life rather difficult for the Israeli composer."*[56] Diese Behauptung, die scheinbar in gewissen Kreisen Fuß gefaßt hat, ist hier ohne jeglichen Beleg vorgetragen. Eine empirische Studie hat dann vor kurzer Zeit nachgewiesen, daß diese Behauptung nicht den Tatsachen entspricht: 71 % einer Stichprobe der Musikhörer des Programms „A" des israelischen Radios sind an gemäßigt moderner Musik (von Bartok

---

53 Lissak, M., *Social Mobility in Israel Society* (Jerusalem, 1969), S. 102.
54 Greenberg, M., *Music Education in Israel in its Cultural and Educational Context...*, Ph. D., Columbia University, 1962.
55 Greenberg, op. cit., S. 413; Yarden, „The Israeli...," S. 131.
56 Michman, J., *Cultural Policy in Israel* (Paris: Unesco, 1973), S. 33.

bis Strawinsky und Britten) „interessiert" oder sogar „sehr interessiert", 22 % hatten eine solche positive Beziehung zur Avantgarde (von Stockhausen bis zur elektronischen Musik), und 53 % wollten diese Musikstile im Radio hören können. 40 % der Befragten hatten den Wunsch, die Musik israelischer Komponisten zu hören. Diese Befragten und das oben erwähnte „concert-going public" dürften weitgehend kongruieren, da mehr als 50 % von ihnen mehr als einmal im Monat Konzerte besuchen[57].

Projekte aus dem Bereich der Empirischen Musiksoziologie nach dem Muster dieser Rezeptionsuntersuchung und einiger anderer Arbeiten an den Universitäten Bar-Ilan und Tel-Aviv könnten ein objektives Bild des Musiklebens und der Musikverhältnisse Israels schaffen. Die methodologische Rückständigkeit oder besser Einseitigkeit der Forschung in Israel hat nicht nur isolierte Fehlurteile wie das eben erwähnte zur Folge, sondern führt nach Art der „two-way"-Straße zur Stagnation: Die unzureichenden Erhebungsverfahren, die meist auf Einzelfällen basieren, begrenzen das konzeptionelle Denken; umgekehrt behindert der Konzeptmangel die Erweiterung der Forschungsmethodik und begrenzt die Forschungssphäre insgesamt. Die Musikwissenschaft Israels scheint sich dieser Situation bewußt zu sein. In den letzten Jahren sind einige Arbeiten erschienen, die neue Forschungstendenzen interdisziplinärer und umfassender Natur aufweisen. Einerseits strebt man einer Synthese von Ethnomusikologie und Musiksoziologie zu; andererseits sind sie auch interdisziplinär im weitesten Sinne, da die Sozialwissenschaften einbezogen werden. In diesen Arbeiten wird auch eine Synthese aus neuer Konzeptbildung und empirischer Forschung angestrebt.

Amnon Shiloah (Musikwissenschaftler) und Eric Cohen (Soziologe) haben kürzlich eine Rahmentheorie der Veränderungsdynamik der orientalisch-jüdischen Musik in Israel entworfen.[58] Neun Module kennzeichnen die Veränderungsprozesse von traditioneller Musik durch verschiedene Stadien der orthogenetischen Preservation (konservative und museal bewahrte Musik) und gemischte Formen (neotraditionelle und pseudoethnische Musik) zur hetero-genetischen Innovation (populäre Musik

---

[57] Braun, J. *E-music on the Israel Radio: An Audience Research Report* (Bar-Ilan University, 1981), Manuskript.
[58] Shiloah, A. & Cohen, E., „Dynamics of Change in the Music. of the Oriental Jews in Israel, " in: *Ethnomusicology* 2, 1983, S. 227–252.

und Kunstmusik). Diese erstmals erarbeitete Theorie der Musikkultur Israels wurde von Jehoash Hirshberg in einer Fallstudie verifiziert, die der jemenitischen Sängerin Bracha Zephira gewidmet ist;[59] die Theorie kann offenbar auf viele andere Erscheinungen appliziert werden. Es fragt sich nur, inwiefern die erwähnten Module von orientalisch-jüdischer Spezifik sind, oder ob sie nicht die bekannten Prozesse widerspiegeln, die von der Volksmusik durch intermediäre Abwandlungen zu einem nationalen Stil der Kunstmusik führen und ihr Paradigma z. B. in Ost-Europa haben. Stehen wir also wieder einer Schein-Orientalisierung ganz allgemeiner musikhistorischer Prozesse gegenüber? Die Schlußfolgerung von Shiloah/Cohen ist insoweit interessant, weil hier nicht nur die Idee des nationalen Musikstils aufgegeben wird, sondern vielmehr die Entwicklung der Musikkultur Israels (und nicht nur die der orientalischen Juden) vom Kulturpluralismus zu einem „Pluralismus auf Staatsebene" fortgeführt und als legitim besiegelt wird: „*Our presentation thus indicates a trend away from the idea of more amalgamation of different ethnic traditions into an overall national musical style, but rather the gradual emergence of legitimate pluralism in music on the national level. This shows that the emergend Israeli cultural identity is becoming less monolithic and more pluralistic than it has been conceived of in the past.*"[60]

Das Leitmotiv der „*ethnic musicians*", die „*still face the dilemma of making their work widely acceptable, without erasing its distinct ethnic character and thereby destroying their own particular ethnic identity*" (op. cit.) ist auch hier vorhanden; indessen wird nicht klar, was genau mit „*ethnic musicians*" gemeint ist, und wie sich diese von den anderen Musikern unterscheiden, die sich dem Problem „*of making their work widely acceptable*" gleichfalls stellen. Die Überspitzung des ethnischen Problems zieht sich wie ein roter Faden durch die israelischen soziomusikalischen Wissenschaften und hat ihr Vorbild in einem bestimmten Teil der lokalen Soziologie.[61]

---

59 Hirshberg, J., „Bracha Zephira and the Process of Change in Israeli Music," in: *Pe'amin* 19, (1984), S. 29–46 (Hebräisch).
60 Shiloah & Cohen, „Dynamics of Change...", S. 148.
61 Smooha, S., *Israel: Pluralism and Conflict* (London: Henley 1978); idem., „Three Perspectives in the Sociology of Ethnic Relations in Israel" in: *Magamot* 2/3, 1984, S. 169–206.

Die Suche nach neuen Konzepten, bezogen auf Israels Musikkultur, zeigt sich auch in einer neueren Analyse der Musiktradition des zentraleuropäischen, hauptsächlich deutschen Judentums in Israel. Philip V. Bohlmann stellt hierin das Konzept der „Re-Urbanisation" vor, die erscheint, *„when a society arrives at such a highly urbanized level that it relies on the institutions inherent in that level of development as means of reestablishing its social structure when the society is displaced."*[62] Konzeptsuche und empirische Forschung gehen hier Hand in Hand, und ein für Immigrantenländer charakteristischer Fall von sozial-ethnischer Selbstbestätigung wird für Israel konstatiert: *„Remaining as the bulwark of the traditions are not individual repertoires, but the transformed structures of a musical culture that had already defined the ethnic group prior to immigration."*[63]

Ein weiteres Konzept – das des „Kultursynkretismus"[64] – wurde in der kürzlich abgeschlossenen Studie des Musiklebens der Stadtgemeinde Kiryat Ono (Satellitenstadt von Tel-Aviv) vorgelegt. Ein Team von Musikwissenschaftlern und Soziologen der Universität Bar-Ilan hatte in diesem Projekt kombinierte Forschungsmethoden angewandt (Beobachtung, Interviews, schriftliche Befragung, case studies) und schließlich gefolgert: *„Four main blocks of music were found to build up the musical culture of the respondents: T-music (traditional music), W-music (western type concert music), P-music (popular music) of a western type, and P-music of an Israeli type, the latter, perhaps, to be considered as the new Israeli T-music. Those musical strains act in different directions as far as their function in culture is concerned. W- and T-music are strongly affiliated with narrow groups characterized by age and origin; P-music, on the other hand, tends to be a more integrative force, especially as regards the aspect of origin. All the above-mentioned styles of music, however are more or less equally distributed amongst the respondents as regards the level of education (with some deviation for W-music) [...] W-musik and T-music emerged to be the most powerful centrifugal force in Israeli society, whereas P-music with its broader ethnic basis seems to be*

---

62 Bohlmann, Ph., „Central European Jews in Israel...," in: *Yearbook for Traditional Music* 16, 1984, S. 68.
63 Op. cit., S. 79.
64 Sieh Anm. 6.

of more centripetal nature. Thus, the findings indicate that the musical culture of Kiryat Ono does not represent a melting pot pattern; pluralistic concepts are not quite adequate to describe the findings either, since some types of music do represent integrative processes. Pluralistic aspects, along-side of integrative, contribute towards an emergence of new musical styles and patterns. This phenomena, formed of several authonomously acting components, which enrich and mould the entire structure, may be defined as cultural syncretism. "[65]

In Religionsgeschichte und Ethnologie wurde das Konzept des Synkretismus schon seit der zweiten Hälfte des 19. Jahrhunderts einbezogen. Interaktionsprozesse der Musikkulturen, die verschiedene Formen der Stildiffusion enthalten, wurden als synkretistisch seit der Mitte unseres Jahrhunderts bezeichnet. Die Kultur- und Musikforschung sieht in der Stufe der Homogenität der verschiedenen in Kontakt tretenden Kulturen bzw. Musiken das Zentralproblem des Synkretismus.[66] Synkretismus ist eigentlich eine Funktion des Verwandtschaftsgrades der einander gegenüberstehenden Kulturen,[67] und Bruno Nettl meint: „*syncretism results when the two musical Systems in a state of confrontation have compatible central traits.*"[68] Diese Konstellation kommt in Israel ganz klar zum Vorschein, indem die P-Musik als erster und aktivster Teil der Musikkultur sich synkretistischen Prozessen fügte: Die P-Musiken der verschiedenen *edot* haben verwandte zentrale Charakterzüge. Zudem ist die P-Musik in einem viel geringeren Maße ein Symbol zur kulturellen Selbstidentifikation als die T- und W-Musik, die als Teile der israelischen Musikkultur

---

65 Benski, T., Braun, J. u. Sharvit, U., „*Towards a Study of Israeli Urban Musical Culture: The Case of Kiryat Ono,*" sieh Ch. XV.
66 Herskovits, M. J., *Man and his Works* (New York, 1948); Waterman, R., „African Influence on the Music of Americas," in: Sol Tax, *Acculturation in the Americas* (Chicago 1952), S. 207–218; Karbusicky, V. „Syncretism ve folkloritice", in: *Ceskoslovenska etnografie* X/4, 1962, S. 421–422; Ringgren, Helmer; „The Problem of Syncretism," in: S. S. Hartmann (ed.): *Syncretism: Scripta instituti Donneriani abeonsis* (Stockholm,1969).
67 Merriam, A., „The use of music in the study of a problem of acculturation," in: *American Anthropologist*, 57:28 (1955); idem., *The Anthropology of Music* (USA, 1964), S. 314.
68 Nettl B., *The Study of Ethnomusicology* (Urbana, 1983), S. 354.

polar gelegen sind und einen viel längeren Weg zu einer synkretischen Musikkultur zurückzulegen haben.

Das „melting pot" Modell, und mit ihm das Modell der nationalen israelischen Musik wurde vor etwa 15 bis 20 Jahren zur Seite gelegte (nicht aufgegeben!): *„its radience has paled and its realization has been postponed for a few generations,"*[69] konnte sowohl die Sozial- wie auch die Musikwissenschaft behaupten. Das Pluralismus-Konzept erhielt nun eine dominante Stellung im Geistesleben Israels. Heute stehen wir nicht nur in der Musikwissenschaft vor einem Scheideweg: Wird Kultur und deren aktiver Teil, die Wissenschaft, in der Richtung eines legitimierten Staatspluralismus, der im Falle Israels zur kulturellen Zersplitterung führen kann, weiterrollen, oder kommen wir durch einen Kultursynkretismus, der dem Kulturpluralismus folgt, *mutatis mutandis*, dennoch zur Realisierung des „melting pot"-Ideals und mit ihm der nationalen israelischen Musik?

Anmerkungen

1) *Eda* (Plur. *edot*) – Gemeinde; ethnische Gemeinschaften der verschiedenen jüdischen Bevölkerungsgruppen, die sich während der Diaspora-Jahre auf der Basis regionaler Zusammengehörigkeit gebildet hatten. In einem beschränkten Sinn kann jede Lokalgruppe als *eda* bezeichnet werden. In einem breiteren Kontext ist das ganze Judentum in zwei Grund-*edot* geteilt: Aschkenazim (vom Wort „Aschkenaz" – Deutschland), die die deutsch-europäische Gruppe bilden, und Spharadim (von „Spharad" – Spanien), die die spanisch-orientalische Gruppe bilden. Jede dieser zwei Hauptgruppen zerfällt in größere Untergruppen; z. B. gehören zu den Spharadim die marokkanischen, jemenitischen oder persischen *edot*. In der modernen Musikwissenschaft werden die folgenden regionalen Grundstile der jüdischen Musik unterschieden: der jemenitische, aschkenazische, mittel-, ost-, nordafrikanische, jerusalem-spharadische, und der Nord-Mittelmeere-Stil. Der Terminus *„ingetherings of exils"* (das Zusammentreffen der exil-edot) wurde während der ersten Jahre des Staates Israel im Englischen geprägt. Er bezeichnet den Immigrations-Prozeß nach Israel der verschiedenen *edot.*

2) Zur ersten Generation der israelischen Musikwissenschaftler, die sich im Bereich der jüdischen Musik betätigten (Anfang dieses Jahrhunderts geboren), gehören: Edith Gerson-Kiwi (Schülerin von Wilibald Gurlitt und Heinrich Besseler), Herzl Schmueli (studierte in Zürich) und Peter Gradenwitz (studierte in Freiburg und Berlin). Die nächste Generation (in den zwanziger Jahren geboren) wurde auch in Europa, aber außerhalb

---

69 Lissak, *Social Mobility...*, S. 102.

Deutschlands ausgebildet: Israel Adler, Amnon Shiloah und Avner Bahat an der Sorbonne; Bathia Bayer und Judith Cohen in Zürich; Michal Smoira-Roll (Cohen) und Ruth Katz in Schweden; Dalia Cohen erhielt als erste ihr Ph.D. in Israel. Die dritte Generation entstammt größtenteils der amerikanischen Musikwissenschaftlichen Schule (Don Harran, Jehoash Hirshberg, Uri Sharvit, Eli Shleifer).

3) Beim Weltkongreß für Jüdische Musik (Jerusalem 1978) fanden die folgenden Panels statt: 1. Die jüdische Musik und der Kontakt der Hauptkulturen mit dem Judaismus; 2. Erhaltung und Notation der mündlichen Tradition; 3. Mündliche Tradition im Osten und Westen; 4. Kontakte der Kirchen- und Synagogenmusik; 5. Das hebräische und jiddische Lied: Text und Kontext; 6. Die Schule der jüdischen Kunstmusik in Rußland; 7. Jüdische Kunstmusik.

4) Bis zum 1. Mai 1983 wurden vom israelischen Radiosender „Kol Israel" (Die Stimme Israels) folgende Musik-Stunden pro Tag gesendet:

Programm A	13 Stunden täglich E- (ernste, klassische) Musik und T- (traditionelle) Musik
Programm B	5 Stunden täglich E-, P-(pop) und T-Musik
Programm C	19 Stunden täglich P-Musik
„Galei Zahal" (Sender der Armee)	18 Stunden täglich P-Musik und 4 Stunden wöchentlich E-Musik.
„Gal hamusika" (Musikstimme)	18 Stunden täglich E-Musik (neues Programm ab Mai 1983).

Das Programm A dupliziert zwei Stunden täglich die „Musikstimme;" die anderen Programme blieben unverändert.

5) Teilinformationen über Konzertbesuch, Radio- und TV-Hören, Vergnügungsveranstaltungen (ohne Aussonderung von Musik-Sendungen und -Veranstaltungen) sind folgenden Quellen zu entnehmen:

Statistical Abstract of Israe (Jerusalem: Central Bureau of Statistics, 1958 ff); *Leisure Pattems of Tel-Aviv-Yafo Inhabitants.* Special Survey No. 44 (Tel-Aviv-Yafo: Municipality, 1974); Rahat, R., *Free Time Leisure Patterns: Report on the Population of Haifa and Ashdod* (Jerusalem: Hebrew University, 1969; *Reading Habits and Leisure Activities of the Jewish Population*: 1979, Series of Education and Culture Statistics 101 (Jerusalem, 1979); *Tarbut Israel 1970* (Hebäisch, Culture of Israel 1970), Bde. A und B (Jerusalem: Hebräische Universität, 1972).

Informationen über Israels Musikinstitutionen sind zu finden in:

Bayer, B., *Institutions of Music Research in Israel*, in: *Zmora*, 1962, S. 12–15; *Directory of Music Institutions in Israel* (Jerusalem: The Israel Section of the International Music Council, 1977); *The Israel Government Year Book* (Jerusalem: The Information Centre of the Prime Minister's Office, 1950); *Tatzlil: Forum for Music Research and Bibliography* 1–20 (Haifa 1960–1980).

6) Der Begriff „Kultursynkretismus," auf die Musikkultur Israels bezogen, wurde von Professor Dr. Vladimir Karbusicky in dem Seminar „Musikleben einer Stadtgemeinde" (Bar-Ilan Universität, Musikwissenschaftliche Abteilung, Ramat-Gan, Israel, April 1981) geprägt.

XV. Towards a Study of Israeli Musical Culture: The Case of Kiryat Ono*

With Tova Bensky and Uri Sharvit

Introduction

This paper was a result of our dissatisfaction with the state of socio-musical sciences in Israel, both in conceptual thinking and practical research. This dissatisfaction has prompted the first attempt to conduct a research project combining ethnomusicology and sociology of music in Israel. This approach resulted in a research seminar given in 1981-1982 at the Department of Musicology, Bar-Ilan University. At the first stage of our project, it was necessary to survey the present state of socio-musical scholarship in Israel. Accordingly, this paper was divided into two parts: the first representing a survey of the chief trends in ethnomusicology and sociology of music, and the second dealing with selected aspects of the musical culture of Kiryat Ono (KO). The first part of the subject was discussed in the previous chapter XIV.

In the 1980s it seemed to be obvious that the state of research in the field of socio-musical sciences, i.e. ethnomusicology and sociology of music, dictates the necessity of empirical conceptual and methodological reasoning. An attempt in this direction was made by the Kiryat Ono project.

The present writers[1] have conducted a research project based on a conceptual and methodological approach new to musicological studies in

---

* Published in full in: *Asian Music*, XVII/2, 1986: 186-209 (with T. Bensky and U. Sharvit).
1 Each co-author contributed to this paper drawing from his own particular field, namely sociology (Dr. T. Benski), sociology of music (Prof. J. Braun), and ethnomusicology (Prof. U. Sharvit). See ADDENDUM: "Introduction" in *Studies in Socio-Musical Sciences*, ed. J. Braun and U. Sharvit (Ramat-Gan: Bar-Ilan University Press, 1998), proceedings of the *George Herzog International Forum for Socio-Musical*

Israel. The aim of the project was to examine the musical culture of an Israeli urban community. Because of its novelty for Israeli conditions and because of the limited resources and manpower involved, the entire undertaking was considered a pilot project. For the purposes of our study, Kiryat Ono, a small city near Tel-Aviv, was chosen. The project was implemented during the 1981-1982 academic year at a research seminar on the anthropology of music at the Musicology Department of Bar-Ilan University.

Our theoretical approach was shaped basically by the studies of Theodor W. Adorno, Vladimir Karbusicky, Alan P. Merriam and Bruno Nettl.[2] Already at the preliminary stage of the project, it became apparent that in conducting the type of research we had in mind, previous research experience was limited, and appropriate literature was scanty. Nevertheless, a number of projects conducted in Europe were methodologically valuable.[3]

In line with the above-mentioned studies, we view music as a sociocultural phenomenon, and as human behavior. As such, the study of music contributes in a number of ways to the reconstruction and understanding of culture and society (both in historical perspective and in contemporary perception). The general approach of the project was guided by four basic hypotheses:

Sciences (HISM-88), which was a follow-up of the conducted at the Bar-Ilan University seminar.

2 Adorno, Theodor W., *Introduction to Sociology of Music,* trans. by E.B. Ashton (New York: Seabury, 1976); Karbusicky, Vladimir, *Empirische Musiksoziologie* (Wiesbaden: Breitkopf und Hartel, 1975); Merriam, Alan P., *The Anthropology of Music* (Evanston: Northwestern University Press, 1964); Nettl, Bruno, ed., *Eight Urban Musical Cultures: Tradition and Change* (Urbana: University of Illinois Press, 1978).

3 Blaukopf, Kurt, "Strukturanalyse des Musiklebens," in: *Musik und Bildung,* 1: 11-15 (1971); Bontinck, Irmgard, ed., *New Patterns of Musical Behavior of the Young Generation in Industrial Societies* (Vienna: Universal Edition, 1974); Diesen, Rolf, *Musiklivet i ei Bygd,* Report II (Trondeheim: UNIT, 1973); Karbusicky, Vladimir, *Das Musikleben in einer Stadt: Berichte aus einem Seminar* (Hamburg: Musikwissenschaftliches Institut der Universitat Hamburg, 1982); Ling, Jan , "Musicological Projects in Gothenburg," *International Review of Aesthetics and Sociology of Music,* 2/1: 119-30 (1971); ibid., "Musiklivert i Skaraborg," in: *Svensk Tidsierift for Musikforskning,* 57/1: 69-75 (1975); Nylof, Gunnar, *Musikvanor Sverige* (Stockholm: Statens Ofentliga Utredningar, 1967).

1. In Israel, two musical processes co-exist: (a) preservation of musical tradition as part of a general effort to maintain socio-cultural identity; (b) interaction of different musical cultures as a constant force of cultural change.

2. As a result of the confrontation of the two above-mentioned processes, a new situation occurs in Israel, which depends on the correlation of those processes. We maintain that, as in other societies, the more dominant and established the socio-cultural elite of a certain group, the greater is the weight of process (a) and the greater individual involvement in diverse social activities, the greater the weight of process (b).

3. Musical culture in Israel has primarily an ethnic-cultural division and only secondarily socio-economic one. Consequently, in the effort to build a unified Israeli nationhood and culture, music acts mainly as a centrifugal force strongly opposing integration.

4. The family and communal and national institutions (home activity, synagogues, day-care facilities, schools, etc.) are nuclei of isolated musical culture, preventing cultural integration in Israel. The mass media, in contrast, contribute to integration.

At this stage, we have concentrated our efforts on the following questions pertinent to an Israeli urban community:

1. What are the basic forms and features of musical perception and musical activities in an Israeli urban community similar to Kiryat Ono?

2. What are the dominant musical preferences and tastes in this community?

3. Does the musical culture of Kiryat Ono act primarily as a centrifugal or centripetal force as far as age, sex, ethnic origin, education, and status are concerned?

Kiryat Ono: Methodology and Background Information

The study aimed at understanding the functions of music in a relatively small city and presenting a picture of its musical culture focused on three aspects. The first two aspects involved active and passive forms of musical communication, and the third was concerned with general and specific musical likes, dislikes, and preferences.

Kiryat Ono, a small city located at the outskirts of Tel-Aviv, had at the time of the study in 1981 a population of 22,000, which formed into some 7,000 households. Like many other small towns and cities in Israel, it was established by immigrants from Germany and Eastern Europe prior to the establishment of the State. During the 1950s, it absorbed a large number of immigrants from Asia and Africa. Gradually, it has developed an active musical life through a number of institutions, such as the Community Center (MATNAS), Conservatory of Music, and Scouts ("Tzofim"), and it has even developed its own youth orchestra. This made it an ideal place for studying musical life. Its easy accessibility by public transportation and physical proximity to Bar-Ilan University also had an important role in our choice.

Using probability systematic sampling procedures, a representative sample was drawn from the list of water meters attached to each flat, and interviews were conducted with 208 heads of households, alternately male and female. The interview schedules were structured and included a large number of open-ended questions. The fieldwork was carried out during the 1981 academic year. Data collected through this procedure were supplemented by a number of more specific projects focusing on Kiryat Ono's local institutions,[4] its schools, nursery schools, synagogues, the Community Center, the Youth Orchestra, and the Scouts. These projects gathered information through "key informants," observation methods, archival research, and field recording. A important source of information were official government and institutional publications.[5] Results presented in this paper rely heavily on information collected through interviews conducted within the main study and represent only a fraction of the findings.

The demographic characteristics of the respondents reveal the great attraction that the town has for persons with university education (33%), and with scientific, academic, and professional occupations (55%). This is probably due to its close proximity to Bar-Ilan University and Tel-Aviv, thus making it almost an integral part of the greater, metropolitan area. The town also has a considerable proportion of working-class population, which is reflected in our sample by 20% of the respondents in

---

4   See NOTE 1.
5   See NOTE 2.

the skilled and semi-skilled workers category. The remaining 25% can be classified as lower middle-class, constituting clerical, sales, and service occupational groups. As far as country of birth is concerned, 29% of the respondents were born in Israel, 47% in Europe/America and 24% in Asia/Africa.[6] Generally, the educational level of respondents born in Israel and E/A is higher than that of respondents born in A/A. Thus, some 43% of the Israeli-born and 37% of those born in E/A had some university education, compared with respondents who were born in A/A, most of whom (42%) had only elementary school education, with only 14% of them having some university education. A similar picture is revealed when looking at the occupational structure of the respondents according to country of birth, that is, a higher proportion of respondents born in Israel and E/A were found in occupations with high status (58% and 60% respectively) compared with the A/A group (41%), who are instead highly represented in the lower occupational group (34%). It is clear that most of the respondents are engaged in typically upper-middle-class occupations and that the occupational structure is highly correlated with ethnic origin. Therefore, whereas our KO sample does not reflect the general Israeli structure, it is in line with the ethnic stratification of occupations characteristic of Israeli society.

A. Passive Forms of Musical Communication: Aspects of Musical Perception

In the course of our research project, the following forms of musical perception were examined:

1. Perception of music by centralized mass-media (radio and television).

2. Perception of music by individual technical means (phonographs and tape recorders).

3. Perception of music at social events (concerts, meetings, synagogues).

---

6   See NOTE 3.

1) Radio is the medium providing the largest number of hours of music per day. Television, in contrast, is not considered in Israel as a major source of musical information.

During 1981-1982, the three channels of Kol-Israel and the army radio, Galei Zahal, broadcast a total of 54-56 hours of music every day. The daily distribution of broadcasting hours on these channels is as follows:

	No. of hours of Broadcasting	No. of hours of Broadcast Music	Type of Music[7]
Channel A	19	13	W-music and T-music, 2-3 hours weekly
Channel B	18	5.5	W-, P- and T-music
Channel C	19	19	P-music
galey zahal (army radio)	24	18	P-music and W-Music, four hours weekly

Table 1: Distribution of Broadcasting of Music on Israeli Radio (No. of hours daily per channel)

Because of the clear-cut stylistic division, the listening habits associated with the radio channels are very handy for music-reception research.

According to the *Statistical Abstract of the Central Bureau of Statistics*, 89.7% of the Israeli population listens to the radio.[8] Elihu Katz and Michael Gurevitch present a table which illustrates the claim that "it is education, not age, which is important" in the consumption of mass-media; origin is not included in this context.[9] This is true only when we consider radio listeners *en masse*. Even the *Statistical Abstract* shows that each channel's audience has different socio-cultural backgrounds. Among the listeners to Channel A, age, education, and ethnicity seem to be very important, with a slight tendency for ethnicity to be the most salient factor.[10] The listening patterns associated with Channel C show a dif-

---

7 See NOTE 4.
8 *Abstract* 1982: 722-723.
9 *The Seculariation of Leisure: Culture and Communication in Israel* (Cambridge, 1976), p. 148.
10 *Abstract* 1982: 722-723.

ferent distribution: here the impact of ethnicity and education seems to be less than that of age.

In Kiryat Ono, where the population has a very high level of education and socio-economic status, an impressive 26% from the sample listens to Channel A. [11]

	Age			Origin			Education[12]		
	20-30	31-50	51+	I	E/A	A/A	ES	HS	THE U
Program A	8	23	43	15	39	14	24	20	26 33
Program B	25	35	45	36	32	42	35	38	32 35
Program C	58	39	32	54	32	45	39	42	53 39
galai zahal	65	55	43	70	41	57	50	59	68 45

Table 2: Listen to Radio Every Day (in %)

As Table 2 shows, those who listen every day to Channel A seem to be mostly 51 years of age or older and of E/A origin, whereas the listeners to Channel C (to select the two channels most opposed in musical style) are mostly 30 years old and younger, and of A/A or I origin. In both cases, the impact of education is negligible and that of sex irrelevant. We take this to mean that W-music tends to be centrifugal as far as age and ethnicity are concerned, while P-music has more centripetal tendencies. Representing youth culture, P-music is affected by age more than by any other factor.

As to the selection of channels (or types of music), it is noticeable that polarized tendencies are clearly pronounced among the younger age groups and I and A/A ethnic categories, whereas the listeners who are 51 years of age or older, from E/A origin and with university education are more tolerant of different types of music. The centrifugal forces do not operate uniformly in all demographic groups.

Education does not seem to have much importance in the selection of music. Age and origin, in contrast, are decisive for both the amount of listening and the selection. This could mean that age and origin are of great importance in developing a pluralistic approach to music, and that

---

11 See NOTE 5.
12 See NOTE 6.

education is not a panacea for overcoming the centrifugal powers of music. The difference in listening habits between those with technical higher education and those with university education indicate that the type of education rather than its level could be decisive.

Table 2 also shows that the integrating, or centripetal power of P-music is remarkable for Israel's specific conditions, while W-music is more centrifugal. Regarding listening habits to *galei zahal*, which broadcasts the same type of P-music as Channel C, we notice tendencies similar to Channel C for all the three basic factors (age, origin and education). The similar picture for the two channels broadcasting the same type of music (P-music) confirms the reliability of our findings.

It should be noted here that the two different patterns of reception for W- and P-music are probably a result of the fact that P-music is more easily received and to a great extent ethnically colored in Israel. This makes it more appealing to the different ethnic groups in the country. The listening habits spawned by P-music should certainly be a subject of a separate study in the future.

2) The number of people owning a phonograph or tape recorder (p/r) is much higher among our respondents than the proportion reported for the country in general: 84% of our sample as compared to 51% of the total Israeli population.[13] This fact once more reflects the high socio-economic level of KO respondents. More than half of those possessing p/r own almost 50 records or tapes, and the others own more than 50.

Table 3 indicates that nearly all the younger people have p/r, and that the group among which ownership is most pronounced is formed of those born in Israel. Educational level could be an indication of p/r ownership. The most interesting question, is, however, who is making use of the p/r equipment, and with what frequency? At this stage, we have to modify our first impression. In the A/A category, which has the smallest percentage of p/r owners, the children are the main users, while in other ethnic categories, the p/r are used by the entire family. This could indicate a tendency towards leveling the differences in ownership in the future. It is of interest that in the A/A group, the frequency of p/r use is also much higher: 36.7% of this group listens to music in this way every day, compared to only 20.4% of the E/A group. We should also note that as far as

---

13 Katz/Gurevitch, op. Cit., p. 149.

age groups are concerned, p/r use decreases together with p/r ownership, while a rise in educational level is accompanied by increasing ownership and decreasing use. We must conclude that education and origin do not affect p/r ownership and use in the same way. While p/r ownership represents for those with greater education more a status symbol than the need for listening, for the A/A group we find the opposite, that is, representation of the need for listening. P/r ownership is probably not a direct consequence of education, but more a result of other factors.

	Age			Origin			Education		
	20-30	31-50	51+	I	E/A	A/A	ES	HS	THE U
p/r	96	89	66	95	81	73	65	85	95 92
use every day	40	35	20	34	20	37	24	32	18 25

Table 3: Phonograph and Tape Recorder Ownership and Users (in %)

We should also keep in mind that p/r ownership or use is of an entirely different socio-musical nature from radio listening. Although both are considered in-doors cultural consumption, the radio, to a great extent, is an instrument of cultural imposition, while phonographs and tape recorders are instruments of self-satisfaction, individual choice, or self-fulfillment of cultural needs. P/r ownership and particularly use are signs of striving for the satisfaction of cultural preferences. In this way, p/r channel the centrifugal message of music to a much greater extent than does radio. Referring to our Table 3, we may claim that the university-educated and E/A groups with their high percentage of p/r ownership, but low percentage of use, are less exposed to voluntary centrifugal forces of music than, for example, the A/A group, or the younger group, with very active use and low percentage of ownership.

3) Attendance at musical events is a highly complex matter, and our findings should be considered as preliminary observations. The definition of the term musical event itself is quite difficult because of its mixed nature. A "musical event" is more than just a concert, involving any social activity with music playing a dominant part. The "symphony concert" category, mentioned in the *Statistical Abstract*, in contrast, distinguishes only a small part of concert life, and "light entertainment," frequently referred to in sociological research, is not necessarily a musical event at all.

A characteristic example of the difficulty of definition could be synagogue attendance, which is usually not considered a musical event or leisure. Our study has shown (see below) that the synagogue, alongside its more obvious functions, is also a musical institution. The social function of many institutions should be re-examined with their musical activity in mind (e.g., the cafe, hotel lobby, play room, supermarket, or street gangs). Accordingly, it is possible to deal with the definition of musical events and related activities. Furthermore, neither sociological nor musicological research in Israel has ever considered the musical or stylistic contents of musical events (apart from the gross division into "concerts" and "light entertainment").

The *Statistical Abstract* presents data for 1979, which indicate that symphony concerts were visited by 5.6% of the total population and light entertainment by 13.4%.[14] Katz presents different statistics: concerts were visited by 9% of the population and light entertainment by 27%.[15] If the difference in concert attendance is due to the difference in categorization ("concert" versus "symphony concert"), the remarkable discrepancy in light entertainment attendance is not clear (the *Abstract* 1976 is very close to the time of Katz's/Gurevith's research). In Tel-Aviv-Yafo, 21% of the population had visited a concert during the past six months, and nearly half of the residents had attended some form of light entertainment.[16] The pattern in Kiryat Ono again shows a strong deviation from overall Israeli patterns and more active attendance of musical events than in Tel-Aviv-Yafo. During the six months prior to field work, 54% of our sample respondents had visited musical events, 29% had attended such events in Kiryat Ono, and 41% elsewhere.

	Age			Origin			Education		
	20-30	31-50	51+	I	E/A	A/A	ES	HS	THE U
Overall attend.	65	57	43	69	56	33	37	58	32	68
W-music	26	52	82	50	56	44	35	56	50	55
P-music	58	26	4	33	27	25	18	33	17	32
T-music	16	22	14	16	16	32	48	12	34	14

Table 4: *Attendance of Musical Events (in %)*

14 *Abstract* 1979: 60.
15 Katz/Gurevitch, op. Cit., p. 112.
16 *Leisure Patterns,* op. Cit., pp. 50-54 and 61-68.

Table 4 shows that the tendency to attend musical events is clearly decreasing with age. This contrasts with trends reported for Tel-Aviv-Yafo and for the country in general.[17] The most likely to attend musical events are the Israelis, and the most reluctant the A/A group. This corroborates other findings, the only difference being the narrow gap between the A/A group and E/A group for KO residents. Attendance increases with the level of education, showing a tendency that also coincides with general information. The generally higher percentage of attendance in KO can be explained by the higher socio-economic and educational standards in the city. Differences based on age, however, are not easy to explain: they may be a result of the location of Kiryat Ono, or of changes that have occurred since the earlier studies (both the Katz/Gurevitch project and the Tel-Aviv-Yafo report are more than ten years old).

The distribution of the public that attends musical events according to types of events is most surprising. Among those who attend musical events, 52% attend events featuring W-music, 29% featuring P-music, and 18% T-music and other types of events. This rare preference for W-music is probably the result of Kiryat Ono's demographic nature. Even so, it seems that the preference for W-music, as opposed to P-music, is much more pronounced than previously estimated in this country. This interest in W-music could not be a result of school education, as was shown by the seminar at Bar-Ilan University, which examined two elementary school classes (see NOTE 1). The children of the third and fourth grade attended mainly popular-music events and almost never Western art music, in spite of the fact that the curriculum of the music classes did include such music.

Analyses of musical style preferences by the three basic demographic parameters show more or less the expected picture. All regular tendencies are present: W-music attendance is increasing with age and education, but less so for the A/A group than for I and E/A. P-music attendance shows tendencies opposite of those so clearly presented for W-music regarding age (a decrease in a most drastic way from 58% for the younger group to 40% for the over-50 age group), but keeps nearly the same patterns regarding education. For the ethnic groups, the differences are almost completely leveled. For T-music, age is of no importance. Within

---

17 Katz/Gurevitch, op. Cit., pp. 112-113; *Leisure Patterns,* op. Cit., p. 53.

the A/A group, however, twice as many respondents attend these events compared with the other ethnic groups, and people with elementary-school education attend those events to a much greater extent than respondents with university education. We noted previously the interesting pattern of respondents with technical education being closest to those with elementary-school education.

The clearly centrifugal tendencies of W- and P-music relative to age and of T-music relative to origin and education appear also in the table of attendance of musical events. In contrast, the centripetal tendencies are not very clearly manifested. The reason for this could be rooted in the complex socio-musical nature of the "going-out-to-a-musical-event" phenomenon itself: the attendance at a musical event, for example a concert, is only partly an artistic experience and frequently a matter primarily of socialization.[18]

With regard to traditional music, one type of attendance at musical events should be singled out here: the synagogue visit. One of the Bar-Ilan projects (see NOTE 1) examined the musical life at thirty synagogues in Kiryat Ono (13 Ashkenazi, 7 Yemenite, and 10 Sephardic). The form of musical life at the synagogue may be defined as both passive and active. From the musical point-of-view, perception is as important as participating in singing and praying. Our study has shown that nearly half of the respondents prefer a synagogue with singing (community, *hazan*, or choir) and that nearly 20% have chosen their synagogue for the quality of the musical performance. This clearly indicates the importance of the synagogue as a part of musical life and for shaping musical culture. The musical atmosphere at all synagogues is strictly ethnic. All the key informants (the synagogue *gabai*, or monitor) were guarding their own ethnic prayer melodies (*nusach*) over-zealously and denying any value to other ethnic melodies. As one Sephardic *gabai* has put it: "I can pray only in the synagogue of my *eda* (ethnic group); definitely not in an Ashkenazi place – I do not understand their language (accent), and I do not enjoy their tunes (prayer chants)." In this way, the synagogue may be seen as the most powerful centrifugal force in the context of the entire Israeli musical culture.

---

18 Adorno, *Introduction*..., op. Cit., p. 121-122).

The rigid musical world of the synagogue, with its well-established socio-cultural elite, is reflected also in other forms of musical perception: the high preference for T-music events vis-a-vis a low level of attendance, in general; the high frequency of phonograph and tape recorder use by a low percentage of ownership; and a polarized attitude toward radio listening. These are all links in one chain: the manifestation of the centrifugal power of different types of T-music.

B. Active Forms of Musical Communication: Aspects of Musical Performance

Two types of musical activities were examined:
1. Ownership and practice of instruments;
2. Singing activities.

Regarding the first type, we have found that ownership encompasses 47% of our respondents. This finding challenges that of Katz and Gurevitch, who found that only every fourth Israeli possesses a musical instrument.[19] Several possibilities might explain this difference. We may say the socio-economic conditions of Kiryat Ono are better than is generally the case in Israel. Another explanation is that this relatively high figure reflects the rapid increase in the general Israeli standard of living that has occurred since Katz's/Gurevitch's study. In any case, almost one-half of the Kiryat Ono population perceives musical instruments as part of its culture. An examination of this phenomenon indicates that instrument ownership is the highest among the university-educated (64%) and lowest among those with only elementary education (30%). Also, we find that instrument ownership is very high among the Israeli-born (60%) and lowest among the A/A group (34%), with the E/A group occupying an intermediate position (44%). This could be a result of correlation between educational level and ethnic origin. In any case, it seems that the high percentage of musical-instrument ownership among the respondents and, especially, among the Israeli-born shows that musical instruments are an integral part of Israeli culture and perhaps a manifestation of this culture.

---

19 Katz and Gurevitch, *The Secularization...*, op. Cit., p. 191.

We must take into consideration that musical instruments are not the main vehicle through which T-music is expressed by people of A/A origin. It is, rather, the vocal music that is dominant in the Jewish Oriental musical culture. Indeed, all the instruments owned by our respondents are most frequently associated with P-music or W-music, and no traditional ethnic instruments were found.[20] We conclude, therefore, that the extent to which musical instruments have become part of Israeli culture is highest among the Israeli-born and lowest among those of A/A origin. Nevertheless, the fact that 34% of the A/A group owns instruments associated with popular and Western art music can be interpreted as the result of an acculturation process in modern Israel.

	I	E/A	A/A
Instruments common to Western art music	30%	42%	6%
Instruments common to popular and traditional music	70%	50%	94%

Table 5: *Percentages of Instrument Owned by Respondents According to Origin*

Table 5 supports this point by showing two features of the process: (a) respondents of A/A origin seem to be the most likely to use P-music as a means of expressing ethnicity, and (b) P-music tends to be a more integrative force than W-music.

The highest percentage of active performance is found in the I-group (21%) and among the younger respondents (21%) 20-30 years old, regardless of sex differences. It should be pointed out that there is a large gap separating instrument ownership and practice, with ownership being much more widespread than practice. We can only speculate about the reasons for this discrepancy. However, it is evident that further research is needed to elucidate such a discrepancy.

Singing activities, another type of musical practice examined in KO, were found to be ethnically stratified with the highest participation of respondents from A/A background. If we, for example, focus on *zemirot*, the traditional songs performed at home on the Sabbath, the highest percentage of the *zemirot* practitioners, 49%, was found among those of A/A

---

20 See NOTE 7.

background, compared with 31% among the I-group, and only 20% among the E/A group.

The specific studies that we conducted in Kiryat Ono institutions pinpoint the ethnic stratification resulting from musical participation. We found that only 4% of the participants in the Youth Orchestra, which performs W-music, were of A/A origin, whereas the rest of the participants represented the E/A group. It should not be ignored, however, that the inner structure of music performed by this orchestra shows clear signs of neglecting Western features: Western symphonic music is arranged to emphasize interchange of orchestral colors and dynamics, while simplifying aspects of harmony and texture. In contrast, at the MATNAS, the Municipal Community Center, we found the following three types of musical activity: a chorus, a jazz group, and a Yemenite song and dance group. In the first two groups, performing W-music, 98% of the participants came from E/A background, and only 2% from the A/A category. The third group, purely Oriental in style, consisted of youngsters of Yemenite origin only. In the Scouts, where only about 10% of the youngsters were of A/A origin, P-music was one of the most significant features in diverse social activities.

These findings show that participation in musical activities is much more ethnically polarized than any type of passive musical communication. Musical performance is without a doubt the ultimate expression of intrinsic culture. Therefore, our findings have far-reaching consequences indicating that passive musical communication on its own is an insufficient measure of underlying cultural processes.

C. Attitudes and Musical Preferences

Music plays an important role in the lives of the Kiryat Ono respondents. When questioned, 91% of the respondents thought that music was at least of some importance in their live, and 57% thought that it was either important or very important. Only 9% thought that it was of very little or of no importance in their lives. It is of interest, that almost identical figures are reported by a research in a quite different part of the world, and different social structure – in he USSR.[21] Indeed, when confronted with seven alternative ways of passing a pleasant evening, 23% preferred to engage in some musical activity. These respondents were very clearly stratified by educational level, with respondents who had at least some high school education preferring a musical pastime and placing a higher value on music than respondents of lower educational level. Furthermore, as Table 6 shows, a tendency towards cleavages according to age and country of birth can also be observed. Thus, it seems that music plays a somewhat more important role in the lives of respondents 50 years of age or younger and among those born in Europe, America, or Israel, as compared with respondents over 50 years of age and those of African or Asian origin.

	Age All	20-30	31-50	51+	Origin I E/A	A/A		Education ES	HS	THE	U
music important or very important	57	58	64	46	59	62	45	35	65	47	67
preferred musical pastime	23	19	23	26	18	28	20	4	32	26	24

Table 6: Characteristics of preferences by respondents: "music important role in live" contra "music pastime in the evening" (%)

Having ascertained the high value placed on music, we proceeded to examine the preferences expressed by the Kiryat Ono respondents for specific types of music.[22] In order to identify the underlying regularities in the responses, we performed Principal Component Factor Analysis.[23] This analysis resulted in five orthogonal (independent) factors accounting for 82% of the variance in the responses. The first factor, accounting for 38% of the variance, related to W-music and included twelve composers and genres of classical music, such as Brahms, Bach, and chamber music. The second factor, accounting for a further 23% of the variance, was Western P-music, such as the Beatles and Bob Dylan. The third factor,

---

21 Tcukerman, V.S., *Muzika i slushatel': opit soziologitcheskovo issledovania* (in Russian, Music and the listener an empirical study in Sociology, Moscow: Muzika, 1972), p. 44.
22 See NOTE 8.
23 See NOTE 9.

accounting for an additional 10% of the variance, was Israeli P-music representing the mainstream of institutionalized Israeli music. This factor may indicate a process of crystallization of a certain type of traditional music. The first three factors represent the preferred type of music among the KO respondents, accounting together for 71% of the variations in musical likes and dislikes.[24] The two remaining factors seem to be of marginal importance in comparison with the first three (one of these two additional factors represents a specific type of controversial Israeli P-music, and the other represents less known W-music. Taken together, they add a further 10% to the 71% variation already explained by the first three factors).

The Principal Component Factor Analysis performed by the project sociologist Dr. Bensky indicates that music as a cultural phenomenon can act as both a centrifugal and centripetal force, depending on the type of music and differentiating criteria. Thus, Western art music is clearly a centrifugal force in society, differentiating the respondents along ethnic, educational, and age lines. Western and Israeli popular music can act in both directions, depending on the relative criteria. Western P-music exerts a centrifugal force dividing respondents along age lines, but centripetal as far as ethnic origin and educational levels are concerned. In contrast, Israeli P-music is centrifugal in dividing the respondents along lines of age and, to a much lesser degree, by country of origin, and centripetal as far as education is concerned. Let us recall that liturgical T-music was singled out as the most centrifugal force on the Israeli musical scene. Another point to note here is that education, contrary to expectations suggested by former studies, does not play an important integrative role.

Finally, we refer briefly to a few recent developments on the Israeli musical scene. During the past few years, a new musical genre, drawing chiefly on Westernized oriental styles of music, has developed in Israel. This type of music represents a new development in the sense that it departs from mainstream Israeli music and was not communicated through the main institutionalized channels of communication. Rather, it developed almost unnoticed, for it was recorded on cassettes and sold in special stands in the small outdoor market that has formed around the central

---

24 See NOTE 10.

bus station in Tel-Aviv. Only during the last three years has this type of music reached some visibility in the national media, acquiring the title "cassette music" and designating its performers as "cassette singers." This music can be regarded as a new response to Israeli popular music from Israeli-born with A/A background (and perhaps even a response to Western art music).[25] Being unaware of these developments in 1980 when the interview schedule was constructed, we suggest that the absence of reference to this type of music in the questionnaire can account for our failure to pinpoint the type of music preferred most by respondents with Asian or African background. However, some indications to the development of this type of music have been detected in our factor analysis. More specifically, the fourth factor (mentioned above, consisting of controversial Israeli popular music) did include the more institutionalized end of this evolving musical genre. Furthermore, stepwise multiple regression analysis of this factor showed that predisposition for this type of music is more evident among respondents who were young, first- and second-generation individuals from Asian or African origin, with less than high school educational level. This fourth factor contributed a further 6% to the 71% of the variance in the musical disposition accounted for by W-music and Western and Israeli P-music. We can only speculate whether this factor would have appeared stronger if other, relatively unknown "cassette singers" (in 1980), were included in our questionnaire. At present, however, given the data that we gathered, the strongest statement that we can make about the respondents with Asian and African background refers to the type of music for which they have expressed a particular dislike. However, that in itself may be suggestive, since they have expressed a particular dislike for a highly upper-middle-class, Western type of music, and this dislike showed strong intergenerational continuities, indicating the highly centrifugal direction of W-music.

---

25 This possibility was mentioned by Professor of Sociology Moshe Lissak in a seminar lecture held at Bar-Ilan University in 1984.

Conclusions

This survey on the state of research in ethnomusicology and sociology of music in Israel, as well as the pilot project on the musical culture of Kiryat Ono conducted at Bar-Ilan University, suggests the following methodological points:

a) The musical culture of Israel, in general, and of any locality, in particular, should be approached on an interdisciplinary basis.

b) Combining ethnological, sociological, and musicological methods, research should rely more heavily on empirical and statistical methods, considering musical communication concurrently and investigating questions of social taste (preferences, likes, and dislikes).

c) New research fields should be included for both style analysis and functional analysis, while terminology and definitions of musical institutions, events, and styles of music should be reconsidered, modified, and specified with regard to the Israeli scene.

The study of Kiryat Ono shows that this urban community presents a multi-directional musical culture. Music was found to be an important component of the activities of municipal and other social institutions. The respondents engaged in both passive and active musical communication to a greater extent than the general Israeli population. Patterns common to Israeli musical culture as a whole were exposed, for example, preferences for Western art music by older people and by those of European and American origin. Other patterns unique to Kiryat Ono have been located as well, for example, a very high percentage of musical-instrument and equipment ownership, or unusually high preferences for Western art music. Patterns of passive and active musical life range from the most polarized orthogonal (Western art and traditional music) to more homogenous (popular music). This was clearly manifested in preferences, likes, and dislikes, but even more so in active aspects of musical behavior. The tendency of polarization is clearly pronounced in the nature of all the musical institutions, which form cultural-demographic cleavages.

Certain respondents have developed a pluralistic approach to music, showing highly tolerant patterns of musical behavior. These are respondents above 51 years of age or older, those of European or American origin, and the university-educated. Other categories, such as younger people, those of African or Asian origin, and the less-educated, reveal partisan, highly biased patterns, with an explicit concentration on certain musical styles.

Four main blocks of music were found to constitute the musical culture of the respondents: traditional music, Western art music, popular music from the West, and popular music from Israel, the last perhaps to be considered as the new Israeli traditional music. These musical strains exert different tendencies as far as their function in society and culture is concerned. Western art and traditional music are strongly affiliated with narrow groups characterized by age and origin; popular music, in contrast, tends to be a more integrative force *vis-a-vis* origin. All the styles of music discussed here, however, are more or less equally distributed among the respondents relative to education (with some deviations for Western art music). Any type of musical communication exerts centrifugal or centripetal social significance depending on the type of music channeled. This confirms that centrifugal and centripetal tendencies are dependent on type of music and socio-demographic characteristics. Western art and pre-Israeli traditional music emerged with the most powerful centrifugal forces in Israeli society, whereas popular music with its broader ethnic basis seems to be more centripetal in tendency.

Thus, it seems quite clear that the musical culture of Kiryat Ono does not represent a "melting pot" music culture. Cultural pluralism, nevertheless, also does not adequately describe our findings, since some types of music represent integrative processes. In the Israeli context the concept of acculturation has been treated in a one-sided fashion; while acculturation of Oriental communities to Western culture has been acknowledged, acculturation has not characterized the Western *edot* ("ethnic groups"). Sammy Smooha states clearly: "the Orientals alone bear the cost of cultural assimilation by giving up their traditions."[26] Fearing "acculturation to Western standards" some scholars have built up the concept of pluralism to a kind of general policy, and "pluralism in music on the national level" is advocated.[27] This interpretation prefers penetration of the mainstream of Israeli music by Jewish Oriental ethnic groups to

---

26 *Israel: Pluralism and Conflict* (London, 1978), p. 217.
27 Shiloah, Amnon and Cohen, Erik, "The Dynamics of Change in Jewish Oriental Music in Israel," in: *Ethnomusicology* 27/2: 248 (1983).

the idea of "amalgamation of different ethnic traditions into an overall 'national musical style'" (ibid.).

Our findings seem to describe processes whereby pluralistic aspects, alongside integrative tendencies, contribute towards an emergence of new musical styles and patterns of musical behavior. Such new, holistic phenomena, consisting of several autonomously acting components enrich the entire structure, and may be defined as "cultural syncretism," as suggested by Vladimir Karbusicky at the symposium "Music in Israeli Society" (Bar-Ilan University, Ramat Gan, April 1981).

Since the second half of the nineteenth century, the concept of syncretism was employed to define cultural processes in the ancient world, in the history of religion, and ethnological studies.[28] Interaction of several musical cultures, which showed diffusion of styles, was designated as syncretic in the middle of the present century.[29] Students of culture and music define the degree of relationship between different cultures or musics as the main problem of syncretic processes.[30] We may claim that syncretism is, in fact, a function of the degree of approximation for the cultures in contact. This is close to Alan Merriam's understanding of syncretism[31] and Bruno Nettl quite recently wrote that "syncretism results when two musical systems in confrontation have compatible central traits."[32] It is self-evident that the application of the concept of syncretism in its Israeli context needs further modification and specifications. We consider our interpretation of the case of Kiryat Ono as a first step towards this approach, where a Merriam-Nettl type of syncretism is quite clearly apparent: Israeli P-music, which shows the most common central traits for different *edot* and least symbolizes cultural-ethnic self-identification, is the first and most dynamic to enter syncretic processes;

---

28 Karbusicky, Vl., "Syncretism ve folkloritice," in: Ceskoslavenska etnografie 10/4:421-422 (1962).
29 Herskovits, Melville, *Man and his Work* (New York, 1948), p. 553.
30 Riggren, H., "The Problem of Syncretism," in: Sven S. Hartman, ed., *Syncretism: Scripta instituti Donneriani abeonsis* (Stockholm, 1969), p. 9; Waterman, R., "African Influence on the Music of the Americas," in Sol Tax, ed., *Acculturation in the Americas*, 2: 207-18 (Chicago, 1952), p 207.
31 Merriam, Alan P., "The use of music in the study of a problem of Acculturation," in: *American Anthropologist* 57:28 (1955); idem., *The Anthropology...*, op. Cit., p. 314.
32 Nettl, Bruno, *The Study of Ethnomusicology*, (Urbana, 1983), p. 354.

T-music and W-music, on the other hand, show much more polarity, are identified with a strong socio-ethnic elite, and do not yet exhibit sizable syncretic features.

Given the pioneering nature of the present study, we hope that the insights generated by this project will stimulate future researchers to apply the concept of syncretism to the study of Israel's musical culture; we feel much is to be gained by the elucidation of syncretic processes in this culture.

Notes

1. The Research Seminar, "Anthropology of Music: The Musical Life of an Israeli Urban Community," was conducted by Joachim Braun and Uri Sharvit during the academic year 1981/82. The participants of the seminar collected 208 interviews with Kiryat Ono residents and presented the following papers on Kiryat Ono institutions:
   a) "The Music of the 'Tzofim' (scouts)" (Lea Biber);
   b) "Music at the Kiryat Ono 'MATNAS' (community centre)" (Tami Linkenberg);
   c) "Music Lessons at the Nir Elementary School" (Rachel Kolender);
   d) "The Kiryat Ono Youth Orchestra" (Lydia Oshri);
   e) "Music Lessons at the Shilo Elementary School" (Adina Portovitch);
   f) "Music at the Kiryat Ono Synagogues" (Yael Shai).

This project was sponsored by the Bar-Ilan University Research Authorities and the National Academy for Sciences. Assistance was provided by Lea Lapidot of the KO Local Municipality, Y. Dostis and N. Ronen of the Department of Sociology at Bar-Ilan University, and Y. Shavit and V. Kraus of Haifa University. We are indebted to all the individuals and institutions who have generously assisted us in this project, and first of all, to all the Kiryat Ono residents who kindly agreed to answer our questionnaires.

2. The annual government *Statistical Abstract* of Israel (Jerusalem, Central Bureau of Statistics) provides some tables on radio listening, television viewers' habits, reading, and outdoor entertainment in Chapter XXVI, "Culture and Entertainment" (*Abstract*, 1958-). The information is scanty and appears once in several years. It is presented according to sex, age, education, and origin. The *Abstract* 1981, for example, presents data on listening to Channel "a*lef*" of Israel's radio, "The Voice of Israel," or *Abstract* 1982 lists data on symphony concert attendance. *Reading Habits of Leisure activities of the Jewish population* (Jerusalem: Central Bureau of Statistics, 1979 and 1981) lists attendance of symphony concerts and light entertainment performances, including music. Similar information is provided by. *The Israel Government Year Book* (Jerusalem: Information Center of the Prime Minster's Office) regularly includes a chapter on the Ministry of Education and Culture, its structure, and some of its activities. The *Directory of Music Institutions in Israel* (Jerusalem: The Israel Section of the International Music Council,

1977) provides information on musical institutions, and the journal *Tatzlil* includes a section "Musical Institutions and Events in Israel." *Tarbut Israel* (in Hebrew, Culture of Israel), vol. A and B (Jerusalem: The Communication Institute of the Hebrew University of Jerusalem, 1972), provides information on radio listening, TV viewing, and concert and entertainment attendance according to basic demographic parameters. The same type of information is provided by *Leisure Patterns of Tel Aviv-Yaffo Inhabitants: Special Survey No. 44*, 1974, and Rivka Rahat, *Free time leisure patterns: Report on the population of Haifa and Ashdod* (Jerusalem, 1969).

3. The following divisions from different areas of origin were accepted:

a) born in Israel (I);

b) people of Euro-American extraction (E/A); and

c) born in any country of North Africa or Asia (A/A).

4. This distribution of broadcasting hours was in effect until May 1, 1983, when a new channel, "Voice of Music" was introduced. Since this time the hour distribution has changed, with the new channel broadcasting W-music eighteen hours per day and Channel A only duplicating the "Voice of Music" two to three hours daily. The other channels did not change their broadcasting distribution.

For working purposes, the following main types of music were accepted (the authors were fully aware of the problems involved in any kind music style divisions):

a) Western style "concert hall" music (W-music, in Germany referred to as E-Musik/ernste Musik; in the U.S.A., frequently designated as serious music, in Israel, as classical music);

b) Every type of traditional music, both liturgical and ethnic/folk music (T-music): and;

c) All types of popular music, including dance music, hits, commercial music, jazz, ethnic pop (P-music, referred to also as "light music," or "Unterhaltungsmusik" [in German U-Musik]).

5. In our questionnaire, the musical aspects of listening were specified (Question 38: "With what frequency do you listen to musical programs on the radio?") This could have some impact on the results vis-a-vis the respondents interested only in listening to the radio in general.

6. The following division was accepted for different levels and types of education:

a) no education, or 1-8 years of elementary school (ES);

b) any type of education from 9-12 years, including high school (HS);

c) any type of higher education in a commercial or technical area (THE);

d) university education (U).

7. For our purposes, the following types of instruments were defined:

a) traditional folk instruments such as the *qanun*, *'ud*, or *nay* (T-instruments);

b) instruments of the classical symphonic orchestra, such as the violin, piano, or clarinet (W-instruments), and

c) popular instruments mainly played with "pop" music and Israeli folk music, such as the guitar, electro-guitar, electro-organ, recorder, and accordion.

8. The question of musical likes, dislikes and preferences for specific types of music was dealt with by a large battery of questions. Respondents were asked to name the three songs or musical works that they particularly liked, three types of musical programs that they preferred to listen to on the radio, and three types of musical events that they would have liked to have in Kiryat Ono. Finally, respondents were given a list of 44 composers, performers, and musical genres, and were asked to state whether they liked or disliked each item on a six-point scale.

9. Factor analysis was performed only on the list of 44 composers, performers, and musical genres for two main reasons. First, this was the most extensive systematic data that we had, and secondly, since all these questions had the same layout, wording, and categories, the performance of factor analysis on these questions posed no special methodological problems. For explanations of Factor Analysis, see H. Nie et al., SPSS- Statistical Package for the Social Sciences, 2nd ed (New York, 1975).

10. The resulting factors show almost identical patterning when compared to data collected through other questions of likes/dislikes and musical preferences. As shown in the table below, W- and P-music were preferred more often and liked the best.

The only deviations found were in relation to ethnic music and Israeli songs. These are probably due to the fact that only 136 respondents (or 65%) expressed particular preferences and, therefore, results presented in the table depict the patterning of musical preferences among two thirds of the respondents, whereas the factors were derived from questions answered by all the respondents and are therefore more representative.

Types of Music, Radio Programs and Musical Events
Most Liked/Preferred by the KO Respondents (in %)

Type of Music	N=136*	N=132*	N=123*
W-music	34	38	37
P-music of Western type	29	37	45
Ethnic Music	26	17	13
Israeli songs	11	8	6
Total	100	100	100

* These represent the number of respondents who have expressed a musical preference on each question.

Addendum

Introduction

In: *Studies in Socio-Musical Sciences*, ed. Joachim Braun and Uri Sharvit (Ramat-Gan: Bar-Ilan University Press, 1998), pp. 9-11.

The 1960s and early 70s witnessed the end of separation, segregation, and narrow specialization that had, hitherto, been characteristic of musicology. This development became manifest not only in scholarly work *per se*, but also in the institutionalization of the discipline. While it is true that repercussions of the separatist era could still be heard in 1982 at the IMS Congress in Strasbourg, and even at the ICTM Conference in Schladming as late as 1989, it was clear that both world centers of musicological thought were hastily erasing the border lines which divided them, and were striving for a syncretized theory and methodology. We now seem to have reached the apogee of this splendid inter- and multidisciplinary period, and are perhaps approaching a waning of this development.

In 1987-88, when musicological symbiosis was at its peak, the prevailing conditions and constellations of interest in the Bar-Ilan Department of Musicology (faculty members were simultaneously approaching the field of musicology from historical, systematic, ethnological, and sociological points of view), as well as the conclusion of combined interdisciplinary research projects[1] promoted the idea of a holistic approach to musicology. It was decided to convene a scholarly forum where, at the same time that the various facets of musicology were being represented, methods could be sought to merge them from such extended fields as historical musicology and ethnomusicology to such specialized areas as psychology of music and music therapy into one overall discipline. Under those conditions musical phenomena could be reviewed from all possible angles. In other words, the Forum's task was to contribute to the idea of a holistic approach — an overall, comprehensive research theory and methodology, which would pave the way for new possibilities in the study of music as an integral part of society.

Although this basic idea was too monumental to be implemented in full, or even to any decisive degree, parts of this new approach were plainly evident at the George Herzog International Forum for Socio-Musical Sciences (HISM-88), which was organized by the Bar-Ilan University Department of Musicology and held between May 29 and June 3, 1988.

The choice of George Herzog's name for this Forum was a legitimate one. He was an outstanding scholar, whose work and personality had contributed greatly to this new approach, and, at the same time, his name would emphasize the fact that the event was taking place in Israel. For these reasons the inclusion of his once-published but little known early paper on the anthropology of Jewish music was also considered justified.

Although some of the papers have been abridged, for technical reasons, and a few omitted, this collection is presented according to the general directions of HISM-88. The program of the Forum divides the papers into four groups: papers dealing with theoretical-methodological questions; research on different social groups; papers on Israeli popular music; and papers relating to specific musical cultures and issues. In this volume the papers have been arranged somewhat differently:

Part I: George Herzog – In Memoriam. This section provides a presentation by one of the leading musicologists of our century, Bruno Nettl, who followed in Herzog's wake and developed his ideas; also presented is a completely unresearched and exciting instance of Herzog's collaboration with Bela Bartok (Yves Lenoir); as well as the reminiscences of a devoted participant of Herzog's classes (Edgar E. Siskin).

Part II: the largest and richest section (nine papers), dealing with: a) the state of research in three different parts of the world – the United States, South Africa, and Hungary (Peter Etzkorn, Klaus Heimes, and Zoltan Falvy); b) new theoretical avenues combining research in the different areas of musicology Helmut Staubmann, Wolfgang Suppan, Don Harran, Ann Buckley, and Shai Burstyn); and c) a study of the phenomenon of modus in traditional music (Harold Powers).

Part III: the four papers of this section are devoted to Israeli popular music; in musicology in general, and in Israeli musicology in particular, for the first time Israeli pop music is discussed on a scholarly level, and at an international meeting (papers by Hana Adoni, Motti Regev, Tova Bensky, and a joint paper by Pamela Squires-Kidron, Edwin Seroussi and Jeff Halper).

Part IV: Free Papers: the last section of the Report (eight papers) may be divided into several subsections: cultural politics in Japan and Switzerland (Uri Epstein, Shuhei Hosokawa, Margaret Engeler); Judeo-Spanish music (Judith R. Cohen, Susana Weich-Shahak); Jewish art music (Detlef Gojowy, Max Stern); and two papers on the impact of contemporary mass media (Paul Nixon).

The main point, however, of all the papers presented at HISM-88 as a corpus should be seen in the fact that a strong call was made for a new, all-round approach to musicology uniting the multifaceted fields of our discipline.

We wish to thank Bar-Ilan University Press, especially Mrs. Miriam Drori, the Director, and Mrs. Anne Lamdan, for their assistance in the publication of this book.

The Editors

Conclusion

XVI. The Musical Landscape in Israel/Palestine: 3.000 Years Ago and Today*

Recently I became aware of two new German words, probably, without adequate translation into other languages – *Geschichtsaufbereitung* and *Vergangenheitsbewältigung*. In Germany the terms are applied while dealing with the periods of Nazi Germany and the DDR. They can, however, be applied to the re-evaluation of historiography of broader periods of nations and states. We in Israel, facing similar tendencies, apply them in our Eastern time account while dealing with some three millennia. For the historiography of Israel – and I mean "Israel" in a broader sense covering the culture and people of ancient Israel/Palestine, the Jewish Diaspora and the modern state of Israel – this was made possible only because of and in the framework of the independent state of Israel, when the necessary national consciousness and national self-confidence was acquired. Self-reconsideration of history was hardly possible for an oppressed people on the thresholds of the grate cultures and states.

I.

The central problem of musical historiography of the ancient world is the matter of sources. In most fields scholars years ago surmounted their reverential regard for the Holy Scripture and it became clear, that the primary source for a historiography of ancient Israel/Palestine is archaeology. Musicology, as usually, stayed behind. From the early days of musicology both Jewish and Christian scholars were relying mainly on one and only source, the Holy Scripture. In 1980 the *New Grove Dictionary*, nearly as Abraham Partaleone and Michael Praetorius in the early 17th century briefly mentions the importance of archaeology and presents six

---

* Published in: K. Eberle et al., *Musikkonzepte – Konzepte der Musikwissenscahft: Bericht über den Internationalen Kongress der Gesellschaft für Musikforschung Halle 1998*, vol. ii (2000), pp. 52-61.

pages on Ancient Israel/Palestine *in toto* based on Biblical quotations and devoted to the Biblical tradition of the Jerusalem Temple. Even some years ago scholars (A. Shiloah, H. Seidel) still consider the Bible the principal and richest source of knowledge on the musical culture of ancient Israel/Palestine.

As researchers of the past in a certain field of human activity we are interested in the musical landscape, the *Platz im Leben* of music of Ancient Israel/Palestine rather than in the music theology or music philosophy of the Old Testament. What part of the early oral tradition was delivered unchanged and what was changed, what was written down and later changed or subject to censorship – all this is mainly a question of future research. Only rare examples from the Old Testament prove the process of change in the sense of historical reality, as for example, the two parallel passages in 2. Sam 6:5 and 1. Chr 13:8. Here an orgiastic musical event, accomponied by wood and metall clappers, rattles, drums and lyres (according to the first description) was changed or censored to a regular liturgical musical performance (singing with lyres, trumpets, drums and cymbals) – in the second. The picture of the entire musical landscape of ancient Israel/Palestine appears in new light when based on material relicts. This is, for example, the case of the *kinnor* and *nevel*. On the basis of archaeological evidence the two musical instruments now have to be interpretated as lyres which means the end of the legend on King David's harp.

The contradiction of biblical imaginative reality and historical facts reaches it's heights in the case of the musical culture of the Babylonian/Persian and early Hellenistic I Period, or the, so called, Period of the Second Temple. A picture of musical splendor and grandeur, liturgical and ceremonial parade emerges from written sources – the Books of Esra and Nehamia. The Mishna and Talmud add details on the type and numbers of musical instruments of the Temple orchestra. Musicologists accepted this information and on their part added details. But the historical reality looks different: we are confronted with a surprising lacuna of at least 300 years in archaeological evidence as regards the musical culture in general, and, especially, the musical liturgy.

This does not mean that we have to deny the Biblical evidence on music as a totality; there certainly are cases where we may see a mutual conformation of sources, at least on the surface: the absence of the lute, for example, from the archaeological layers of the Iron Age to the Hellenistic/Roman Age coincides with the Biblical text, which has no name for this instrument. Now it is possible to disclose the undeniable conflict of Biblical texts and archaeological evidence: from the territory of ancient Israel/Palestine there are at our disposal some 700 finds with musical meaning, and modern archeological research has reached a level, which allows to draw the general picture of Israel/Palestine's musical scenery.

Music in this area, as other aspects of social life, was governed by the phenomenon of the *Ungleichzeitige im Gleichzeitigen*, to use the wording of the Helga Weippert, or in regard to music, I would rather say *the hetherogeneous in the homogeneous* i. e. hetherougenous ethno-religious musical units in a homogeneous Near Eastern musical landscape. The mosaic of the musical landscape was created synchronously by different diachronic historical cultural levels of musical culture. In a historical sequence this musical picture may be delineated as follows.

The oldest group of inhabitants which we can identify from a sociomusical point of view belongs to the *Natufian Stone Age* (12th-8th mill. BC) and appeared during the Neolithic Agrarian Revolution. It is confirmed by the work-cult-sound syncretism of sound producing stone, bone and shell tools – mostly string-rattles (10th mill. BC, see **Fig. IA-1**) and bull-roarers. In the 4th mill. BC the Acoustical/Organological Revolution occurred: in the Near East and in ancient Israel/Palestine in particular, complicated chordophones (harps and lutes) and membranaphones appeared and the first signs of musical active shamanism and individual professional virtuosity may be detected.

In the second large period the *Bronze Age* (late 4th – end of 2nd mill. BC) Canaanite culture shows signs of early urbanization and rich archaeological finds confirm a high degree of musical development. The main local traits are connected to the beginning of an autochthon tradition of mass-performance: the mass-use of cult clay-rattles (avoided by the Biblical text), individual forms of musical instruments and performance practices of string and wind instruments (lutes, lyres and reed doublepipes), advanced for the Near East professional and folk forms of performance. A great part of the musical terminology of the Old Testament was born at this time in North Canaan, Ugarit. Along with the two neighboring great ancient musical cultures – the Messopotamian and Egyptian

– a third entity is now attested on the East shores of the Mediterranean Sea from the Sinai to Ugarit, the Canaanite musical culture.

During the *Iron Age* (1200-586 BC) along the shores dominated the Philistine and Phoenician cultures, in the hinterland and highland the Kingdoms of Edom, Moab, Ammon, Judah and Israel ruled. At the initial stage of monotheism, however, and at least till Hellenistic-Roman times, the orgiastic Canaanite musical tradition was a considerable part of musical life. Material relicts from the Iron Age of Ancient Israel/Palestine confirm the presence of a multitude of different religions and cults, different ethnic traditions and languages, different stages of historical and socio-political development and different musics. There was hardly one dominating Judaean/Israelite musical culture, an impression the Biblical texts may have created. The musical culture was rather a colorful mosaic, created by a number of local musical cultures. As result of a process of acculturation, however, on the very restricted territory of Israel/Palestine an autochthon culture emerged, which presents the musical landscape of ancient Israel/Palestine. The cult stand from Ashdod (11th cent. BC, see **Fig. IA-6**), for example, is so closely related to different traditions that was interpretable as a stand depicting Philistine cult-musicians and compared with the passage from 1.Sam 10:5-6; by latest research the musicians may be explained as a group – if not first one – depicting Cybele priests. Local lyre players and female singers were highly regarded in the entire Near East. They excelled as priestly musicians over the entire country, although with different features in each sub-culture. In the 9th-7th century B. C. there was a general diminishing of the number of strings of the string instruments, which seems to indicate some kind of musical *ars nova* in Israel/Palestine. Mass-instruments, as clay rattles, were distributed over the entire country, as were the reed double-pipes and the round frame-drums. These folk instruments, however, were also the carriers and symbols of distinctive ethnic layers and different believe systems. In this way in some socio-cultural settings they, probably became also symbols of dissent, and fall victim to violence (see **Fig. III-3e**). The birth of the *zumra*-type instruments, which soon were accepted over the entire country, could be detected only in Edomite culture. The lute is absent from Biblical texts, and is completely absent from the Bronze Age to Hellenistic times. The total absence of the harp remains an unanswered question, while the absence of the lute, parallel to the absence of cymbals, may be attributed to the increasing pressure of orthodox monotheistic circles. It is a picture of hetherogenous ethnic/national musical sub-cultures in a larger area of a homogeneous Levantine musical landscape.

As mentioned, for the *Babylonian-Persian Period* (6th-4th cent. BC) we are confronted with an archaeological gap of some three centuries. Archaeological evidence is, in fact, completely absent from this period. This state of the art puts in question the entire picture of the rich musical culture described in the books Ezra, Nehamia and Chronicles.

For the *Hellenistic-Roman Period* (late 4th cent BC – early 4th cent CA) the abundant archaeological and written evidence creates a florid mosaic of a multicultural and multi-religious society, typical for Hellenistic cultures. Musical styles from the Dionysian, Nabataean, Idumaean, Sidonian to Israeli, Samaritan and Syrian interacted. It is remarkable that the relationship and affinity of the different ethnic and liturgical life styles at this historical period is frequently seen in and attributed to the musical behaviour of human communities. This is confirmed by both Jewish and Roman sources. Musical life includes now a broad spectrum of musical instruments: ancient (cymbals, rattles) and modern (bells, crotals) idiophones, new mobile and virtouse string instruments (lutes, harps; for the obsolete lyre the place of a symbol is secured), mono- and double-pipes build in new advanced forms which allow a broad use of different tone-rows and by use of metall a more brilliant sound, horizontal flutes and shrill conical double-tongue instruments. Mosaics, depicting musical events, decorate Jewish and non-Jewish buildings. At this time the *shofar* is broadly accepted as the second most important after the *menora* symbol of a Jewish symbol-group. In the 4th century the organ is attested in Samaritan communities as liturgical instrument. Josephus describes musician competitions and Ben Sira praised the delights of music. This time shows, however, also the beginnings of strong pressure from Jewish autocratic circles to supress alien music and musical instruments and the use of musical instruments in general. The Greek melody was proclaimed synonymous with adultery and the *Oraculla Sybillina* prohibits the use of musical instruments in front of the altar. In this syncretic landscape of both acculturation and confrontation the ancient times disappeared and on the eve of Christianity and Diaspora Judaism a new musical era was brought to life.

II.

It is the concept of this paper that the musical landscape of modern Israel basically reminds the one of Ancient Israel/Palestine with most processes and tendencies intensified and in some cases brought to painful hostility. The gap in the *Ungleichzeitige im Gleichzeitigen* has become wider, over more distant periods, which makes it harder to create homogeneity; the traditions have become more distant, from wider geographical, chronological and cultural areas, which makes acceptance and tolerance more difficult; communication and information channels are faster and highly factual, which activates reaction, competition and rivalry.

On the border of the pre-Christian and first Christian millenium the fragile harmony of the Hellenistic musical life was revolutionized. For the Israelits and Judeans it was the end of a geographic concentrated and restricted musical culture which in the forthcoming nearly two millenia changed into more than hundred fragmented, often distant musical subcultures. The different Jewish *'edot* (ethnic communities), now at the sources of Israel's musical culture, break up roughly into the *Ashcknazi* (Europe and North America), *Sephardic* (South Europe, Near East), Yemenite, North African and Asian groups. The traditional music of the different *'edot,* an ongoing process of change in form, nature, and contents of the oral tradition, to-day may only vaguely represent, if at all, the core of the musical material at the beginnings of this tradition. Although mostly a musical kernel of sounds is present in similar genres of most *'edot,* we may call it a "identity gene," we hardly will recognize similar sections of a certain prayer if performed by different *'edot.* The strict monotone recitation tone of the Ashkenaz style changes unrecognizably into a highly interwoven ornamented style of nasal singing when performed in Yemenite communities and both are far from the hurried chanting of Iraqi Jews or the Samaritan vocal polyphonic "organized chaos" of sounds. Even the exophonical sign-system, which was added to the Biblical texts in the 9th-10th century, the *t'amey hamikrah* did not secure a constant musical and performance tradition.

What was it than that was keeping together the distant musical structures? The prayer text, liturgical or para-liturgical texts of the events of the Jewish "life-cycles" (birth, puberty, marriage, death) and "season-cycles" (festive days, holidays). It was not the musical pattern, nor the performance tradition – it was the liturgical sacred text.

The inconsistency of the musical oral tradition and the interaction with a great number of neighbouring cultures changed the music unrecognizably and sometimes to the opposite. Music itself does not allow to follow up the process of change, while the history of a musical instrument, e.g. the organ, provides an excellent documented example of this process. A 3ed century B. C. invention from Alexandria and later Hellenistic/Roman arena instrument, the organ was not accepted at the Temple and branded from Jewish life by Talmudic and Midrashic writings both as pagan Greek invention and for the Temple unacceptable inferior musical instrument. The confusion of names of the organ and a clear case of misunderstanding by Joshua ibn Gaon brought to life the legend about the organ as Temple instrument (the Gaon using wrongly the term *magrepha* for the organ depicted a phantasy-instrument in his hand written Bible, 1306). From that time on the organ was frequently depicted in Hebrew manuscripts of sacred texts and after this accepted in some Jewish communities: a unique case of change in symbolic meaning and function of a musical instrument on the basis of a misunderstanding in Biblical iconography (see Ch. V).

With the beginning of the emancipation of European Jewery (18the century) the first steps towards Jewish secularism were made and the building of a Jewish nation not necessary identical to religion started. Music became an integral part of this process. The establishment of a modern secular national school of art music, which featured a national music language became the central challenge of Jewish musicians in many parts of the wold from Russia to Switzerland and the USA. In the first decade of our century music itself, supported by all means of expression of national tradition rather than a sole sacred text, became a decisive force of national amalgamation. This process reached new dimensions and received a new meaning in the State of Israel.

The musical culture of modern Israel occurred from the multicultural tradition of late 19th century Palestine under the rule of the Ottoman Empire. Simultaneously, the accumulating process of increasing Jewish emigration from different parts of the world decisively shaped the culture and mentality of pre-state conditions. Thousandth and later millions Jews with different musical traditions met in Israel.

The early attempts in the 20's to establish a professional musical culture were not successful and for the pioneers in some cases even tragic (for example, Yoel Engel, one of the founders of the St. Petersburg Jewish National School of music could not find in Palestine of the 20s a suitable frame for his professional and social life). The first local major confrontation occurred in the 30's with the massive influx of musicians with Western musical education, mainly emigrants from Nazi Germany. Faced with the local dominating Jewish and Arab traditional music and local Western dilettantism they became disillusioned and desperate. The landscape of Palestine, nevertheless, soon changed: professional activities increased when in 1936 Bronislav Hubermann founded the Palestine Orchestra (at present, the Israel Philharmonic Orchestra, IPO). The institutionalization of Western art music started. Jewish and Palestinian traditional musical cultures were pushed aside and ignored by the musical establishment. A striking example of the confrontation of local Near Eastern pop-music and established Western art music is the, so-called, "cassette-singers movement" by musicians of Jewish-Arab origin who performed Eastern commercial traditional music. From the 70's this trend gained popularity and small partisan pop-groups developed to one of the main strains of contemporary Israeli popular music. One of the inter-Jewish conflicts – Ashkenazi (Western) musical images *versus* Sephardi (Eastern) musical images was launched.

The creation of a national school of Israeli art music dominated compositional thought from the 30's till today. Musicians of different background, different concepts of aesthetics and taste were united in Israel by the idea and notion of a new national culture, national responsibility facing a national mission in a new age of a new Jewish nation, the Israeli nationality. Although well known Israeli composers (Stefan Wolpe, Erich Sternberg), advocated modernism and innovation and rejected any attempts of a national musical style, the new ambiance – the geography and landscape, the new national majority and the statehood – all of this was to strong not to provoke new music. Guided by the concepts of 19th-20th century European national schools of art music the Israeli composers created the "Mediterranean style."

"It is only on his own soil that (the artist) is "allowed" to address his listener and to develop a free dialogue based on a clear and known common basis," wrote Uriah Alexander Boskovich (1907-1964), the composer considered to be the founder and ideologist of the new style. On his orchestral song "The Lord is my Shepherd, Ps. 23" he commented: "It is evident that the Israeli musical canticle abandons the enclosed realm of the synagogue, of theology and of official religion and reached to the origin of psalmodic poetry." The raw material for his music was the sound-world of Israel from ancient Jewish prayer-tunes to Bedouine double-pipe improvisations, from East-European Jewish dance-tunes to Arab drum-rhythms. Boskovich was followed by a number of composers of the older generation, everyone in his own way: Paul Ben-Haim created music which fused Sephardic and Western musical styles; Oedon Partos' music was based on an amalgamation of Western art music and the Yemenite idiom; Joachim Stuchevsky preference was his own *klezmer* tradition, while Marc Lavry's source of inspiration was the new Israeli folk song. It was the last one, who proclaimed "that there is something which can be found only in the works of Israeli composers, which could not exist had they not lived here, something that we call 'Israeli music'." Modern techniques of composition were not alien to Israeli composers and some (Joseph Tal) used dodecaphony as well as electronic means of expression. This did not, however, deprive his music from its Israeli nature: there existed a conglomerate of features – musical, textual, visual, ethnic, social and others, which all together crated the phenomenon of the Israeli. This was the time of the "melting-pot"-ideas.

Soon (60th – 80th), with the second and third generation of composers, mostly educated in Israel and furthered by studies in Europe and the USA, the time of fragmentation of styles in art music started: from folklore transcriptions to electronic music from diverse use of traditional styles to avant-garde. One of the leaders of the new developments was once again Boskovich, who turned to the meaning of numbers in the *Kabbalah* for a musical purpose. The composer died early but his central idea adequate to the historical developments of his time – the enclosure and integration of all aspects of the Jewish and Israeli cultural heritage, historical, religious, traditional, or pure musical – emerged now as the uniting force of Isareli art music. Jewish musical pluralism is now represented by Israeli secular art music. Only a brief selection of composition titles by Israeli composers of the second and third generation may represent the picture: *Judith* and *Jerusalem Symphony* (Mordecai Seter), *The Writings of Hezekiah* and *Be Not as Your Father* (Abel Ehrlich), *Mizmo-*

rim and *The Old Decrees* (Ben Zion Orgad), *Festival Prelude* and *Confession* (Noam Sherif), *Elegy* on the 1967 war and *The Destruction of the Temple* (Tzwi Avni) and so on. *This is a Gate Without a Wall* and *About an Old Tune* by Marc Kopetman, a emigrant of the early 70s from the former Soviet Union, are of special significance: blending the high musical professionalism of the Russian newcomers from the former Soviet Union and the national strivings of the Israeli musical culture, Kopetman's technically refined and nationally conscious musical language represents a new level of intellectual and emotional symbiosis typical for the new strains in Israeli music. Israeli composers, accepting diverse advanced composition techniques strive for one central human and artistic idea – the musical expression of the Israeli reality, of the thoughts, feelings and longings of an Israeli musician in the second half of the 20th century, the incorporation in his music of the musical collective memory of the Jewish and Israeli people.

Israel has one of the finest symphonic orchestras in the world. Active concert life is featured by at least twenty periphery symphonic and chamber orchestras, a opera theater, and several permanent music festivals. There are several splendid concert-halls, four departments of music at local universities, and two academies of music, and a special channel of the Israeli Radio is broadcasting classical art music some 20 hours per day. The international fame of Israeli musical culture is based mainly on the artistic level of the IPO, which only in Tel-Aviv presents every season some 300 concerts. The listeners of the IPO and art music radio channel are, however, hardly 3% of the population.

Art music can not be considered to be the main stream of music, which shapes the Israeli local musical landscape. Western art music remains an island in a sea of musical whirl. A major tradition is collective singing of the so called *schir yisraeli* (a type of early 20th century Russian socialist mass-song acculturation in Israel) at social gatherings in overfilled halls, where people meet regularly for the performance of this repertoire. Alongside the oriental or Arab/Jewish popular music is nowadays one of the strongest strains in the Israeli musical landscape. Numerous popular music groups, frequently of mediocre artistic level, dominate audio-video media. Most ethnic religious communities, concentrated on a certain block of music, at this stage seem to resist a broader process of integration or acculturation. Besides the International Folk Music and

Dance Festival, regularly take place festivals of the Eastern song, *hassidic* music, *khasanut*, each with its own audience, own ideology. In the 70s-80s the general picture has moved from the "melting-pot" to a pluralism reality.

Ethnic, religious, social and cultural pluralism has produced not only common peaceful existence and syncretism. It has produced also conflict, estrangement, even aggressive confrontation. The central feature of the Israeli musical landscape in the last decade is the politicization of both art and popular music. Extreme examples of pop-music appeared, as, for example, the song "We are the fucked off generation..." and by the same author-pop-singer a lament on the tragic death of Israel's Prime Minister Izkhak Rabin. The performer of the songs was ostracized by the new right-wing establishment. Recently an avant-garde pank-group named Dir-Yasin (an Arab village were during the War of Independence, 1948, most of the population was killed by a Ezel riot, a right-wing Likud group, who later were sentenced) started concert tours. In 1993, the time of Rabin's social-democratic government, the highest prize for music, the Israel Prize in sciences and arts was awarded to an avant-garde composer for his opera on texts of the Kastners trial and a cantata on texts of letters by German war prisoners from Stalingrad; in 1997 during the reign of the right-wing government the same Prize was rewarded to two compositions in a hotchpotch style, the cantatas *The Fanfare of the King* and *Mishneot* which used Jewish liturgical texts and elements of music. In both cases the political predisposition was clearly felt.

A research project conducted in 1984/5 by a team of musicologists and sociologists at the Bar-Ilan University (see Ch. XV) came to the conclusion that four hardly comparable main blocks of music constitute the musical culture of the Jewish Israeli population: Jewish traditional music, Israeli popular music, Western type art music, and Western type popular music. In this modern mosaic of musical styles the *Ungleichzeitige im Gleichzeitigen* or the 'hetherogeneous in the homogeneous' is manifested in a new more vehement way. Already the non-simultaneity of Western art music and Jewish traditional music by itself are very large, and the two are of rather distant ideologies also. Israeli popular music, strongly divided by ethnic and political biased Ashkenazi and Sephardi patterns, is a secular phenomenon and opposed to Jewish traditional religious music, even in similar ethnic groups. Moreover, the last one, divided by theological and ethnical partisanship is, in fact, opposed to any style of art music and is not simultaneous to any of the other three blocks of music. This is the picture of musical life without even taking into account Palestinian traditional, popular and meanwhile non-existent art music. In this musical reality Jewish traditional music and Western art music emerged as the most powerful centrifugal, even aggressive forces of Israeli society, while popular music both Israeli/Palestinian and Western style with its broader ethnic basis seem to be more centripetal in tendency. The research results stressed the interdependence of acculturation and level of education. The demographic tendencies of Israel (a strong increase of the Palestinian and Jewish orthodox population), however, and political developments of the late 90s resulting from this, hamper the process of acculturation. In this landscape the 'hetherogeneous in the homogeneous' of ancient Israel seems to have changed to its opposite – extremely homogeneous blocks of music in a society of an aggressively heterogeneous musical culture.

Related bibliography

Aspects of Music in Israel. Israel: Composer League & National Council for Culture and Art, 1980.
Joachim Braun: *Music in Ancient Israel/Palestine*, Grand Rapids/Oxford U.K., 2002.
Joachim Braun & Judith Cohen, "Jüdische Musik", in: *Die Musik in Geschichte und Gegenwart,* 2. Neubearbeitete Ausgabe (1994), Sachteil Bd. 4:1511-1569.
Jehoash Hirshberg: *Music in the Jewish Communuity of Palestine 1880-1948*, Oxford, 1995.
Amnon Shiloah: *Jewish Musical Tradition*, Detroit, 1992.
Helga Weippert: *Palästina in vorhellenistischer Zeit*, München, 1988.
Eric Werner, *The Sacred Bridge*, vol. I and II, New York, 1959-1984.

Figures

Fig. IA-1.

Fig. IA-2.

Fig. IA-1. Pelvic bone withh fox teeth string rattle, Hayonim Cave (10th mill. B. C.), IAA 79.536
Fig. IA-2. Ivory plaque, Megiddo, lyre player at symposium of ruler (12th-13th cent. B. C.), IAA 38.780

Fig. IA-3. *Terracotta plaque relief, Dan (15th cent. B. C.), Hebrew Union College (Jerusalem), No. 23.095*

Fig. IA-4.

Fig. IA-5.

Fig. IA-4. Drawing, tomb of Khnumhotem II, Beni Hassan, lyre player with a group of Semitic nomads (20th cent. B. C.), fragment (from Newberry, 1893, pl. XXXI)

Fig. IA-5. Alabaster relief, captured Jewish lyre players, Nineveh (8th cent B.C.), BM 12497

413

Fig. IA-7a.

Fig. IA-6.

Fig. IA-7b

Fig. IA-8.

Fig. IA-6.   Clay stand with five musicians, Ashdod (11th cent. B. C.), IAA 68.1182
Fig. IA-7.   Mosaic floor, Sheikh Zouede, Gaza, Dionysian procession (3ed-4th century C. E.), Ismailia Historical Museum, (a) relief drawing from Hickmann 1949, (b) fragment (photo by Prof. A. Ovadia)
Fig. IA-8.   Mosaic floor, Sepphoris, Dionysian POMPI, in situ (3ed cent. C. E.)

Fig. IB-1.

Fig. IB-2. Fig. IB-3.

Fig. IB-1. Wall drawing, Idumaean Necropolis, hunting scene with trumpeter, in situ (3ed cent.)
Fig. IB-2. Bar-Kokhba coin (132-135 C. E.), lyre – probably, kinnor, EIM K- 4676
Fig. IB-3. Bar-Kokhba coin (132-135 C. E.), lyre – probably, nebel, EIM K- 4649

Fig. IB-4.

Fig. IB-5.

Fig. IB-4. Terra-cotta figurine with double-pipe, Achziv (8th-7th cent. B. C.), IAA 44.56

Fig. IB-5. Mosaic floor, synagogue, Hamat Tiberias (3ed cent. C. E.), shofar with menorah (seven-branch lampstand), mahta (incense pan), etrog (cirus fruit), and lulav (palm frond), in situ.

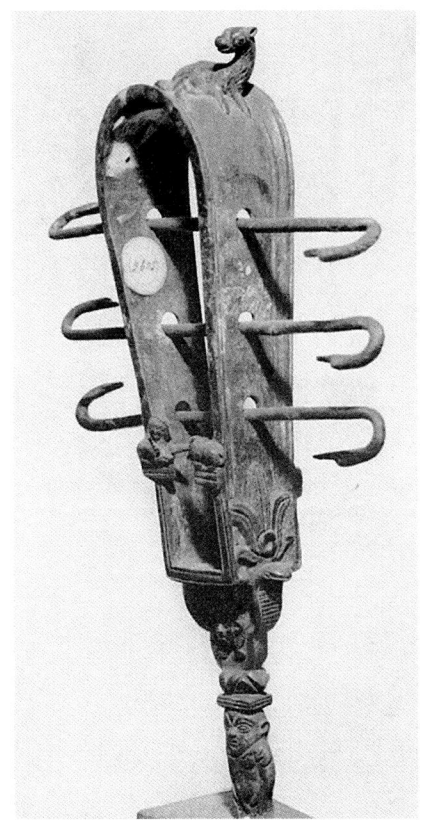

Fig. IC-1a. Fig. IC-1b.

Fig. IC-1. Sistrum, (a) Egyptian (from Hickmann 1961, MGB II/1, fig. 25, 11th -8th cent. B. C.), (b) Sumerian (from Rashid 1984, fig. 42, first half of 3ed mill. B. C.)

Fig. IC-2a.

Fig. IC-2b.

Fig. IC-3.

Fig. IC-2.	Rock etching, Negev, drawing of (a) lyre players and (b) drummer and dancers (from Anati 1963), in situ (first half of 2nd mill. B. C.)
Fig. IC-3.	Mesopotamia, chordophone-membranaphone duet lyre with drummer (from Rashid 1984, fig. 59)

Fig. IC-4a.

Fig. IC-5.

Fig. IC-4b. Fig. IC-4c.

Fig. IC-6.

Fig. IC-7.

Fig. IC-4. (a) Basalt etching, Harra Desert (1st-4th century C. E.) arghul player with dancer, AM J1886, (b) Terra-cotta figurine, double zurna player, Tel Malhata, IAA 94.3394 (7th cent. B. C.), (c) Beth-Shean, mosaic floor, (6th century C. E) Convent of St. Mary, mono zurna player
Fig. IC-5. Wall painting, Thebian necropolis No. 52 (15th century B.C.), harp, lute, and double-pipe players (from Hickmann 1961, MGB II/1, Fig. 61)
Fig. IC-6. Mesopotamia, vertical harp (from Rashid 1984, Fig. 152, Ninive, 8th-7th cent. B. C.)
Fig. IC-7. Silver bull-head lyre, Mesopotamia. UR King Burial (from Rashid, fig. 4)

Fig. III-1a.

Fig. III-1b.

Fig. III-1d.

Fig. III-1c.

Fig. III-1a. Clay rattle, spool form, Hazor, IAA 67.1160.
Fig. III-1b. Clay rattle with handle, Tell el 'Agul, IAA 35.4157.
Fig. III-1c. Clay rattle, anthropomorphic form, Tell el Far'a South, IAA I6936.
Fig. III-1d. Clay rattle, bird form, Ashdod, IAA 60.1031.

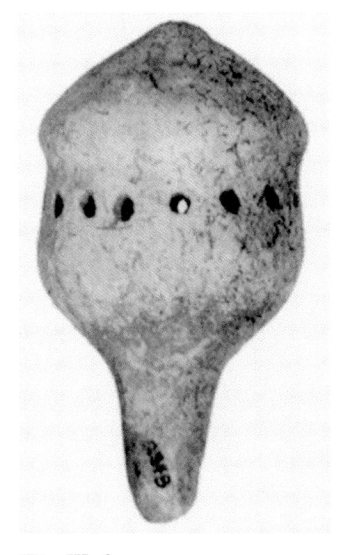

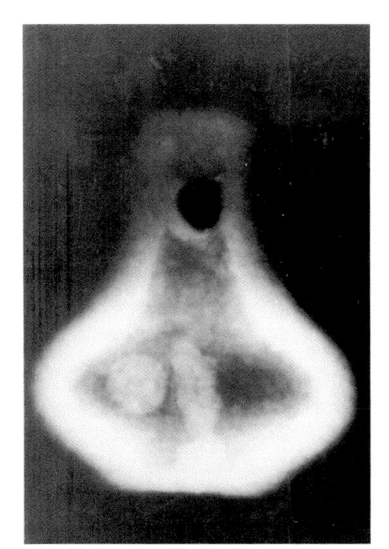

Fig. III- 1e.   Fig. III- 1f.

Fig. III-1g.

Fig. III-1e.   Fruit form, Megiddo, OI A18362.
Fig. III-1f.   Bell form (x-ray), Hazor, HUIA 45288.
Fig. III-1g.   Terracotta figurine, idol with rattle on his head, Qitmit, IAA 87.117.

421

Fig. III-2a.

Fig. III-2b.

Fig. III-2a.   Symmetrical lyre with rounded resonance body, Ashdod (original lost).
Fig. III-2b.   Symmetrical kithara type-"concert" lyre, Gaza (copy in IM).

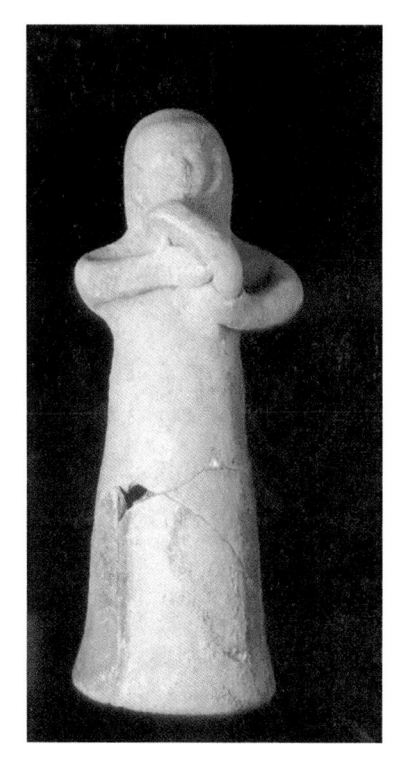

Fig. III-3a. Fig. III-3b.

Fig. III-3a. Bell-shaped figurine of female drummer, Achziv (from Mazar 1996, fig. 53:8).
Fig. III-3b. Plaque relief of female drummer, Tell el-Fara'a, North EB F3426.

Fig. III-3c.

Fig. III-3d.

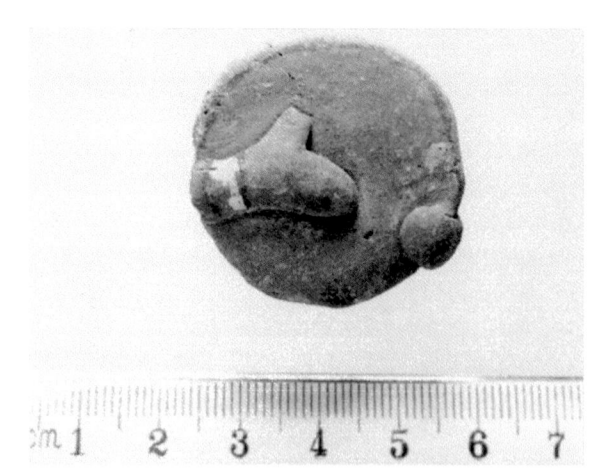

Fig. III-3e.

Fig. III-3c. Plaque relief of female with disk and hands in a symmetrical position, Taanach, AAM J.7285.
Fig. III-3d. Bell shaped figurine of female drummer, Nebo, SBF M1072.
Fig. III-3e. Broken drums from terra-cotta plaque figurines, Amman, AAM ATH 66-3/4

Fig IV-1a.

Fig IV-1b.

Fig. IV-1. Dura-Europos Synagogue, (a) wall painting, 2nd-3ed century (From E. R. Goodenough, Jewish Symbolism..., vol. XI, pl. xiii); (b) idem., drawing of destroyed.objects, among others two lutes

Fig. IV-2a.   *Fig. IV-2b.*

Fig. IV-2c.

Fig. IV-2.   Parma City Library, Ms. 1870, (a) fol. 105r/ Ps. 76, (b) fol. 89r/Ps. 67, (c) fol. 198r/Ps. 137.

Fig. IV-3.   Farhi Bible, fol. 186r, 1366-1382, Sasson Collection, Jerusalem.

Fig. IV-4.

Fig. IV-5.

Fig. IV-4. Golden Haggadah, fol. 15r, British Library, BL-Add. 27210.
Fig. IV-5. Barcelona Haggadah, fol. 61r, British Library, BL-Ad 14761fol.

Fig. IV-6.

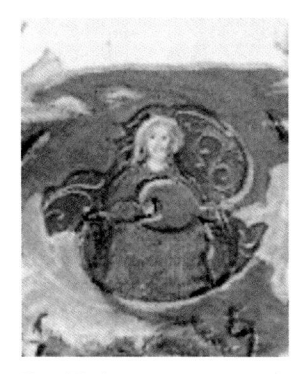

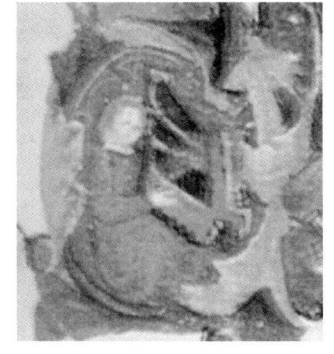

Fig. IV-6a.   *Fig. IV-6b.*

Fig. IV-6.   Arba'a Turim, Vatican Library, 1435, Cod. Rossiana-555, fol. 292/293, frame with (a) lute and (b) organ player.

429

Fig. IV-7.

Fig. IV-8.

Fig. IV-7. Miscellany, Ms. Rothshild-24, fol. 322v, IM Jerusalem.
Fig. IV-8. Miscellany, Ms. Rothshild-24, fol. 464v, IM Jerusalem.

Fig. IV-10.

Fig. IV-9.

Fig. IV-11.

Fig. IV-9.   Siddur, Bodleian Library, Ms. Opp. 776, fol. 79v.
Fig. IV-10. Bible, 1411, British Library, Royal 19.D.iii, fol. 458.
Fig. IV-11. Hagaddah Yahudd, Israel Museum, Jerusalem, Ms. 180/50, fol. 17r.

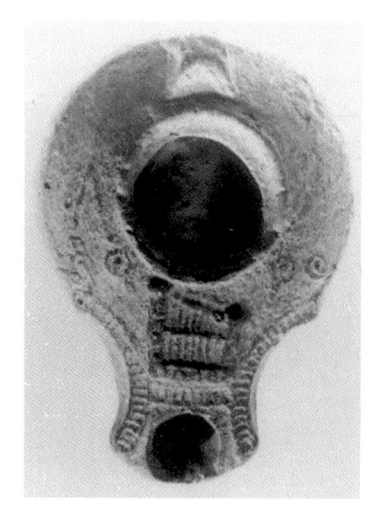

Fig. V-2.

Fig. V-1.

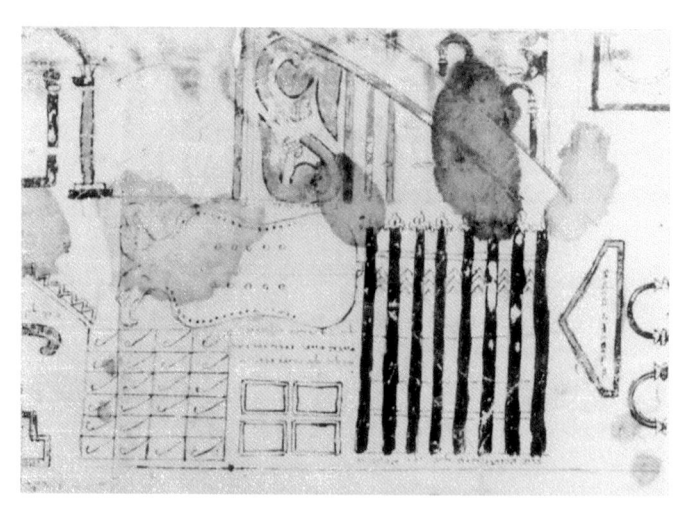

Fig. V-3.

Fig. V-1. Terra-cotta oil lamp, 3ed-4th century, Ein Hashofet, Israel, IAA 71.5080.
Fig. V-2. From Abdul Rizaq Zaqzyq and Marcelle Duchesne-Gullemin, "La mosaique de Mariamin," in: Annales Arabes Syriennes, XX/1 (1970), pp. 93-125, Pl. 1-2.
Fig. V-3. Drawing, representation of the Talmudic magrepha, Second Kennicot Bible, 1366-1382, Bodleian Library, Ms. Kenn.2, fol. 1v.

Fig. V-4. Fig. V-5.

Fig. V-4. Kaufmann Haggadah, late 14th century, Budapest City Library, Kaufmann Collection, Ms. A 422, fol. 3v.
Fig. V-5. Lobkovitz Prayer Book, 1494, Prague, Klementinium-Universitni Knihovna, Ms. XXIII F202.